DYING TO
BE THIN

NIKKI GRAHAME
DYING TO BE THIN

THE TRUE STORY OF MY LIFELONG BATTLE AGAINST ANOREXIA

JOHN BLAKE

Published by John Blake Publishing Ltd,
3 Bramber Court, 2 Bramber Road,
London W14 9PB, England

www.johnblakepublishing.co.uk

First published in hardback in 2009

ISBN: 978 1 84454 743 2

British Library Cataloguing-in-Publication Data:

A catalogue record for this book is available from the British Library.

Design by www.envydesign.co.uk

Printed in the UK by CPI William Clowes, Beccles, NR34 7TL

1 3 5 7 9 10 8 6 4 2

Papers used by John Blake Publishing are natural, recyclable products made
from wood grown in sustainable forests. The manufacturing processes
conform to the environmental regulations of the country of origin.

Every attempt has been made to contact the relevant copyright-holders, but
some were unobtainable. We would be grateful if the appropriate people
could contact us.

I would like to dedicate this book to my mum, dad and sister, for dragging them to hell and back.

I would also like to thank all of the doctors and carers who looked after me: Brian Lask, Dee Dawson, Paul Byrne and Sam Swinglehurst.

CONTENTS

Foreword   xi
Prologue   xvii

Chapter 1   Fun, Food and Family   1
Chapter 2   Things Fall Apart   9
Chapter 3   A Big, Fat Lump   23
Chapter 4   Never Give In   35
Chapter 5   The Maudsley   47
Chapter 6   I Don't Belong Here   65
Chapter 7   Hillingdon Hospital   77
Chapter 8   Collingham Gardens   89
Chapter 9   Too Uncool for School   103
Chapter 10   Raw Anger   115
Chapter 11   Death Pact   123
Chapter 12   Zombie Child   145
Chapter 13   Get On and Die   159

Chapter 14   Sedgemoor   169

Chapter 15   Huntercombe   179

Chapter 16   I'll Never Have to Eat Again   195

Chapter 17   Rhodes Farm   211

Chapter 18   I Want to Live   227

Chapter 19   A New Struggle   239

Chapter 20   Never Going Back   251

Chapter 21   *Big Brother*   265

Chapter 22   The Magic and the Misery   281

Chapter 23   A Life Worth Living   301

Further reading and resources   313

In order to protect their identities, many names of patients in the hospitals and institutions have been changed.

FOREWORD

BY DR DEE DAWSON

Even though the age of onset of anorexia nervosa is forever decreasing, it is still very rare for a child of eight to develop this life-threatening illness.

I have treated just a handful of very young anorexic children and they have all left Rhodes Farm and stayed fit and well. It is vital that this illness is treated well in a specialist unit if it is to be prevented from developing into a chronic long-term illness which blights a person's entire life.

Unfortunately, Nikki was sixteen when she was referred to us – eight years after the illness started. It is so much more difficult to treat when the person has become entrenched and can remember no other life. Nikki could only remember anorexia and battling with food which, in some way, was giving her something she lacked in her life. It might have been that she was frightened to give it up because she would no longer be special and everything I have seen about Nikki shows me she needs to be special. Maybe Nikki without anorexia would have meant she was a normal person and that was too frightening to contemplate. Nikki not only wanted to cling onto her anorexia but she wanted to be the best anorexic that had ever been. Of course, the very best anorexics die very young and so would Nikki have done had she had not been admitted repeatedly to a succession of hospitals and clinics. Thankfully, Nikki has, either through maturity or choice, decided to no longer take her anorexia to the limit of life as she has in the past. She is in perfect control of her diet and her weight but clearly she still has huge body image issues.

Like so many of the patients I have treated over the years, Nikki did not listen to my doom and gloom prophesies. Children who starve or restrict themselves to a very limited range of foods do not develop normally. The most obvious outward sign is that they do not grow and, for example, a girl will not develop breasts. At puberty a girl's body changes from being straight up and down to having a waist and hips. Nikki never went through puberty. She deprived her body of food throughout her teenage years, either not caring what happened to her or, like so many, believing it would never happen to her. As well as the retarded growth, girls who starve do not develop normal ovaries and this has two major effects. Firstly they are unable to have children and secondly they damage their bones, which become thin and brittle.

A few years ago, I had a letter from a 26 year old who, like Nikki, had never reached puberty and thus had never had a period. She wrote to tell me that at 25 she had decided to stop worrying about her weight, began eating normally and a year later at 26 had her first period. It is so rare for someone in their twenties who has been ill for ten years or more to suddenly change their attitude to food as this woman did. I know of no other cases like this to compare her with, but it shows how resilient the human body can be and that Nikki might still be able to have children if she were to eat normally. It might not be too late.

When Nikki came to me following a long stay in Great Ormond Street Hospital, she came with a despairing letter from the referring doctor. We were lead to believe that Nikki would not survive and that she was an impossible case.

Nikki weighed just 31kg when she came to us 10 years ago. She needed to gain 14kg to reach a safe weight. From the start, Nikki was adamant that she did not want to gain weight and used every trick she knew to avoid eating. All the patients at Rhodes Farm gain a steady 1kg a week and it is rare for anyone to get behind. If a patient does manage to avoid gaining a kilogram one week, they have to put on two the next, they always have to catch up.

Initially, Nikki appeared to be gaining sufficient weight but after a few weeks we discussed that she had been drinking water and doing various other things to disguise how much she weighed. She was, in reality, about five kilograms lighter than we had thought. She spent the next five weeks on one-to-one supervision whilst she caught up the weight.

In the twenty years Rhodes Farm has been open, no child has ever managed to pull the wool over our eyes for so long. Nikki must have known she would be caught (we spot-weigh the children from time to time to prevent water drinking). She lived for the moment and never worried about the future.

After a few weeks, Nikki decided she would like to be on the winning side and in true Nikki style began to co-operate. Instead of putting her heart and soul into bucking the system and upsetting the nurses, she turned model patient and decided that she wanted to get better. From then on until the end of her stay she never looked back; she put every ounce of energy into being perfect. Nikki went from being especially bad to especially good but she never stopped being special.

It was very nostalgic for me to see Nikki's tantrums on *Big Brother* and *Princess Nikki*; they has been an everyday occurrence at Rhodes Farm when she invariably did not get her own way. In the end, we won the battle to make Nikki gain weight and she was discharged weighing two kilos more than she needed to be. It looked as though she had turned the corner and was going to stabilise her weight. Unfortunately, Nikki began to lose weight soon after she was discharged and, despite offering to readmit her when she had lost only a kilo or two, she never returned to Rhodes Farm and her weight was allowed to slip once more.

I remember Nikki as having a great enthusiasm for life and a very bubbly personality. Throughout her teenage years she used her enormous perseverance and iron will in a destructive way to damage her health and punish her body. In latter years, she has used her drive and determination in a much more positive way and this has brought her to be the celebrity she is today.

Since Nikki left *Big Brother* she has visited Rhodes Farm several times to talk to the children. They always take more notice of someone who has experienced what they are going through than they do mere doctors and nurses. She has desperately wanted to stop youngsters going down the path she took and her help has been much appreciated.

I wish Nikki every success in her ongoing fight against this evil illness that has taken over her life for so long. I hope she is able to continue the path to the end and finally overcome her struggle with food. She has won so many battles – she can win this one too.

Dr Dee Dawson is the medical director of Rhodes Farm, a clinic which cares for children with severe eating disorders.

PROLOGUE

I was clutching the gleaming metal award so tightly in my hands that my knuckles had turned white.

In front of me, around each of the six golden tiers of the Royal Albert Hall, were more than five thousand people, clapping, cheering and even screaming my name.

Through the bright lights I could see Simon Cowell, David Walliams and Billie Piper, all applauding ... me!

It was the most amazing moment of my life.

I'd just been presented with the award for Most Popular TV Contender 2006 at the National Television Awards for my time in the *Big Brother* house earlier that year.

My mum and I had spent hours searching for the perfect dress for that night and here I was in a £275 Betsey Johnson bluey-green silk gown and a pair of £375 Gina shoes. It was the most I'd ever spent on an outfit and I had never, ever felt so special.

I'd been dropped off at the Royal Albert Hall in a limousine and as I walked down the red carpet, hundreds of people stood 20 deep at either side, calling my name and elbowing one another out of the way to ask me to sign autographs. Beyond them was a bank of paparazzi photographers taking my photograph from every angle.

For anyone, that night would have been special. But for me it was miraculous. Because for so long no one had even imagined I would still be alive then, let alone receiving a coveted television award.

I had been just eight years old when I began a determined and resolute campaign to starve myself to the brink of death. Or beyond that if need be, as I wasn't much bothered if I lived or died.

At that time, the late 1980s, I was one of the youngest people in Britain to have ever been diagnosed with anorexia nervosa – a psychiatric illness which makes people, usually teenagers, desperate to become as thin as possible and develop an obsessive fear of gaining any weight at all.

For the best part of the next decade I stumbled around a miserable circuit of hospitals, specialist units, my own home and foster care, as doctor after doctor tried and failed to make me eat.

My childhood was shattered and I grew up in institutions surrounded by kids with the most horrific mental problems. At night there was no one to kiss my head as I curled up in my hospital bed. In the morning there was no one to cuddle me when I woke up sleepy and scared.

I became brutalised, like a wild child who had lost touch with normal behaviour. I'd scream and scratch and yell and fight when people tried to make me eat.

A perfectionist from the start, I was determined not just to be anorexic. I wanted to be the best anorexic Britain had ever known. Many of my doctors think I achieved that. They stuck tubes up my nose, stitched tubes into my stomach and pumped me so full of drugs to control me that I became like a zombie. But still I wouldn't willingly give in to their demands that I should eat.

Once I lay in a hospital bed just 15 minutes from death as my mum begged me to cling on to life. Twice I took overdoses in a bid to end my misery. The first time I was just 13 years old.

But gradually, miraculously, I discovered that there could be a special life for me outside of hospitals and institutions if I chose to live it.

This is the story of that choice, and it is the choice I hope and pray other kids with anorexia will one day find the strength to take.

CHAPTER 1

FUN, FOOD AND FAMILY

Looking back to the house at 37 Stanley Road before everything went wrong, it always seems to have been summer. Back then everything was good, better than good. I had one of those childhoods you normally only see in cereal adverts.

We didn't have bags of money or live in a huge mansion, but we had fun. There were summer holidays to Greece, Mum and Dad would cuddle up on the sofa to watch a video on a Saturday night, I had a grandad I adored who had an endless supply of corny jokes, and sometimes my older sister/occasional friend/usually arch enemy Natalie even let me play with her collection of scented erasers!

There was Mum and Dad and Natalie and me (and Rex, our dog). And it worked. My mum, Sue, was tall and slim. She was shy compared with other kids' mums but she doted on me and Nat. She worked as a dinner lady but was always home in time to cook our tea – and she was an amazing cook. Nothing fancy, but proper home cooking that we all sat around the table to eat. Every night it was something different – spaghetti Bolognese, lasagne or a macaroni cheese that was worth running the full length of Stanley Road for.

Then there was my dad, Dave. And while of course I loved Mum, with Dad it was something more – I adored him.

Mum always laughs that the love affair between me – Nicola Rachel-Beth – and Dad started within minutes of my arrival at Northwood Park Hospital on 28 April 1982. After Natalie, Dad had been hoping for a boy but when I burst into the world screaming my lungs out he was, for some reason, totally smitten. From that point onwards I was the apple of his eye.

After the birth, the nurses wheeled Mum away to stitch her up. She left Dad sitting in a corner of the room by a window, holding this little bundle with jet-black, sticky-up hair and chubby cheeks.

When Mum was brought back an hour later, the sun had gone down and the room was pitch-black but Dad hadn't even got up to switch the light on. He was still sitting in exactly the same position, transfixed by the new arrival – me.

As I got older the bond only grew stronger. But it was kind of OK because there was an unspoken agreement in our house – Mum had Natalie and Dad had me.

I couldn't leave Dad alone. And for him little 'Nikmala' was pure delight.

By the time I was four or five, every time Dad left the house to go to work or pop down the pub I'd go belting down the road after him, begging to be allowed to stay with him.

I'd spend hours standing outside the betting shop at the corner of our street after Dad disappeared inside, rolled-up racing pages clenched in his hand as if armed ready for battle. Kids weren't allowed in and the windows were all covered over, but whenever the door was pushed ajar I'd sneak a glimpse of that mysterious male world of jittery TV screens, unfathomable numbers and solitary gamblers, all engulfed in thick cigarette smoke.

It became a standing joke in our family that whenever Dad emerged from the bookies' with a brisk, 'Right, off home now, Nikmala,' I'd reply, 'Can't you take me to another betting shop, Dad? Please?'

By the age of five I'd started going running with Dad. He loved keeping fit and so did I. More than that, I was developing a fiercely competitive streak and it made me rotten to Natalie. If she couldn't keep up, Dad and I would just speed off, leaving her puffing and panting behind.

Dad worked shifts at a big bank in London, looking after its computer system. It meant he wasn't around a lot of the time but the moment he stepped inside the door I was all over him.

Everyone wanted to be around Dad, to laugh at his jokes and hear his stories. Well, at the time I thought it was everyone, but looking back I think it was probably just women. In fact even at seven I knew that Dad was a bit of a ladies' man. He couldn't take us for a plate of chips at the Wimpy without chatting up the girl behind the counter.

You name her, Dad would try to turn on the charm for her – my nursery school teacher, the lifeguards when he took me swimming on a Sunday morning, holiday reps; pretty much anyone really. But at that point it just seemed harmless, a bit of a fun. I had no idea what was really going on in my parents' marriage and how it would soon tear our family apart.

We also spent a lot of time with my Grandad, my mum's dad. He always had a pipe sticking out of the corner of his mouth and Natalie and I called him 'Popeye'. He had just one tooth in his bottom gum which he'd wiggle at me, ignoring my squeals, as I sat on his lap, cosy in the folds of his woolly cardigan.

Up until I was seven everything was fun. With just two years separating us, Natalie and I were constant playmates. Then, as now, our relationship veered between soul mates one day and sworn enemies the next, but hey, at least things were never boring.

We were always very competitive with each other. Natalie was a jealous toddler the day I first appeared home from hospital in the back of the family Morris Minor. And we still fight over Mum's attention now. Mum always went out of her way to treat us fairly and make sure we both felt included in everything. But it was never enough to stop the bickering. If I even thought about touching one of Natalie's favourite Barbie dolls, she'd go mad. But I was just as protective over my toys.

When I was five or six I would pore over the family photo albums and jealously interrogate Mum about any pictures I didn't appear in.

'Why are you cuddling Natalie in this picture and I'm not there?' I'd demand. 'You weren't born then, Nikki,' Mum would explain. But that wasn't good enough for me. I'd just rage inside, furious that there had been a life before me.

In another picture from that old album Dad is pushing

4

me in the buggy while Mum holds Nat's hand. 'But why weren't you pushing me that day, Mum?' I yelled. Even though I had Dad's total devotion, I wanted Mum's too. And if that meant trampling all over Natalie to get it, so be it.

My competitive nature and quick temper had probably been bubbling under since birth. I cried pretty much continuously for the first fortnight after I was born, which should have given Mum a bit of a clue what she was in for.

And as a toddler I was pretty tough. Certainly any three-year-old who ever went for a spin in my favourite bubble car at the Early Learning Centre in Watford never made that mistake twice. Mum found me pulling one kid out of the car by his jumper before leaping in and driving off round the shop myself.

At play school I had to stand in the toilet on my own one morning for putting a wooden brick on one of the other kids' heads. Another time I was hauled up for kicking one of the boys.

At infant and then junior school I was always up to something, getting into scrapes. Dad called me his 'little bruiser' but I knew he was proud of me for sticking up for myself. But I was popular in class too – I had a big group of friends and I was always the leader.

I was in the Brownies, went to the church's holiday club, loved swimming at weekends and was always out playing on my bike after school with kids from our street. My friends Zanep and Julidah from down the road were always round our house and we'd play for hours in the twin room I shared with Natalie.

Our house was a fairly typical chalet bungalow in the north-western suburbs of London, with two bedrooms overlooking the street at the front and above these a big attic which we used as a playroom. Our garden was magical. Back then it seemed huge to me, with its long slope of grass stretching from a wooden-boarded summerhouse all the way down to the living room window. To one side of the garden was a 'secret' passageway which got narrower and narrower until it reached the special spot Natalie and I used for burying treasure – well, Mum's old jewellery from the 1970s. In another corner there were swings, a slide and a climbing tree.

On the patio at the top of the garden, we would help Dad light bonfires in the winter and in summer we would stage our theatrical productions there, prancing and dancing up and down.

Sometimes I think that house in Stanley Road will haunt me for the rest of my life – I was so happy there and I was a kid there. Because what I didn't know then was that the time spent living in that house up until I was seven *was* my childhood – all of it.

The only thing that made it OK to be called inside from that magical garden was the thought of one of Mum's dinners. Up until the age of seven I would eat pretty much anything she put in front of me. I was never one of those 'just three chips and half an organic sausage' type of kids.

I'd fed well as a baby and as soon as I went on to solids, anything Mum served up, I'd eat. On Sunday it would be a big roast and then midweek we would have home-made burgers, meatballs or liver and veg. And that would be followed by a proper dessert – a steamed pudding or fruit with custard. I loved Mum's food. We all did.

And going out to restaurants was a real treat too. I was only two when we all went on holiday to Crete and I ordered a huge plate of mussels in a restaurant. 'You might not like those, Nikki darling,' Mum warned, but I wasn't going to be dissuaded.

When my meal arrived everyone in the restaurant was staring at this tiny little toddler tucking into a huge plate of shellfish – but I loved it.

Back then food was fun and a big part of our family life. But within a few short years there was no fun left in either food or our family.

CHAPTER 2
THINGS FALL APART

'Will you please stand on your feet and not on your head?' Mum yelled at me one Saturday morning. 'You spend more time upside down than the right way up,' she grumbled.

It was about the millionth time she'd had a go at me about it, half jokingly, half worried I might do myself some permanent damage by spending so much time performing handstands. I'd even watch TV upside down. And when I wasn't doing that I would be cartwheeling and backflipping my way up and down the wooden floor of our hall.

'OK,' Mum finally said, 'if you love all this acrobatics so much we might as well put it to some use.' The following week she'd signed me up for the Northwood Gymnastics Club. I was beyond excited. I was still only six years old but getting dressed up in a royal-blue leotard, my long, dark-brown hair pulled back in a pony tail, I felt so important – like a proper gymnast.

All those hours spent on my head had obviously been worth it, because I quickly showed a real ability at gymnastics. And I loved it all – the training, the competitions and just messing around with the other girls afterwards. Cartwheels, somersaults and flips on the mats, vaulting and the asymmetric bars – I couldn't get enough of it.

Within a couple of weeks the coach must have decided I had some natural talent because I was selected to become part of the gym's squad.

I was so proud of myself. It was amazing. But being part of the squad instantly meant a lot more pressure. I was representing the London Borough of Hillingdon and there was a gala every six months and a new grade to work for every couple of months. And that meant a lot more training. Within a couple of months this had shot up from gymnastics once a week to sessions three evenings a week and for three hours on a Saturday morning. We'd often do a full hour of tumbling followed by an hour of vaulting. It was exhausting and any sense of enjoyment quickly seeped away.

Being the way I was, I couldn't be happy unless I was the best in the squad and unfortunately there were girls there who were clearly better than me. One Saturday morning we were in the changing rooms, messing around in our leotards at the end of a tough, three-hour session. One of the other girls was standing behind me, staring at me, when she suddenly said, 'Haven't you got a big bum, Nikki?'

I could feel myself going bright red but I just laughed and pulled my shell suit on quickly. How embarrassing.

That evening I crept into Mum's bedroom when she and

10

Dad were watching telly downstairs. I opened their wardrobe door and stood in front of the full length mirror bolted to its inside.

I analysed my bum carefully. Then I stared at the slight curve of my tummy and then my fleshy upper arms.

Maybe that girl at gymnastics was right – maybe my bum was a bit on the lardy side. Maybe that was why I still couldn't get those flips right.

After all, that other girl's arms were much thinner than mine. And she had a tiny bum and virtually no tummy at all and she was brilliant at flips. In fact she was better than me at almost all the routines. Plus, she was really popular with the other girls too.

And I guess that is how it all began. Somewhere in my seven-year-old brain I started to think that to be better at gymnastics and to be more popular, I had to be skinny. And because I didn't just want to be better than I was at gymnastics, but to be the best, then I couldn't just be skinny. Oh no, I would have to be *the* skinniest.

'I'll keep my tracksuit bottoms on today, Mum,' I said as I went into the gym the following week. She didn't think anything of it then, but I'd decided I didn't want anyone laughing at my fat bum ever again.

Yet it would be too easy to say that one girl's catty comments sparked off the illness which was to blight the next ten years of my life and which will inevitably be with me in some way until the day I die.

No, I think that was just what brought things to a head. Looking back, I think I was already vulnerable to any kind of comment that may have been made about my size. Because already a whole truckload of misery was slowly building up behind the front door at Stanley Road.

11

Dad was having a really rough time at work. Things had always been rocky for him there, but it was getting worse. He kept clashing with his bosses and felt everyone was out to get him. After he joined the union and became heavily involved with it, he felt his bosses were out to get him for being an activist.

'They're destroying me,' I'd hear him rant at Mum.

'Just keep your head down and stop causing trouble, Dave,' she would tell him. 'We need the money.'

But that would just drive Dad into a fury. 'You don't understand what it's like working there,' he'd rage.

For 18 months he was involved in disciplinary action and subject to reports. It sent him – and all of us – crazy.

Because Dad was convinced he was about to be sacked, he started working part-time at a stamp shop he set up in part of his dad's jewellery shop off the Edgware Road. So, on top of all the stress at work, he was also working really long hours in his second job, desperate to keep paying the mortgage so we could stay in our perfect home.

He was angry all the time. Looking back, he was probably suffering from depression or stress, perhaps both, but at seven all I could see was that the dad I adored had turned overnight into some kind of raging monster.

In many ways I feel sorry for my dad because he'd had a really tough childhood. He was born in America but at six his father moved to London with a new wife while his mother, Magda, stayed in New York with her new husband. Magda had custody of Dad but, according to the family story, his dad went over there and brought him back to Britain. Having got him back, though, his dad and his new wife realised they didn't really want him. They didn't take care of him and he ended up stuck in a children's home.

12

Magda still lives in Manhattan in some plush apartment but my dad doesn't have much contact with her and he doesn't speak to his father at all. So Dad has had it hard himself in life – he says that's why he can't show emotion in front of his kids. But I tell you, he could certainly show anger back then.

And although I can see the reasons for his behaviour now, at that time I was just a little girl who desperately wanted her daddy. And Dad had changed so much – he didn't want me following him to the betting shop any more and there were no more runs around the streets.

One day I entered a gymnastics competition and won second place. I was so proud of myself and sprinted straight from the gym to Dad's stamp shop, my silver medal bouncing around my neck as I ran down the road.

I walked into the shop and said, 'Hi,' waiting for Dad to notice the shining medal on my chest and to throw his arms around me and tell me how proud he was of his favourite daughter. I waited as he looked up and gave me half a smile over a book of stamps. Then I waited some more. And some more. He didn't notice, and it was soon obvious he was never going to notice. He hadn't seen my medal and, worse still, he hadn't registered the sheer joy on my face. In the end I said, 'Look, Dad, I came second.' I can't even remember how he reacted. Whatever he did or said, that isn't the bit I remember about that day.

Dad began missing my and Natalie's birthday parties. And if we had friends round after school and were being noisy he'd go mad. One evening I had my friend Vicky Fiddler round to play. We were busily brushing each other's hair at the kitchen table when Dad burst into the room in a fury. 'Who's this?' he yelled, glaring at us both.

I was devastated he could act so mad in front of one of my friends.

He was always so angry. For as long as I can remember he had called me 'Fatso' and 'Lump' but it had always seemed like a joke. Now the things he was saying seemed more cruel. He said to Natalie that at night sawdust would fall out of her head on to the pillow because she was so stupid.

At that time Dad was working a lot of night shifts too, which meant Natalie and I had to creep around the house all day, terrified we would wake him up. And when he was on normal day shifts we would skulk around when he was due home, waiting for the sound of his key in the lock, at which point we would run upstairs and hide.

One afternoon we accidentally scratched his back-gammon board with my shoe buckle and were so terrified of how he'd react that we spent the entire afternoon hiding in Mum's wardrobe.

Dad wasn't violent towards us – although I can remember the odd whack if we were playing up – but just really, really angry. Most of his anger he was taking out on Mum and they were rowing all the time. A lot of their fights happened first thing in the morning when Dad came in tired and grumpy from a night shift and got into bed with Mum. Natalie and I didn't need to eavesdrop at their door to hear what was going on. We'd wake up and look at each other as we heard every word being hurled across their bedroom. Often it was about stuff I just didn't understand, other times it was Dad's problems at work or how we'd keep our house if he didn't have a job.

As the months went by it felt like they were rowing about everything, right down to what dress Mum was wearing. One time I remember her coming downstairs all dressed up for an evening out. 'Why are you wearing that?' Dad barked. Mum's face crumpled and she looked totally lost. 'You've never had any class,' he sneered at her as she turned around and slowly went back upstairs to change.

I understand now how complicated marriages can be and that there are two sides to every story. And there were probably times when Mum was nasty to Dad or wound him up, but I don't remember them. I just remember Mum becoming less and less sparkly, less and less pretty and more and more ground down. She stopped having friends round to the house and looked exhausted all the time.

One day I heard Dad tell her she was hopeless and had no vision.

'You and your family have never thought I was good enough,' Mum shouted back at him. Mum had been brought up a Catholic and Dad's family hadn't liked it, although by this point the two of them couldn't even agree what channel to watch on the telly, let alone on big things like religion. They never went out the way they had once done and there was no more cuddling up in front of a video.

I was seven and all I wanted was for my daddy to play with me and Natalie and to talk to us, but all we saw of him was him arguing on the telephone with this massive firm, being horrible to our Mum and shouting at us.

Things took a turn for the worse around about the time I turned eight, in the spring of 1990. Mum sat me and Nat down one day and told us Grandad was ill – really ill. People kept talking about the 'C-word' and although I didn't really have a clue what it really meant, it was clearly bad.

Mum took me out of school to visit Grandad one afternoon at the Central Middlesex Hospital, where he was being treated. She'd popped into the baker's on the way to collect me and she gave me a gingerbread man to eat on the train on the way there. It all started out feeling like a real treat.

But as soon as I saw Grandad in the hospital I knew something was badly wrong. I think it was the first time I'd ever seen him without his woolly cardigan on and that was enough of a shock. Instead, he was wearing a white hospital smock which seemed to smother him, he was so thin and pale. There was no pipe sticking out of his mouth any more and any Popeye strength had clearly been sapped away.

I sat on Grandad's bed and chattered about gymnastics and Brownies and the latest dramas at Hillside Infant School while Mum squeezed into an adjoining toilet with a doctor 'for a word in private'. It was the only place they could find to tell her that her father was dying.

When Mum walked back into the room her whole body was shaking except for her face, which was totally rigid.

The doctor had just told her the results of surgery on a blockage in Grandad's bowel. 'We opened him up but saw immediately there was no point in operating – it was too far gone, so we just sewed him up again. Mrs Grahame, I'm terribly sorry, but there is nothing further we can do for your father.'

Mum nearly passed out from shock but pulled herself together to come back into the room, where I was still talking Grandad through my flip routines.

We chatted for a bit longer, then Mum and I walked back to the station. When we got home she told me run out and play in the garden while it was still sunny. It was years later that she admitted to me that, while I cartwheeled up and down the lawn, she slid down our living room wall and sobbed and sobbed and sobbed.

Mum had always adored her father and it was obvious there was something special between them. I think that is why she had always understood and accepted the closeness of the bond between me and Dad.

Mum's childhood had been pretty tough. Her family were hard-up and Grandad had a fierce temper, but no matter how violent or angry he had been, she always idolised him and never blamed him for any of the troubles between her parents.

When Grandma died of cancer when she was 51 and Mum was 18, Mum had been upset, but not devastated. But, faced with the prospect of losing Grandad, she just went into freefall – she couldn't cope at all.

Grown-ups don't use the word 'terminal' to kids and even if she had done, I don't suppose I would have known what it meant. But I could see myself that every time we went to visit Grandad he was thinner, paler and more ill-looking. He didn't have the energy for corny jokes any more and seemed to find it exhausting enough just breathing in and out. He was fading away in front of us.

And as Grandad slipped away, it seemed Mum was going the same way. 'But he's never been ill in his life and he's not even 70,' she would repeat again and again. She would get choked up at the slightest thing and tears were never far away.

So there we were that summer of 1990. Mum sad all the time, Dad mad all the time. Mum and Dad fighting, me and Natalie fighting. Grandad dying.

Then Rex fell ill and was taken back and forth to the vet. He was diagnosed with a tumour on his back leg and the vet said there was nothing more they could do. He'd have to be put down. Dad adored Rex, so when I saw him crying as he stroked his head one morning, I knew what it meant.

Rex was 18 and he'd been there all my life. The house felt so quiet without him. No mad mongrel racing up and down the hall every time the doorbell went. Just silence.

It was tough going back to school at the start of that new term. I'd never been academic but I'd always had fun at Hillside and been popular with the other girls. But even teachers noticed I had lost my energy and enthusiasm. Now there were so many more things to think about in my life than there had been a year ago.

And rather than just playing French skipping in the playground with all the other girls, I would spend more and more time staring at my friends, asking myself the same old questions: 'Is my bum bigger than theirs?', 'Are my legs chubbier?', 'Is my tummy fatter?'

Nicola Carter was one of my best friends even though her bum was smaller than mine, her tummy flatter and her legs thinner. She had long, brown hair like mine and freckles scattered across her nose but oh, she was so skinny. She looked amazing.

All the kids in our class called us 'Big Nikki' and 'Small Nikki'. Well, you can imagine how that made me feel. I was clearly just too big.

With so much bad stuff going on at home I threw myself into gymnastics more and more. And the more gymnastics I did, the more competitive I became about it. I may only have been seven but I was incredibly determined and driven. I only ever wanted to be the best. I knew I wasn't as good as the other girls, not as pretty as them and not as thin as them. But rather than just think, Oh well, that's the way it goes, I was determined to become the best, the prettiest and the skinniest.

Gymnastics had become a constant round of grades and competitions and although there wasn't much enjoyment left in it for me, I was still desperate to excel.

One evening I was standing in the gym with the other nine girls as we waited for the results of our grade five to be read out. Finally the coach got to me. 'Pass,' she said. 'Not distinction this time, Nikki. That's a bit useless for you, isn't it?' She probably didn't mean anything by it and if she did she was probably just trying to gee me up a bit, but all I heard was the word 'useless'. It stuck in my brain like a rock and I just couldn't shift it.

Shortly afterwards Mum was watching me line up to collect my badge at a county trials competition. She remembers that as I waited my turn she looked at my face and all she could see was torment and misery. I was only seven and I'd reached a pretty good standard as a gymnast but I felt useless.

I had to improve, I had to get better. And for that, I had to get thinner. I also deserved to be punished for not being as good as I should have been. Well, that's what I thought. So I started denying myself treats.

Every week Mum would buy me a Milky Bar and Natalie a Galaxy to keep in our sock drawer. It was up to us when we ate them but we were both ultra-sensible and limited ourselves to one cube a day as that way they lasted longer. I'd also treat myself to a cube before training on a Saturday morning.

But when I started feeling more and more useless at gymnastics and more and more unhappy finding myself in the crossfire between Mum and Dad at home, I thought, I'm not going to have my cube of Milky Bar today. I don't need it.

That very first time I denied myself, it felt good. Like I'd finally achieved something myself. And I liked the feeling so much that I did it again.

The other treats I had loved as a little kid were Kinder Eggs. I'd always been an early riser, which drove my parents mad, so years earlier Mum had made a deal with me that if I stayed in bed until seven o'clock I got a chocolate egg.

For ages it was just brilliant. Early in the morning I'd be wide awake but as soon as seven o'clock came round on my panda bear alarm clock, I'd go rushing into Mum and Dad's room, climb into bed between them and claim my Kinder Egg.

But when I started wanting to be skinnier I started opening my reward, throwing away the chocolate and just keeping the toy inside.

And if anyone else, like my auntie, offered me a bag of sweets I'd just say I was full up or I didn't like them. When I deprived myself it felt good. But even then I knew this had to remain a secret – I couldn't tell anyone.

During that long, miserable summer the rows between Mum and Dad just grew more vicious. Mum was usually teary and weak, Dad raging or sullen. And Grandad was fading away. Everyone was pulling in different directions, caught up in their own personal tragedy.

For me, how to avoid eating became something to think about instead of what was going on at home.

By the end of the summer Grandad was really ill. One evening all four of us went to visit him. After a while Dad, Natalie and I went and sat in the corridor so that Mum and Grandad could have a bit of time alone together. We'd been sitting there about 20 minutes when she came out of his room shaking. She didn't need to say anything. Grandad had gone. He was 69.

All the way home in the car I wailed until we got back indoors and Dad tipped me into bed exhausted.

Mum was utterly distraught and lost the plot entirely. She was 36 but felt her life was over too. It was like she was drowning but had no idea how to save herself.

'Pull yourself together,' Dad would shout at her when he found her crying yet again. It was his idea of tough love but Mum couldn't pull herself together. Dad couldn't understand why not, so they drifted even further apart.

Mum went to the doctor and said she was in a mess, she couldn't cope any more with her grief, Dad's anger and their fighting. The doctor said she would talk to Dad about things if he'd make an appointment to see her.

'Please go to the GP, Dave,' Mum begged one evening as she washed the dishes. 'You need support for all the stress at work otherwise we're not going to survive this. I haven't got any energy left to fight you any more. We need proper help.'

But Dad just refused. 'I'm not going,' he said. And I think at that moment, with Mum leaning against the kitchen sink and Dad standing in the conservatory, my parents' marriage ended.

A couple of days later – about a fortnight after Grandad died – Mum woke up and thought, Right, this is it. Life really is too short for all the rowing and fighting. I want a divorce. Just like that, after 15 years of marriage, she decided she'd had enough. Natalie and I would have had to be blind, deaf and very stupid not to realise that this time things were really bad. But, because divorce is such a big thing for a kid to get their head around, I don't think either of us had really thought it would happen.

One morning, soon after Natalie had left for her school and I was waiting for Mum to walk me to mine, she came into my room, knelt down in front of me and just hugged me and burst into tears. I said, 'Mum, why are you crying?' And she just wouldn't tell me. I kept asking her why, but she couldn't say.

It was a Saturday morning a couple of weeks later when Dad and Mum told us what was really happening. They had been rowing for hours, shouting and screaming at each other. Nat and I just wanted them to hurry up because Dad always took us swimming on a Saturday morning.

Then they came out of the kitchen and took us into the living room. 'Right,' said Mum, 'Your dad and I are going to separate.'

I felt numb. Mum was crying, then Dad started sobbing like a baby. Every time she went to speak, he would shout over her. Then Mum was screaming, 'Let me speak, let me speak,' but when she began he stormed out of the room. It was like something out of *EastEnders* – I didn't think this could happen in real life.

My whole childhood had been blown apart.

Half an hour later, Dad took me and Natalie swimming and we had a really cool competition to see who could stay underwater the longest. Weird, isn't it?

CHAPTER 3
A BIG, FAT LUMP

I pulled my Benetton stripy top over my head and slid my jeans with the Minnie Mouse patches down over my ankles, then just stood and stared.

I was standing, again, in front of the floor-length mirror inside the door of the wardrobe in Mum and Dad's bedroom, wearing just my knickers. In reality I was probably a tiny bit chubby at the time, but all I could see was someone mega fat compared with everyone else at gymnastics *and* everyone else in my class at school, if not the rest of the world.

By now I was spending more and more time analysing my body and staring at the bodies of other girls around me to see how I compared. At that time cycling shorts were really in fashion and everyone was wearing them. I'd look at anyone wearing them and if their thighs touched when their feet were together they were fat. If their thighs didn't touch they were skinny and I wanted to look like them. Mine touched. And Natalie's touched even more. She's so fat, I thought. I never want to look like that.

School swimming lessons were a total nightmare – all those girls in their swimming costumes looking slim and gorgeous and athletic, and then there was me. I was just a big lump. I felt fat compared with all my friends and virtually everyone else.

I spent ages working out which girls in my class had bigger thighs than me, which had rounder tummies and which had chubbier arms.

And just when I thought I couldn't look any worse plodding from the changing rooms to the swimming pool, the unthinkable happened – Nicola Carter got a green swimming costume with ruffles on it. Exactly the same as mine! Now it would be obvious to everyone that my bum was totally massive next to hers. I'd never ever live down the 'Big Nikki' label.

I hated the way I looked. Giving up chocolate had made me feel good but it hadn't really done anything to make me lose weight, so I had to take more drastic action. At eight years old I was too young to understand about calories, but I knew – like all kids do – that some things are 'bad' for you. For goodness sake, adults never stop going on about it: 'Don't eat all those crisps, they're bad for you' or 'Eat your cabbage, it's good for you.'

So really it was quite easy to know what to do – just follow the grown-ups' rules. I started denying myself all the 'bad' things that Mum, Dad, my friends' parents and teachers had ever talked about – chips, pastry, custard, puddings, chocolate and crisps. If Mum was going to cook 'bad' foods I'd suggest something else instead, saying I'd gone off chips or wasn't in the mood for custard. And at first, preoccupied with her own losses and sadness, Mum didn't have a clue what I was up to.

I took any opportunity I could find to deprive myself of 'bad foods'. One Saturday afternoon it was Joanna Price's birthday party. Her parents had arranged for a swimming party but while everyone else was chucking each other in the pool and screaming crazily, I stood quietly at the shallow end, checking out their thighs and tummies. Afterwards, back at Joanna's house, I carefully picked all the fruit out of a trifle, leaving the jelly and custard at the bottom of my bowl. I was determined I would be the skinniest girl in a swimming costume for the next party.

Then I started giving away my food at lunchtime. Every morning Mum would send me off to school with my yellow teddy-bear lunchbox filled with sandwiches, a bag of Hula Hoops, a Blue Riband chocolate bar and a satsuma. And every night I returned with the box empty except for a few crumbs stuck to the bottom.

What Mum didn't know was that I'd hardly touched the food she had put inside. It was easy to offload the crisps and chocolate to any of the greedy-guts who sat near me at dinner break. After a couple of months I started depriving myself of the sandwiches too. They were more difficult to give away, so I'd stick them straight in a bin instead.

With a couple of hundred kids all sitting eating their lunch in the school hall, there was no way a teacher could notice what I was doing. One day my friend Joanna asked why I kept giving my food away but I just laughed and changed the subject. I didn't really have an answer for that question myself.

As I never, ever felt hungry, I didn't care about going

without lunch. I just felt good inside when I denied myself. I felt kind of victorious, as if I had won a battle that only I was aware was taking place.

By the autumn of 1990 my thinking had moved determinedly into a place where I was going to eat as little as possible and become as skinny as possible. Then I started skipping breakfast. Before, Mum had always made me and Natalie sit down for a bowl of Frosties or Ricicles. But it was so frantic in our house in the morning that it was dead easy to chuck them in the bin or ram them down the plug hole of the sink without Mum or even Natalie noticing.

Mum would be dashing in and out of the shower to get dressed and make her own breakfast and I quickly learned how to get rid of any evidence very fast indeed. Other mornings I'd say to her, 'Don't bother sorting any breakfast for me. I've already made myself a couple of slices of toast.' Even then I was like a master criminal – I'd crumble a few crumbs of bread on a plate, then leave it on the draining board to make my story appear believable.

At first Mum bought it, but then she noticed I was losing weight and her suspicions were aroused. One afternoon I walked in from school and instead of her normal cheery smile and 'Hi, darling,' she just stared at me. I could see the shock in her eyes. She had noticed for the first time that I had dramatically lost weight. My grey pleated school skirt was swinging around my hips whereas before it had sat comfortably around my tummy. And my red cardigan was baggy and billowing over the sharp angles of my shoulders.

'Nikki, you're wasting away,' she half joked. 'You'll have to eat more for your dinner.' But behind the nervous laugh there was strain in her voice. Maybe in the back of her mind she had noticed I'd been getting skinnier for a while, but now it was blatantly obvious.

It didn't bother me how worried she was, though. I was losing weight and it was good, good, good.

From then on Mum watched me like a hawk at every meal. The next breakfast time I used my 'I've had toast earlier, Mum' line she was on to me in a flash.

'Well, if you have, young lady, how come the burglar alarm didn't go off when you went into the kitchen, because I set it last night?' she said.

She angrily tipped a load of Frosties into a bowl, doused them in milk and slapped them down in front of me. I spent the next 20 minutes pushing them around the bowl with my spoon until she nipped into the hall to find Natalie's school shoes or something and then I leapt out of my chair and shoved them down the sink. Ha, ha, I'd won after all!

Dinner times got a lot harder too. For a long while I had been eating the meals Mum made me at night – I'd allowed myself that much, but no more. But that autumn, as the days grew shorter and the weather colder, I just got stricter and stricter on myself until there were only certain bits of dinner I would allow myself to eat.

Why was I doing it? I had started out just wanting to be thinner and a better gymnast but quite quickly my eight-year-old mind had come to see not eating as something I *had* to do. It was like a compulsion. I had to eat less and be in total control of what I was eating. And if Mum tried to stop me I had to find a way to get away with it.

By now, depriving myself was just as important as, if not more than, becoming skinny.

27

Dinner times became a battleground. As soon as the front door slammed shut behind me as I walked in from school there would be the usual yell, 'What's for dinner, Mum?', that is heard in millions of homes across the country every afternoon. But while most mothers' replies are normally greeted with a 'Yeah, yummy' or at worst a 'Yuk, that's gross,' in our house Mum's evening menu was just the beginning of a negotiating session that could last for hours.

Usually Mum gave in and made me whatever I demanded because she was desperate for me to eat something and she thought that if she gave in to me, at least I would have something. But even that didn't always work. Often she would slave for ages cooking something that she thought I might find acceptable, chicken or fish, only for me to shove it away the moment she laid it down on the table.

Mum tried everything to make me eat. She tried persuading me: 'Go on, Nikki, just for me, please eat your dinner up.' And she tried disciplining me, threatening that I wouldn't be allowed to go out with my friends or to gymnastics unless I ate.

Sometimes she got so frustrated with me that she totally lost it and started screaming and shouting. But that was fine. I'd just scream and shout back.

Other times she simply sobbed and sobbed, begging me to eat while I looked at her blankly. Getting Mum crying was always a result. It meant she hadn't the strength to fight that particular mealtime and it was a victory for me. Dad was still living in the house but he was normally at work at mealtimes, which meant Mum was desperately trying to cope with me on her own — as well as watching her marriage collapse and trying to come to terms with having lost Grandad.

Although only eight, I was already an accomplished liar. 'Did you eat your lunch at school today, Nikki?' Mum would ask. 'Yes thanks. The egg sandwiches were great,' I'd say. I always gave just enough detail that Mum couldn't be entirely sure whether I was lying, although deep down she must have thought I probably was.

I'd also discovered a brilliant new way of getting thin – exercise. I started with sit-ups every single night in my bedroom. It was great because Natalie now slept in the attic room, which meant I could get up to anything in my room and no one would know.

'Night, darling,' Mum would say, tucking me into bed and kissing my forehead. 'Night, Mum,' I'd call out to her as she shut the door, already throwing back the duvet, ready for at least 200 sit-ups before allowing myself to sleep.

Soon the bones started to jut out at my elbows and my legs looked like sticks. Mum was becoming more and more worried. She was equally concerned by what she saw in my face – a haunted, troubled look and eyes that had lost every bit of sparkle. My sense of fun had disappeared and I was withdrawn, distracted and sullen.

One Sunday lunchtime all four of us went to the Beefeater for a roast. It was a birthday 'do' and so we were all making a show of togetherness.

When we got to the table, Mum, Dad and Nat all sat down while I hovered at the edge. 'Sit down, Nikki,' said Mum. But I couldn't. I had to keep moving, had to keep using up that energy inside me to make me thinner. And I didn't want to be near all that food – it felt disgusting.

I refused to sit down for the entire meal. Mum and Dad both tried to persuade me and got mad with me, but nothing could make me sit at that table. That was when they really started to worry there was a major problem emerging. And they were scared.

It was about this time that *The Karen Carpenter Story* was on television. It was on too late at night for me but Mum saw it and immediately spotted the similarities. And it was then that the presence of 'anorexia' as an illness first entered our lives.

Anorexia – the name given to a condition where people, usually women, starve themselves to reduce their weight – has probably been around since the end of the 19th century. In Victorian times it was thought to be a form of 'hysteria' affecting middle- or upper-class women. It was only in the 1980s in America that it became more recognised and clinics began treating sufferers.

The death of Karen Carpenter, one half of the brother-and-sister singing duo The Carpenters, played a huge part in increasing understanding of the illness. She had refused food for years and used laxatives to control her weight before dying in 1983 from heart failure caused by her anorexia.

It was only after the film of her life, made in 1989, was aired in Britain that people here had any idea about what anorexia really was. And even then it was regarded as a condition which only affected teenage girls. That's what made Mum think at first that it couldn't be what was wrong with me. I was only eight, so how could I possibly have it? But still she was worried.

'Right, if you won't eat your dinner, I'm taking you to the doctor – tomorrow!' she yelled at me at the end of another fraught meal.

The following evening after school – it was towards the end of 1990 – Mum marched me into our local surgery in Northwood. Our family GP was off on maternity leave, so we saw a locum instead. Mum explained to him how I would agree to eat only certain things and how at other times I'd refuse to eat entirely or shove food in the bin or down the sink when I thought no one was watching.

The doctor was one of those types who treat children as if they're all a bit thick. 'So, my dear,' he said slowly, 'what have you eaten today?'

This was going to be a breeze, I just knew it.

'Well,' I said quietly and hesitantly, my very best 'butter wouldn't melt' look on my face. 'I had a slice of toast for breakfast, then my packed lunch at school, although I didn't have the crisps because they're not very good for you, are they?'

Mum looked at me in disbelief. 'Tell the truth, Nikki,' she hissed.

'But I am, Mum,' I lied effortlessly, thinking of the one mouthful of sandwich that had passed my lips all day.

'Well, Mrs Grahame,' said the doctor. 'I can see she's a bit on the skinny side but I don't think it's anything to worry about at this time. It'll all blow over, no doubt. You know what girls are like with their fads and fashions.'

'She's not faddy,' insisted Mum. 'I know my daughter and it's more serious than that.'

'Well, let's just keep an eye on her and see what happens,' said the doctor, his decision clearly made.

We drove home in silence, Mum feeling defeated again and me victorious once more. No way was anyone going to be 'keeping an eye' on me!

And when I wasn't doing the screaming and shouting it

was Mum or Dad's turn. After their initial decision to split they had decided to give their marriage another go. Then the rows just became even more vicious and after a torturous couple of months they returned to the idea of divorce. But because they couldn't agree on what to do about selling the house and splitting the money, we all carried on living under the same roof.

In my eyes Dad was still acting like a monster. He'd gone from someone I would chase down the road every time he left the house to someone so bitter and angry that I didn't want to be around him. I transferred all the intensity of my feelings for Dad straight over to Mum. And now I'd lost Grandad and Dad, I clung to her, both emotionally and physically. I reverted to acting like a toddler. If we were watching television I'd insist on sitting on her lap and if she went out I'd stand by the window waiting for her to return. If it was evening time I'd lie on her bed until she got home.

Mum became the focus of everything for me – both my intense love on the good days and my anger and frustration on the bad. I wouldn't let Natalie get anywhere near her. I needed her all for myself. So poor old Nat had her close bond with Mum smashed to pieces.

By worshipping Dad rather than Mum I'd probably backed the wrong horse, but I wasn't going to lose out now. No, that would have to be Nat. That caused big rows between me and her then – and it still does even today.

But even though Natalie and I both desperately needed Mum, she didn't really have much left to give us. She was weak, crying all the time, and I was just so needy that she felt exhausted, which in turn made me feel abandoned.

My world was falling apart.

When Mum couldn't stand sharing her bed with Dad any more she decided that she, Natalie and I would all move up into the attic and live there. From now on I slept on a double bed with Mum as I couldn't bear to be physically apart from her. Natalie slept on an old brown sofa. All our toys were still scattered around the room, so it seemed like a bit of adventure having Mum up there with us, but it was kind of weird too.

By now I was struggling at school. The less I ate, the harder I found it to concentrate. And so much of my energy was being spent thinking about how I was going to dodge the next meal, how much I'd eaten so far that day and what Mum might be thinking about making for dinner that night, that I just couldn't focus on lessons at all.

Then at break times I started going to the girls' toilets and doing sit-ups. I would do dozens in a session before the bell, then dash back to my desk all hot and sweaty. One of the girls in my class must have told on me because one day a teacher came in and found me and said I wasn't allowed to do it any more.

That must have been when school started getting really worried about me and called Mum in for a meeting. They said they were concerned about my rapidly falling weight and that I didn't seem able to concentrate in class any more.

Mum hauled me back to the doctor again. It was a different locum, so we went through the same charade of my pretending to be eating a healthy if meagre diet and the doctor believing me. Again we were sent home, Mum even more dejected and me even more triumphant.

Dad was seldom around at mealtimes despite still living in the house, so he rarely saw the battles. When Mum tried

33

to talk to him about me, it just ended up in another row as they tried to blame each other for my getting into such a state. Although what kind of state it was exactly, they still weren't sure themselves.

One night Dad was in the pub when my friend Sian's mum walked up to him.

'Are you Nikki's dad?' she asked. Dad nodded and this woman he'd never met before grabbed his arm with a terrible sense of urgency.

'My daughter is really worried about Nikki,' she said. 'She's hiding in the toilets at school doing exercises and refusing to eat. Are you aware of what's going on?' she said.

Dad looked blank and was forced to admit he didn't really know the extent of what was happening at all.

'Well, you need to be worried,' my friend's mum told him. 'If you don't do something, your daughter is going to die.'

CHAPTER 4

NEVER GIVE IN

So why was I doing it? I can imagine that a lot of people reading this will find it totally weird that someone should want to put themselves through the pain and misery of starving themselves. Not to mention all the upset and stress it causes for their family.

As an eight-year-old I had no idea about the big 'why' behind it all – it was just something I *had* to do. A bit like other girls had to get every single badge at Brownies or had to get 100 per cent in a spelling test. But this was obviously more compulsive. And potentially fatal too.

Some of the anorexia counsellors I've had have said that maybe my eating disorder started as a bid to make myself literally disappear in the warring situation at home, as if by physically getting smaller I would just fade from view. And another expert said he thought I simply went on a hunger strike that got out of control. He thought I was so angry and devastated at how my perfect life had been shattered that I was refusing to eat until someone picked up all the pieces and put them back together again.

Counsellors have also quizzed me endlessly about my mum and whether she was to blame in some way but I really don't think so. Mum has always been slim but not skinny and I never remember her dieting. But I do once recall her taking me and Nat to Folkestone for a weekend just when things were starting to go badly wrong with Dad. She was really stressed and hadn't been eating properly. She stood in the hotel bedroom admiring her flat tummy in the mirror and said, 'Ooh, I've really lost weight.' But I honestly don't think that alone could have caused it – there can't be a woman in the country who hasn't said something similar at some stage and not all their daughters have become anorexic.

Another counsellor – trust me, I've seen dozens – thought that on some subconscious level I was trying to copy the way Grandad had just faded away from life. He reckoned it was a 'mourning reaction' and I was trying to identify with Grandad by losing weight myself. And while I guess there might be some truth in that, part of me still thinks I would have become anorexic whatever happened. It was in my nature from before I was born, and the events of that year only brought it on at that particular time.

I also believe that anorexia just gave me something for myself that year as my life fell apart. I felt unhappy about everything that had happened, useless at gymnastics and inadequate at keeping my family together. But not eating was something I was good at. Not eating became my hobby, something that was all mine and that I could be in control of while my family and my perfect life fell apart around me.

In fact how much I ate was about the only thing I could control in the deepening chaos. And maybe I began to realise that not eating actually brought me quite a lot of control. Very soon I was pulling all the strings in my family. Mum's every waking moment became filled with begging me to eat, pacifying my moods, sorting out my medical support and worrying about me. And while I remained anorexic, all her attention remained focused on me.

And as I'd always wanted to be the best at everything I did, long before I'd even heard the word 'anorexic' I'd set about becoming the very best anorexic ever.

I didn't tell Natalie what I was doing and she never asked. I didn't tell my friends and certainly not Dad. And when Mum asked, begged or pleaded with me to tell her what the problem was, I simply denied there was a problem.

Even though I'd started depriving myself of food to get skinnier for gymnastics, that soon went out of the window and before long losing weight became an end in itself. In fact my gymnastics was only getting worse as by losing weight I was also losing muscle. I couldn't do the flips, I couldn't jump, I couldn't do rolls any more – and that made me feel even more useless.

Then, just as you might have imagined things couldn't have got much worse at home, they did – with bells on! Dad found out that Mum had started seeing another man. Even though they were supposed to be separated despite living under the same roof, he went mad.

It wasn't even as though Mum was having some mad, passionate affair. She'd just struck up a friendship with a bloke called Tony who used to pop round to fix her old

Morris Minor whenever it broken down – which was pretty often!

Natalie and I had always quite liked Tony. We'd usually be playing out in the street on our bikes while he messed around under the bonnet. He'd talk to us and ask about school and he seemed harmless and friendly. After he had finished on the car he would go inside to wash the grease off his hands and have a cuppa and a chat with Mum. And that is how it all started. Tony's marriage had been a bit rocky and I think he and Mum were two lost souls clinging to each other for a bit of comfort.

Natalie and I worked out what had been going on when the rows in our house reached volcanic proportions.

But, despite Dad's jealousy, there was no way Mum was ditching Tony and having Dad back. Because what I didn't know then was that, all through what I'd thought of as my perfect early years, my dad had been having a string of affairs.

Natalie was just nine months old when Mum and Dad had decided to have another baby and Mum fell pregnant almost immediately. But around the same time Dad started going out most nights with his mates, leaving Mum looking after a small baby alone and expecting another.

It was only one day when she found a long blonde hair wrapped around one of his socks as she filled the washing machine that everything became clear. Dad admitted it all. It was a woman who worked in one of our local shops. What a cliché! But it was easy, I guess – and so was she.

I love it when Mum tells the story about how she threw her best coat on, strapped Natalie in the buggy and marched up to the counter of the shop, pushing in front of all the other customers.

'I hear you've been screwing my husband,' she said calmly to the woman, suddenly finding herself the centre of attention in the shop as all the other customers listened in.

'Leave him alone,' Mum said determinedly.

'Are you threatening me?' the woman sneered.

'You're bloody right I am,' said Mum, spinning the buggy round and storming out.

I've always liked to think that moment was Mum's victory over a woman with the stunted imagination, let alone morals, to shag a man with kids. But it was a hollow victory. That weekend Mum miscarried the baby. She'd lost an unborn child and her belief in what her marriage had been.

Mum said everyone was entitled to make a mistake and agreed to take Dad back so long as he promised never to do it again. He said he couldn't promise but he'd try. Some commitment, eh? Anyway she took him back.

Mum says a string of 'other women' followed over the years, which is why when she finally called time on the marriage, she really couldn't go back.

It wasn't until I was older that Mum told me about Dad's affairs, but I picked up enough information from ear-wigging their rows at the time to have a pretty good idea what was going on.

I'd always been such a Daddy's girl, I'd adored him, and finding out that my dad wasn't who I thought he was hit me hard. I felt betrayed.

Tony started coming round quite a bit in the evenings. He would hold Mum when she cried about Dad, and Grandad, and me. If he'd known at that time what he was taking on by getting involved with Mum and all of us, he would probably have run for the hills! But he was kind and caring and he stuck around. He would come round a lot when Dad wasn't there, which was another huge jolt for me and Natalie. It just confirmed for us that we were never going to get our old life back. The only thing that softened the blow was that we both liked Tony. We called him Hog because his hair stuck up like a hedgehog's bristles. He didn't even seem to mind too much when we took the mickey out of him.

Mum, Natalie and I were still living in the attic because Dad was refusing to move out of the house. There was a court battle pending over who would keep the house and it was becoming really nasty. Dad instructed one of his American cousins, a hotshot lawyer from New York, to act on his behalf. And then a few times this really scary heavy bloke came round saying, 'We're going to make you an offer – you should take it.'

But Mum had nowhere to go to, so we stayed in the house, living like normal downstairs during the day when Dad was at work, then scuttling up to the attic each evening. We'd sit up there watching television and hear Dad walking around downstairs singing manically. It was like something out of a horror film.

One night it kicked off really badly between Mum and Dad. There was screaming and shouting downstairs, a smashed teapot and so much anger. I lay in bed, the pillow over my head to dull the noise as I cried and cried.

After that night Mum applied for a restraining order against Dad. In the end, though, she let him back into the house and the court case over what they should do with our home rumbled on.

In January 1991 Mum filed for divorce and my perfect life was well and truly over. That same month Dad finally lost his job and it was obvious that sooner or later we'd have to move out of my beloved Stanley Road.

Things at school were going rapidly downhill too. I started spending most of my days sitting in the medical room with the school nurse, Mrs Bullock. My teachers didn't mind because they could tell I was very weak. I looked awful and hadn't been concentrating on my lessons for months. Mum had told them about the problems at home and maybe they thought I was just going through a difficult patch and I'd pull through soon.

Mrs Bullock became a surrogate mother for me in the hours when I had to be away from my real mum. I loved her and wanted her total attention all the time. If another pupil dared to come to the medical room with a cut knee or something wrong with them and needed Mrs Bullock, I couldn't bear it. I would pace up and down, feeling angry and anxious. This is my room, I'd say to myself. I need Mrs Bullock – she's for me and me only.

By the beginning of 1991 I had reduced what I would allow myself to eat more and more until it was virtually nothing. For breakfast it would be one small glass full of hot orange squash and four cubes of fruit salad. Then Mrs Bullock would give me tea and two digestive biscuits in the medical room, which would be my lunch. Obviously she knew that wasn't enough, but I think she too was grateful to think I was getting something inside me.

I negotiated with Mum – or should I say bullied her? – into letting me eat my evening meals out of a peanut bowl. If she ever tried to serve something up on a normal dinner plate I'd just freak, push the whole lot away and refuse to eat anything at all.

But even a peanut bowl-sized portion was no guarantee

I would eat. For a normal dinner I would allow myself ten strands of spaghetti or two small potatoes with some vegetables. And when I had eaten the amount I'd decided was acceptable, that was it, I'd stop eating and however much Mum begged, cajoled or shouted at me, nothing would change my mind.

And all the time she was growing more and more terrified and frustrated as the weight fell off me.

We went to the doctor four or five times but each time it was a locum and he was insistent it was 'just a phase' or 'girls being girls' and 'something I would grow out of'. How wrong could he be?

My doctor's notes at the end of 1990 recorded my weight as 21.4 kilograms (3 stone 5 lb). By February 1991 it had dropped to 21 kilos (3 stone 4 lb). The locum described me as: 'Very quiet, introvert and controlled. Reluctant to open up. Kneading her hands and tearing up the Kleenex given to her when she started to cry.' But he still sent me home again.

I was also suffering from Raynaud's Disease, which affects blood flow to the extremities and means you are incredibly sensitive to the cold. But by then I had so little body fat protecting me that it was hardly surprising.

One evening things hit a new low at home. Mum had cooked dinner, so again I trailed up to the table, sat down, looked at my peanut bowl and point-blank refused to eat. Normally Mum would try to persuade me at first, but this time she just lost it.

'I can't stand this any more,' she screamed. 'Are you trying to kill yourself?'

She dragged me to the floor and with one hand held me down by my hair while with the other hand she scooped up fistfuls of pasta and tried to force them into my mouth. I was screaming, clawing at her and trying to push her off me. Then I clamped my lips shut. Whatever she did, she wasn't going to make me eat.

Another time Natalie and I had gone shopping with my auntie and Mum for bridesmaids' dresses because my cousin was getting married. We were in the restaurant in Debenhams and Mum ordered us fish and chips. But when it arrived I picked at a few peas, then pushed it away.

Mum went mad. She held me down on the chair with one hand and tried to force the chips in my mouth with a fork. I was shouting and crying at her to stop but she was raging. My auntie was shouting, 'Sue, stop it! Calm down, Sue. Leave her.' But Mum couldn't. She was terrified at what was happening to me and overwhelmed with frustration that she couldn't do anything about it. Nothing she had tried was working, the doctors still weren't taking her seriously and I was fading away in front of her eyes.

As the weeks went by I became weaker and weaker and was feeling so out of it at school that one day the headmistress called Mum in for a meeting. She said the school couldn't deal with the responsibility of having me there any longer while I was so ill and I'd have to take some time off.

So that was it, no more school. But by then I was so tired and weak I was beyond caring. I became so weak and helpless that I'd get Mum to carry me around the house. I loved that. I could still have walked if I'd had to, but being carried made me feel like a baby again – it felt safe.

The state I was in gave Mum and Dad a whole new subject to row about. Dad blamed Mum, saying I'd got worse since she'd filed for divorce. Mum blamed Dad for, well, everything that had happened really.

Then, by the February of that year, I'd reduced what I would allow myself to water – which I'd only agree to drink out of one particular sherry glass from the kitchen cabinet – vitamin C pills and the occasional slice of toast or shortbread biscuit.

I was painfully skinny but not only had all my body fat gone, so had my spirit, my energy and my childishness.

Lying on our battered brown corduroy sofa watching television, I was locked in a world far away from everything going on around me. I was unable to concentrate on anything, play with toys, think or even move very much.

For a fortnight I ate virtually nothing at all. I chewed gobstoppers to keep away hunger pangs. And I screamed and lashed out if Mum or Dad tried to make me eat. I was so weak that at night I had to crawl up the stairs to bed as Mum tried to help, tears rolling down her face on to the carpet.

You might wonder why she wasn't dialling 999 or camping outside the doctor's front door, but she had been told so many times I'd just 'snap out of it' that she had lost all confidence in the system – and in herself. Her self-esteem was shot to pieces after everything she had been through and she had no strength left to fight. But one morning at the beginning of March she knew she couldn't leave it another day. She helped me into the car and drove me to the GP's surgery.

When we arrived she helped me out of the car and we found ourselves a seat in the stuffy waiting room. Mum went up to the receptionist and quietly but determinedly stated her case. 'My daughter is very ill,' she said. 'I can't cope any more. We are going to sit here and we're not leaving until someone does something to help her.'

This time it took the doctor just one look at me to tell I was dangerously ill. I was malnourished and extremely weak. But most urgent was the fact that I had become severely dehydrated.

I was so tired I hadn't got the strength to lie when the doctor asked what I'd eaten that day. And Mum was doing all the talking this time anyway. The previous day I'd had a quarter of a slice of toast for breakfast, no lunch and two slices of bread and a fish finger for my dinner. That was all.

The doctors weighed me and I was just 20 kilos (3 stone 2 lb). I had a BMI of 12.4, which meant I was severely underweight. A normal eight-year-old would be around 27 kilos (4 stone 4 lb) – that's 7 kilos, or more than a stone, heavier than I was.

The doctor promised Mum that by the following day they would have found me a specialist unit where I could be assessed and helped. He turned to me and said, 'Now go home and eat something – it'll be your only hope of staying out of hospital.'

When we got home Mum heated up a Cornish pasty for me in the microwave and I ate the lot. It was delicious. After so many weeks of eating almost nothing, it felt amazing.

But within an hour of finishing it, a huge wave of guilt surged over me. I hated myself for being so weak and giving in. You must *not* do that again, I reprimanded myself.

I went to bed feeling angry at myself and guilt-stricken about how much I'd eaten. And I was terrified of what the morning would bring.

CHAPTER 5
THE MAUDSLEY

I was lying on the sofa wearing a billowing white dress dotted with huge purple lavender flowers when the call came saying they had found a specialist unit for me.

That morning I'd crawled up to the attic and dug the dress out of our big red dressing-up box. I had a porcelain doll that had an almost identical dress and I decided I wanted to look like her. It must be easy being a doll, I thought.

I put the dress over my head, then, exhausted by the effort, returned to the sofa, where I lay and watched Mum vacuuming around me. By this point I was so sick I could barely move.

'We've got a place for your daughter at the Maudsley Hospital in south-east London,' the official-sounding woman on the phone told Mum. 'Can you come straight away?'

'Oh yes,' Mum replied. 'I'd go to hell and back to save my daughter.' She didn't know then that hell and back was

47

precisely the journey she would be making over the next nine years.

The following few hours were a flurry of activity. Mum rang Dad, who came straight home from work, picking up Natalie from school on his way. We drove to the station, then set off on the tube journey to the Maudsley.

The Maudsley Hospital is the biggest mental health hospital in Britain. It treats people with all sorts of horrific mental problems, including kids with emotional and behavioural problems, obsessive-compulsive disorder (OCD), post-traumatic stress, depression and other serious psychiatric conditions. When we turned up there that day, 5 March 1991, I had no idea I was being bracketed with kids so seriously ill.

The journey from Northwood Hills tube station to the other side of London was exhausting. When Mum helped me off the train at Elephant & Castle, people were staring at me. I must have looked like a kid dying of cancer. And when I saw the stairs leading up out of the station, I thought I couldn't do it – I just didn't have the energy to get up there. But somehow Mum and Dad helped me and we clambered up into the daylight and through the dirty doors of a red London bus. After about ten minutes the bus lurched to a stop and the doors flew open again. In front of us was the Maudsley.

It was certainly a serious-looking building, with two grand pillars flanking a flight of stone steps that led up to the main entrance. I felt tiny as I crept up the steps and entered the monstrous great building.

Inside we were greeted by a smiley nurse who showed Mum and Dad into a side room for a meeting with Dr Stephen Wolkind, the hospital's expert in child psychiatry.

Natalie and I were taken into another room by a nurse –
let's call her Mary – who gave us crayons and paper to
keep us occupied. It felt like Mum and Dad were gone
for hours. After Natalie and I had coloured and drawn
everything we could think of we wandered outside and
sat on the low bars of a climbing frame in the fading
spring sunshine.

'I wish Mum and Dad would hurry up so we can just
clear out of this place and go home,' I said to Natalie.
It had never occurred to me I wouldn't be back in time
for *Neighbours*.

Then Natalie pushed me on the swings for a bit. I was
too weak to push her. But still Mum and Dad didn't emerge
from their meeting. What could they be talking about?

Finally Mary, the nurse, came out to the swings and told
me it was time to go in. She led me down a corridor and
into a small cubicle. Inside there was a narrow single bed,
a table and a chair. She sat me down at the table and told
me to wait a moment. A couple of minutes later she
returned carrying a glass of milk, a couple of cream
crackers and some cheese.

'Here's a snack,' she said, placing it in front of me, then
sitting down herself on the edge of the bed.

I looked at the plate, barely able to hide my disgust at the
big chunk of cheese plonked in the middle. Didn't these
people know cheese was about *the* most 'bad' food around?

'Oh no, I don't fancy that at the moment, thank you,' I
said quietly.

'Nikki, you have to eat your snack,' replied Mary. 'I'll
talk to you when you have finished it.'

For more than an hour we sat in silence. A few times I
tried to engage Mary's eyes, buried deep in her pudgy face,

but each time she looked away. It was only later I discovered that it was the Maudsley's policy to avoid any interaction with eating-disorders patients during mealtimes. So instead I silently gazed out of the window watching aeroplanes etching white lines across the sky of south London.

Finally, another nurse came into the room.

'Right, Nikki,' she said brusquely. 'Your mum and dad are going home now, so you'd better say goodbye to them.'

Mum was standing in the doorway behind the nurse, her gaze flickering between me and the floor. I could tell by the red puffiness around her eyes that she had been crying. Even Dad looked shell-shocked.

At first I couldn't quite understand what was happening. I'd always thought we were just here for a meeting with specialists. It hadn't occurred to me for a moment that they might want to keep me here. But the look on Mum and Dad's faces told me in a second that this was exactly what was happening.

'No, no. Don't take my mum away,' I pleaded, my voice high-pitched but starting to choke with the realisation of what was happening.

'I need my mum. Please don't make her go. I need her.'

As Mum and Dad moved towards me to kiss me goodbye, I started to wail. This just could not be happening. Mum couldn't be abandoning me. Not her, surely? OK, Grandad and Dad had left me, but Mum wouldn't do that. Would she?

My screams grew louder and louder, like the howling of a wounded animal. I watched the nurse gently take hold of Mum's elbow and lead her back out into the corridor. 'No, no, noooooo,' I screamed.

I lunged forward and flung my bony arms around Mum's thighs, my screams now subsiding into loud sobs as I begged her not to leave me in this strange place surrounded by strange people.

Tears were sliding slowly down Mum's face as she tried to untangle my arms from her legs and steady herself.

'I've got to, Nikki,' Mum kept saying. 'I've got to – the doctors are going to make you better. You'll be home soon, I promise.'

But I didn't hear any of that. My head was thumping and my ears were filled with a strange howling – I didn't realise then that it was me making such a horrific noise.

Mary and the other nurse peeled me away from Mum but I started screaming and lashing out at them. I was so angry, so furious that everyone would gang up and do this to me. Why me? After everything else, why me?

I flung myself around the room, banging into the bed and table, flailing my arms and legs.

Eventually, Mary pinned me to the floor to stop me smashing my head while the other nurse gently pushed Mum and Dad into the corridor.

For a moment I stopped struggling and took a breath. Through the glass window of the door I could see Mum looking back at me over her shoulder as she walked away. She had walked away and left me sobbing on the floor. Mum, who'd been there me for every second of every day, who carried me like a baby from room to room, who cuddled me to sleep and kissed my tears. She had left me.

I lay totally still and heard the lock on the door at the end of the corridor click shut. I was eight years old and totally alone. I cried until my head pounded and I was shaking with exhaustion.

After five minutes Mary picked me up from the floor and eased me back into the chair by the table.

The two cream crackers and lump of cheese were still sat there on the plate. My whole life had been upended once again but that chunk of cheese wasn't going anywhere.

'Now, Nikki,' she said, 'we're going to work you out an eating programme which is going to make you better.'

She was fat and spoke with a strict, headmistressy voice that I could tell meant she wouldn't put up with any negotiation. I was so scared.

'If you stick to the programme and eat your food you will see your Mum in a couple of weeks,' she told me. 'As for now, eat your snack up and then we'll talk to you.'

'When am I going to see my mum?' I mumbled through my tears.

'Eat your snack and then we will talk to you.'

'But I need her. I need her.'

'Eat your snack and then we will talk to you.'

'Please let me see her. Please.'

'Eat your snack and then we will talk to you.'

And that is how it went on. Me, sobbing, begging and way beyond being able to think about eating. Them, refusing to talk to me, comfort me or even look at me unless I started eating.

At six o'clock they took away the plate of crackers and cheese and replaced it with a plate of chicken nuggets, beans and chips. Again I looked at it and refused to eat. Again they sat near me at the table, refusing to speak unless I ate.

'Please, when can I go home?'

'Eat your dinner.'

At eight o'clock they took the cold, congealed food away and brought a glass of milk and a small KitKat.

'When am I going to see my mum?'

'Eat your snack.'

At 8.30 the chocolate and milk were taken away and the nurse said it was bedtime. I looked over to the bed where the pyjamas Mum had sneaked into her handbag on the way here had been laid out for me.

The only time I'd ever been away from home before was at a Brownie camp and then I was so miserable I'd wet the bed. How on earth was I going to manage in this place with absolutely no one I knew around me and no idea when I might be going home?

I was shaking as I swung my legs in between the plain white sheets. I thought of my teddy-bear duvet cover. I thought of my sticker collection. I thought of Mum and Dad and Natalie all doing just what they had done last night, last month, last year – but without me.

How could this be happening?

One of the nurses sat on the bed as I lay there and closed my eyes. It can only have been exhaustion from that long day that made me able to sleep.

Next morning it all began again. I was woken by a nurse and got up and dressed myself. At eight o'clock a tray was put on my table with a bowl of cornflakes, a slice of bread and butter and a glass of orange juice on it. I allowed myself the orange juice and left everything else.

Then they set about weighing and measuring me. My weight had dropped to 18 kilos (2 stone 12 lb) – the average weight for a four-year-old. And I was a month off my ninth birthday.

The doctor's reports from that assessment say I was

'finding reality of life too hard to bear and wished to be dead to be reunited with her idealised grandfather'. I was the worst anorexic case they had ever treated at the Maudsley and there was a real concern that unless the weight went back on immediately, I could die.

'You are dangerously underweight,' Mary, my key nurse, told me. 'You will not be allowed to see your Mum until you eat. And you will not be allowed to speak to your Mum until you eat. And if you still refuse to eat we're going to take you to a medical ward, put a tube into you and force-feed you.'

No one ever asked me if I wanted to put the weight back on. No one ever considered I might not want to get better.

But I realised then that this woman was totally serious and this wasn't a battle I was going to win.

And, young as I was, I was old enough to know that my only option was to play the system.

OK, I'll comply with their rules, I thought. But as soon as I get out of here I'll eat whatever I want and get as skinny as I can as soon as I can. I'll eat whatever they serve me up and pretend I'm better.

The food's just like medicine, I told myself. I'll take it to get them off my back. So every mealtime I sat obediently at the small, square table, pushed up against a blank wall, and slowly yet surely cleared my plate.

It was real old-fashioned school food, like liver with potatoes and green beans, steak and kidney pie and shepherd's pie. All of it was disgusting but I got my head down and got on with it.

During mealtimes there was no one to talk to, nothing to look at and nothing to do. In some ways eating the food relieved the boredom – and knowing this was just a game, something I'd do to shut everyone up, made me feel like I was still in control too.

And when I ate my food everyone treated me so much more nicely. If I ate my meals I'd be allowed out of my cubicle to play with the other kids on the ward. There were about ten of them, but I was the only one with an eating disorder. The rest were just oddballs.

A girl called Janey used to run up and down the ward shouting and swearing at the nurses. She'd been kicked out of school and seemed totally out of control.

Then there was Anna, who was about the same age as me, and she had behavioural problems and Down's Syndrome. At that stage I was really into Felt by Numbers, a cross between Fuzzy Felt and Painting by Numbers. I was mad about it and for a while Mum had been buying me a box of it every weekend. When I'd finished my felt works of art I Blu-Tacked them up all around my room and they looked amazing.

One morning Anna came into my room when I wasn't there and pulled every single one of my Felt by Numbers off the wall and threw them on the floor. When I returned and saw hundreds of pieces of felt lying higgledy-piggledy all over the floor I was heartbroken. I squatted down, picked them up and stuck each tiny piece back in its correct place. It took hours.

Next morning Anna came back and did exactly the same again.

The boys on the unit were really naughty too – some had behavioural problems and others would shout and swear at any time of the day or night. And we had another couple of Down's Syndrome kids too.

I'd never come across kids with mental problems before

and it was utterly terrifying. The screaming and shouting at night, the dramatic mood swings and violent outbursts were all alien to me and I felt so isolated. If one of the kids was having a temper tantrum at night, I'd pull the sheets and blanket over my head and try to block out the noise by thinking about home.

But the other kids' rages and fits taught me something too – it got them attention and for a short while it gave them control. I think that on some level this sunk into my brain because within the year I was ranting and raving like the rest of them.

My first week at the Maudsley seemed to last for ever but within a month I understood the system and just got on with it. As a child you become institutionalised very quickly.

I made friends with a couple of the other girls and even the really weird kids started to seem more normal with every day that passed. There was a girl called Emily who used to shout all the time and couldn't stop lying. She probably had Tourette's Syndrome or something similar, but at the time I thought she was just mental. Even so, we became friends and would hang around together. Well, it was either that or being on my own all the time.

I'd been in the Maudsley for a fortnight before Mum and Dad were finally allowed to visit. When it was time for them to leave I cried hysterically again, grabbing hold of Mum's leg. After that they came every week and I got more used to the partings, but it was never easy. Mum was relieved that I had a bit more meat on me and that for the moment I was safe, but they didn't dare look any further forward than that.

Natalie came to visit a couple of times but only because she was ordered to by Mum. I could tell from the way she looked around the place out the corner of her eyes that she hated it. I don't blame her at all. She was still just a kid herself and it was a dark, horrible, looming building filled with all these nutcase kids.

I think she also felt sorry for me having to live there. As my big sister, she felt bad I was there and not her, but at the same time she couldn't help feeling glad it wasn't her too.

Spending all weekend on the ward was really miserable. All the other kids went home on a Friday evening so I'd be on my own apart from a couple of nurses who were called in especially to look after me.

Chesney Hawkes's 'The One and Only' was number one in the charts at the time and whenever I hear that song I'm instantly transported back to the Maudsley with that playing on radio and me playing the hundredth game of KerPlunk with a nurse in a deserted day room on a Saturday afternoon.

Those weekends dragged on for ever. Sometimes one of the nurses would take me out on a little trip but other times I'd just watch films or write letters to my friends.

Then, after three months, I was told that as long as I continued to reach my target weight each week I would be allowed to go home at weekends. I was over the moon.

I was weighed every Friday afternoon and if I hit my target, Mum and Dad could come and collect me. If I didn't hit the target, though, there was no way on earth I could persuade the doctors to let me go.

The first weekend I was allowed home, I was so excited. Mum and Dad came to pick me up and we went home together on the tube.

I kept thinking about climbing into my old bed, seeing

Natalie and my friends. And best of all, I wouldn't have to eat as much as in hospital. Re-sult!

'Am I going to have to eat this weekend?' I asked Mum as the train doors slid shut at Elephant & Castle.

'Yes, you are,' Mum replied firmly. 'We've been instructed by the hospital exactly what you have to eat – they have given us menu sheets and told us how much weight you've got to maintain over the weekend. So you have to eat.'

Mum and Dad would take it in turns to pick me up for 'home weekends'. Their divorce was finalised in July that year but they were still living under the same roof and on reasonable enough terms to present a united front to me. You didn't have to dig far below the surface, though, to hit a wall of mutual resentment between them.

The moment I walked out of the gates of the Maudsley on a Friday evening, rush-hour traffic roaring up and down Denmark Hill, I felt elated, free and victorious that Mum and Dad were there together to pick me up.

But by the time I'd stepped through my front door an hour and a half later my thoughts had already turned to how I was going to get out of eating between then and Sunday night. My goal for home weekends soon became purely to lose the weight I'd had to put on during the week – and I'd do my damnedest to achieve it.

Relations with Nat could be pretty fraught on my home weekends too. In the months I'd been away she had been transformed from 'Natalie Grahame' to 'Nikki Grahame's sister'. At school she felt other kids and teachers only wanted to talk about me and how I was getting on, when I might be back and if I was feeling any better.

Things were tense between Natalie and Dad too, as she

was mad at him about the divorce. She had always been closer to Mum than to him and in some ways had been quite pleased at first that they were splitting up because she felt he had been so horrid to Mum. But then Nat didn't want Tony being close to Mum either. So she was mad at Dad for allowing that to happen too.

There was certainly a lot of anger in our house back then. Some of the doctors were concerned about me returning to that environment at weekends but Mum and Dad could have been attacking each other with chainsaws as far as I was concerned – I just wanted to be at home.

Yet as the weeks rolled by, home visits became more and more about skipping meals and exercising secretly in my bedroom than about seeing my family. In fact the longer I stayed away from home the less I cared about Mum and Dad, Nat, friends, school, gymnastics, everything really. All I could think about was how I was going to lose all the weight they had made me put on in hospital. But while I was at the Maudsley I complied with their rules.

Each morning after breakfast of a bowl of cereal and a slice of toast we would go to the hospital's classroom. It wasn't like a proper school but it was OK. I did a project about flowers, learning their names and colouring in pictures. That took us up to lunchtime – and one of their stomach-churning meals.

Then, in the afternoons, we would either go to the park or play outside. The Maudsley offered us lots of things to do and sometimes we did have fun. There was a toy room, an art room, a gym and a Sega room where you could play computer games. We could watch telly and videos too. My favourite video was *Willy Wonka and the Chocolate Factory*. I watched it over and over again and loved the bit

59

where the Golden Ticket-winning kids were allowed inside the factory. I'd look at all the chocolate and think, Oh, I wish I could eat that. But I knew there was absolutely no way I could allow myself – the guilt would be too unbearable.

There was also a day room where we'd sit around and do jigsaws or play board games like Buckaroo and draw Spirograph pictures.

In the evenings I'd write letters to Mum. Each week she sent me writing paper and stamps and I'd spend hours drawing pictures and writing notes for her and my friends from school. By now I'd been gone a matter of months and almost every day letters decorated with childish colourings and stickers arrived from my old classmates. I glued them up all around my room.

Evening was also the time for us kids to visit the tuck shop. Of course all the other children were beyond excited about that – but I hated it. The doctors encouraged Mum and Dad to give me 50 pence a week to spend on sweets. But why on earth would I want to do that? I was already eating massive meals every day. I didn't want to spend money on sweets in the evenings. I wanted to buy comics and magazines but the staff weren't having any of that. It was Chewits, Chewits and more Chewits. Sweets felt like a punishment to me.

There were some good times at the Maudsley, though. One time they took us camping in the New Forest for a few days. One of the nurses, Clive, left a trail of red paint through the woods and we had to follow it. It was such a laugh just doing normal kids' stuff.

But even that trip had its moments. Mary was there and one morning she said to me, 'It's snack time, Nikki. You can have a packet of crisps and a fizzy drink.'

'I can't eat crisps,' I said. 'I can't.'

Mary barely looked up and just threw four biscuits at me instead.

The following evening everyone else was making warm bananas with melted chocolate around the camp fire. 'Can I have my banana cold, on its own, please?' I asked. Mary tossed the banana in my direction with a look of disgust.

They also took us on trips around London and to the Water Palace in Croydon, an indoor water park. It was fun, but there was a lot of crying and shouting too.

At the hospital there was an occupational therapist called Charlotte. Her job was to help me express my feelings through art and crafts. I liked making things but I just wasn't interested in her constant questions about my mum. Did she watch what she ate? Had she encouraged me to diet? Did I get on with her? It all seemed so irrelevant. Why couldn't everyone just leave me alone to eat – and not eat – exactly what I wanted? What none of them realised was that I couldn't give a toss about getting better. I just wanted to get out.

The staff did try really hard to make us kids feel comfortable. There was a young nurse called Billy who everyone thought was really cool. And there was lovely Pauline who used to cuddle me when I was sad.

Clive was cool too. But one morning he said to me, 'You're filling out a bit.' Surely anyone – most of all a qualified nurse – would know that is not the sort of thing you say to an anorexic. That had a massive effect on me. I already hated what they were doing to my body. I could feel my thighs become softer and see my tummy getting rounder and it disgusted me. I was gutted that they were undoing all the work I'd done to my body over the past year. So for Clive to then say I was filling out threw me into a new depression.

But worst of all the nurses was Mary. I remained terrified of her until the day I left the Maudsley. She would stand behind me during meals and make me scrape every last scrap of food off my plate. If I didn't finish it, she'd tell me off. I was still just a child and found her really frightening.

If any of us played up we were given a certain number of 'minutes' to stand and face the wall. Mary was always handing out the minutes to me for being cheeky by saying 'Shut up' to the nurses or even a couple of times 'I hate you' when they made me eat something I couldn't face.

One of the nurses would read me a story when I got into bed but when she turned the light out there were no cuddles or goodnight kisses like at home. Often I would lie there and quietly cry. About missing Mum, missing Dad, being stuck in hospital and another destroyed Felt by Numbers.

Other nights I'd feel stronger and make plans about what I'd do when I got out of there, how I'd set about losing the weight they'd made me put on and how I'd get back in control of my life. All I could focus on was the day they would let me home. To reach that day, though, I knew I just had to get on with doing what I was told and so I did start gaining weight.

After a couple of months of eating all my meals properly, sitting at the table in my cubicle, I was allowed to eat in the main sitting area, although my table was still shoved so that I was facing the wall with a member of staff sitting next to me.

When I'd done that OK for a month, I was allowed to eat in a downstairs office, although still it was only a blank wall and a nurse for company.

Then finally, four months after arriving at the Maudsley, I was allowed to eat my meals with the other children in the main dining room. Chatting and giggling during meals again was fantastic. I felt normal. There were three tables in the children's dining room: the Dinosaur table, the Happy Eaters table and the Care Bears table. They put me on the Happy Eaters table! What a joke that was. If only it had been funny.

It had taken me virtually my entire stay at the Maudsley to work my way up to that table but it meant I was one of the kids who behaved during mealtimes and, most importantly for my doctors, I was eating my meals.

At the beginning of September, after six months at the hospital, I was told I would be going home. I'd gained 4 kilos (9 lb), to bring my weight up to 26 kilos (4 stone 1 lb) and although still skinny I was closer to the average weight for a child of my age.

But although on the outside I appeared to have recovered, inside my head I was still as intent on starving myself as the day I'd arrived there. If anything, I was more determined than ever. The big difference was that I was now far cleverer at fooling people about what I was thinking.

To celebrate my last day at the Maudsley the staff treated all the kids on the unit to a McDonald's. I ordered a hamburger, chips and a strawberry milkshake and hated every minute of it. For me the entire trip was a nightmare, although the other kids were having a great time. I ate and drank with a smile on my face, making sure everyone thought I'd come through my problems and was as right as rain again.

But in my mind there was no doubt – as soon as I was home the starving would begin. And this time it was going to be serious.

63

CHAPTER 6
I DON'T BELONG HERE

Brand-new, neatly pressed grey skirt, new red woollen cardigan and new Kylie pencil tin. It was the beginning of the school year at Hillside Infants when I emerged from the Maudsley in September 1991.

After six months in hospital I'd gained more than 3.2 kilos (7 lb). There was colour in my cheeks, a slight curve around my thighs and tummy and a shine to my hair. And I hated it. I hated every millimetre of fat they'd made me put on my body and I wanted it starved off my bones as quickly as possible.

I found it hard to settle back into school. In fact I loathed it. I hadn't been away that long but, at nine years old, things move fast. My old friends Joanna, Emily and Erin had found new best mates and I felt I was constantly hanging around the edge of conversations.

And I felt different. I was different. In the six months I'd been away I'd seen things my classmates didn't know existed – kids with severe psychiatric problems, others

65

torn from their families, girls who had been abused by their dads. And I too had behaved in ways I'd never thought possible, being rude, aggressive and hysterical when pushed to the limit. The way other kids acted in hospital had rubbed off on me and I'd seen how being naughty and rude could get you attention when you needed it.

Everyone I bumped up against at school wanted to know where I'd been and what I'd been doing, even though I'm sure they all knew already.

Kids would come up to me in the playground and say, 'Where have you been?'

'I've been at private school for a while,' I replied, not batting an eyelid. I'd become a pretty accomplished liar.

But even though I was back at school, I still stood out as different. Mum had to pick me up every lunchtime, take me home and try to get me to eat my lunch before bringing me back for afternoon lessons.

'Why do you go home at lunchtime?' one nosy parker after another would ask me. Sometimes I'd just ignore them, other times I was more inventive. 'I've got diabetes and can only eat certain things,' I'd lie. It was none of their business. It was none of anyone's business.

As the weeks went passed I suppose it became a bit more normal but I felt as though from now on I was never going to be plain Nikki Grahame ever again. Oh no, I was always going to be Nikki-the-girl-who-got-so-skinny-she-had-to-leave-school-and-go-into-hospital-Grahame. I hated it.

Things at home were no better either. Mum, Natalie and I were still living in the attic bedroom while Dad was downstairs on his own.

The only good thing about being home was that I was able to control my eating again – and that meant only eating what I wanted. Within weeks of leaving the Maudsley I'd cut right back on what I was eating – just like I'd planned all the time I was away.

At first, breakfast was cereal and a slice of toast. Then at school I got a free packed lunchbox which Mum took me home to eat. (Since the divorce she'd been struggling for money, so we qualified for free school meals.)

Dinner would be something hot like spag Bol or fish pie. Again, at first I'd eat what Mum put in front of me but within a couple of weeks I started hiding food again and was back to all my old tricks – and more.

Mealtimes became a war zone. I'd seen so much bad behaviour, fighting and swearing in the Maudsley that I had emerged from there a very different child. I knew what kind of behaviour could get results because I'd seen it close up day after day. So I'd shout and swear at Mum in a way I'd never have thought of doing before. I hadn't even known the words existed.

'You can shove that up your fat fucking arse!' I'd scream when she tried to put a meal in front of me.

Mum must have wondered where this monster had come from.

Part of it was copying what I had witnessed in hospital but I think being away from my family for so long had made me more brutal. I didn't care who I upset with my antics any more. The slightest thing could tip me into a full-scale tantrum. And, as I got older, I was physically stronger and less scared of Mum or anyone else who might try to force me to eat.

I had to go to my GP every week to be weighed and I

knew that there there they would quickly realise what I was up to, hiding food and refusing meals. But that didn't stop me. I'd only been home a month when Mum first suspected I had vomited up my dinner one evening and marched me back to the doctor.

To be fair to myself, I never made my anorexic career out of vomiting. It was just something I did if I felt really uncomfortable about the amount I'd eaten.

A bigger problem for me was my obsession with exercise. After school I ran up and down the slope outside our house until I was breathless. And I never sat down in the evenings, ever. I would pace up and down the living room while Mum and Natalie watched television. And when they'd finally had enough of me disrupting their viewing and were shouting at me to stop, I'd stand by the fireplace. I couldn't bear the thought of sitting down – you don't burn any calories like that. Then, once everyone was in bed, it was more sit-ups, hundreds of them.

Once again I was feeling very low. I was unhappy at home and school and took my misery out on both myself and those around me. I hit myself and bit myself during temper tantrums if Mum tried to make me eat. My arms and legs would get covered in bruises and I pulled my hair out in clumps.

And I was spiteful to Natalie too. I wouldn't let her near any of my toys and would lash out violently in our fights.

'I just want to be dead,' I said to Mum one evening. 'Why can't I be dead?' And I meant it.

Then, in the run-up to Christmas, Dad finally moved out. I felt split down the middle. Part of me was glad he was gone because I was still so angry with him for everything that had happened. But another part of me was devastated that any hopes of my life returning to how it once was were totally dashed.

What was worse, Dad's old employer, the bank, had called in our mortgage, so it was just a matter of time until we would all have to be out and the house sold. It was a Monday lunchtime and Mum had picked me up from school for lunch when she broke the news. We were sitting in the kitchen when she turned and fixed me with one of those despairing looks that left even my nine-year-old mind in no doubt there was more trouble coming down the line.

'I'm so sorry, Nikki,' she said, 'but we're going to have to sell the house. Your Dad's not working any more and the bank want their money back.'

It was just awful. I immediately started to cry. Stanley Road had been about the only stable thing in my life over the past three years and now that was being taken away from me too. It felt like the unfairness of it all was never going to end.

There were so many memories of that house and its amazing garden. There were the good memories: water fights with Natalie in the back garden and playing hide and seek in the attic. And, more recently, there were the bad memories: the screaming matches between Mum and Dad and the tears rolling down Mum's face as she stood at the kitchen sink staring out past those dreadful orange curtains she loved so much.

If I ever become ridiculously rich I'll buy that house in Stanley Road again and move back there. Maybe one day I'll get the life back that I lost.

But that lunchtime, sitting in front of a tired-looking ham sandwich, I just couldn't take in what Mum was saying. 'But leave here, Mum? We can't. No way. *No way.*'

But whether I liked it or not, soon afterwards there was a For Sale board up in the front garden and Mum was packing up our clothes and toys into old banana boxes. Dad leaving and the house going up for sale hit me hard. Life seemed so unsettled again, so I went back to focusing on the one thing I could control – eating. I cut the amount I would allow myself more and more until I was on tiny portions.

Mum tried to keep a close eye on me during mealtimes but I was hiding food again. Chips would go up my sleeve, pasta inside my knickers and meatballs down my T-shirt. I was an expert at it by then and it only took Mum to lose concentration for a moment and food would disappear from my plate.

I was also negotiating with her again about what I would and wouldn't eat and as I gradually wore her down I was getting away with smaller and smaller portions. She still feared that to fight me might mean I ate nothing at all. I think the state I was in when I was admitted to the Maudsley had so terrified Mum that she would agree to anything if she thought she could prevent that happening again.

She couldn't, though. I liked to give her the illusion she had some control over what I was doing but in reality she had none. It was me and me alone who would decide how much I would eat.

Mealtimes became horribly bitter and fraught. I would scream and throw tantrums if Mum served up something I wouldn't eat. The first time I threw an untouched plate of food at the wall, she gasped in shock before going mad at me.

'How dare you?' Mum finally yelled, visibly taken aback at what her little daughter had turned into.

I didn't even reply, I just pushed my chair away from the table and stamped upstairs to my bedroom.

But within a couple of weeks that behaviour had become the norm. Anything I didn't like went straight up the wall until you could tell what we'd had for dinner recently by checking out the stains Mum couldn't scrub off the walls of her once cream-coloured dining room.

Worse still, I was becoming increasingly violent towards her. I felt furious that she wasn't letting me starve myself the way I wanted to and I wanted to hurt her for that. I'd push her away and lash out if she tried to make me eat.

Christmas 1991 has entered family folklore because of one of my terrible outbursts. Tony had assured Mum there was no point in rushing out early to get a turkey, even though we had my auntie, uncle and three cousins coming over for lunch on Christmas Day. 'Everyone just makes a big fuss before Christmas,' he laughed. 'There'll be plenty of turkeys left if we wait until Christmas Eve *and* they'll be half-price. You'll see.'

Well, what we didn't see when we turned up at the shops on Christmas Eve was a single turkey – not one. All we could find was one very sad and scrawny-looking duck. Not that it bothered me – I wouldn't be eating much of it.

Mum spent hours cooking for everyone, trying to make it an extra-special Christmas after the grim year we'd all had.

But as soon as I saw the duck lying on my plate I knew I was in trouble. I couldn't bring myself to eat it. I just couldn't eat all that fat. Mum could sense the danger too as my face took on that haunted, troubled look that I would get so often at mealtimes.

Everyone was chatting and joking around the table when suddenly there was a loud smash. I'd picked up my plate and thrown it across the festively decorated table straight at the wall.

'I'm not fucking eating it!' I screamed, watching the gravy sliding down the wall like a slow-moving oil slick.

'For God's sake, Nikki,' Mum screamed. There was silence as my auntie and cousins stared intently at their Brussels sprouts, not daring to look up. But suddenly Mum, Natalie and I broke the silence by all starting to giggle hysterically at the same moment. Then everyone joined in and we were all laughing uncontrollably. I think we were probably laughing at the sheer awfulness of everything – it was a real laugh-or-cry situation. Now we always call it the Flying Duck Christmas.

But it wasn't normally like that. By then there was rarely much laughter at mealtimes in our house. It was far more likely to be screaming and shouting, particularly when I'd just hurled another dinner plate across the room.

Soon I was eating virtually nothing again and my weight fell dangerously low. I was mentally and emotionally tormented too. I felt isolated and alone at home and school and I found it hard to concentrate or even think about anything other than food. I became totally focused on what I was trying to do – not eat. I was locked in a vicious circle because the less I ate the weaker I became and the more incapable I was of finding any pleasure in anything. Food and avoiding it occupied my mind every waking hour.

At the beginning of 1992 I was pulled out of school again. In less than four months since I had been discharged from the Maudsley I had lost three kilos (nearly 7 lb) and was down to just 23.3 kilos (3 stone 9 lb) – 75 per cent of the weight I should have been.

I was pale, sickly-looking and covered in a layer of lanugo hair, which anorexics get when they are seriously ill. It's a fine hair, almost like fur, which grows all over your body in a bid to keep it warm when there isn't enough body fat left to do that. I had loads on my back and all down my arms. It was horrible.

The whole family was attending family-therapy sessions in the hope it might help me but when I was there I refused to get involved. These people still didn't get it – I didn't *want* to eat and get better. I couldn't let myself do that.

My medical notes show that I then went down to consuming just one glass of water and a biscuit each day. It was critical.

Soon after that I stopped eating entirely. I just couldn't do it any more. Eating was giving in and I refused to do it. I was going to be strong and deny myself everything. At mealtimes I stopped sitting down at the table. Instead I would stand in the corner of the room and watch as they all tucked in. I'd watch Natalie's every move as she nudged the food on to her fork, lifted it to her mouth, chewed then swallowed. It looked so simple but I just couldn't do it. The guilt would be too much for me. I'd feel like I had done something too awful and I couldn't let that happen.

By this time Mum, Dad and my GP were frantically worried about me again.

Our family doctor, Sara, was back from her maternity leave and was brilliant at trying to find me specialist care. But that wasn't so easy. Letters flew backwards and forwards in an attempt to secure the funding from my local health authority for a bed in an eating-disorders unit.

But then there were no beds available and I was put on a waiting list. It dragged on like that for weeks and all the time I was getting thinner and weaker.

Then one week I ate nothing except vitamin C pills. During all the times I had starved myself before I had never felt hungry, but this time even I felt the need to eat – yet still I couldn't do it. Something inside me just wouldn't let me give in to food. 'You can't do that, Nikki,' I'd hear in my head. 'You'll be giving in. You have to stay strong.' And I did. I stayed strong in my head and I didn't eat. But physically I was weaker than I'd ever been.

My GP's notes show that when I visited her on Friday, 24 January I hadn't eaten anything since the Wednesday. I was terrifyingly thin. On the Saturday and the Monday I was back at the surgery but still I wasn't eating. I was so hungry I was unable to think straight. I told Mum I wanted to die and threatened Natalie with a fork.

Mum was buckling under the strain. One or other of us was in tears most of the time and the tension was unbearable. And still the battle to find a bed at a suitable unit continued.

Then I stopped drinking too. I became more and more dehydrated and was desperate for a drink but I just couldn't allow myself to give in to that either.

I remember watching Tony and Mum sitting in the kitchen drinking tea and I was just desperate for it, desperate – but I couldn't do it. I couldn't give in.

One morning, truly desperate, Mum took me back to our GP again and pleaded with her for help. The doctor told my mum to drive me straight to the nearest hospital.

I was nine years old and weighing just 19 kilos (just under 3 stone) and I hadn't drunk any fluid for a week. I was now a critical emergency case because I was so severely dehydrated and was rushed to the local Hillingdon Hospital and placed on the Peter Pan Ward, a general children's medical ward.

'It'll only be for a night, won't it, Mum?' I asked as we climbed into the car to go there.

'We'll see, darling,' Mum replied. 'We'll see.'

CHAPTER 7

HILLINGDON HOSPITAL

As Tony drove us to the hospital I stared numbly out of the back window of the car. I was too tired to talk and too weak to pay much attention to the people going about their everyday lives, scurrying up and down the busy streets.

Then something in a shop window caught my eye. It was a huge poster, the height of a man, advertising bottles of water. In the picture, water was splashing out of the bottle and falling into a glistening pool beneath it. I stared at the image, transfixed by the wetness. Oh, I so wish I could drink that, I thought. I'm so thirsty. Because I hadn't drunk anything for three days I was seriously dehydrated, but still I hadn't been able to permit myself even a drop of water.

I knew from being in the Maudsley that once I was in hospital they would be making me drink and eat – and part of me was relieved. I would be able to hand over control to the nurses and it would be like having a holiday from myself.

We pulled up outside Hillingdon Hospital and I looked up, half scared and half comforted by the solidity and plainness of the huge building.

Inside, a lovely nurse introduced herself as Geraldine, the ward sister. She helped me with my overnight bag – stuffed full of comics, clothes and my teddy bear – as we walked along the ward and into the cubicle which was to become my virtual jail for the next three months.

'Now, Nikki, we're going to start off by getting you a nice drink,' Geraldine said, smiling. I didn't even bother to fight the suggestion. But I did lean down, unzip my bag and pull out my sherry glass. 'Can I have it in this, please?' I asked, holding up the tiny tumbler. 'I only drink out of this glass.'

'Really,' replied Geraldine. 'Well, I think you're going to need a bit more than that, dear. You've got to drink a litre of lemon squash by midnight or we'll have to put you on a glucose drip.'

She was really lovely but clearly wasn't going to take any nonsense from me, and her threat worked a treat. As she poured out the first large glass of lemon squash from a plastic jug, I held out my hand and grabbed it.

The first mouthful tasted amazing. It felt like I could distinguish every single ingredient and I loved it. I was so thirsty that soon I was gulping down the squash. But however much I drank they just kept topping up my glass in a bid to rehydrate me.

The next step was for staff to weigh and measure me, take my blood pressure and assess my mental state. The notes on my admission sheet make grim reading: 'She shows feelings that life not worth living, sad, tearful and irritable, obsessed with weight and once thought of drinking her sister's chemistry set in attempt to kill herself. Digs forks into herself.'

I can't remember the chemistry set incident now and I'm not convinced it ever really happened, but I must have told them it did. Certainly I'd reached a point where there didn't seem anything in my life worth living for.

After all the tests, Geraldine sat on the edge of my bed and handed me a programme of what my life would be while I remained at Hillingdon. I still have the two pages of typed notes which were to provide the format for my every waking moment during my stay there. They are decorated with my childish felt-pen pictures of a rainbow, balloons and a flower, but not even my pretty doodlings can take away the harshness of the regime.

During stage 0, which lasted until I had increased my weight from 19 kilos (3 stone) to 19.95 kilos (3 stone 2 lb), my day consisted of:

Bedbath, not hairwash
Bedpan
Schoolwork for half an hour each day
Mum to visit for half an hour each day
Dad to visit for 20 minutes every other day
Reading half an hour each day
No other visitors.

And that was it – my entire day's activities. All of it was to take place in my hospital bed, which I was not permitted to leave even to use the toilet.

There were hours and hours every day where there was just nothing at all for me to do except lie on my bed and stare into space.

Stage 1 – until I reached 20.3 kilos (3 stone 3 lb) – introduced the 'perks' of a hairwash once a week and drawing and colouring for half an hour each day. Everything else remained the same.

Stage 2 – until I reached 20.8 kilos (3 stone 4 lb) – increased schoolwork, reading and Mum's visit to one hour each per day and Dad's to 20 minutes daily. Natalie was also allowed to visit once a week with Mum.

And so it went on with extra privileges at each stage. But it all came accompanied by the threat that if I lost weight at any point I would be fed through a tube.

I'd been told enough times about 'tube feeding' and it sounded terrifying. The mere thought of having a tube shoved up my nose and all the way down into my stomach made me gag. Worse still, it meant I'd have no control at all over the number of calories they were pumping inside me.

Mum and I had talked about tube feeding too. 'If you ever have to be tube-fed I won't be able to visit you,' she'd said. 'I couldn't face seeing you like that.'

The doctors at Hillingdon must have thought that the privileges they were offering plus the fear of tube feeding would be enough to make me eat. But they can't have dealt with anyone with such ruthless self-control before.

I decided in my head how much I would allow myself to eat, and then nothing more. And no amount of privileges or threats would make me change my mind. There was no way I was giving in just to have an extra half-hour's colouring or an extra half-hour with Mum. Hugging my mum? By then I could take it or leave it. That's what being locked up in hospitals had done to me.

I didn't even make it to Stage 4 and after my weight had crept out of the critical level to reach 21 kilos (3 stone 4 lb) it stayed pretty static until I left there.

All my meals were brought to me in my cubicle and served up on one of those narrow tables that swing across the bed. I wasn't even allowed to go for a shower or to the toilet, so my whole life was contained for three months within those cubicle walls.

It was cripplingly boring and enough to send anyone mad, let alone someone who was obviously struggling to keep their senses together, as I was at the time.

I guess they thought that if my life was so unstimulating I'd start to find food interesting and give in to it. But they hadn't reckoned on my cast-iron will.

For breakfast I would allow myself to eat a Weetabix with water and black tea. For lunch it would be half a jacket potato and dinner would be something like minced turkey. They made no effort to force me to eat and would just leave the food in front of me until the next meal if I hadn't touched it. Meal after meal I would pick at few vegetables or anything else I felt I was 'allowed', then leave the rest for hours on end until eventually it was cleared away.

I suppose they didn't feel the need to encourage or force me to eat because they thought the combination of privileges and punishments was enough.

So I sat there for hour after hour, day after day, my head aching with boredom, but still refusing to eat up all the food in front of me.

I'd sit and stare out of the window or peer through the gap in the curtains at the comings and goings of the nurses up and down the ward. But if one of them caught me looking she would just pull the curtains tight shut – looking out was far too much like entertainment.

Bed-wash in the morning, when the nurse would come

round with a bowl of warm water and some soap, became one of the high points of my day. At least it was some human contact.

'Hello – do you like working in the hospital?' I'd ask my bed-wash nurse, in a desperate child's attempt to strike up a conversation. I'd do anything to make them stay for just 20 minutes and talk to me. Most of them were pretty on the ball, though, and knew I was just trying to relieve the boredom. And that was against the rules. So they'd just give me a friendly smile, finish the wash and walk away, leaving me in silence in my cubicle jail all over again.

When I arrived at Hillingdon I was still young enough to be scared about being told off by nurses and doctors. But as the weeks rolled on and I became more and more bored, I became rebellious and cheeky. I started getting off my bed to do star-jumps when no one was around. But I was usually caught by the nurses and sent back to bed.

One day, some charity workers came to our ward, handing out toys to all the kids. There were He Man and Action Man figures for the boys and Barbie dolls for the girls.

I was sitting in my cubicle, trying to hear what all the excitement was about, when a lady from the charity poked her head through my partially opened curtain and said, 'Hello, dear, would you like this?' She handed me the most beautiful Barbie I'd ever seen. She was wearing a pink ball gown and came with her own hair brush.

'Oh, thank you, she's lovely,' I murmured. And I'd never been so grateful for a present in my whole life.

She really was beautiful. I sat on my bed and brushed her long, blonde hair with the tiny pink hair brush and unfastened her clothes, then put them back on her again, until she looked perfect.

I felt so lucky. I had my very own doll to play with.

It was about half an hour later that Alison, a ward sister, came into the cubicle and saw me dancing my doll up and down the bedcovers.

'You're not allowed that,' she said, before walking over and snatching it from my hand. 'It's got to go.'

Hot tears swelled in my eyes as Alison stomped out of my cubicle, Barbie's glossy blonde hair bouncing on her shoulders as she disappeared from sight in the sister's hand. 'I hate you,' I gulped as she pulled the curtains shut behind her. And at that moment I did.

I was getting harder, tougher. They were treating me like a prisoner and I was starting to act like one.

I counted the hours until visits from Mum and Dad. They were the only thing that broke the boredom. I didn't normally have much to say when they were there but it felt good being near real people again.

Mum would come to see me every day. I used to look out of my bedroom window and wait for her Morris Minor to pull into the car park. Just seeing the familiar curve of its bonnet and knowing Mum was nearby made me feel better. But as soon as her allotted visiting time was up, that was it and she was sent packing again.

It was a very tough time for Natalie. That was when she learned to cook – and look after herself. Mum was so caught up in trying to get me better that it was hard for her to look out for Natalie too. Even now I think Nat hurts a lot when she remembers how she would have to walk home from school and cook her own dinner if Tony wasn't around. Then she'd spend the evening tidying the house and watching telly on her own until Mum got back from visiting me. She was trying so hard to be the perfect child, to make everyone else feel better in this awful situation – it was only later when her anger and resentment for all that came pouring out.

Dad used to visit too. Once he smuggled me in copies of the *Beano* and *Dandy*, which I'd loved reading at home. I lifted my blankets over the bed-table to create a den, then sat underneath reading the comics with a torch.

Yeah, I've fooled them. They won't know what I'm doing, I thought. But it was only a couple of nights before I was spotted, the comics were confiscated and Dad was banned from visiting me for the rest of my stay at Hillingdon.

They were incredibly strict there and Mum and Dad had to agree to their rules. In any case they were terrified that if they brought me home I would die.

The nurses were very tough on me too. One day I asked one of the agency nurses if I could have a bath. I knew I was chancing my arm but I was desperate. She let me walk all the way down the corridor on my own, which was a treat enough. Then, in the bathroom, I soaked for 20 minutes, feeling my weightless body resting effortlessly in the water.

But when Sister Alison came round and discovered what the agency nurse had done, she went mad. I never saw that nurse again and think she might have been sacked.

If I needed the toilet I had to ring a buzzer and a nurse would appear and snap at me, 'What do you want?' Five minutes later a bedpan might be brought.

One afternoon a nurse called Heather had gone off to get me a bedpan but after ten minutes she still hadn't reappeared. I was desperate for a wee and after another five minutes I couldn't hold it any longer. I picked up the bowl used for my bedbath every morning, squatted down and weed into it.

Sure enough, Heather chose that exact moment to walk back in. My cubicle was opposite the nurses' station and as she opened the curtains all the other ward staff could see me. I felt that they were giggling and nudging each other as I squatted there in full view. I felt so humiliated that I crawled on to my bed and cried.

Some people may find it difficult to believe that nurses could be unkind in the ways that I have described but I don't think they were nasty – they just didn't have any time for me. I was on a medical ward alongside kids with 'real illnesses' and they must have thought I was a self-indulgent little madam taking up a valuable bed. That's certainly how I felt they thought.

There was a boy in the cubicle opposite me with leukaemia and they must have made comparisons between us. He used to wave at me when he went past the window of my cubicle and apparently he wanted to come in and visit me but he wasn't allowed as it wasn't on my privileges list. Instead he made me a card and one of the nurses delivered it.

In the first few weeks I spent a lot of time crying for Mum, Dad and Natalie. But I'd already survived the Maudsley and I was getting tougher all the time.

Natalie wrote me a letter once and was telling me that she was totally in love with Marti Pellow, the lead singer of Wet Wet Wet. She copied out all the lyrics to their song 'Goodnight Girl'. It was in the charts at the time and writing lyrics was all the rage among girls our age.

The night after I received Nat's letter I woke in the early hours and could hear the song playing quietly on the radio in the nurses' station. I lay there and thought about my love and promises – for Mum, for Natalie, for Dad.

Then I rang my buzzer. When the nurse came, looking tired and a bit tetchy, I said, 'I want to get well – can you bring me a glass of milk, please?'

She returned with a large glass of milk and I drank the whole lot down in one go. It must have been a month since I'd drunk milk like that and it tasted good.

It was an amazing moment. That could have been my happy ending and this book would be over here. But it wasn't to be that simple. Next morning when I woke all I felt was guilt and self-loathing at having drunk the milk. It was clear to me I didn't want to get better that much.

I went back to refusing food, and spent more days and weeks watching time pass by outside my cubicle window. My weight had gone up a bit after I arrived at Hillingdon but once I felt they were trying to push it up too far I just refused more and more food.

I didn't hit a couple of stages on my chart, so – as threatened – out came their nasal tube. As soon as I saw a nurse carrying the long, white tube towards me one afternoon, I felt physically sick. At the side of my bed she coated the end of it in gloopy KY Jelly and then began to insert it into my nostril. The pain was acute.

'Keep swallowing, Nikki,' the nurse said as she thrust the tube further and further down. But I could feel it coming out through my mouth and I was gagging. There were huge globules of KY stuck at the back of my throat and I was crying, begging her to stop.

When she finally realised she couldn't get the tube any further down my throat, she whipped it back out, making me gag and choke. It was a size-10 tube – one of the large adult ones – so I begged them, if they had to do it, to use something smaller. In the end they agreed to one of the feeding tubes they use for babies.

When the nurse tried to insert that one it was only slightly less painful and I still cried as I felt it slip down into my stomach. Once it was inside me, the nurse then attached the tube to a bag of milk feed connected to a pump which began flooding the liquid into me. I pulled a hand mirror out of a drawer, opened my mouth and watched as the milky feed slipped down into my body. There was nothing I could do to stop it. I'd lost control and I was devastated.

I did soon start to do something, though. The next time they tried to tube-feed me, I started writhing around the bed, pushing the nurses away and clamping my hand over my nose. For 20 minutes I screamed and shouted, adamant I would not let them get the better of me again by tube-feeding me. Fighting made me feel good, as though I still had some control over my life, like I was still alive. But what happened next was to change all that.

I'd been lashing around so much on the bed, I hadn't seen another nurse enter the cubicle with a huge hypodermic needle in her hand. It was only when her hand was by my thigh and jabbing the point towards me that I had any clue what was happening.

'This will just help you sleep,' the nurse said as she broke the surface of my skin with the needle.

Maybe I should have screamed out in protest at this, the first of literally hundreds of times I would be beaten into chemical unconsciousness over the next few years. Maybe I should have fought harder at being treated like a troublesome zoo animal. Maybe I should have screamed as my last ounce of fight was being drugged out of me. But in reality all I thought was, Oh my God, I wonder how many calories are in that?

The sedative was of a thick, syrupy consistency. That has *sooo* got sugar in it, I thought, before I slumped backwards against my pillows, unable to care any more.

Clearly I'd become too big a problem for them. Pacifying me or negotiating with me had become too much bother, so they went for the easy option – a quick jab in the leg and a perfectly docile patient.

It was like something out of *One Flew Over The Cuckoo's Nest* – I was being drugged into submission. But for them it worked and meant they could at least get a nasal tube in quickly while I was out for the count.

I still ripped out a couple more nasal tubes during my time at Hillingdon but, by using sedatives and tube feeds, within three weeks they had lifted my weight out of the danger level. Even so, with it still hovering around 21 kilos (3 stone 4 lb), they realised the Hillingdon regime just wasn't working for me. They needed somewhere that could help me get to the root problem of my anorexia and try to bring an end to it. It was felt a medical ward wasn't the best place for that.

And so, at the beginning of April, I was transferred to a psychiatric unit for young people. My weight was still desperately low and getting better was a very long way away.

CHAPTER 8

COLLINGHAM GARDENS

'Celery? Yuk. Not even an anorexic who knows celery contains no calories at all likes celery!'

I turned my nose up in disgust at the first meal laid out in front of me at my new 'home'. Then, when no one was looking, I lifted my T-shirt with one hand and with the other hand slipped the celery beneath the waistband of my jeans and into my knickers. Done in a flash and no one had spotted a thing. This place was going to be a walk in the park.

It was 7 April 1992 and I'd been transferred straight from Hillingdon to Collingham Gardens Child and Family Centre, a psychiatric unit for children. Again, at that time I was the only kid there with an eating disorder, but at least they had the specialist expertise that might help me.

And, as I soon learned, they were wise to anorexics' food-dodging tricks. It was only half an hour after that first celery salad and my new key nurse, Erla, said I could go and play in the cosy room with some of the other young patients.

We were rolling over the sofas when I suddenly felt the stick of celery slide down my trouser leg and out on to the carpet. I kicked it behind the sofa and wandered off to the other side of the room as casually as I could. But Erla wasn't daft and within minutes she had found the offending item and knew exactly who was to blame. She pulled me to one side and knelt down, staring me straight in the eye. 'While you are here, young lady, you do not hide food. If you hide any item of food whatsoever your entire meal will be replaced and you'll have to start it all over again.'

I was terrified, both of Erla, a big, imposing woman who seemed to growl rather than speak, and the prospect of double portions for misbehaviour.

Until that point my first impressions of Collingham had been good. It was housed in one of those huge mansions that line the back streets of Earl's Court, west London.

One of the care assistants from Hillingdon, a lady called Pat, had taken me for a day visit before I was admitted properly. The other kids in there mainly had behavioural problems or learning disabilities. Some had been in care, others had been abused by their parents. But even though we'd all been through some really bad stuff in our lives, we still managed to have a good laugh together. We all kind of picked up why each of us was there without ever really discussing it, and we just got on with kids' stuff instead.

Everyone seemed a bit more normal than at the Maudsley. What a relief that was! Also, the Maudsley was a secure unit whereas at Collingham we weren't locked in and that gave it a far more casual atmosphere.

There were some really cool boys there too. I was a

couple of weeks off my tenth birthday when I arrived and just beginning to realise boys could be nice to hang around with. There was Simon, who had been abused by his dad, and David, who had been thrown out of school for getting into trouble, and Mikey, who had behavioural problems. But none of that mattered. To me they were just fun and a bit cheeky and I could be a total tomboy hanging around with them.

At first I even quite liked the regime at Collingham. They started off by giving me meals like salad with a bit of bread and butter and I felt OK about that. They'd make up the calories with FortéCal, a glucose drink which contained 450 calories in each 200-millilitre bottle. But I was OK with that as I knew exactly what FortéCal contained – it didn't feel like anyone was trying to trick me into having more calories than I wanted. And they didn't make me eat anything I didn't want, like sweets or chips.

I stopped having tantrums and became a lot calmer. I was happier because I felt I had some control again over what was going inside me.

But things went a bit wrong the day Mum and Natalie made their first visit to see me there. I had been in only a week and was having my lunch. They'd given me just a salad and everything was fine. But when the nurse brought over a Complan high-calorie build-up drink to go with it, I went potty.

'You've filled this mug up too far,' I screamed. 'Are you trying to con me? I'm not drinking it,' I yelled. 'You might as well take it away.'

I was still sitting there 40 minutes later when Mum and Nat arrived at the door of the unit. I heard a nurse saying to them, 'We're very sorry, Mrs Grahame, but I'm afraid

Nikki has refused to eat her lunch, which means she won't be able to have any visitors this afternoon.'

A raging anger which had been lying inside me for months suddenly burst to the surface and I became like a demon. I screamed and swore at the nurses, waving my arms around like an out-of-control windmill. 'I hate you!' I shouted. 'You're all horrid. You won't let me see my mum. I hate you.'

One of the nurses walked slowly towards me, making soothing noises and holding her hands out, but I wasn't having any of it. I lashed out at her, kicking her shins and flailing my arms about.

I ran towards the stairs to try to get down to where Mum and Nat would be. But by now I was out of control and on reaching the top of the stairs I flung myself forwards, down the steep marble staircase. I don't know if I even thought about what I was doing – I just wanted my mum and I needed someone, anyone, to listen to me. I hurtled downwards until I rolled to a stop halfway down the steps, crying and shaking in a pathetic heap.

The nurses ran down to pick me up but I still wouldn't let them near me. I hate you!' I kept screaming. 'I *need* my mum.'

I smashed my head against the banister and pulled at my clothes and hair with my hands in a frenzy of screaming and sobbing. It took nearly a quarter of an hour for me to calm down enough for the nurses to be able to help me up the stairs and back to my cubicle.

Things were only going to get worse at Collingham, though. To begin with they must just have been getting me used to eating again because after the first fortnight the salads stopped and they started giving me the same food as all the other kids – and that was terrible.

Chips were on the menu twice a day. Now, I can understand why they did it. They were catering for children and their thinking was 'kids love chips'. Except me of course. I was the only one on the ward with an eating disorder and being given chips was about the worst thing I thought possible.

As soon as I smelt the deep-fat fryer warming up in the kitchen my stomach would turn in revulsion. Normally the chips were slapped on the plate with burgers or fish fingers or, when Erla was in charge, Cornish pasty! All that pastry as well as chips. It was foul.

My stance hardened. Now my day fell into a routine of meals that I would eat and those I would refuse. I would always eat breakfast because it was always the same, a bowl of cereal, a piece of toast and cup of tea. It was safe for me – no surprises.

After breakfast I had to have half an hour's bed rest. Like at Hillingdon, the staff knew I would take any opportunity to exercise, even if it meant just stepping on the spot in the corner of a room. And bed rest was the only way they could stop that.

Afterwards, I'd have time for a quick play with the other kids before snack time at 10.30. But I'd never eat that snack, which meant I'd have to sit there with it in front of me until lunchtime at 12.15, when they'd take it away. It was all part of a carefully worked-out plan. I'd realised that if I ate that snack – usually a Complan drink and a couple of biscuits – I'd then have to have another half an hour's bed rest, before just 45 minutes' play, then lunch. For the sake of that 45-minute play, it was not worth drinking a 450-calorie Complan drink. I might as well sit it out until lunchtime.

I rarely ate lunch either – again, it just wasn't worth it to me because lunch finished at one o'clock, followed by an hour of bed rest, then an hour of play before the afternoon snack at three. I wouldn't eat a full lunch in return for just one hour's play in the afternoon. No way.

I saw the afternoon snack differently. It was normally only a Complan build-up drink and a biscuit, followed by half an hour's bed rest, then two hours' play before supper. Two hours running around made eating the snack worthwhile. I'd use that two hours to stomp up and down the corridors or run around the garden, anything to burn up some calories. That playtime also provided some mental stimulation after having spent most of the day sitting at a table staring at food I was never going to eat.

By the evening meal I was usually back to not eating again. Dinner finished at quarter to seven, bed rest for an hour took it to quarter to eight and then bedtime was half past eight. Again, it just wasn't worth it to me and I might as well just sit in front of my untouched meal until bedtime.

I sat at my meal table for hours on end, bored out of my nut. Occasionally some of the nurses would try to encourage me to eat but most of them just ignored me – that's what they had been told to do as I wasn't supposed to get any interaction or attention until my plate had been cleared.

The Queen singer Freddie Mercury had died six months earlier and I'd been given the band's recently released *Greatest Hits Volumes I and II*. I was a massive fan of Queen – I always had been since Mum and Dad used to listen to their records at home when I was little. While I was at Collingham, Mum even took me on a day trip to lay flowers outside the house where Freddie had lived.

Every day at Collingham, to pass the time, I'd sit at the dinner table and go through in my head the lyrics of each Queen song in the exact order they appeared on the albums. I knew every single lyric to every single song. Lunchtime would start with 'Bohemian Rhapsody' running through my mind, then 'Another One Bites The Dust'. Often I'd still be sitting there three hours later in front of a cold plate of sausage and chips when 'One Vision' finally came to a crashing finale in my head.

But we did have good times at Collingham too. The manager there was called Paul Byrne and he was lovely. He took me under his wing and looked after me. He was good to me and for the first time in years I could laugh again. Paul played all those 'Dad' tricks that other kids got at home. Once I was in the bath and he dangled a broom down from the floor above and banged on the window. I nearly jumped out of my skin. Another time he put custard in my bed – it was disgusting but very funny. And he was always jumping out on me from behind curtains and doors.

Paul made Collingham fun. When he was around I could even forget about food for a while. But he was strict with me too and if I didn't eat he would really shout at me. 'Come on, Nikki, stop staring at your plate and eat.' But if I did eat it I got loads of extra treats. He'd get one of the nurses to take me to the pottery room or let me go with the other kids when they walked down to the local shop for a magazine.

One day, he said if I ate everything they gave me until Wednesday lunchtime he'd take me to the zoo. I did it and he took me. It was brilliant.

There was a really cosy day room at Collingham with amazing board games and a Nintendo and there was also a classroom where kids who were well enough had lessons. To help us with our French lessons Paul fixed up for us all to go on a day trip to Boulogne. It was so exciting going over on the ferry and trying out our 'Bonjours' on every shop owner we met.

The only downside for me that day was the food. All eight of us piled into a restaurant and of course everyone except me instantly ordered burger and chips. I couldn't face the burger and thought omelette at least sounded a bit healthier. But when it arrived it was the size of a dustbin lid and oozing bright-yellow grease.

Paul took one look at my plate, then at my face and laughed out loud. 'Serves you right for trying to be smart and not having burger like the rest of us,' he chuckled. 'You can eat the lot now!' But he didn't make me eat it all – so long as he knew I was trying to eat he never pushed me too far.

Another time we went on a camping holiday in the New Forest, like I'd done at the Maudsley. We had a camp fire, made dens and bridges and one of the nurses dressed up as a ghost. It was so much fun. Best of all, I got away with eating hardly anything.

After I had been in Collingham for a few months I had to move rooms and share with a girl called Lucy. I'm still not sure why exactly she was there but she was pretty strange. She was a real goody two-shoes and would grass me up to the nurses at any opportunity.

For months I'd been getting away with offloading loads of food on to the boys' plate at mealtimes. Whenever it was lamb chops, say, I'd slice off all the fat and lob it on to my mate Lee's plate and he'd swallow the lot. It was a perfect system. But once Lucy saw what I was up to she wasted no time telling the nurses. Paul came in and screamed at me, 'What do you think you are doing, Nikki? Well, you won't be getting away with any more of your little tricks.'

I was so angry at Lucy for dropping me in it and we didn't speak for days. But after a while we made up and sometimes we even got on OK. Once I persuaded her to get up with me really early in the morning to jump out on the nurses turning up for their morning shift. We hid at the bottom of the stairs at the crack of dawn to play our trick and when we leapt out on the nurses as they came in, they all screamed. Once they'd recovered from the shock they saw the funny side. They were cool. And I think they must have realised there weren't a lot of other laughs for us kids in that unit.

Collingham was only open on weekdays but at first I wasn't trusted to go home at weekends, so Paul would drive me back to Hillingdon Hospital instead. On a Friday evening, as we sat in traffic jams in the Sunshine Variety Bus, I'd make him listen to my Queen tapes.

The weekends back at Hillingdon were grim. I'd spend hours tidying up the playroom because it was good exercise and something to do, then I'd lie on my bed watching Queen videos and singing to myself, trying to kill the hours until it was time to return to Collingham on Monday morning.

At Collingham I had my own bedroom. It was quite big and I decorated it with colour posters of Freddie Mercury I'd bought in the Virgin Megastore and my collection of helium balloons. Every time Mum visited I'd drag her out to a card shop for another balloon. I was also really into stickers and had them all round my room – the furry ones and scratch 'n' sniff ones that I got out of Frosties packets (without eating the Frosties, of course).

The only problem with my room was that it was right next to the nurses' station, which had a massive observation window so that they could keep an eye on me at any time of day or night. I also had to sleep with the door open in case I was up to any exercise or being sick. That meant I had no privacy, even when I was sleeping. It was like living in a goldfish bowl.

After I'd been at Collingham for two months, Mum was allowed to come in and sit with me during meals. They were trying to work out some kind of strategy to help her cope with me when I eventually went home. Everyone was just terrified that otherwise, as soon as I was discharged I'd just go straight back to my tricks and tantrums, Mum wouldn't be able to cope and I'd get really sick again.

First of all at mealtimes Karl, my clinical nurse, sat down with us. But once he was happy that Mum could be strict with me if she needed to be, he would leave us alone. Of course as soon as he was gone I started pushing my luck again. I'd still try to wrap Mum around my little finger.

But I was making progress and my weight did start increasing. In my mind, though, I still firmly believed being skinny was perfect and that was still the way I wanted to be.

What the doctors didn't know was that I had been using my time wisely at Hillingdon and Collingham, devouring every women's magazine and newspaper article I could find about losing weight. I'd become a child expert on food and nutrition and could recite the calorific values of hundreds of different products. And I'd worked out exactly how much exercise would burn off how many calories too. I had an almost encyclopaedic knowledge of slimming.

So when I did start to go home at weekends I was already several steps ahead of Mum – even though I was only ten. The moment I arrived home on a Friday evening I'd have a set amount in my head that I would allow myself to eat that weekend. And no matter what instructions Mum had been given by Collingham, it wouldn't make any difference.

I was tricky too. One weekend at home I invited my old boyfriend Nicholas Richards round for tea. We'd been at Hillside School together and written to each other during my stays at the Maudsley, Hillingdon and Collingham. I was so looking forward to Richard coming round but I still couldn't help obsessing about how to reduce the calorie count of our tea.

'Oh, but Mum, can we have Quavers instead of the normal Salt 'n' Shake crisps? I love Quavers,' I said. Mum was just delighted to think I was eating crisps. What she didn't know is that a packet of Quavers is 85 calories and Salt 'n' Shake is 146. Mum could be such a soft touch.

And I'd still argue with her about everything she prepared for dinner. If she tried fish fingers, for instance, it would be the same old argument.

'Collingham say you have to eat three of them, Nikki,' she would say.

'Fine,' I'd reply like a right little cow. 'But if you give me three I won't eat anything. If you give me two I'll eat them all.'

What could she do? I had her over a barrel.

Mum was still very brittle. She would cry a lot about what I was doing to myself and everything that had happened. I may only have been ten years old but I could sense she was weak and I used that to my advantage.

Another thing Mum was always trying to feed me was waffles. I hated them and would squeeze them on to kitchen paper to blot all the oil off before I ate them. Mum would huff and puff about it but it was either that or they went straight in the bin. I'd hide food in my knickers too and on a bad day there would be plates thrown at the walls again as well.

I think I regressed whenever I went home for a couple of reasons. Certainly it was easier to bully Mum than the nurses. But also it may have been because at home I got so much more attention when I played up, and on some deep level that was what I wanted. I knew Mum was desperate for me to eat – my life depended on it and by now she felt hers did too. But in hospital the nurses, even the nice ones, weren't as emotionally connected. Whether I ate or not, at the end of their shift they would go home and put their feet up in front of *Corrie*.

Because I liked Collingham, though, my mood was much better and I was far calmer there than at home or Hillingdon. The only tantrum I ever had was the day Mum and Natalie were turned away at the door. They never gave me sedatives or tube-fed me there, so I must have been far easier for the nurses to handle than I'd been at Hillingdon.

Collingham was a very warm, caring place and I liked it for that. It didn't necessarily help me sort out my anorexia but maybe that would only happen when I was ready. But my weight did gradually creep upwards.

I was allowed home for Christmas and I knew I was only weeks away from getting out permanently. I still didn't want to eat but I knew I had to go through the motions to get everyone off my back.

They finally discharged me on 14 January 1993. I weighed 28.5 kilos (4 stone 7 lb) and was 132 centimetres (4 feet 4 inches) tall.

As Mum helped me load my bags into the boot of her car outside the unit, I felt I had won another battle. I was being allowed home – free at last. But to me it was clear that even if victory in this battle was mine, there was still a long, painful war ahead.

CHAPTER 9

TOO UNCOOL
FOR SCHOOL

'Ninety-eight, 99, 100.' I took a quick breath of air as I finished my second set of sit-ups, then jumped off the floor and started pacing up and down the room.

It was three o'clock on a freezing February morning and it was still pitch-black outside my bedroom window. But, like the night before, and the night before that, I'd been awake for the past three hours exercising silently while Mum and Tony slept in the room next to mine.

I'd start with sit-ups, then walk up and down the room until my head spun. Then I'd do lunges and star-jumps, although they were more tricky as sometimes the floor shook and Mum would wake up. My bed looked inviting and sometimes I felt so tired I could die but I had to keep going, had to keep burning off those calories.

As soon as I returned home, away from the watchful eyes at Collingham, I had thrown myself back into an almost constant exercise regime. Again, I couldn't even sit down in front of the telly in the evenings. Instead I'd stand in the corner of the room, stepping from one leg to the other.

I'd gone back to Hillside School but was finding it really tough to settle back in. I didn't feel I belonged there – or anywhere – any more. I'd only just got things back on an even keel after the Maudsley when I'd had to leave for Collingham. And this time it was even harder to fit back in.

Before, I'd always been a leader in my group but all the friendships had changed since I'd been away. There was a girl called Amanda Turbeville, who had joined the school while I was away. Joanne and Emily and Erin were all hanging around with her now and I was totally left out. That's what it's like with girls at that age – you're either in or you're out and I was most definitely out.

Maybe my old friends thought I was just a bit too weird or uncool to hang around with now. I don't know what it was but I felt rejected all over again.

Mum told me to stick at it and things would get better, so I kept turning up, hanging around the edge of my old group and waiting for acceptance. And waiting.

It didn't help that I was really behind in my schoolwork too. We'd had lessons at the Maudsley and Collingham but they were only really giving us a basic education as best they could in the situation. I was never destined to be a great academic. I'm more of a doer than a thinker and it didn't really bother me that I was behind except it was just something else which marked me out as different.

As the months rolled by Mum would encourage me to ask friends round for tea but there really weren't many girls for me to invite. Then I made one new friend, a girl called Lena, who was Russian and had just moved to the country and couldn't speak English very well. She was stunning, with long, dark-brown hair, but the other girls were mean to her because she was different. We were both outsiders and clung together. Lena would come round my house after school and we would play games and make circuses. We kept each other going for a long time.

Things at home were tough too. While I had been in Collingham, Mum had moved into a new house in Tolcarne Drive, five minutes' walk from our old home. It was a nice house and Mum had bought me a lovely new bed and decorated the walls with Forever Friends teddy-bear wallpaper and curtains. But I still desperately missed my old bedroom and our old house.

Tony was living with us permanently now, which also bothered me as it was just someone else battling for Mum's attention.

Everything felt wrong. Mum was upset too as she knew in her heart that I'd been happier at Collingham than I was at home. It was true. Collingham had given me a stability that I didn't feel at home. And despite the bad times I'd had fun there too. There wasn't much of that at home.

I was continuing as an outpatient at Collingham, which meant once a fortnight Mum and I would get on the tube down to Earl's Court for a weigh-in. Also, once or twice a month, I was having outpatient psychiatric treatment with Dr Matthew Hodes at St Mary's Hospital's Department of Child Psychiatry at Paddington Green. I hated those sessions – just another nosy parker asking me a load of questions I didn't want to answer. Sometimes I wouldn't even sit down in his room.

We had family therapy sessions too. Natalie had to take afternoons off school for them, which she hated too – to her it was just another example of me causing more upset in her life.

For about six months I trundled on at a fairly steady weight. I was still exercising and very fussy about what I would agree to eat, but at least I wasn't losing a lot of weight.

If it was a meal I 'allowed' myself, like two fish fingers and one potato, things were usually fine. But if Mum made something with more fat, like macaroni cheese, it was back to the same old tears, screaming and tantrums. She wasn't allowed to fry anything and pastry was a definite no-no. It must have been a nightmare for her every single evening. Before Mum even turned the oven on I would demand to know what she was planning to make. Then there would be the lengthy period of negotiation until we found some way of cooking it that we could agree on.

Collingham had left Mum with strict instructions about how much I should eat every day. But I knew she would bend the rules so long as I was getting some calories every mealtime. I was all too aware that her greatest fear was me throwing my plate at the wall or simply refusing to eat anything. I used that fear to blackmail her into giving me my own way. Once Mum started preparing the meal, I would stand behind her supervising, watching every single ingredient go in and calculating the calories in my head. But at least I wasn't losing weight. And my mood was a bit brighter during that spring too. Things settled down at school a bit in the early summer and I even got invited to a few of the girls' birthday parties.

But shortly after that, things took a turn for the worse again. Everyone around me suddenly started growing up – and I was being left behind.

'Have you started yet?' a girl in my class asked me as we sat in the playground one morning break time. It was the same conversation all the girls in my class had been having for the last couple of months – periods, time of the month, 'coming on'. They couldn't shut up about it – they were obsessed.

'Er, no, not yet,' I replied, looking intently at my scuffed school shoes.

The doctors had told me that my puberty might be severely delayed by my anorexia. At first it hadn't bothered me. Who'd want to go through that yukky business every month anyway? But as more girls in my class began to have this mysterious experience and turned into young women I felt more and more of an outsider.

Then at PE I noticed how loads of them were starting to get pudgy bits around their chests – they were growing boobs. They'd arrive at school on Monday mornings wearing bras, the tell-tale straps showing through their white cotton school shirts.

'Are you still wearing a vest, Nikki?' Amanda asked one warm day, peering at my childish white vest through my summer blouse. I was mortified. My chest was still as flat as a pancake.

That Saturday Mum took me to British Home Stores and bought me a little cami top which I wore just to make myself feel better. By now I was 11 and wanted boobs and periods. I wanted to be normal but the doctors were warning me that, because of the ramifications of anorexia, it might not happen for years, if ever. In the meantime I had to continue living in the body of a child.

I started slipping back mentally and physically. I could feel it sweeping over me over a few weeks. I felt so isolated again. I became quieter and introverted and as hard as Mum tried to reach me by talking to me and trying to comfort me, there was nothing she could do. I dealt with my torment the only way I knew how – more exercise and less food.

As soon as I got home from school I would lock myself in my bedroom. Sometimes I'd lie on the bed and cry. Other times I'd just exercise – it was the only thing that made me feel better.

The dining-table screaming matches escalated again. Each mealtime started in the same way. Mum, Tony, Natalie and I would be sitting down together but Mum would barely be able to concentrate on her own food as she would desperately be trying not to take her eyes off me for a moment in case the food started disappearing down my top or trousers.

I'd begin by pushing the food around my plate and separating it into piles so nothing touched anything else. Then the food would just sit there getting colder and colder while I stared silently at the wall or floor, withdrawing further and further into myself.

Mum would beg me, 'Please eat it, Nikki. You said you'd eat this. Please?'

As the minutes passed she would become more forceful. 'Look, if you don't eat, you'll have lost weight when you go for your weigh-in next week and they won't let you home again. You'll be sent back to Hillingdon Hospital.'

Sometimes that threat would work, because I was still haunted by the regime at Hillingdon and hated the thought of going back there.

I began drinking litres and litres of water and would put bars of soap in my pockets to make me heavier for my fortnightly weigh-ins at Collingham. As long as I could get away with these tricks there was less need to eat at home.

But soon, even the threat of Hillingdon meant nothing to me. I wouldn't even look up when Mum mentioned being sent back there. There wouldn't even be an eyelid flicker. I don't care about Hillingdon, I thought. I don't care about anything. I don't even want to be alive, to go through this, any more.

Tony, too, tried hard to make me eat, praising me when I did eat a mouthful, persuading me when I wouldn't. But there must have been loads of times when he thought he'd wandered into a total nightmare.

After half an hour or so Tony and Natalie would drift off into the other room, leaving Mum and me sitting there, my plate still piled up between us. Some evenings it felt like we were enemies on either side of a battlefield. And sure as hell I wasn't going to be the one to give in first.

Things got so bad that after a couple of months Mum made me eat my dinner wearing just my knickers so she could tell if I was hiding food. I felt the cold really badly then because I was so skinny and I would be covered in goosebumps, but it was the only way she could see what I was doing.

An hour or more would drag past and still I'd refuse to eat. That was when Mum would sometimes lose it with me and start shouting at me in her frustration. 'Just eat it, Nikki!' she'd scream. 'You're killing yourself and you're expecting me to sit back and watch you.'

Once she had started I'd join in too, screaming and lashing out at her. 'I'm not fucking eating it. Understand?' I yelled back. 'I don't want your food. You can fucking stuff it.'

Even after I had finished my food, or the whole thing had been abandoned, I'd then have to sit in front of Mum for an hour in case I was sick.

If I'd eaten everything, I'd be allowed out to see Lena and some of the other kids from our road who used to hang around on their bikes. But if I felt I'd eaten too much I'd make my friends stand and wait as I vomited it all up.

Other times I just ran out of the house straight after dinner, before Mum could stop me, and threw up against someone's garden wall. One night she tore round the streets in her slippers looking for me by following a trail of vomit.

I was never a bulimic, though – someone who constantly controls their weight through vomiting. For me, being sick was simply a last resort if I'd been made to eat something that I really couldn't cope with.

I knew Mum was finding it draining because I was constantly outwitting her. She was truly stuck in the middle. Collingham had given her strict guidelines about what I *should* and *shouldn't* do. But I was giving her ultimatums about what I *would* and *wouldn't* do. 'It's your choice, Mum,' I'd say. 'I'll either eat what I agree to or nothing at all – you decide.'

Collingham had told Mum that if she allowed me to leave food on my plate she was helping me kill myself. So every time I didn't eat a full meal, which was most days, she was consumed with guilt.

Mum was trying to please everyone and constantly feeling like she was failing everyone.

Her every attempt to outwit me failed. Collingham had told her to buy double-cream milk to help build me up. She knew I would point-blank refuse to drink it, so she had to pour it all into semi-skimmed milk bottles when I wasn't around. But she didn't get away with that for long as I could tell the milk was thicker and creamier and it made me gag. Then she tried buying higher-calorie Tesco cakes and putting them in boxes of McVities low-fat cakes.

'These don't taste the same, Mum,' I said after the first mouthful. It was like I could taste calories and she couldn't get away with anything.

Mum was tired of the constant battle. Every day she was reliving the same nightmare but there was no alternative. If she gave in to me, the chances were I'd die. I was making her life a misery.

All the counsellors had told Mum she had to be strong for me. Because while anorexics like to think they are in control, their behaviour is actually totally out of control. And that is why they need to feel their family is strong, like a fortress protecting them.

Deep down, I guess I did want Mum to be strong to protect me. But I also wanted her to be a push-over, to give in to my outrageous food demands and tempers. It was like I was constantly testing Mum to see exactly how strong she was. And sometimes she did cry, and sometimes she did lose it. And then I could see the despair in her eyes as she realised she wasn't being as strong as she ought.

Natalie was becoming so angry that everything at home revolved around me and what I had or hadn't eaten. Mum's every waking thought was consumed with me and whether I'd live or die. There wasn't much time or energy left for Natalie and she resented me like hell for that. She started rebelling in her own desperate bid for attention. She would be rude and stroppy to Mum and would stay out late, giving Mum even more to worry about. Natalie and I were getting on worse than ever, bickering all the time. Our house was so full of anger and violence that it was impossible to believe that we'd once been so happy. How could things have slipped this far?

During that autumn my weight started falling quite quickly as I became more and more withdrawn and unhappy. I'd slipped back into this hellish cycle where I could only make myself feel better by not eating, but not eating was just making me feel weaker and more sick again.

I began bunking off school and hanging around the shops. When Mum found out she went mad. It didn't stop me, though. I was angry, threatening suicide, rebelling and being a complete pain in the arse.

The fortnightly trips to Collingham to get weighed became even more of an ordeal. I'd tried bars of soap but now I'd fill my pockets with paperweights and anything else heavy I could find to boost my weight. But even the combination of that and drinking several litres of water wasn't enough to disguise the fact that it was slipping dangerously low.

At that point I think Mum in a way gave up on me – she was exhausted and just felt there was nothing she more could do. Then one day in December I simply refused to go to see Dr Hodes at Collingham and be weighed. Mum tried persuading me, then we started screaming at each other, but still I wouldn't budge. I refused to leave my bedroom.

'Please come, Nikki,' Mum begged. 'Otherwise they'll send you back to hospital and it's Christmas soon.'

'I don't care!' I screamed. 'I hate you, I hate hospital and I hate my life – I wish I was dead.'

I'd been saying things like that more and more, talking

about killing myself. I don't know whether I seriously meant it at that age or even understood what death meant. But I certainly knew I wasn't happy in the life I was in.

Mum had made an appointment for me at Collingham and I knew I would be readmitted. I had no idea how long I'd be away for this time, so the night before the appointment I persuaded Mum to let Lena and my other friends Suzanne and Jennifer come round for a Christmas party sleepover.

We lay in our sleeping bags on the lounge floor, chatting and giggling. At times like that I almost felt normal.

When Mum and Tony went to bed we lit a cigarette and passed it round between us. I knew it could be months before I saw my friends again and there was nothing I could do about it. I was being thrown along by events out of my control.

The next morning Lena, Suzanne and Jennifer went home and Mum helped me pack a suitcase for my stay in hospital.

As we walked down to the station I looked at all the toys and decorations in the shop windows. It would be Christmas in a fortnight but try as I might I couldn't see much to celebrate.

CHAPTER 10
RAW ANGER

'Here we go again,' I mumbled to myself as I forced my emaciated frame back up the steps at Collingham Gardens.

It was a bitterly cold day and the gusts of wind stabbed at my body, now unprotected by even the merest layer of fat.

There was a huge Christmas tree in the entrance hall at the unit, and tinsel neatly wrapped around the staircase, but I was long past enjoying that sort of thing. I was down to just 23 kilos (3 stone 8 lb) and didn't care about anything much at all.

I was put straight on total bed rest and not even allowed to walk down the corridor without permission. Yet it was almost a relief to be back. It felt like coming home. Again, someone else was going to take control for me for a while. All I had to do was comply.

And it was good to see Paul Byrne again, even though I knew he and the others were going to make me eat. A few days before Christmas there was a big dinner for all the kids and they made me finish the lot – turkey, sprouts and stuffing. It was foul.

As Christmas got closer all the other kids gradually drifted away with their parents and the unit prepared to shut down for the holiday. But there was no way they would allow me home for a fortnight. Instead I was transferred to the Chelsea and Westminster Hospital to be kept under observation. I was allowed home for just Christmas Day and Boxing Day.

Mum and Tony came to collect me in the car on Christmas Eve. It was another bitterly cold afternoon but when we arrived at our front door I didn't even step inside. Instead I started running up and down the road to burn off some of the calories they'd been ramming down me at Collingham. It might have been Christmas for other people, but to me it was just a chance to exercise.

When Mum finally persuaded me to go inside, I stood shivering next to the open fire in the living room, keeping the exercise going by rocking from one leg to the other.

Mum looked at me in despair. 'I see nothing has changed then, Nikki,' she said.

Christmas was OK. It was good to be home and to see my friends, but hanging over me all the time was the thought that I had to go back to the Chelsea and Westminster after Boxing Day – and there they were going to make me eat again.

Back in Collingham after New Year, things weren't as good as they had been during my first stay.

A lot of the old nurses had moved on and the new ones weren't as much fun. Many of the kids were new too. They were a nice group, but they weren't my real mates. Yet again I felt like everything had changed around me and I was the odd one out. That was becoming such a familiar feeling. At first it hit me hard, so I had a wobbly start back at Collingham, exercising furiously whenever I could until I dropped another kilo.

I remember one afternoon talking to a couple of the new girls. We were all moaning about how much we were being made to eat. 'This is a walk in the park compared with Rhodes Farm, though,' one of the girls said. 'Wait until you're in there!'

I'd heard the name 'Rhodes Farm' bandied about for the past couple of years by other anorexics and experts. People always spoke of it with a certain awe. The place was regarded as the Alcatraz of anorexic centres – no one got out of there without being made to put on weight.

'I'll never go to Rhodes Farm,' I said confidently. 'Not me.' Cockily, I thought I'd always be able to outwit the system.

At Collingham they had me straight back into counselling sessions too, which I still loathed. One session I spent the whole hour listening to my Walkman rather than answer their boring questions.

I made the decision I just had to get out of there as quickly as possible, which meant going along with whatever they wanted me to do – and that was eat. So I started eating whatever they put in front of me and gave myself a break from my constant battling.

I began to make some progress, clearing my plate at mealtimes and my mood improved too. And the less miserable I felt, the more inclined I was to eat. And the more I ate, the better I felt. Somehow I'd drifted out of the bad cycle I'd got stuck in at home and was in a better phase. I even started concentrating more in classes.

Paul said if I could reach 34 kilos (5 stone 5 lb) I would be allowed home at weekends again. The alternative was misery weekends at the Chelsea and Westminster, and I'd have done anything to avoid those.

So I pretty much complied and ate what was put in front of me, and my weight crept up. Of course there were still times when I'd try to hide food but there were none of my tantrums and plate-throwing routines. I was much calmer at Collingham.

There were other treats too if I ate my meals. One day Paul took me shopping to Kensington High Street because I'd been making such good progress. For some reason we wandered into a Thorntons Chocolate shop – bizarre, I know! They had a raffle on and Paul got me a ticket. And what do you reckon? I won an Easter egg and it was huge. I felt so proud when I carried it back into Collingham. I didn't eat it of course – I just kept it in my room – but it was great to look at.

Although I was eating more, I was still obsessed with exercise. Mum would come and visit me at weekends and if I'd been eating OK she would be allowed to take me shopping. But what Paul and the other nurses didn't know was that once we were out of the front door I'd break into a run, desperate to burn off a few calories. Mum would be left trailing behind, trying to keep up.

But I knew she wouldn't shop me to the nurses as that would mean she'd be barred from visiting. So again I had her over a barrel.

By the spring I had reached that golden 34 kilos (5 stone 5 lb) and was allowed to spend weekends at home again. But of course it was back to dodging food and exercising every weekend. If I didn't take every opportunity to do that at home I'd feel guilty, as though I'd failed in some way.

Even when Mum came to collect me on the tube I'd run to the top of each escalator at the station for the exercise.

'Please don't do that, Nikki,' she would say.

'Oh, don't worry about it,' I'd tell her. 'Let's just get home.'

In April it was my thirteenth birthday. Hurray, I was a teenager at last. Still no boobs or periods but I felt sure they had to come soon.

Just after my birthday I was allowed a weekend at home, so to celebrate I went with Lena and Jennifer to an under-18s disco. It was brilliant.

Still in a better frame of mind, I continued to gain weight. They were giving me enormous meals – plates piled high with chips, and custard on every pudding. There was no choice but to eat them. If I didn't eat it or tried hiding anything then I'd just get the whole lot replaced and would have to start all over again.

On 21 June I hit my target of 38.2 kilos (6 stone). I was 142.2 centimetres (4 feet 8 inches) tall. Two days later I was discharged and allowed home.

Mum and Dad had been having loads of sessions with the doctors at Collingham while I was there about how they were going to prevent me losing all the weight again the minute I came out. They were trying to build Mum up, to teach her how to be strong with me when I was in a rage or negotiating myself down to one cream cracker for my dinner.

Mum had to make it clear to me that she was never going to let me die. The doctors thought that once I truly understood this I would feel more secure and stop trying to control situations myself by refusing to eat. It was a good idea in theory. But in practice, no chance.

When I got home the weight fell off faster than ever before. My willpower kicked in and just wouldn't let me give in to eating anything more than an allowance set by myself. It was like everything that had gone before, with bells on. It was during this autumn that my illness reached its peak.

There were still some meals that Mum could cook me which I was OK about. A slice of roast beef in a gravy from a packet was allowed because I knew there was 120 calories in the gravy and roast beef was only 100. With that I'd have one potato cut into four (120 calories) and carrots (virtually none).

I remember thinking to myself, I wish I could eat food, not numbers. But I couldn't. My entire life was dictated by calorific values.

Mum was trying to get tougher with me and would make lasagne (500 calories) or macaroni cheese (500 calories) as 'punishment meals' if she thought I'd been hiding food or exercising a lot. But I knew exactly how many calories a lasagne contained and would just go mental about it.

So it was the same old battles. Several times I scalded myself on my stomach when I tried to hide spag Bol and other food down my knickers. Another time Mum found pasta inside my school sock. Most of my clothes got food stains on them somewhere before Mum returned to insisting I ate in my knickers.

I threw Complan drinks in the plant pots, shoved food behind the cooker until we got rats, and would often fill my mouth with food but then spit it out when no one was looking.

If Mum even considered giving me the kind of portions I had meekly eaten up while at Collingham, the whole lot went straight over the dining room wall. Poor Mum spent so many evenings wiping off all the pasta sauce and grease.

I was being sick, throwing food around, hiding food and doing everything I possibly could to get my weight back down again.

Mum looked so sad and so hopeless. But I still thought this was all her fault and she deserved my outbursts – she shouldn't be making me eat when I didn't want to.

Our neighbours just hated us because of all the screaming and shouting. They kept complaining about the noise but they were the least of our worries. It was a house so full of anger that nothing would keep us quiet.

I was angry at Mum, angry at Natalie and angry at myself. Some days I would hit my stomach again and again, screaming, 'I'm so fat. I hate myself.'

All the time my weight was dropping perilously low.

I was still attending outpatient appointments at Collingham, but even they were unsure how to save me. Whatever good work they did while I was in there was all undone immediately I returned home.

By the start of October my weight was down to 29 kilos (4 stone 8 lb). I'd lost 9 kilos (1 stone 6 lb) in just four months. I was sullen, spiteful, having temper tantrums and rowing with everyone. I was vomiting up food soon after meals, and even several hours later if I felt the need.

Mum says the haunted, troubled look had taken over my face again and she gave up the fight herself – she couldn't see anything left that she could do to help. Then, one morning at the start of October, she told me we were going to an appointment at Great Ormond Street Hospital for Sick Children in central London. Great Ormond Street is a general hospital, I thought. This will be a walk in the park! I was so angry inside and so full of pain that I wasn't bothered what happened to me next. It couldn't be any worse than the present.

On 16 October 1995 Mum, Tony and I trooped up to the Mildred Creak Unit at Great Ormond Street, which specialised in psychiatric and eating disorders. When we walked in, it looked more like a youth hostel than a hospital – it was really cosy with posters on the walls and lots of armchairs. A group of kids were sitting around having their afternoon snack and chatting.

The nurse took me into a side room before guiding Mum and Tony down a corridor away from me. She returned a few minutes later with a glass of lemon squash and a couple of biscuits.

'I've brought you this for your afternoon snack, Nikki,' she said.

I took one glance, smirked at her and replied, 'No thanks, I'm going home soon.'

How wrong I was – it was to be almost three years of pain, sadness, anger and loneliness before I properly returned home once more.

CHAPTER 11
DEATH PACT

I'd been at Great Ormond Street Hospital for about a week when Vicky arrived. Tall and super-skinny, with dark-brown hair which fell either side of her angular face in long plaits, she looked amazing.

She was dressed really grungily in brown corduroy trousers and a Radiohead T-shirt. She was so severely anorexic and so cool. I was desperately jealous. Vicky was the first anorexic I had ever met and to finally find someone else who felt and thought like I did was incredible. In the four years I'd spent at the Maudsley, Hillingdon and Collingham, I'd always been the only anorexic. That had just made me feel even more of an outsider.

So meeting Vicky was fantastic. She was like me, but better, because she was skinnier. Vicky was 12, just a year younger than me, and we became best friends instantly. We thought we'd be soul mates for life. The staff put us in the same room and that first night we stayed up talking for hours, sharing our secret thoughts and dreams. It was obvious to us that we both had the same problem, although we didn't really discuss it then or later.

It was just as well I found a friend, though, because the rest of the kids on that ward were, quite frankly, nuts. They weren't anorexic but they were some of the most seriously messed-up kids in Britain at the time. What I didn't realise then was that I too probably qualified as seriously messed-up. But all I could see was myself surrounded by total oddballs. Sometimes it was funny the way people behaved but other times it was just horribly scary.

At one end of the ward there was a girl called Isobel who spent every day propped up in a big wheelchair. She was very pretty but she didn't speak or communicate with the outside world at all. She needed to be fed through a nasal tube, was incontinent and had to be carried or pushed in a wheelchair everywhere she went.

But the incredible thing was that there was nothing physically wrong with her. Nothing! What she had was a psychiatric problem called Pervasive Refusal Syndrome, in which kids just shut their body down and go back to being babies. When her parents came to visit she would lie there and scream and scream. Isobel was at Great Ormond Street for two and a half years, then one day, all of a sudden, she started talking and walking. She returned home and went back to school. It was unbelievable.

Then there were a couple of kids at the Mildred Creak Unit with Attention-Deficit Hyperactivity Disorder (ADHD) – to me they just seemed incredibly naughty and would run up and down the corridor screaming and shouting at all times of the day and night.

Then there was a great big fat boy called Jonathan who we

used to call Pugsley after the character in *The Addams Family*. He used to lie in bed all day and the nurses would have to bring his food to him because he claimed he couldn't move. They even had to wheel him into the schoolroom.

And there was another boy called Shane. He had this weird thing going on in his head where he claimed he couldn't see or walk. I used to fight with him all the time. I could tell he was a liar and couldn't see why everyone made such a fuss about him. When I saw him crawling past my room for a wee, I'd follow him down to the toilets, then look under the door and see him standing up for a pee. I knew I was right.

Honestly, these kids were nuts and sometimes when they were having fits or tantrums it was terrifying. I'd come from a pretty ordinary middle-class home in a nice area with nice friends and there I was in a scene like something in a horror film. Often I felt Vicky and I were the only sane ones in there. Although looking back, we probably had a lot of problems ourselves.

At first they only gave me portions I was happy about, so I pretty much ate what was served up to me. My first dinner there, the day I arrived, was spaghetti hoops (a Great Ormond Street speciality), mashed potato (another of their favourites), one sausage and for pudding a fruit salad. So, although that was a lot more than I'd been eating recently, it was still bearable.

After dinner, one of the nurses searched my bags for laxatives, which some anorexics use to flush food through the body, and razor blades, in case I was thinking of killing myself.

Breakfast the next morning was OK too – one Weetabix, a piece of toast and a cup of tea.

I felt I was doing really well and told myself I was fine again now. They should let me home in two days, I thought. But if they don't, I'll start refusing things. What I didn't realise at first was that they were just warming me up with small portions and there was no question of them letting me home for quite some time. When I saw how wrong I was I began to refuse food.

All of the kids in the unit would sit around the dining table together, watched by a nurse. There would be Isobel with her drip feed and Pugsley Boy Jonathan, whose bed had to be wheeled right up to the table. Every mealtime would be the same. 'Come on, you need to make a start, Nikki,' the nurse would say over and over. But I'd just carry on sitting there, staring miserably at my plate and shaking my head.

I'd eat on Mondays because afterwards I'd be allowed down to Radio GOSH, the hospital's station. But other days I just wasn't interested.

The policy at Great Ormond Street was that I had to stay at the table until I had eaten everything on my plate. I wasn't allowed into the schoolroom or day room until it had all gone.

If, after a couple of hours, I was still refusing to eat, everything left would get carried over to the next meal. So if I refused a snack, later on I'd have to have lunch *and* a snack. And if I refused lunch as well, that evening they would give me dinner, lunch and a snack.

If it got to bedtime and I still hadn't eaten anything, I'd got away with it – and I did. But then they'd threaten me that if I did the same the following day I would be tube-fed. So I'd go a few days eating a bit more before refusing again. It was a case of staying one step ahead of being 'tubed' for as long as possible.

Vicky and I were equally obsessive about food and our conversations went round and round. 'What do you think will be for lunch?' 'What will they make us eat for dinner?' 'How many calories do you think were in that casserole?' 'How many sit-ups will it take to work off that cheese sandwich?'

But there was one big difference between us – Vicky was cooperating with the nurses. She would beg for smaller portions and say things like, 'Please don't make me eat this,' but in the end she would give in. Great Ormond Street was her first admission and she was still compliant and polite, like I'd been at the Maudsley.

But my time there and at Hillingdon had made me fearless and far harder to control. I'd watched kids have screaming fits and rages and learned from them. I was well on my way to becoming a psycho child myself.

After being kept away from my family for the best part of four years, I really wasn't sure where I belonged any more. I'd been drugged up and dragged face to face with the horrors of mental illness and I felt deeply damaged by it. I was going into fits and tantrums more and more often and crying a lot of the time. My mind was utterly tormented. And although my anorexia had begun with a desperation to be skinny, now it was almost as much about beating the system as about being thin. It was Me against Them.

One afternoon Mum took me down to the hospital shop to buy a helium balloon for my collection. I was standing in the aisle waiting for her to pay when I saw a plastic bottle of paracetamol pills. I wasn't even thinking about what I was doing, or why, when my hand instinctively reached out, picked them up and slipped them in my jeans' pocket.

I might have been only 13 but I knew exactly what taking the contents of that little bottle could do and it felt very possible. After Mum had left for the day I called Vicky over to my bed and turned out my pockets.

'Where did you get them?' Vicky asked, staring at the bottle of pills and immediately realising the seriousness of the situation.

'I nicked them downstairs and I'm keeping them,' I replied. 'I'll put them in the second drawer of the cabinet between our beds in case either one of us ever really needs them. For if things ever get too bad.'

'OK,' Vicky whispered. 'It's our secret. But we've got to promise that whichever of us needs to take them will tell the other one first.'

'Pact,' I replied solemnly.

'Pact,' repeated Vicky.

We should have been little girls making pacts no more serious than about which boys we fancied. But it was too late for that. We had already been propelled into a hideous other world far removed from childhood.

I was still eating as little as I could get away with and was weak and listless. One day, Vicky and I were allowed to go to nearby Covent Garden as a treat but I had to be taken there in a wheelchair because I couldn't afford to use up any energy by walking. When we got there I bought a milkshake and a Baileys-flavoured Haagen-Dazs ice cream and ate the lot – it was fantastic. But the guilt I felt afterwards was overwhelming and I didn't eat a thing the next day.

After I'd been at the unit a month the doctors called a meeting with Mum and Dad because they were concerned I hadn't really gained any weight since my admission.

Dasha Nicholls, the registrar, said to Mum, 'Things aren't getting any better, Mrs Grahame. We might have to think about tube feeding.'

When Mum told me what they were proposing I felt sick. I hadn't forgotten the tube feeding at Hillingdon and exactly how painful and disgusting it had been. But worse still, I knew it meant I'd have no control over how much I was eating. But even though that threat was there I still refused to eat. I knew I couldn't cope with the guilt I'd suffer if I gave in to their food.

One morning I saw a nurse approach my bed pushing a trolley. On the trolley was a long tube. I knew exactly what this meant – they were going to tube-feed me through my nose.

Dr Bryan Lask, my specialist doctor, came over and talked me through it. Dr Lask is a professor of child psychiatry and one of the leading experts in his field but he always talked to me as an equal. I really liked and respected him, so I listened.

In the end I agreed to be tube-fed so long as I was allowed to follow a 1,000-calorie-a-day diet. That's about half what a girl of my age should have been eating but I think Dr Lask hoped to be able to increase the amount later and felt that in the meantime anything was better than nothing at that point.

The deal was I would eat normally during the day but whatever I didn't eat in proper food would be made up for at night through the nasal tube. For instance, if I ate 100 calories of crackers at lunchtime and another 100 calories of fish at dinner, they'd give me the remaining 800 calories by tube during the night.

It was a metre-long tube made of pure silk, which meant

it was much softer and less painful to push into me than the hosepipe-like one they favoured at Hillingdon. A vanilla-flavoured milky drink containing calories, fibre, protein, fat and vitamins called Ensure was pumped through the tube and down into my stomach.

After a couple of weeks my weight stabilised and Dr Lask wanted to increase my daily intake to 1,500 calories. I went schizo. I felt I'd been betrayed and was furious. 'There's no fucking way you're doing it!' I screamed at the nurse as she tried to fit up a larger bag of milk feed.

I went on yelling and throwing my body around until Dr Lask had to be called. Finally we agreed he could increase the calories by 100 every other day.

But the day it hit 1,800 I went mad again. As soon as the nurse inserted my tube that night I ripped it straight out and tore it in half. The pain as the tube came shooting up my throat and down my nose was hideous. But I didn't care. It was a victory to me.

I was raging. A second nurse came and had to hold me down while they inserted another tube. But again as soon as she stepped away I pulled it out with one sweep of my arm and threw it across the room. That happened again and again until I'd destroyed six tubes. One of the nurses told me later that each tube cost £45. On top of everything else I was costing the NHS a fortune – but I couldn't have cared less.

For weeks I would rip out up to six tubes a day. I did it so often I became anaesthetised to the pain. Even now my nose still clicks because of the damage I did by pulling those tubes out so roughly.

Sometimes six male nurses would hold me down, trying to keep my arms from the tube, as it was connected to the feed bag and pump. I was like a mad thing. Screaming, kicking, punching them, pulling their hair and scratching their faces to get them off me so I could grab hold of that hateful tube before it started poisoning me with calories.

I was obsessed with keeping that tube away from my body. On different occasions I punched a couple of nurses quite hard and spat in the registrar's face. Another time Nicky Harris, the ward sister, had to sit on me to hold me down because I was demented with anger.

By now I was little more than a bag of bones but my desperation to stop them from feeding me gave me an inner strength. And I would never give up. It was like I was being driven by some demon to claw and punch and spit – anything to win.

In the end the nurses got sick of fighting with me time and time again and one morning as I started screaming and lashing out, I suddenly felt a sharp prick in my bum. The sensation of drowsiness I'd known at Hillingdon soon surged over me and within a minute I was lying there unable to fight any longer. It was Diazepam, a sedative and muscle-relaxant which basically just knocks you out.

That became the norm. They didn't have the staff to spare six nurses to hold me down six times a day as they tried to feed me – there were another nine kids on the ward who needed looking after too. A 'chemical cosh' was both quicker and more cost-effective, I guess.

In addition to the emergency Diazepam jabs, I was already on a daily cocktail of other drugs designed to knock the fight out of me and make me compliant. I was on Thioridazine, a tranquilliser, Amitriptyline, an anti-depressant, and Chlorpromazine, an anti-psychotic drug which was supposed to reduce my anxiety.

I went from being a real live wire, always slightly hyper and ready for a fight, to a total zombie. I was 13 years old and one of the living dead. My eyes were glazed, my expression blank and inside my mind it was like stumbling through a deep fog. It was like living my entire life buried under a huge pile of blankets, warm and comfy but suffocating too. I knew things were going on around me but every noise was muffled, every sight fuzzy and every sensation dulled.

I'd fall asleep in classes or halfway through a sentence when Mum came to visit. I couldn't concentrate on anything.

At first I tried to fight the drugs by drinking litres of black coffee but then the nurses worked out what I was doing and limited me to one cup a day.

Whenever the drugs wore off, though, I'd become even more angry than before. I was like a wild animal who'd broken out of its cage and wanted revenge knowing that it would soon be recaptured. I'd hit myself and the nurses, claw and spit. Often I'd go up to the playground on the roof, where there was an area for kids to shout and let off steam. I'd scream for hour after hour until patients all over Great Ormond Street Hospital could hear me.

Even in my most docile state, I never totally gave in to the system. At every opportunity I would turn off the machine next to my bed which pumped the milk feed into my nasal tube. The milk feed dangled next to my bed in a bag connected to a machine, but I soon worked out how the machine worked. I would press a button at night to see exactly how many millilitres had gone through and how many were left to go, then lie awake for as long as I could manage to watch those calories flooding my body.

Sometimes I switched off the machine but that was only ever a brief victory as the nurses would soon spot what I'd done.

A craftier trick was to unscrew the connector which linked my nasal tube to the bag of Ensure liquid, then let the milky fluid drip from the tube on to my mattress. Sometimes I'd lie all night in a soaking-wet mattress that stank of vanilla-flavoured milk. But even that was preferable to having it go inside me.

One time I kept the tube disconnected for three days, letting the feed drip each night on to the carpet beneath my bed. But when my room started stinking of rancid milk it became clear what I'd been up to.

The machine pumped feed into me at 250 millilitres per hour. But then they replaced it with a super-duper new machine that they were very proud of as it could pump in 400 millilitres per hour. When they used that I could feel the liquid pouring into my stomach. I felt like a car being filled up with petrol. I felt bloated and sick as the rich liquid swilled around my stomach.

One night as they hooked up the new pump to begin feeding me, I just lost it. I couldn't face another night of it and I exploded with rage, ripped the machine off the stand and lobbed it across the room. That was the end of their smart new machine. Well, until it returned from the menders.

All that time, every mealtime, after a bit of a cry and a half-hearted attempt to negotiate with the nurses, Vicky would dutifully put her head down and eat. I felt she was betraying our special bond. And couldn't she see she was putting on weight? It was disgusting and only made me more determined to never let that happen to me.

133

I became so angry about how much they were pumping into me at night that I started refusing all food during the day.

My weight was now dangerously low. At around 27 kilos (4 stone 3 lb) it was less than half what a 13-year-old girl should weigh.

Dr Lask decided to give me an incentive – if I complied and reached 29.5 kilos (4 stone 9 lb) by Christmas, I could go home for the holiday.

As desperate as I was to go home, I wanted even more to win my battle to be skinny – so I carried on fighting. I couldn't give up anyway, because the guilt would be too great if I caved in after having achieved so much.

The big weigh-in was set for a week before Christmas. As I stood on the scales and looked down I could see I was 2 kilos (4½ lb) short. My first feeling was simply joy that I'd kept the weight off so well. And I didn't believe they'd really keep me in over Christmas.

Mum and Dad were called in for another big meeting with the doctors. As soon as Mum came into my room afterwards I knew it was bad news. 'Sorry, Nikki, but they're going to make you stay in over Christmas,' she said. It took a couple of seconds for it to sink in, then I went mad. I didn't feel anything but rage. I whacked my head against a wall and scratched my face with my fingernails. I raged for an hour with no one able to calm me down until I finally collapsed, exhausted.

This is it then, I thought. I'll show them how much trouble they have caused not letting me go home and not letting me starve myself to death. This will teach them that all their efforts to keep me alive were just a total waste of time.

I turned and walked quietly back to my room and dug out the paracetamol pills from my bedside drawer. I got a cup of water from the kitchen, then sat on my bedroom floor and swallowed the lot. The water ran out after the first half a dozen and I was gagging as I forced the rest down my throat.

I didn't think about Mum and Dad or Natalie. All I could think was how sorry everyone would feel when they saw what they had made me do.

I wandered into the day room and lay down on a sofa. The next thing I remember is being carried down to a medical ward. I opened my eyes and there was Vicky, in tears as she looked down at me. 'Nikki, I can't believe you've done this without telling me,' she said. 'What about our pact?'

I felt so tired I couldn't answer. I just closed my eyes and thought how nice it would be for all this pain to be over.

Vicky had seen me lying on the sofa, totally out of it, and guessed what I'd done. When she checked the drawer and found the pills missing she had alerted the nurses straight away.

Mum and Dad were called and came straight to my bed on Victoria Ward, a medical ward at Great Ormond Street, where my liver function was being monitored. Although I probably hadn't taken enough pills to kill myself there was still a danger that with my critically low body weight I could have seriously, even fatally, damaged my liver.

'You could have died, Nikki,' Mum kept saying. 'Please don't leave us, Nikki. Me and your dad love you so much. We want you to live.'

After a couple of days I rallied but I still wasn't eating

and I felt more depressed than ever. The thought of returning to the nasal tube just filled me with fury all over again.

Then one morning Dr Lask came and sat by my bed. 'OK, Nikki, you've got your way,' he said. 'We'll give up on the nasal tube for a while – but you have to eat.'

He explained they had decided that Mum would have to visit all day, every day, to look after me, bath me and try to get me to eat. The nurses couldn't cope with me on their own any longer and, besides, the doctors thought I might respond better to treatment if Mum was around more.

But still I wasn't eating enough and in the last couple of days before Christmas they became desperately worried about me again. I was refusing fluids too and they feared I was becoming dehydrated. All over Britain kids of my age were working themselves into a frenzy of excitement about Christmas. But I was being given a stern warning that if I didn't get food or drink inside me soon, I was going to die.

On Christmas Day, Mum, Tony and Natalie came up to visit me. I've got a photo of me and Vicky from that day. I'm wearing a blue Oasis T-shirt and my brand-new Ellesse trainers, which I loved. But I look so haunted and sad in that picture. At that point I was totally out of it from all the drugs they were giving me to keep me quiet plus the paracetamol I had taken. It was a struggle to even stand up, I was so ill. But in my mind I was stronger than everyone.

The four of us sat at the table for a Christmas dinner but it was pretty hard to find much festive cheer. After pulling a cracker with Natalie I sat there utterly miserable. I ate an orange, then watched as everyone else piled into their hospital turkey and sprouts.

Mum must have been desperately forcing out that 'ooooh' noise everyone makes while pulling crackers because one look at her pale and frozen face revealed her true terror. She knew full well that it would need a miracle for me to still be alive the following Christmas. In fact the way I was going I'd be lucky to make the New Year.

That evening Dad came up to visit me with Trudi, his new girlfriend. We all did a jigsaw puzzle, although I stood up the whole time – sitting burned no calories.

On Boxing Day morning Mum made the three-hour round trip to see me again. I was so weak and sleepy I couldn't even speak to her.

'I'm going to go now, Nikki,' she said, stroking my head. 'I've got Tony's son and his girlfriend coming for their lunch, so I'd better get back.' Her brittle tone told me that she was trying not to cry but I couldn't do anything. Certainly I couldn't reassure her everything was going to be OK. I didn't know – or care – whether it was. And I didn't want her leaving me for a moment – I was supposed to be her main concern. I stood at the door of the ward looking lost and alone as she walked away, knowing that would make her feel guilty.

Soon afterwards Dad came back to visit. He bounced in the room beaming at me, just like the Dad I had adored all those light years ago. 'Hello, Nikmala,' he said. He helped me off the bed and we went into the day room to watch telly. I lay down on the sofa, my head on Dad's lap, his arm around my shoulders. It felt so safe, so warm.

We must have been there for about half an hour when Emma, one of the really cool nurses, came in and sat down next to Dad.

'Having a good time?' she asked Dad, smiling, before her gaze moved down to where I was lying.

Suddenly her expression froze and she leaned forward and grabbed my wrist, feeling for a pulse.

'Oh my God, she has passed out,' Emma shouted out to the corridor. 'Quick, get one of the doctors in her *now*.'

Dad was horrified. He thought I'd been lying there quietly enjoying the telly but I'd actually slipped into a coma. It was caused by the combination of the drugs I was on, the paracetamol overdose and my critically low weight.

Mum was just taking off her winter coat in the hall at home after getting back when the phone rang. She knew it would be Great Ormond Street.

'You're going to have to come back,' said the nurse. 'Nikki is critically ill.'

I was rushed down to Helena Ward, another medical ward, for immediate observation. It turned out I was severely dehydrated. The nurses were desperately trying to insert a drip to try get some fluid back into me when Mum and Natalie arrived.

Time and again the nurse searched for a vein to put the drip into. But I was so ill and so weak that my veins were almost impossible to find. Even when she found one, it was so weak that it collapsed.

By the time Mum and Natalie got back to the hospital, I was still unconscious. Mum was terrified that this time it really was the end.

'What's happening?' she asked desperately. 'My baby's dying, isn't she?'

'We've got to get a line into her otherwise we can't guarantee anything,' the doctor replied. 'She is severely dehydrated. If we don't get fluid into her within the next 15 minutes we could lose her.'

Most other people would have been cracking open another tin of Quality Street in front of the Boxing Night Bond movie. But inside Helena Ward my family was facing up the reality that I might finally have succeeded in starving myself to death.

Mum clung to the side of the bed as if by holding on tight enough she could keep me there.

Finally a nurse found a usable vein and they hitched up the drip and gradually began to rehydrate me. But I still wasn't out of the woods and my condition remained severe.

Mum stayed all night with Natalie. She held me next to her, willing me to live. 'You've got to fight, Nikki,' she kept saying. 'There is a life out there for you.'

Poor Natalie was so exhausted that in the early hours of the morning she climbed into bed next to me. But even her warmth couldn't bring me back to my senses.

It was almost 24 hours before I finally woke up, surrounded by doctors. There was my social worker Peter Honig, Dr Lask, Dasha Nicholls the registrar, my key nurse Sam and Dad all standing around my narrow hospital bed.

As I opened my eyes all I could feel was a dryness in my mouth and a grogginess in my head. But then a far stronger feeling hit me – anger. Because to my side was a bag of glucose connected to a drip which they had finally managed to feed into my arm.

'What've you been doing?' I said. I reached up to the bag, trying to see the calorie count written on it, but I was still so disorientated I couldn't work out what it said. So instead I reached for the needle that was piercing the back of my hand and yanked it out.

'Calm down, Nikki,' said one of the nurses as she set about trying to reconnect it. But this vein had collapsed too, so there was nothing she could do but try to find a new one. I wasn't having that, though, and went into the most horrific rage at Dr Lask, Dad and the nurses. 'Did you knock me out so you could fill me with this shit?' I shouted, feeling utterly betrayed.

Dr Lask must have been called in from a day off because he was still wearing a hand-knitted jumper that he must have been given for Christmas. He kept trying to calm me down and talk to me as I thrashed around the bed, clawing at any nurses who dared approach me with a needle.

After a while, exhausted, I slipped back to sleep. But I drifted in and out of consciousness, picked up snatches of the conversation going on around my bed between Dr Lask, Peter Honig, Dasha Nicholls, Mum and Dad. I wasn't even sure who was saying what – it was just words and voices rolling around in my head. They were saying things like: 'It's a huge risk' ... 'But we haven't got a choice' ... 'Stitch it in?' ... 'Gastrostomy' ... 'General anaesthetic' ... 'Tube'.

The words bounced around my head like bumper cars at a fair. But there was one they kept coming back to: 'gastrostomy'. In my fuddled state I was trying to work out what it could mean. But they can't do anything to me now, I thought. I'm dying now. I'm winning, so what can they do to stop me?

It was a couple of days later, when I'd come back to my senses, that Mum explained to me the true, horrific

Above left: Daddy's girl – and blissfully unaware of what I would endure later in my childhood.

Above right: Big sister Nat taking care of me.

Below left: Aged four, wrapped up for a winter walk in the park with Natalie.

Below right: Nurse Nikki.

Happier days, before I got ill.

Above left: The family, together, before my parents' marriage fell apart.

Above right: A day out with Julidah, Zanep and Natalie.

Below left: Puppy love – me and Rex.

Below right: Fun, food and friends – my seventh birthday party.

Above: Our house at Stanley Road. I was so happy growing up there until about eight years old.

Below left: A bleak day for my family: Granddad's funeral.

Below right: Fanatical gymnast – as with everything I do, I felt I just *had* to be the best.

Nine years old, and the change in me is clear from these photos. I'd lost my sparkle and looked pale, thin and sad.

Above left: Nat in the attic room in Stanley Road; me, Nat and Mum moved up there while Mum and Dad were separating.

Above right: The day I refused to sit at the table during a family meal out at a Beefeater restaurant – even at such a young age, the thought of being around all that food disgusted me.

Below left: My ninth birthday – a weekend when I was allowed home from the Maudsley.

Below right: Ready to go back to school after six months at the Maudsley hospital.

Collingham Gardens.

Above left: Wasting away. You can see how large my head looks compared to my body in this photo.

Above right: My tenth birthday, spent at Collingham Gardens – a birthday cake would have been the last thing I wanted.

Below: With Paul Byrne, the unit manager (*left*) and Karl, my nurse (*right*)

Above: Days out with Collingham Gardens which, to my horror, seemed to involve quite a bit of eating. *Left*: Looking ecstatic at a trip to McDonald's and, *right*, a camping trip. I'm quite sure that I argued with them about whatever was on that plate.

Below left: My childhood was spent going in and out of institutions. This was one occasion when I was at home with Dad. You can see how thin my legs were.

Below right: Alarmingly thin at ten years old. Everyone around me was shocked but I wanted to be even thinner.

Above left: February 1993, and I must have reached a target weight to have been allowed back home. This wasn't the end of my illness, though, not by a long way.

Above right: Great Ormond Street – you can see the naso-gastric tube I was forced to have.

Below left: With 'Vicky', another anorexic at Great Ormond Street.

Below right: At Huntercombe with Mum – I was 14 in this photo, and 60% of the weight I should have been.

meaning of gastrostomy. 'They're going to give you an operation to stitch a tube directly into your stomach,' she said quietly. 'Because you keep pulling the nasal tube out, there's no other option left. You won't be able to pull this stomach tube out. They have to do it to keep you alive.'

What Mum didn't tell me was that Dr Lask had described me as the worst case of anorexia he'd had to treat in 32 years and that my chances of long-term survival were slim. I was also to be the first anorexic patient ever at Great Ormond Street to have a gastrostomy – and the danger of my undergoing anaesthetic and surgery at my critically low weight were extremely high. They were only doing the operation because they thought the alternative was certain death.

I felt sick as Mum talked on and on about the op and how it was all for the best. I was scared by the prospect of surgery but terrified to think there would be nothing I could do to stop them feeding me once the tube was fitted. Then they would have won the battle for control over my body once and for all.

By the next morning, when Dad arrived on the ward a couple of hours before I was due to go down for surgery, I was hysterical.

'Please, Dad, please don't let them do it', I begged. 'Please, I'm going to be good from now on. I'll eat, I promise.'

Dad looked so confused. He desperately wanted to believe me and he didn't want me to have this hugely risky operation either.

'Go and get me a Complan build-up drink from the kitchen now and I'll drink it. You'll see, I'm serious,' I said.

Dad walked out of my room and returned five minutes

later with a large glass of chocolate Complan – it's a high-calorie drink which they used to build up the anorexic kids.

He handed it to me saying, 'OK, if you drink this maybe I can persuade them not to do the op. But you've got to drink it.'

It tasted delicious. It was so long since I'd drunk anything like that and I loved it. And I didn't even feel overwhelmed with guilt like I would have done normally – because I knew it was my last chance to avoid the operation.

I swallowed the lot and kept it down. I had to.

'So they won't do it now, will they, Dad?' I asked.

I'd barely finished speaking when Dr Lask walked into the room, saw the empty glass and went berserk.

'What on earth is going on here?' he demanded, staring at Dad. 'Nikki is supposed to be on nil by mouth in preparation for her general anaesthetic. Are you trying to sabotage this operation, Mr Grahame?'

Dad flared up in retaliation. 'She is going to eat again,' he said, pointing in my direction. 'She has promised me, haven't you, Nikki?'

Dr Lask didn't even look at me to see my response. 'Nikki has had the last two weeks to show she could eat without a tube but she hasn't taken that opportunity,' he said. 'Why should we give her the benefit of the doubt now?' Then he spun round and left the room.

I don't think Dad realised I was on 'nil by mouth' and I'm pretty sure he didn't give me the drink to stop the operation going ahead. I reckon he was just hoping I had turned a corner and might start eating again. He was as desperate as I was that I shouldn't have a bloody great tube stuck into my stomach.

But the operation went ahead anyway. They must have

stuffed me full of sedatives again because I don't remember much more until opening my eyes and seeing the stars on the ceiling of the lift. That meant I was going downstairs for surgery. Dad was on one side of the bed and Mary, one of my nurses, was on the other.

As I stared hazily up at the stars sparkling above my head I thought, This must be what it feels like to be in heaven. Comfy, warm, safe. Kind of nice.

I looked across at Dad. 'It's all right, Nikki,' he said, squeezing my hand. 'Go back to sleep.'

CHAPTER 12
ZOMBIE CHILD

The stars were still twinkling in the dimmed light of the lift when they brought me back up to the ward from the operating theatre.

I felt groggy and my head seemed to be weighing a ton. But the strongest feeling was an incredible pain in my stomach.

Back on the ward, I lifted up the sheet and looked down at my tummy. There was a bandaged area on the left of the lower part and sticking out of it was three inches of clear plastic tubing. This was clamped to another tube stretching under the sheet and up to a feed bag suspended beside my bed. I felt disgusted as I watched the milk feed slowly seep into my body, but even I didn't have the energy to fight it at that moment.

My weight had been so critically low that the doctors had started tube-feeding me as soon as the operation was complete. They had just hours to get calories back into my body before it went into total shutdown.

I was pumped full of so many sedatives that I don't remember anything more about the next few days, until I was wheeled out of my bed just before midnight to sit with the other kids in the television room.

It was the countdown to New Year 1996.

'Ten, nine, eight...' everyone was shouting. I just sat there in silence, my face blank. I was so doped up and weak that I was like a scrawny shop dummy, propped up in a wheelchair watching expressionlessly as the rest of the world celebrated being alive.

They'd barely finished the countdown when my eyes closed again and they wheeled me back to bed.

After that I was sedated for more than another week. So in total I was in a zombie-like state for a fortnight, unable to speak or hear, and with a catheter fitted to drain away my urine and faeces.

I was again on Diazepam, Chloropromazine, Thioridazine and Amitriptyline, plus Carbamazepine, a mood stabiliser. The drugs were syringed into my feed tube three times a day, but if I started to come round they quickly topped them up.

I was totally at their mercy. For the time being, they had won.

Mum visited me every day during that fortnight and Dad came a lot too, although I had no idea at the time that either of them were there. Mum would brush my hair or sit and look at me or read the papers. Dad would wander up and down, talking to kids who didn't have visitors.

After two weeks I'd put on a couple of kilos – enough to bring me out of the danger zone. Only then did they gradually reduce the sedatives.

When I finally came round I opened my eyes and saw a

blank wall. They'd turned my bed around to make it easier to get to my tube. I stared at the dried brush strokes on the wall for a few minutes before slowly scanning the room.

To my left was a bag of milk feed still attached to me, the pump forcing the Ensure liquid into my body. On the other side of me sat Evelyn, one of the Dutch agency nurses who worked on the ward.

I moved my hands over my tummy and hips and could immediately feel I had put on weight. That immediately triggered a full-on rage. I'd been lying there zonked for a couple of weeks and all the time they had been fattening me up like a pig.

I can't believe they've done this to me, I thought. After all the hard work I've put in to be thin and they've treated me like this. Well, this is it now. The fight really begins. At that moment I was so angry I could have fought a giant.

The first thing I did was try to yank the tube out of my stomach. I grabbed hold of it and pulled as hard as I could. It was stitched in, so there was no way it would come out, and the pain was so agonising I screamed. But I still kept pulling.

Nurses ran into my room and tried to get hold of my arms but it was like my superhuman strength had come back to me and it took two of them to hold me down while another stuck a sedative jab in my bum.

And so it continued over the next few days. Whenever I regained consciousness I would straight away pull at the tube or try to prise it out with my fingers. But as soon as the nurses heard my gasps of pain they'd be there with their syringes to sedate me again.

I poked and prodded that wound every moment I was conscious. I became obsessed by the hole in my stomach and couldn't keep my hands away from it. Within days it was infected from so much fiddling, oozing a green goo and giving off a foul stench of rotting flesh.

Even that didn't stop me, though. I'd just dig my fingernails deeper into the pus and flesh, trying to unpick the stitches which held it into me.

There was about an inch and a half of tube inside my stomach and another six inches hanging out which was attached to my feed bag. My constant quest was to get my fingers to the bottom of that inch and half inside me. Some days I got my fingers right down into my stomach by poking about so deeply. The pain was excruciating but I couldn't stop myself. I stretched the hole by pulling it so much and have left a permanent scar.

One morning, about two weeks after the operation, I was sitting at the dining table with some of the other kids when suddenly everything felt distant. I could still hear them all chattering but I felt a hundred miles away. The next moment I was lying on the ground, jerking and twitching.

The nurses and other kids ran around me, trying to put me in the recovery position while a Crash team was called from Accident and Emergency.

At that moment Mum arrived at the unit but the nurses wouldn't let her in because everything was in a state of total confusion. 'Let me in,' she was shouting, banging on the door. She thought I must have dropped down dead. She'd been half expecting this moment for so long and now she was terrified it was going to happen with her unable to reach me in time, stuck behind a locked double door.

I lay on the floor, unaware of anything, for several minutes before coming to. Then, a couple of days later, I was watching television with Mum when the same thing happened again. More seizures and blackouts followed.

The doctors were really worried. But so they should have been. It was a problem they had created by giving me so many fucking drugs.

Over the next couple of months I had nine seizures – they started with something like an epileptic fit and then I'd black out. I was taken to a neurology ward for tests but they couldn't work out what was causing them. Then they stopped as suddenly as they had started.

My life fell into a routine where they would attach the feed bag to my stomach tube every evening. About half an hour beforehand they would give me a sedative to shut me up and then hope I would sleep through the entire feed.

I became desperate to fight those drugs. They were stripping out of me what little energy I had left. So, when they'd given me my evening jab, I would sit bolt upright in bed chattering to Vicky long after she had drifted off to sleep. Then I'd be up and down to the toilet dozens of times – anything to prevent myself nodding off.

The drugs always won in the end, though, and soon I'd be slumped against my pillow. But I often woke in the night and if I saw the feed still pumping into me, all hell broke loose.

As the weeks passed, though, I realised that if I really wanted to win this battle I needed a plan more sophisticated than just screaming and shouting every time they tried to feed me. Soon my every waking hour was dedicated to dreaming up methods to beat the tube.

Each night after the feed had finished, a nurse would disconnect my stomach tube from the feed bag tube, slip a cap on the end of it, then tape it up against my skin to stop it getting caught when I rolled over in bed. That process normally woke me up and I'd lie there dozily watching her do it. One night, though, I noticed some of the feed came dribbling back out before she capped the end of the tube. Aha, I thought, this is worth trying.

As soon as the nurse moved away from the bed I ripped the tape off my tummy, slipped the cap off the tube, rolled on to my side and held the tube pointing downwards. Soon the feed was pouring out of it like vomit on to my mattress.

Brilliant, I thought. I'm back in control.

From then on I was doing it every night. The feed went everywhere, over my clothes, my pyjamas, my duvet. Even my teddy bears got soaked. The carpet was sodden under my bed where I hoped no one would notice. Within days the entire room stank of stomach juices. I stank of stomach juices. It was disgusting and made me wretch but I didn't care.

After a week the nurses worked out what was going on and as soon as they heard me moving around after a feed they'd be straight over armed with their syringes.

But still I didn't give in. There were fewer nurses on during the night shift and I knew that if one of them was busy with Isobel or one of the other demanding kids, there wasn't much one of them could do to stop me on their own.

Some nights they would have to call for emergency doctors and nurses from other wards because they couldn't cope with me. I was like a demon child again. Because if I knew there was a chance of getting that feed out of my body, I'd do anything to achieve it.

They decided they would have to return to feeding me

during the day as then there were more staff around and it was easier to control me.

But it remained a constant battle and I never, ever got tired of fighting. I was stronger than they thought and I was determined to prove it.

By now, winning had become an end in itself. Yes, of course I still wanted to be as skinny as I could but beating the system had become my main obsession.

When I was being fed by the pump during the day, I would have to pull it along on a stand with me everywhere I went.

On days when I was well enough I would have lessons in the Great Ormond Street classroom. In I would go, pencil case in one hand and pushing the stand with the other. As the weeks and months rolled by I lost all sense of time, as had happened in all the other institutions I'd been in. One minute I'd be making Christmas cards to send home, the next it was Easter baskets, then Halloween pumpkins. Sometimes it felt like those art and craft lessons were the only thing connecting me to the rest of the world's calendar. I never did much other school work beyond art but I liked listening to what was going on.

Then one day I came up with a brilliant plan. The next morning I put on four pairs of socks before I arrived for morning classes. Sitting behind my desk, I carefully disconnected the bag from my tube and let the feed drip on to the floor. After a couple of minutes I wiped up the milky pool with the outermost pair of socks still on my feet. Then I leaned down, slipped the dripping-wet socks off and put them in my pocket. Five minutes later I did the same again with the next pair of socks. And again. And again.

Brilliant. That was 20 minutes' worth of calories wasted. Another victory to me.

I got away with that for a couple of months before one morning one of the members of staff helping out in the classroom screwed up his nose and sniffed suspiciously.

'I can smell Ensure,' he said after a couple of minutes. 'Nikki Grahame, if you have disconnected your tube...' he went on, walking menacingly towards me. As he reached where I was sitting he looked down to see a large, milky puddle under my desk. So that was the end of that.

Then I came up with another scheme. Isobel, the girl who had reverted to being a baby and couldn't walk or talk, was tube-fed through her nose. Her milk feed was 1 calorie per millilitre and mine was 1.5. Every morning the milk feeds would come up from the dietician's office on the hospital trolley. I would wait until the nurses were busy with one of the other kids, then go down to the trolley and swap the labels so that Isobel was getting 1.5 cal per mil and I was getting just one. Genius!

After a couple of weeks Isobel started putting on weight and I started to lose weight and no one could understand how. I got away with that for a good few months until one morning I wasn't quite careful enough and one of the nurses noticed a corner of a label had peeled up. Everything fell into place and it was all over.

As a punishment I was put on total supervision, which meant I had a nurse with me all the time – even when I went to the loo and had a shower.

But even then I came up with new scams. At night there were only two nurses on duty but if Isobel woke up and needed looking after, both of them would be occupied with her for quite a while.

I'd seize my opportunity and sneak into the nurses' station, to rifle through their drawers and pigeon-holes, looking for any notes on my treatment. I'd read my notes and see if there were any plans to increase my calorie intake. Any information like that would help me in my battle.

Because they didn't trust me they began feeding me through my bag at mealtimes so they could keep an eye on me while I sat at the table with the other kids.

I desperately needed a new way of sabotaging their schemes. One night I was lying in bed when 'ding' went a bell in my head – I'd had a brainwave. I already knew that if I pushed out my stomach muscles after a feed some of the milky fluid would drip out of the tube. But it was never enough to make much difference. And that was when I came up with the idea of using a syringe to suck it out. Clever, eh?

Next morning when the nurses were doing bed rounds I wandered casually up to the trolley and snatched three syringes. Then, straight after mealtime, I dashed back to my room, plunged the syringe into the end of my tube and sucked out some liquid. It was so easy. I squirted the fluid – a mixture of Ensure and stomach juices – into an empty water bottle. Within a couple of minutes I'd removed almost a litre of liquid from my stomach.

Before long I was nicking syringes at every opportunity. Immediately after every mealtime I would hurry back to my room to start work. I was never allowed to close my bedroom door in case I was up to something, so I'd have to stand with my back to the corridor, pretending to look inside my wardrobe as I sucked the feed out of my stomach. Once I'd transferred it into an empty water bottle, I'd open my bedroom window and lob the bottle out.

It all went brilliantly for a couple of months. My weight wasn't going up and I was delighted. Then one morning one of the office staff from downstairs turned up on the ward and I could hear a commotion going on outside my room.

Five minutes later my key nurse stormed in. I loved Sam so much and felt we had a special bond – I even became obsessively clingy about her and didn't like her treating the other kids. But this time I knew I'd upset her really badly from the red flush across her face.

'We've had someone from the office downstairs up here complaining,' Sam said, her normally laid-back voice stretching in irritation. 'She says she can't see out of her window any more because the fire escape next to it is piled high with plastic bottles filled with what appears to be rock-hard milk and stomach juices. Would you care to explain, Nikki?'

Of course I didn't fucking care to explain. I'd been sussed out. I stormed out the room in a seething rage. From then on, only one syringe was allowed on the ward at any time as they couldn't risk me stealing them again.

I still tried to force liquid out of my stomach after feeds by pushing out of my tummy muscles. But it was only drips and drops. Even so, the stench of vomit and stomach juices became overpowering in my room. And the carpet by the side of my bed was hard with dried stomach juices.

For more than a year I didn't eat anything properly at all. It sounds incredible but the only things that went into my mouth were water and one cup of black coffee a day.

Finally they decided to give me another chance and put me on three very high-calorie glucose drinks, called Forté

Juice, each day. Each carton was the equivalent of a meal, so it was a pretty big deal for me. But they were still making up the calories by tube feeding as well.

For a while it worked OK, although as my weight crept up I became increasingly unhappy. By June 1996 I'd reached 40 kilos (6 stone 4 lb) and I hated it. I could feel the fat gathering around my hips and stomach and it repulsed me. In the ward bathroom there was a mirror but it only showed down to my waist. I'd stand up on tiptoes trying to see my whole body but it was difficult. What I could see was bad enough, though.

One night I was lying awake in bed when the bell in my head sounded again. An even more ingenious plan.

I slipped out of bed and sneaked into the open kitchen on our unit. I picked up an armful of Forté Juices and then went to the toilets, where I squeezed each of them down the sink until they were all empty. Then I hid them in my wardrobe until the next morning, when I stuffed one up my jumper before leaving my room.

At breakfast I sat down and waited for the nurse to bring my normal morning carton of Forté Juice. I opened it but as soon as she turned away I switched it with the empty carton. For the next 20 minutes I sat there sucking a straw, pretending to empty the carton. 'Finished,' I said holding it up at the end.

'Well done, Nikki,' the nurse replied. But I hadn't drunk a thing. It was another massive win for me. Later on I emptied the still full carton of Forté Juice down the toilet, leaving me another empty carton for the next mealtime. I got away with that every mealtime for months. The weight was really dropping off me again. I was back on top and it felt brilliant.

By this time I was sharing a room with a girl called Parjeet. She was a small, skinny girl who had anorexia but also had to permanently walk around with an oxygen tank because she had breathing problems. It was more a psychiatric problem than a physical one, though.

We never got on. Maybe it was 'professional' anorexic jealousy because she was desperate to be skinnier than me. There were no more late-night chats like Vicky and I had enjoyed. It must have been awful sharing a room with me and my mad tantrums and screaming. But it wasn't great sharing with Parjeet either. Her oxygen pump used to wheeze away all night and she would grass me up at every opportunity. One day she discovered my secret stash of Forté Juice cartons and went running to the nurses.

I didn't even find out what she had done until the next mealtime when I sat down and the nurse poured my Forté Juice into a glass. I knew the game was up from the smug look on the nurse's face. I was so angry they'd found me out that I flew into a rage. *'Fuck that!'* I screamed, pushing the glass across the table. 'I'm not drinking it!' And I didn't.

I hated Parjeet for that. But I knew she'd do anything to stop me from being thinner than her.

From then on I refused Forté Juice at every mealtime but it was hardly a victory as they just put me back on full tube feed instead. For a while I was gutted. But I never gave up. I kept on pushing feed back out of my tube and exercised like crazy every moment I was alone. At the same time I made sure they thought I was gaining far more than I really was. Sam had a set routine for weigh-in days. She pulled the scales slightly away from the wall and made me jump on. But what she didn't realise was that I was still close enough to the wall to lay my palm flat on it and push down with all my strength while she was looking at the reading.

I could add a good 3 kilos (6½ lb) by doing that and pretty much decide how much I wanted to weigh on any particular day. I refused to be weighed by anyone but Sam. All I had to do was throw a tantrum if anyone else was on duty and they would decide it was easier to wait for Sam's shift.

I did all the obvious stuff too. I'd drink loads and loads of water before they weighed me to make myself heavier. A 1.5-litre (1¾ pints) bottle of water weighs about 1.5 kilos (3½ lb) and I could easily drink two or three of those before a weigh-in.

But that's one of the oldest tricks in the book – any dimwit anorexic could tell you that 'waterloading' is vital to boost a weigh-in. What is amazing is that Great Ormond Street didn't realise I was doing it and the doctors couldn't understand how the scales said I was putting on weight when I was looking skinnier than ever.

Then one day my luck ran out. I was sitting in the classroom when the ward sister, Nicky Harris, came to the door and said, 'Nikki, come with me, we need to weigh you.' I knew at once there was no fooling Nicky. She took me to a different room and placed the scales slap bang in the middle of the floor. They showed I was 4 kilos (9 lb) less than at my last weigh-in.

It was another skirmish they'd won, but the war went on.

CHAPTER 13

GET ON AND DIE

I felt like a prisoner who keeps digging escape tunnels only for each of them to collapse or be discovered.

Every attempt to keep the calories out of my body failed. I was more depressed, angry and obsessed with being thin than ever before.

I was having weekly sessions with the unit's counsellor but that wasn't helping my mood. I still couldn't see any good raking over a load of stuff I'd been asked about a million times before. Sometimes I'd sit in the armchair in front of the counsellor, close my eyes and pretend to be asleep. Other times I'd stare out of the window or hum for the entire hour.

Mum visited me almost every day for the 17 months that I was at Great Ormond Street. To get there and back could take three hours, but she never complained even when I was a total bitch to her. Sometimes if she was late I would scream down the ward at her. Other times I wouldn't speak or even acknowledge her for the whole

159

time she was there. She'd sit at a table and I would move my chair around so my back was facing her. I felt so angry that she had sent me there and that she could take me away at any time but instead chose to leave me there being pumped full of calories morning, noon and night.

Several times she turned up only to be greeted by me screaming at the nurses, 'Tell her to fuck off. I don't want her near me. Unless she has come to discharge me she can fuck off.' It wouldn't be anything specific that she had done. I'd just be having 'one of my days'.

When Mum visited she was allowed to take me up to the hospital's roof garden or, if I was stronger, out for a walk. But Mum wasn't my mum any more. She was just an excuse for me to lose weight. As soon as we got up on to the roof I'd run up and down like a loony, trying to burn off calories. And if we went out of the building I'd speed walk along the streets, leaving her desperately trying to keep up, begging me to stop.

Some days we went to the park but once we were in the gates I'd instruct Mum, 'Sit there while I do 20 laps.' Each time I shot past her she'd try to start speaking but I'd just ignore her and hare off on another lap. In my mind the sole purpose of her being there was to give me an excuse to get out of the unit and to exercise, and she had to realise that. And there was nothing she could do to stop me.

'If you tell the nurses what I've been doing I'll say I don't want you visiting me any more,' I'd threaten her. I was so, so cruel to Mum because I was using her huge love for me as my weapon.

Sometimes she would sit with me during my meal and I'd hide food in full view of her. 'If you tell, though, Mum, you know you won't be coming back again,' I'd snarl. It was the same when I was allowed home for day visits. They never trusted me enough to let me stay there overnight and I think Mum was relieved as she knew she couldn't control me.

Mum would be tortured with guilt every time she gave in to me because she knew she wasn't doing the best for me, but she was terrified I'd ban her from seeing me. I think she was scared of me physically too. In my constant anger I lashed out at her regularly. I gave her black eyes and bruises on her arms and legs. But the next moment I'd be hugging her and crying, desperate for a cuddle from my mummy. It must have been so confusing for her, like being stuck in an abusive relationship with someone who says they love you but can't stop hurting you.

Some people would say she should have stopped visiting me if it was only endangering me, but she couldn't just abandon her youngest daughter in an institution surrounded by seriously mentally ill kids. In any case, the doctors had warned her that my hideous behaviour was a way of testing how much she really loved me. If I was ever going to get better I had to know deep down that she would always be there for me however much I pushed her away.

I was so self-obsessed. Even after Mum had a car accident and hurt her back, the first thought in my mind was, Who's going to come and visit me now she's too ill?

Mum also felt she had to keep visiting me because she truly thought I would be dead soon. I was so out of control that she couldn't see any other conclusion to the hell of the past five years.

Yet only once can I remember her really getting angry and losing it with me. One day I dragged her out for a walk to Covent Garden. Well, she was walking and I was jogging up ahead, burning off every calorie that I could. It was only when I stopped at a corner that Mum caught up with me, out of breath and boiling hot despite a chilly breeze. She started screaming at me like I hadn't heard her do in years. And all the nervousness in her voice had disappeared, replaced by a raw anger.

'I'm sick of this, Nikki. I've had enough,' she yelled. 'Why don't you go and die? Starve yourself to death. Run yourself into the grave if that is what you really want. Because I can't cope with it any more. I'm sick of you dragging me around like a dog on a lead.'

I stood there totally stunned, aware of people in the street staring at us, but unable to take my eyes off Mum's flaring eyes.

'Because this isn't just your life you're screwing up here, you know,' she went on. 'It's mine and your Dad's and Natalie's and Tony's too. But you're the one getting all the help and all the attention and you're still choosing not to get better. So just do whatever it is you want.'

Then she spun round and, propelled by fury, rushed back to Great Ormond Street. For the first time in years I was the one scurrying along behind, desperately trying to catch up and win favour. For a short while the tables were turned.

When we got back to the hospital one of the nurses grabbed Mum and said, 'Well done, Mrs Grahame – someone saw you in the street standing up to Nikki. This is what you have got to do.'

They'd been telling Mum for ages that she had to get angry with me but she had found it too hard.

That day was a big turning point for Mum. I didn't ban

her from visiting for standing up to me, so it taught her that she did have some power in our relationship. And it taught me I could have a strong mother.

Dad used to visit at least a couple of times each week. Some days I'd get him to take me swimming and I'd pound up and down the pool while he stood there watching me, uncertain how to stop me. Other times he would run around the park with me a couple of times, thinking if he let me do a bit of exercise it would stop me overdoing it. But however many laps we did, it was never enough for me.

Some afternoons Dad would bring a football and we'd go down to the park for a kick-around. He thought it was a bit of father-and-daughter bonding, like the old days. But it wasn't – we were there for just one reason and that was for me to burn up the calories.

Natalie was really supportive too and would visit me on a Friday evening, coming on the tube straight from college in Stanmore. We got on better then than we had for years. Maybe it was because we had been apart for a while or maybe we were simply growing up. Whatever it was, at least we had stopped acting like banshees every time we were in the same room.

At that time, Natalie was hanging around with a load of hippies, learning the guitar, smoking spliffs and getting her nose pierced. I'd got into all that too through Vicky, so finally Nat and I had something in common. She'd turn up with tapes she had recorded for me of bands like Kula Shaker, Blur and Oasis and I thought she was dead cool. On her sixteenth birthday I sent her a card and inside I wrote, 'I'm so proud to have a sister who is 16.' I meant it.

All this time my weight was gradually increasing and every day my flesh felt a little more padded. I knew it was time for desperate action.

To hell with the pain, I thought. I'll cut it out. My next perfect opportunity was during a visit to the Great Ormond Street classroom. We were doing art and crafts and there was a box of scissors lying on a table. I didn't think for a second. I pulled down the waistband of my trousers, pulled the tube out as far as I could and snipped just where the plastic entered my stomach.

I felt victorious again.

The next time a nurse came to feed me, she pulled up my top looking for the end of the tube. I watched the look of shock on her face as she realised it had gone.

'What've you done, Nikki?' she said in horror. 'If we don't reopen this gastrostomy immediately the wound will close up with the rest of the tube inside you.'

Yeah, like I was bothered about that!

But they weren't giving in either. I was hauled back to my bed, where a group of doctors and nurses hurriedly planned their next move.

They decided to insert a new style tube. It worked by being inserted and then injected with a little water to create a balloon just inside my stomach which I wouldn't be able to pull back out. Imagine it like pushing a round balloon through a letterbox, then blowing it up so you can't pull it out again. The feed was to be pumped through another tube attached to the balloon. Fairly simple really, but apparently very effective.

The inflatable tube worked for a good few months before I came up with my counter-attack. Oh my God, I thought. Why didn't I think of this five months ago? It was obvious – all I had to do was deflate the balloon and then it and the tube would simply slip out. But what I needed for that was a syringe. They were still counting the syringes on our ward, so that was no good. Then a week or so later, by sheer good fortune for me, Parjeet became critically ill and was taken to the Accident & Emergency Department.

We may not have been buddies but as her room mate I was allowed to visit her. I was sitting chatting to her when out of the corner of my eye I spotted a syringe lying on a trolley. The whole time I was talking to Parjeet, my eyes kept going back to the syringe. I was determined I wasn't leaving that ward without it. As I got up to go I wandered over casually, slipped two syringes into my pocket and walked back up to the Mildred Creak Unit.

That night after lights out I stuck the syringe up the tube and sucked out the water. The balloon deflated immediately and with one gentle tug it was out. No pain, nothing. I'd won again. Brilliant.

The following morning I woke up and looked at my stomach under my pyjamas and the hole had already closed up. This time I had really won, I knew it. I was so proud of myself, I felt jubilant.

Half an hour later, at breakfast, the nurse came over with her breezy morning chorus, 'Right, Nikki, time to connect your feed now.'

That's what you think, I thought, smiling broadly at her.

Again she lifted my top and again the tube had disappeared. Her face was a picture of confusion.

'Where's your tube gone?' she said.

'Oh, I don't know,' I said innocently. 'It's just gone.'

Afterwards I heard the nurses panicking about how they

were going to explain it to their bosses. That was two tubes I'd managed to magic into thin air without any of them noticing.

When Dr Lask arrived on the ward later that day even he looked exhausted with me.

'OK, Nikki, I'm going to have to book you in for another operation,' he said.

But I'd already planned my response.

'No,' I said. 'I'll eat. I want to eat.'

It was the early spring of 1997 and by then I hadn't put anything solid in my mouth for more than a year but I just couldn't face another day of the tube.

Dr Lask agreed to give me one last chance to prove myself.

They started me off on Forté Juice high-calorie drinks, then after a fortnight introduced baby food because it was easy for me to digest. It was disgusting and Mum and I would wander around the hospital shop looking for jars which looked slightly more appetising than the usual chicken and potato mush.

It was a really weird sensation having food in my mouth and it took a while before I moved on to soup and bread and biscuits. But it wasn't long before the bread and biscuits were going in my knickers and I was back to my old ways again.

One afternoon Dr Lask called a meeting with Mum and Dad. 'I'm sorry, Mr and Mrs Grahame,' he said. 'But I honestly don't think there's anything more I can do for Nikki. We've tried everything over the past 17 months but nothing has worked.

'She has driven herself to the point of death, is destroying her body, will probably deprive herself of ever having children, but we can't stop her.'

Dr Lask was one of the leading authorities on anorexia in Britain but even he couldn't save me.

'Nikki is not the worst case of anorexia I've ever had to deal with in my 32-year career,' he said slowly. 'She is *by far* the worst.'

Mum was desperate, begging him to try a bit longer.

But Dr Lask was adamant that keeping me in a hospital environment was starting to do more harm than good and felt I might fare better in a more relaxed setting. He recommended a foster home called Sedgemoor in Taunton, Somerset, which might kick-start me into getting my life back.

Mum and Dad were worried at the thought of my being so far from home and away from medical support with foster carers. But, like me, their options had run out.

So on 27 March 1997, a month before my fifteenth birthday, I walked out of the Mildred Creak Unit for the last time. I weighed 29 kilos (4 stone 4 lb) and was 150.1 centimetres (4 feet 11 inches) tall. In the time I'd been there I hadn't managed to keep on any weight at all.

Mentally I'd made no progress either. I still wanted exactly the same things as the moment I'd walked into the place – to be as skinny as possible and to fight as hard as possible anyone who prevented me achieving my goal.

Great Ormond Street had admitted defeat – they couldn't cope with me any longer and were sending me away, to somewhere it would be even easier to avoid food.

I was triumphant.

CHAPTER 14
SEDGEMOOR

Fields and trees skidded past the back seat window of our Volkswagen Golf as I sat staring out on that long drive down the M4 to Somerset.

I gazed out, excited to be in the real world again after so long in Great Ormond Street. But it felt scary too, being sent so far from home without Mum or Dad or Natalie. Yet I was pleased there'd be no doctors and nurses telling me to eat any more. Now I could starve myself just as much as I wanted.

The doctors had decided that as hospital just wasn't making me any better it might be better off to put me in a more normal home-like environment. But going home was not an option. Towards the end of my time at Great Ormond Street there had been a mammoth meeting between my doctors, social worker, family therapist and Mum and Dad. As soon as I was called into the meeting room for the last ten minutes I could tell by Mum's blank expression that something bad had happened.

169

'We've been talking and have decided you won't be going home until you are at least 18 years old,' Dr Lask explained. 'If you go home we have no confidence that you won't just go straight back to starving yourself.'

It was a total body blow. It made everything so pointless. If I was never going home – because that's what it seemed like to me – what exactly was the point of being alive? I started screaming and went into one of my temper fits, throwing my body around as people tried to restrain me, arching my back and whacking my head against the wall. It went on for almost two hours before eventually I collapsed from exhaustion and fell asleep.

The doctors felt foster care at Sedgemoor was a better option for me than home in that relationships I'd create with foster carers would not be as intense as with Mum and Tony and might prevent me relapsing. But the doctors were also aware my family was in no real state to take me back either. My anorexia had taken a terrible toll on them all.

Mum had borne the brunt of it and was in a bad way. Depression had swept over her gradually. She was still in a low place after Grandad's death and the divorce. But it was knowing that there was nothing she could do to make me eat which really plunged her into torment. Worse still, whenever I was with her I seemed to be an even more successful anorexic.

It is quite common in families where there is an anorexic child for something called 'reverse parenting' to take hold. Basically it means the kid is in charge while Mum and Dad do what they are told by them because they're so scared their child might die or shut them out if they don't. That is exactly what was going on between me and Mum.

Then Mum had a car accident and suffered constant back pain for months which only added to her depression. On top of that she heard people gossiping about her, questioning whether she was to blame for my anorexia. 'Well, Sue's always been thin herself,' they were saying. 'Makes you wonder if she encouraged it.' If those silly old cows had seen just one of Mum's amazing sponge puddings they'd have known there was no way that was true.

But rather than fight back, Mum just shrank into herself. There was no fight left in her.

And if all that wasn't enough to deal with, Natalie was still furious about all the attention being lavished on me and was staging a full-on teenage rebellion. Mum felt she had failed me and Natalie and so was a failure as a mother – as well as as a wife and daughter. She was tearful a lot of the time and found it harder and harder to do even the simplest jobs around the house. Gradually it reached the point where she was spending every day just lying on the sofa, unable to face the world.

She'd get up in the morning thinking, Right, today I'll go down the town, do some shopping, come home and have a good tidy-up. She'd shower, put some nice clothes on and come downstairs, up and ready for the world. But once Natalie and Tony were out of the house her resolve would start to slip and her strength would ebb away.

Some days she would make it out of the house and round the corner. But by then the outside world would all seem too much and she would run home crying and gasping for breath. She'd collapse on the sofa, crying in front of the telly, and only get the energy to tidy herself up when Natalie was about to come in from college. The only time she could get herself out of the house was to visit me.

For a while she managed to lie quite convincingly to Tony and Natalie about how she was feeling, but she was sinking fast. Then one evening she received the call from Great Ormond Street saying I had cut my gastrostomy tube out. It was the final straw.

She and Tony were sitting at the kitchen table talking and for the millionth time trying to make sense of it all. Then Mum calmly walked over to the draining board, where she kept the big bottle of ibuprofen pills she needed for her back pain. She undid it, tipped a handful of pills into her palm and shoved the lot into her mouth. She swallowed as many as she could get down her, then did it again.

Tony leapt across the kitchen, snatched the bottle from her hand and slapped her on the back in an effort to bring the pills back up.

Obviously if she had really wanted to kill herself she wouldn't have done it in front of her boyfriend. So I think it was really Mum's way of showing how desperate she felt. She couldn't cope any more.

The GP put her on anti-depressants and she had group therapy with other anorexics' parents at Great Ormond Street. It all helped but nothing was able to help her shake off that constant feeling of sadness.

So all that meant that going home just wasn't an option. Which was why I was speeding down the motorway to Taunton.

Sedgemoor was then one of Britain's biggest residential care businesses, which placed kids in a number of children's foster homes around Taunton. Then the kids all attended a special school nearby.

Some of the kids had been kicked out of school, others had run away from home because they didn't get on with their parents, some had family problems and some were total delinquents – really rough, tearaway kids.

There were two other girls living in my house. Julie was a big fat girl who had ended up there because she didn't get on with her mum and had been thrown out of school for behavioural problems. She couldn't stop nicking stuff. It was obvious she came from a really rough home, and she stank. She'd go into my room when I wasn't around and steal my CDs and shower gel. They even had to lock up the food in the kitchen otherwise she'd have had the lot.

My other housemate, Karen, was lovely but very, very disturbed and into self-harming. She spent most of her time in her room listening to Radiohead and really depressing music with candles burning all around her bed. When they called her down to dinner she would often have candle burns all up her arm and hot wax over her clothes.

We had three women carers: Margaret, who was a bit unfriendly, Wendy, who was a real soft touch and didn't know the first thing about calories or food (result!), and Kath, who was OK. Each morning one of them would drive us to school, where we did proper coursework, aiming towards our GCSEs. I felt more normal than I had in years.

The first day you arrived at Sedgemoor, the staff would hand you £1,500 to buy a stereo and television for your room and anything else you wanted to decorate it with. And there was still loads of cash left over for new clothes and make-up. I think the idea was to kit yourself out for a new life. If you stayed six months you got to keep all the stuff you had bought. But if you didn't stay, you lost it all.

Each week we got an additional allowance of £5 to spend on magazines or to go bowling or to the cinema.

After having to obey the rules and regulations at Great Ormond Street for so long, foster care was like arriving in heaven. I had so much freedom, I didn't know what to do with it. First off, I dyed my hair pink. I was still into that hippie look that Vicky and Natalie were into.

Then one Saturday afternoon I went into Taunton and got my nose pierced. It was so cool. Then I had five holes pierced in one ear and four in the other.

We were living quite near Glastonbury, so on Saturdays we would get the bus there and go shopping, returning with bagfuls of multi-coloured flowing skirts and lacy white tops.

And one day we went to Stonehenge because it seemed a cool thing to do. I didn't drink because of the calories but I smoked a couple of spliffs with some of the other girls. I didn't like it much, though, because it made me feel lethargic, which I hate.

Vicky, my friend from Great Ormond Street, visited me for a day at Sedgemoor. It was brilliant to see her, but secretly it was even more brilliant to see her looking fatter than me. However much we loved each other, we were still hugely competitive.

Most girl friends would have spent the day together agonising over which nail polish to buy or slobbing out at the cinema, but not me and Vicky. We filled our day running around the streets of Taunton, trying to burn off calories.

It had been arranged that once a month Larry, my key

social worker, would take me back to Great Ormond Street to be weighed. When I left there, Dr Lask had threatened me that if my weight fell dramatically I would be straight back in for emergency feeding. But even that thought wasn't enough to make me eat enough. The house I was staying in wasn't an anorexic unit, so the staff there had little idea about dealing with me and I got away with loads of dodges.

Also, because it was foster care, we could make our own breakfasts and lunches if we wished, which for me was perfect. At first I had one Weetabix for breakfast with water and black coffee. For lunch I had a Weight Watchers' soup and a packet of Ritz crackers. Then for dinner it would be steamed vegetables and some fruit or a low-fat yoghurt. Before bed I would have an Options drink which the carers thought was hot chocolate – they didn't realise it was only 40 calories.

Sure enough, when I went for my weigh-ins at Great Ormond Street my weight had dropped. I was allowed to return to Taunton but told I had to start eating and my weigh-ins were increased to once a fortnight. I didn't want to go back into the Mildred Creak Unit permanently, but once I started losing weight again I liked it and I couldn't bear the guilt of eating more than I felt was enough. Soon I was skipping breakfast entirely. Because it was like living in your own home I just went back to the crumbs-on-the-plate trick, claiming I'd already eaten if anyone challenged me.

I started buying low-calorie crisps and having them for my lunch – that was about 90 calories. And for dinner I'd have a tray of button mushrooms – they are only 13 calories per 100 grams (3½ oz). Then I found something even better – water chestnuts at just seven calories per 100 grams!

The carers would cook evening meals but I'd just say I didn't fancy it and they let me off. They saw me eating my water chestnuts or Weight Watchers' soups and thought that was OK. They had no idea about calories.

I cut back and back until for about a month I lived on nothing but Weight Watchers' soups, black coffee and cigarettes. I'd started smoking every now and again out of our bedroom window at Great Ormond Street with Vicky. We'd nick cigarettes from the nurses' station and think we were really cool. In foster care, everyone smoked and I was soon on 20 a day. I'd read they suppressed appetite and made you skinnier, so what wasn't there to like about smoking?

I'd been at Sedgemoor for two months when one morning in May I was due to return to London for my next weigh-in. As I'd barely eaten for a fortnight, I knew I was going to be in big trouble. I was painfully thin again and feeling incredibly weak. I couldn't even run down the street because my legs would ache, and my clothes billowed around me because I was so scrawny.

I was lying on my bed thinking, How am I going to get through this one? when my eyes settled on the metal doorstop in the shape of an owl that held my door open. It must have weighed a few kilos but I picked it up and wedged it down the front of my navy-blue flared dungarees. (I'd chosen them as the best clothes I had for disguising how much weight I'd lost.) Perfect, I thought, slipping on a chunky wool jumper over the top.

All the way back up the M4 we went with the doorstop stuck inside my dungarees.

When I arrived at Great Ormond Street one of the nurses took me upstairs and put me on the scales. I'd slipped off my boots but was still fully clothed. But when I looked down at the numbers of the scales I saw instantly that my weight was dramatically low – I'd lost 6.5 kilos (1 stone) in just seven weeks. The nurse diligently wrote my weight down on her chart, then scurried off to find a doctor.

Mum had met me at Great Ormond Street and as I trudged out into the corridor she put her arm round my bony shoulders. We had a couple of hours left until the doctors decided what we should do next so we decided to wander down to Covent Garden for a bit of window shopping.

It was only a ten-minute walk but by the time we got there I was exhausted. We were crossing the Piazza when my feet, too tired and clumsy to move properly, tripped up on the cobbles and I landed in a heap on the ground. I must have looked such a pathetic figure – a little bag of bones, pale, scraggy and sickly, too weak to even pull herself to her feet. A few people stared at me as I sat there and I didn't even have the energy to look away.

Mum saw the horror on the faces of passers-by as they looked at me, and tears started rolling down her face. As another couple of shoppers turned to stare at me, Mum just lost it. 'What are you looking at?' she screamed. 'Stop staring at my daughter – can't you see she's ill.' It was just awful.

But of course people were going to look at me. Why wouldn't they? I was a walking skeleton, except I could scarcely even walk.

Mum helped me up and we went back to the hospital.

There the nurse told us to go straight to the Middlesex Hospital for a bone-density scan. Anorexics tend to have very low bone density, which means they are vulnerable to fractures and osteoporosis. The doctors wanted to assess my risks.

We climbed into a taxi with Larry, my social worker from Sedgemoor, and off we went. The doorstop was still in my dungarees as I quietly congratulated myself on getting away with it so brilliantly.

CHAPTER 15

HUNTERCOMBE

I lay on the padded bed as the scanner glided up and down my body, checking out exactly what damage I had done to my bones.

Then, all of a sudden, the nurse froze as she stared at the screen.

'What on earth is that?' she said, pointing at a dark object on the monitor.

She pulled up my T-shirt and as her eyes fixed on the 3-kilo (6½ lb) lump of iron that had been secreted inside my dungarees all day, everything became clear.

My fate was sealed – although naively I didn't yet realise it.

Outside the Middlesex Hospital, Mum, Larry and I picked up another cab, which jerked its way through the afternoon traffic.

'Which train for Taunton do you think we'll make?' I asked Mum as I gazed dreamily out of the window.

She looked at me, a mixture of fear and frustration in her eyes.

'We're not going back to Sedgemoor, Nik,' she said. 'The doctors have said you are too ill – you have to go straight to Huntercombe Manor.'

I didn't need to ask what Huntercombe Manor was. It was well known on the 'anorexic circuit' as a specialist centre for teenagers and adults with severe eating disorders and in desperate need of refeeding and help. I'd been threatened with it loads of times when I was at Great Ormond Street.

There was only one place 'worse' than Huntercombe and that was Rhodes Farm. No one came out of Rhodes Farm without being fattened up. Huntercombe was supposed to be tough too, although I knew a few people had managed to beat the system there.

But I still didn't want to go. I went mad in the cab, shouting and throwing myself around the back seat. God knows what the driver must have thought, but I didn't care.

Mum held on to me, trying to calm me down. 'Please, Nikki, we want you to live,' she kept saying. 'We want you to live.'

'I hate you!' I screamed, pushing her violently away from me. 'All you want is to ruin everything.'

But as we pulled up on the gravel drive outside Huntercombe Manor, even I, through my angry tears, couldn't fail to be awestruck by the place. It was like a scene out of *Four Weddings and a Funeral*. Set on the outskirts of Maidenhead, in Berkshire, Huntercombe was a beautiful old house surrounded by stunning grounds of neatly trimmed grass, mature shrubs, an orchard and even a secret walled garden.

We climbed up an imposing flight of steps into a main

hall where the floor was laid with deep carpet and the walls lined with huge oil paintings. There were grand murals everywhere, even on the ceiling.

It was probably the most beautiful building I had ever been in. But I didn't really care about any of that then. I'd been locked away inside so many hospitals and institutions that I couldn't give a toss what they looked like inside or what the staff and other patients were like. The only thing that mattered was what they were going to do to me there.

As I walked through the hall I saw a girl that I knew from Great Ormond Street going through the door for an evening out with her parents. I didn't even say hello but grabbed her arm and asked, 'Gemma, how much are they going to make me eat?'

'Probably about a thousand,' she replied grimly.

'No, I won't eat more than three hundred. I won't.'

Gemma gave me half a smile as she walked off with her mum. All us anorexics followed the same code. It wasn't about being friendly and having a chat about old times and mutual friends. The only thing that mattered was calories – how many and how to avoid them.

Three hundred calories a day was the top limit of what I'd been allowing myself during the past few weeks at Sedgemoor. It is a pitiful amount and not enough to survive on. That's why I was literally skin and bones the day I arrived at Huntercombe, my translucent skin drawn tightly across the jutting bones of my face.

I must have looked like the living dead because as my eyes met those of another girl of about my age standing in the hallway, she literally flinched in horror. I saw her take a small gasp, unable to take her eyes off my emaciated frame, and she stepped backwards slightly, as if repulsed by me.

It is strange that after such a violent reaction she should become my best friend at Huntercombe and probably the person who helped save my life.

'Hi, I'm Carly,' she said, in a girly little voice which seemed quite at odds with the troubled, world-weary look in her eyes.

Carly had been at Huntercombe for nine months and was approaching a normal weight, although still skinny by most people's standards.

Hello, I thought, instantly assessing her weight. Not as thin as me, I decided with satisfaction.

Then one of the staff came over and guided me up a flight of stairs to a kitchen where they sat me down at a table and brought me a banana and a glass of fruit juice. Carly followed me into the room and sat down opposite.

I wasn't allowed to talk to anyone until I'd eaten my snack, so Carly just sat there watching me in silence. But she didn't need to say anything. Just being there was enough to tell me that she would be a real friend.

The next step was to be weighed and measured. My weight was then just 27.7 kilos (4 stone 5 lb) and I was 152 centimetres (4 feet 10 inches) tall. I was 60 per cent of the weight I should have been at that age and height.

Huntercombe had an adolescent unit and an adult ward. I'd arrived as an emergency case and there were no beds free in the adolescent unit, so I was put in with the grown-ups. I'd never met an adult with an eating disorder before and it was really shocking. There was a woman called Jane, who was 20, who looked so thin and so old already that it was sad to watch her move around the ward. Then there was another woman, Fran, who was not just painfully skinny but sad-looking too.

But the good thing about being on the adult section was that there was more freedom. The first night I went into my bedroom, closed the door and started exercising immediately. I must have done 300 star-jumps that night and no one noticed.

Obviously it was good for shedding calories but it also kept me warm. My body weight had fallen so low that I was constantly freezing and the high ceilings and old-fashioned windows at Huntercombe meant draughts howled through the place at night.

When I finally lay down in bed, I rolled on to my side and put my hands between my thighs for warmth. But when my knees met there was a gap above them – I was that thin.

When I woke up, at 5am, I was still freezing cold, so I got up and inspected my new room properly. I opened the door of my new wardrobe and inside noticed a full-length mirror. I immediately pulled off my clothes and inspected my naked body for the first time in three years – there had been no full-length mirrors at Great Ormond Street or Sedgemoor.

I was so shocked at what I saw that I couldn't quite believe it was me at first. I had to keep touching my legs and stomach to make sure it wasn't an illusion or one of those magic mirrors that I remembered looking in with Dad when we went to Blackpool Pleasure Beach.

The figure looking back at me was little more than a skeleton with just a thin layer of tissue paper for skin, drawn over the stick-like bones. I stood staring for a good couple of minutes, considering what I'd become.

And my verdict?

Brilliant, I thought. It's been worth every moment of all that hard work.

I pulled my clothes and Dr Martens boots on and thought, I'm going for a jog now.

Now I'd seen what I'd achieved through all those years of starving myself, I was more determined than ever that I couldn't let anything destroy all my good work.

But I knew that meant I was going to have to fight even harder than I had ever done before.

I slipped quietly out of the door downstairs and started running around the garden, hoping no one would wake and notice me.

I managed a few days of dawn jogs before one morning one of the nurses came rushing across the grass towards me.

'What do you think you're doing, Nikki?' she scolded. 'Come inside right now. And if you do this again you will be put on extra calories immediately.'

I later found out a girl called Paula, a total bitch, had seen me out of the window and snitched to the nurses.

I'd only been there a couple of days and I was already loathed by all the girls on the adolescent unit. I was the thinnest, most ill-looking girl they'd ever had there and they hated it. When it came to anorexia, I was the best. They could see it and they were jealous. At this time I was so immersed in my anorexia that I was unable to think or concentrate on anything else. I was desperately sick, but didn't realise it.

I'd been at Huntercombe less than a week when Mum came to visit and brought with her my old schoolfriend Lena. We'd kept in touch by writing letters to each other but I hadn't seen Lena for almost two years. When she walked into my room I was stunned. She had turned into a young woman – she had boobs! And hips! She was wearing a pair of trendy white patent wedges, an A-line skirt and a skimpy little top. I looked at her and thought, Wow, you look like a model in a magazine.

There was me in my tie-dye trousers and pink hair with a ring through my nose, looking like a skeleton being propped upright by a pair of Doc Martens.

We were both 14, but I knew then that we were worlds apart. I thought, You're not the little girl I used to run up and down the street with in a shower cap and a swimming costume, knocking on people's doors and running away. You're not the little girl who came for sleepovers in a tent in the garden on Halloween. You're doing your thing now and I'm doing mine. So I just ignored her for her entire visit.

I wasn't jealous of Lena and what she looked like. I couldn't even think that far – all I could think about was what was happening to me right there, right then.

'Mum, please get me out of here,' I pleaded as Lena stared at me with a mixture of shock and revulsion. 'Take me back to Sedgemoor. I can't stay here. They're going to make me fat. They're going to make me eat.'

Then I'd repeat the same thing over and over again.

Mum and Lena left after a couple of hours. They were barely outside the building when Lena burst into tears. 'She's dying, isn't she?' she said to Mum.

Mum couldn't say 'no', but she couldn't bring herself to admit the answer might be 'yes' either. Lena was just a kid herself and had never seen anything as shocking before.

'Nikki didn't even notice I was there,' she said. 'She's so

185

caught up in her illness. That's all that she can see.' Mum nodded. Lena was absolutely right.

I didn't care about any of them then – Mum, Dad, Natalie, Lena. All I cared about was not eating.

After a fortnight I was moved into a bed on the adolescent unit and then my battle really began.

There were two kitchens in the unit: a downstairs one for residents on the road to recovery, who were allowed to prepare their own food, and an upstairs one where nurses supervised everything. That's where I, Carly and the other four really sick kids – Debbie, Hannah, Paula and Simon – all ate. Simon was the first boy I'd ever met with an eating disorder. He was from North America but had to come to England because it was the only place he could get treatment.

Simon and I were the sickest. Hannah was pretty ill too but she hated me as she knew I was her main competition and much skinnier than her. Paula and Debbie were just weird. Paula used to regurgitate all her food and Debbie wasn't really a proper anorexic – she just pretended to be by not eating, because she wanted attention.

Every week the Huntercombe dietician, Yvonne, would plan out our individual diet sheets.

When I arrived, my breakfast was one box of cereal from a selection pack with one cup of milk and a cup of fruit juice. Snack time was one digestive biscuit and another cup of juice and lunch was a hot dinner off the menu – either fish, chicken or vegetarian.

They allowed us to be vegetarian at Huntercombe – and so of course all the girls were and I joined in too. It gave us something else to be in control of.

My first lunch there was fried veggie sausages with fried

parmentier potatoes and spinach creamed in butter with nutmeg. It was horrific for me – so many calories and so much fat. When I picked the spinach off my plate there was a disgusting yellow puddle of melted butter where it had been sitting.

At the first opportunity I shoved one of the sausages up my sleeve. There were eight of us at the table, all trying to get away with similar tricks and the nurses couldn't look at all of us all the time. So next a few potatoes went down my knickers. They were scalding hot, but I was desperate to get rid of them.

I managed to hide one and a half sausages and quite a bit of potato but what I hadn't reckoned on was the 45-minute time limit at Huntercombe for every meal. That meant you had to finish your main course, fruit, yoghurt and juice in the time otherwise you'd have to eat the whole lot again.

Disaster.

My time was up and I still hadn't drunk the juice.

'You were told the rules, Nikki,' said Adam, my key nurse, plonking another plate of veggie sausages and potatoes in front of me. 'You're going to have to do it all again.'

'No way!' I yelled. 'I'm not eating all that again.'

I sat there furious, glaring at the full plate and refusing to even pick up my knife and fork. And I was still there at afternoon snack time at 3.30, when a piece of fruit and a juice were added to the pile of food in front of me.

Adam tried desperately to persuade me to eat but I wasn't having any of it.

Normally, when dinner came I would then have been expected to eat my lunch, snack *and* dinner all in one go.

187

I begged Adam, 'Please, can we just forget about lunch and snack and start afresh at dinner. Please?'

Finally he agreed and I stomped off into the garden. He thought I was still seething but secretly I was very pleased with myself. It was another victory to me and charging around the garden for an hour was a great way to lose calories.

When the other girls looked out of the window and saw what I was doing, though, they weren't fooled for a minute. They were allowed only ten minutes' exercise a day and they were furious that I was outside burning off calories while they were stuck indoors.

Every mealtime all of us would sit round a long dining table and wait for the meals to be served up. 'You Might Need Somebody' by Shola Ama seemed to be on the radio constantly as we each battled with our plates of food every day.

It was the same rule of getting your entire meal replaced if you left anything on the plate or if you hid food or ignored three warnings from a nurse about playing with food or separating items of food on the plate. Separating food, moving it around the plate and cutting it up into tiny pieces are all anorexic traits. Lots of anorexics don't like the idea of one type of food touching another. For instance, chicken must never touch vegetables, so they'll separate them. Then they'll eat the items in strict order, starting with the one lowest in calories. I was always getting into trouble for separating food and for pressing food down on my plate with a fork to squeeze all the oil out of it.

For my first couple of weeks at Huntercombe I was allowed to start off on fairly low-fat foods – I think it was probably just to get me used to being there. But after that I was put straight on to 2,500 calories a day. I'd got used to eating just 300, so that was a terrible shock.

Meals suddenly became things like pizza and chips. But chips were horrific for me. I hadn't eaten them in literally years and I couldn't handle it at all.

There were other nightmare dinners too. Bubble and squeak was horrendous because it was fried, and spaghetti soya (like spag Bol but veggie) always came in huge portions and was really filling. Macaroni cheese and the risotto were killers too, as they came drenched in cheese and butter. They were delicious but you could feel the calories melting into your body.

I'd always hide anything I could get away with but if I was spotted and had my meal replaced I'd go mad. I could feel anger building up inside me like the engines of a space rocket about to blast off. The anger would build and build in my chest and then I'd explode, shouting and lashing out at anyone who came near me.

I'd cry hysterically, screaming for my mum and to be allowed home. I'd fling myself around the room, hurl my chair and writhe around the floor, clawing at my skin and pulling clumps of hair out of my scalp.

It must have been horrible for people to watch. The anger would come pouring out of my body, leaving me shattered. At the same time I was fully aware that my fits were pretty good for burning up calories too!

I really think my mental torment did help me avoid putting on weight. I was always so anxious and stressed thinking about how to avoid the next meal, and how to get out of there, that it must have had an effect.

My fits were happening more and more frequently –

most days and sometimes every mealtime. The other girls hated me for them.

'Just fucking get on and eat it, Nikki,' they would shout if I was refusing food and building up to an hysterical fit.

A characteristic of this eating disorder is the competitive urge to be the thinnest and most celebrated anorexic in a particular place. So the other girls were already jealous because I was the thinnest and the illest. I was top-dog anorexic.

Hannah was particularly jealous. She was an incredibly clued-up anorexic, just like me, and between us we must have known the calorie content of every food in the world.

I'd say to her things like, 'Hannah, how many calories do you think were in that lentil cutlet?' She'd sigh deeply and say, 'Ohhh, what do you care, Nikki? You're *sooo* skinny already. I don't want to talk about it.'

Hannah could be really mean. She would always copy what I chose on the menu just to make sure I wasn't getting away with fewer calories than her. And if she ever saw me hiding food at mealtimes she wouldn't hesitate to tell a nurse. But I'd land her in it if I saw her hiding food too. It was every anorexic for herself.

I'm sure a lot of the nurses hated me. They were always having to tell me off and I was probably just too much trouble for them. Every mealtime I would be refusing to eat, yelling and getting hysterical and violent, so it must have been really hard work looking after me. In the end I think some of the nurses just stopped challenging me every time I hid food or refused to eat and they just let me get on with what I wanted – which was not eating.

I can't blame them. A lot of them were in their late teens or 20s and probably just wanted an easy life. They got paid the same amount whether they chased me around trying to make me eat all day or just didn't bother. And I'm sure it was much more enjoyable for them to spend their shift sitting with a compliant kid who was making progress than some shrieking nightmare like me.

I was foul to some of the agency nurses. I was so rude, telling them to fuck off at mealtimes and pushing food away. One day I was having a screaming fit about being made to eat something when one of the agency staff, Sharon, really lost her rag with me. She shoved me under the desk where she was working, pulled her chair in tight so I had no chance of escaping, then left me there for over an hour. I was trying to scratch and bite her legs but she just carried on typing away on the desk above my head.

Sometimes I think Carly was the only person at Huntercombe who liked me at all. She wasn't like the others. In fact she wasn't even properly anorexic. She was more obsessive-compulsive, although she had been dangerously thin when she was admitted. Her problem was that she couldn't eat anything which she thought might have been contaminated by someone's fingers. So she didn't even mind foods that were higher in calories so long as they came out of a sealed wrapper. She wouldn't eat a piece of fruit because anyone might have touched it but she would eat a chocolate bar if she opened it herself. And she would only eat a slice of bread if it came out a fresh bag that she had opened.

In the kitchen at Huntercombe there would be 12 cartons of juice or ten bottles of milk open at any one time, because Carly could only drink something she had just opened herself. She and I had had similar upbringings and as soon as we met it felt like we had loads in common. She'd been at stage school and I wanted to be an actress, so we would put on shows in the day room, singing songs from *Bugsy Malone* and *Starlight Express*. Carly loved doing it and I enjoyed it too – but for me the chief motivation was always that it was a way of moving around and exercising. The rest of the time the nurses would make me sit down so as not to use up calories.

Sometimes at night Carly and I would sneak into the grounds of the manor house and slip into the walled garden, looking for ghosts and trying to scare each other. We were both very immature for our age and acted more like five-year-olds than 15-year-olds. But we'd both missed out on so much growing up that we were just catching up with other people.

In the adolescent unit I had my own room and Carly was sharing with Debbie but she still spent every evening in my room until the nurses threw her out. Sometimes the nurses would let her bring cushions up from her bedroom and put them on my floor and stay for a sleepover. We'd be awake chatting for hours and could talk about anything – although never about our illness.

We terrorised the nurses and made up songs about them. 'More ag, more ag,' we'd shout at one called Morag every time she walked past.

After dinner Carly and I would often go and sit in the phone booth downstairs and ring our mums. In the evenings there was a receptionist on the front desk called Barbara who would sit and knit. One night, Carly and I thought it was hilarious to keep ringing the front desk from the phone booth, pretending we were Chinese and trying to get through to a takeaway. 'Harro,' we shouted down the phone. 'We want chicken noodles and egg flied lice, prease. You deriver?'

After about the fifth call Barbara must have realised what was going on, and she stormed round to the phone booth and yanked us out. 'I'm fed up with you two,' she shouted. 'I don't wanna be working 'ere, do I?'

We ran off laughing until our stomach muscles ached.

We'd have a great laugh in classes too. There were lessons every day, although I was too sick to concentrate on English or maths for very long. For a while the only thing I could focus on was art.

After my first fortnight at Huntercombe my weight had increased by about 1 kilo (2 lb), but from then on it hardly rose at all.

I'd become determined I would never ever go above 33 kilos (5 stone 2 lb) and so the closer I got to that figure the more difficult I became to control.

CHAPTER 16

I'LL NEVER HAVE TO EAT AGAIN

By the midsummer of 1997 – three months after arriving at Huntercombe – it was very clear I wasn't getting any better.

I remained adamant I would not go above 33 kilos and was exercising at every opportunity. Each night I would pace up and down my bedroom before doing a round of star-jumps and sit-ups. And if there were no nurses around I would run up and down the stairs over and over again. Once, I even managed to lock myself in a room with an exercise bike. I was in there for 15 minutes before a nurse found me and pulled me off it. I felt particularly victorious that day.

Even in the day room I stood up all the time, stamping from foot to foot. But all the girls in the unit would stand whenever they could to burn off calories. We must have looked so strange to people who came in.

I also used a relentless succession of scams to avoid food. I hadn't been at Huntercombe very long when one day I

195

saw a member of staff returning to the kitchen, tapping her security code into a keypad and pushing open the door. The next time she went back to the kitchen I stood closely behind her and committed the security code to memory. What a brilliant bit of ammunition, I thought.

That night I waited until all the nurses were busy elsewhere, then I went up to the kitchen, typed in the code and I was in. I didn't really have any specific plan – it just felt that I was having one over on the system.

Inside the big kitchen, lined with cupboards and worktops, I began rummaging through boxes of food and inside the fridge. I took a couple of large, half-full cartons of milk out of the fridge and filled them up with water. That'll be a few less calories on our cereal in the morning, I thought. Another little victory.

A few weeks later I sneaked back into the kitchen and went through all the paperwork until I found my personalised diet sheet. Then I picked up a pen and drew a neat line through my afternoon snack. No more two-finger KitKats!

The next time the dietician checked my list she saw what I had done, so it was a very brief victory, but worthwhile all the same. From then on the dietician had to sign every single alteration made to anyone's diet sheet.

By now I was supposed to be on a 2,500-calorie diet but because of hiding food and exercising I still wasn't putting on much weight.

Every meal was a battle and the doctors wanted to take action before my condition deteriorated further. They decided there was only one solution – I'd have to go back to being tube-fed directly into my stomach.

'We're going to have to reopen your gastrostomy,' a

charge nurse called Kate told me one afternoon after I'd refused yet another lunch.

Just the mention of gastrostomy made me feel ill. 'I'll eat,' I said immediately. 'Please, anything but that.

'You can't talk your way out of this one,' Kate said firmly. 'You're having the op to put a tube back in whether you like it or not' – she paused – '*but* we promise we'll only actually use it at night if you refuse to eat during the day.'

The night before the operation I was so nervous I couldn't sleep. I was desperately tired but I couldn't close my eyes, I was too scared of the coming morning.

In the end I got Mum, who was there, to push me downstairs for a cigarette. I was still on about 20 a day at that point – menthol after meals and before bed and Silk Cut the rest of the time. I'd even got a collection of empty fag boxes stuck all over my bedroom wall. Well, at least it was different from my helium balloon collection at the Maudsley.

Once again there were huge risks in my having a general anaesthetic and such major surgery when my weight was so low. But if the alternative was death, the doctors believed it was a risk worth taking. As for me, I didn't care about the op, only about how much food they could pump down the tube.

In the morning I was transferred by ambulance to Great Ormond Street. It felt strange being back there again, almost like going home.

A few hours after my second gastrostomy operation in 18 months, I was back in Huntercombe. There the doctors gave me a choice – 3,000 calories a day if they used the tube, or a couple of hundred less if I ate proper food. To me that 200-calorie difference was enough to make me, eat proper food and so for the first couple of days I complied and ate their enormous meals during the day to avoid being tube-fed at night. I could feel the tube sticking out of my stomach and it remained a constant threat of what would happen if I refused to eat.

But the food was too much. One day, after a massive bubble and squeak, they served up profiteroles with cream. I can't do this any more, I thought, looking sadly at the mountain of choux pastry and chocolate. How could they expect someone like me to eat all that? Even someone with a huge appetite would find it intimidating.

I was also clashing with the nurses all the time and found it exhausting. They were trying to prevent me from walking anywhere to lose calories, so every time I stood up they'd say, 'Sit down, Nikki. What it is you want, we'll get it for you.'

My mood was very low. I was having big meal after big meal and not even being allowed to move around in between times. Imagine how you feel slumped in the chair after Christmas dinner. Well, it was like that every single day.

I knew I couldn't take any more – of the food or of any of it. I was sick and tired of everything. I didn't even get any joy from Mum and Dad's visits any more.

Once Dad came to see me and he said, 'Sit down, will you?' as I paced about the room.

'No,' I snapped. 'I won't. You can go home if you want me to sit down.'

Having him there meant nothing more to me than an excuse to be out of sight of a nurse and to be walking up and down using up calories.

I'd rather stand up and walk around than have a visit from him, I thought. I don't want to see him that much.

I knew Mum and Dad weren't going to take me out of there – I'd been told I wouldn't go home until I was at least 18. If they're not coming to take me back with them, I'd think, what's the point of their coming at all? I was angry at them for leaving me there and felt very alone.

It was during one of Dad's visits a couple of months earlier that I had slipped a bottle of paracetamol into my pocket one afternoon when he'd taken me to Sainsbury's to buy toiletries. I'd kept them in my bedside drawer as a kind of security measure in case things ever got really bad. And now they really were bad.

One night I climbed into bed with the bottle and sat staring at it. I knew exactly what I was going to do. I just can't be bothered with any of this any more, I thought. I can't face the food. I'm going to be stuck in here – or somewhere pretty similar – for years and I hate Mum and Dad for letting it me go through it.

The first time I'd taken a paracetamol overdose, at Great Ormond Street, was to show everyone how angry I was they hadn't let me home for Christmas. That was a 'this'll teach them' protest. But this time, this was it – I wanted to die. I'd run out of steam, I'd run out of energy for fighting and I wasn't winning any more. They'd beaten me with their tubes and their sedatives and their drugs. They were going to feed me whatever I wanted, so what was the point of carrying on?

I wasn't scared or worried or tearful. It just seemed the logical thing to do. There really wasn't anything worth living for. I just wanted the whole nightmare to be over.

My bedroom door was wide open as I wasn't allowed to

close it any more in case I was exercising, but I was still able to swallow the pills without anyone noticing. I got out of bed and went nearer the door so I could hear if anyone was coming. The first pill tasted sour in my mouth as I jerked my head back and swallowed it down. The second was easier and by the third I was used to the metallic flavour on my tongue.

I didn't have any water, so it became harder and harder to swallow each pill as the moisture in my mouth dried up. But nothing was going to stop me and I kept on swallowing them, sometimes ramming two down at the same time, sometimes gagging as a pill stuck to the back of my throat. Then I started to retch with the effort of getting them down. A couple of times one came straight back up again but even that didn't stop me. I just swallowed it again.

I didn't give Mum and Dad a single thought. I didn't give a shit about them.

Pill followed pill followed pill. And I felt glad. Just another couple of hours and this would all be over. No more calories, no more screaming, no more injections, no more hospitals.

I remember getting to 25 and thinking that was probably enough.

Then I climbed back into bed and closed my eyes. This is it then, I thought. This is the end of it. I've finally got what I want. I can go to sleep and I'll never have to eat again. I'll never have to put on any more weight.

Then I slipped into unconsciousness.

But it wasn't to be that simple. Two hours later I came round, feeling more sick than I'd ever felt before. I managed to swing my legs off the bed and staggered down the corridor to the toilet, where I was violently sick. I was roaring sick over and over again until I was bringing up acid-green stomach juices. I lay on the floor of the toilet for hours, too weak to move.

Eventually a nurse came in and found me and asked what was the matter. I couldn't even answer and they assumed it was an extreme tummy bug and took me back to bed.

I lay there totally gutted that I had failed. I was crying, desperate and furious. The pills had been my last resort and they hadn't worked.

The next day they said there was no point in giving me any food because I was still being sick, so I stayed in bed all morning, sipping Diet Coke because I felt so thirsty.

When they called Mum she guessed immediately that I had overdosed. She rushed to the hospital and, without questioning me first, went straight to the nurses and told them what she feared.

'It's impossible – she can't have done,' said the charge nurse, Pauline. 'She has been on close supervision, so there's no way she can have got hold of any tablets.'

But Mum knew me better than anyone. And she knew the look of utter hopelessness in my eyes. She came and sat with me but I couldn't speak to her or even look at her. I was just so traumatised that I'd failed.

What I didn't realise, though, was that I was still in grave danger of dying from liver failure, which can happen up to two days after an overdose. A paracetamol overdose is particularly dangerous in anorexic cases because of the effect that continual starvation has already had on the liver.

After sitting with me for a while, stroking my head and holding my hand, Mum went back downstairs to the nurse. 'I'm telling you my daughter has overdosed,' she said firmly. 'And if you don't do anything to help her and anything happens to her I will be blaming you.'

Still nothing happened – and I didn't admit a thing – until Mum finally made the doctors give me a blood test a couple of days later. The results immediately showed a high dosage of paracetamol in my system. All of a sudden it turned into panic stations and I was immediately wheeled into an ambulance and taken to A&E at nearby Wexham Park Hospital.

There I waited an hour and a half to be assessed. Mum was terrified I could be dying in front of her eyes and still no one was doing anything to help.

'Please, please, will you get her on a ward?' Mum begged one of the nurses.

The unit was heaving with people and the nurse just looked at Mum with irritation and said brusquely, 'I'm sorry, but your daughter has put herself here. She can wait. We've got sick patients who haven't chosen to be here and they are our priority.'

We waited some more and finally I was put on a ward, assessed and placed on a drip.

By then I was feeling a bit better. I hadn't had to eat a thing for three days, so that alone had made me happier. But I was still angry I hadn't succeeded with the overdose.

After a couple of days' observation I was free to return to Huntercombe. But first I asked to speak to my specialist, Dr Lask, on the phone as he was still overseeing my treatment.

'I just can't do it, Dr Lask,' I said. 'I just can't face all that food you are giving me.' I really liked and respected Dr Lask. I felt he listened to what I was saying.

'I can only come back to Huntercombe if I can go back to 1,000 calories a day.'

He agreed.

So one week after the overdose I was back in Huntercombe, my weight down to 28.3 kilos (4 stone 6 lb) as I hadn't been eating at Wexham Park.

I was put on 1,000 calories a day and I got away with murder with the nurses. They were all terrified that if they confronted me about anything I'd try to top myself again. It was all cool by me.

I was also allowed to negotiate my diet sheet with Yvonne, the dietician. She was lovely but she could be a bit of a soft touch and I got away with a lot with her. On my sheet it said I had to have two digestives as my bedtime snack but I came up with a far better idea. 'Yvonne, I really want to try and have chocolate again,' I said one day. 'So maybe I could have one Jaffa Cake at night instead of the digestives.'

And she agreed! So, instead of two 78-calorie digestives, I was having one 45-calorie Jaffa Cake. Result!

Within days all the anorexics had suddenly developed a passion for Jaffa Cakes. And I had a great trick of holding one next to my hot night-time drink so that all the chocolate melted off on to the side of the mug.

I was constantly wiping chocolate, grease, cream or anything else I didn't want on to cups, plates, clothes or even my hair. My tops were always stained and dirty – but I didn't care, so long as I'd avoided some calories.

Back in Huntercombe my condition only deteriorated, though, as I again refused to eat.

I went back on the nasal tube but when I returned to ripping that out again and again they decided they would have to start using the gastrostomy tube, as they had threatened. But each time I managed to talk them out of it at the last moment by agreeing to eat again for a while.

My fragile mental state was even more precarious. I was having more and more temper fits. If the nurses tried to make me eat or I felt anything was getting out of control, I would start shouting, screaming and hyperventilating. I would flail around until my body became rigid and my back arched right back. It's a condition called opisthotonos, which I've since learned can be caused by a depressed brain function or is in some cases a side effect of a large amount of medication.

They injected me with a sedative a couple of times at Huntercombe but it wasn't as common as at Great Ormond Street.

The only person who could calm me down when I was having a fit was Carly. The nurses would shout at me, 'Come on, snap out of this! Get out of this, Nikki.' But Carly would wrap her arms tight around me and keep cuddling me and soothing me as I sobbed and screamed.

I'd still be trying to smash my head and my body against walls and the floor but she would hold me and protect my head. I really didn't care if I knocked myself unconscious or even killed myself – ever since the last overdose I'd had no fear of dying.

But whatever I did, Carly never let go of me. She would stroke my hair until eventually exhaustion overwhelmed me and I calmed down. I guess all I really wanted was to feel cuddled and loved, and that is what she did.

Other days I would go out into the grounds to the 'screaming tree', which was where kids could go to get their anger out. I'd stand there for hours screaming into

Above: Once I was back out in the big wide world, I decided I wanted to study dance. Here I am aged 16 with a friend.

Below: A still from my audition tape for *Big Brother*.

I was amazed and honoured when I won the Most Popular TV Contender award
at the National Television awards.

Above left: With my dear friend Carly, who I met whilst at Huntercombe.

Above right: Mum and I on holiday in Dubai – now that I'm financially independent, I like to enjoy what I've earned!

Below: My two gorgeous chihuahuas, Baby and Thumbelina.

Above left: I do a lot of work with *OK!* Magazine – here I am at their Christmas party.

Above right: I like using my profile to raise money for charity – this was the celebrity driving challenge in aid of Help for Heroes.

Below left: Talking to Pete Doherty at the Celebrity Soccer Six match at Milwall.

Below right: Glammed up for the Vodafone Live awards.

the wind, trying to force out of my body this ball of fury which was dominating my life.

Sometimes I'd feel as though I was going to explode with the poison that was swilling around inside me. Most of the time I felt anxious, agitated and fat. Sleep gave some relief but often I would toss and turn for hours, locked in my misery.

I'd become too sick to even consider getting better. I could hardly think about the next five minutes, let alone the future and what I wanted from it. I couldn't imagine any other existence than the one I was living at that moment. Maybe I'd become institutionalised within my own anorexia. Certainly I'd known nothing else and thought of little else for the past seven years.

In my head I was just stuck where I was and nothing could shift me.

At that point I was on all sorts of drugs, including Prozac, as I'd been diagnosed with depression by then. After a while I was put on a different anti-depressant, Seroxat, as Prozac was making me twitch. Then there were the sedative pills at night to keep me calm and help me sleep – but also to prevent me getting out of bed and exercising.

One evening we all had a Chinese takeaway for dinner. Supposedly it was a treat but for me it was horrific. It was stir-fried vegetables, wallowing in grease – which was, and still is, my worst food fear. As I looked at the greasy pool of food on my plate I thought, Just eat it and then you can run away. You can exercise off the fat and then you'll never have to eat anything like this again. That thought was the only thing that got me through that awful meal.

Afterwards I waited until the front-desk receptionist went home at nine o'clock, then slipped out of the main doors. Huntercombe isn't a locked unit and it was so easy. We were allowed lunchtime strolls, so I knew exactly where I was going. I ran down the lane that led to the main road, then jogged straight to Taplow railway station.

It was pitch-dark but quite a warm night. I waited for 20 minutes on the platform, then jumped on a train to Paddington. There I changed on to the tube, all the time dodging ticket collectors and any commuters staring at my emaciated frame in concern. I jumped off the train at Northwood Hills and ran all the way home. It felt so good to be back.

I banged on our front door and waited breathlessly. I thought Mum would be shocked to see me, but surely she'd be glad too – she'd throw her arms around me then we'd snuggle up on the sofa in front of the telly. Wouldn't we?

When Mum opened the door she didn't look at all shocked – just angry. Huntercombe had already called her to say I was missing.

'You're not staying, Nikki,' she said. 'You've got to go straight back.'

'But I want to come home!' I yelled. 'I'm not going back.'

Ten minutes later, though, Mum had started the car and was bundling me into the back with Tony's help. It took both of them to haul me in there and slam the door shut on my kicking and screaming.

And then back we went. I hadn't even seen my bedroom. Hadn't even had a night snuggled under my own Forever Friends duvet. Instead it was hell once again for me.

I'd probably only been gone about three hours when Mum guided me back into the massive entrance hall at Huntercombe, the ceiling murals gazing down on me as I stood there beaten and exhausted. At least I've missed evening snack, I thought dismally. That's some calories avoided.

Soon afterwards, in January 1998, Mum and Dad were called to Huntercombe for another big meeting about my future.

My weight was at 32.4 kilos (5 stone 1 lb), which meant that in the eight months I had been there, I had put on just 4.7 kilos (10½ lb). Dr Lask had reached the point where he had to accept Huntercombe wasn't working for me. I sat in the dining room and waited to be called down to join everyone in the main office. Although I had no idea what they were discussing, I knew instinctively it wasn't going to be good news for me.

Finally one of the nurses called me into the meeting. She suggested Carly go with me – they must have known I was likely to have a major fit and Carly would be the only one able to calm me down.

Carly and I walked into the grand, wood-panelled office with huge sash windows looking over neatly mowed lawns. Mum, Dad, Dr Lask, a man from the Social Services' funding department and Dr Mark Tattersall and Dr Lakintosch from Huntercombe were all sitting round in a large circle.

Carly shot me a reassuring smile as we sat down and Dr Tattersall began talking.

'Now, Nikki,' he said. 'We've spent a very long time discussing the best way to help you get better and we've come to the conclusion that you could really benefit from some time at Rhodes Farm. It's an excellent place with all the facilities to really help you.'

Well, I think he said that last bit, but I didn't really hear much after the words 'Rhodes Farm'. The two words pulsated in my head – it was every anorexic's nightmare come true.

I didn't need any explanation of what Rhodes Farm was like – everyone on the anorexic circuit knew all about it. It was the stuff of horror stories told in hushed voices late at night: deep-fried fish in batter, cheese sandwiches, cream with everything and mayonnaise shoved up your nose through a tube if you didn't comply.

Vicky and Debbie had both been at Rhodes Farm and their stories of plate after plate of huge-calorie meals had left girls in terror of the place. And there was no healthy-eating regime at there at all. You would get one apple a day and everything else was microwaved meals already engorged with calories and then laden with extra cheese. Just mentioning the name sent a shudder of fear through the girls at Huntercombe.

'No,' I said quite simply. 'No, I'm not going. Not me. I'm doing OK here, I don't need to move.'

Rhodes Farm was for other girls, for losers who'd get beaten by the system. It wasn't for me – I was too good at getting away with stuff, with winning. Going to Rhodes Farm meant no chance of winning any more. My battle would be over. And that was terrifying.

'I'm afraid there is no choice, Nikki. You have to go,' said Dr Tattersall.

'But I'm not going there – I'm really not,' I kept repeating, aware of the terror in my voice as it became clear their minds were made up. I could feel, too, that familiar sense of anger building up inside me and I knew I was going to flip.

I sprang out of chair and darted for the door but Mum

jumped up and stood in my way. I lashed out at her with my arms, then spun around and made for the partly open window. No one was quick enough to stop me as I flung myself through the gap and jumped four feet down to the garden. Then I ran until my legs buckled and I went sprawling.

In moments Carly was with me, holding me as I cried, and then I threw myself back, slamming my head into the ground and clawing wildly at myself.

'No, no, no. I'm not going!' I kept screaming.

I went totally mental and this time there was nothing even Carly could say to help me.

They were going to send me to Rhodes Farm. After all those years of fighting, they had beaten me.

CHAPTER 17
RHODES FARM

'Right, Nikki, listen and I'll explain. Monday it's a four-finger KitKat, Tuesday is a Toffee Crisp and Wednesday is a Lion Bar.'

It was my last night at Huntercombe and Debbie was talking me through the feeding regime I would face on my arrival at Rhodes Farm the following morning. 'Thursday is a Picnic and Friday it's a Caramel,' she continued. 'You have to eat a chocolate bar every single day.'

I was lying on cushions between Debbie and Carly's beds. As a special treat before leaving I'd been allowed a sleepover in their room. Although I'd never been particularly good friends with Debbie I needed her that night, and she and I lay awake for hours as I pumped her for information about life at Rhodes Farm.

Poor old Carly, my best mate, who for months had held me when I cried and been the only person who could make me laugh when everything seemed so bleak. That night she didn't get a look-in. In the end she fell asleep, leaving me and Debbie dissecting every detail of the Rhodes Farm regime. Debbie had spent several months there and, like all its other patients, she had piled weight on during her stay. It was only afterwards that she had lost it again and had to be admitted to Huntercombe.

'But there must be some way I can beat the system, Debbie,' I said for the hundredth time.

'I've told you, Nikki,' she replied. 'There isn't.'

When Debbie finally fell asleep I cried into my pillow, terrified of what was going to happen. My only hope was that I wasn't just any other silly anorexic off the street, but I was the best anorexic out there and if anyone could beat Rhodes Farm I could.

The next morning I said goodbye to Carly. She'd been such a good friend to me and I loved her. But at that point I was so stuck in my illness that all I could think about was what was waiting for me at Rhodes Farm.

I climbed into the back of Mum's car and we set off for London. Soon we reached the western suburbs and the traffic grew thicker. This is it then, I thought. I'm just going to have to give myself over and let them get on with whatever it is they want to do to me.

I didn't have to wait long to find out exactly what that was. Within a couple of hours of arriving at Rhodes Farm I was sitting in front of a mammoth plate of chicken Kiev and chips, followed by a large KitKat.

From the outside, Rhodes Farm Clinic, in Mill Hill, north-west London, looks like a large, detached family house. Inside too it was like a proper home, with a cosy blue-tiled kitchen complete with long dining table and Welsh dresser. There were lounges with sofas you could sink deep into and floral curtains at the windows. Upstairs it was a rabbit warren of one-, two-, three- and four-person bedrooms, each decorated in a different theme with matching duvet covers and curtains.

Rhodes Farm had been the home of Dr Dee Dawson when she first started taking in teenagers with eating disorders back in 1991. But by the time I arrived it had been turned over entirely to caring for up to 32 kids at any one time.

Mum and I stood on the front step and rang the doorbell. After a couple of minutes it was flung open and there stood Helen, one of my nurses from Great Ormond Street. She didn't even need to say hello for me to hear her voice in my head again. 'Neeekkeeee, I reeeally want you to eat that bisceeeeet,' she had used to say to me time after time in her thick Geordie accent. Oh great, this is all I need, I thought as I summoned up all my energy to flash her a forced smile and step into the main hall.

As soon as I arrived I was weighed and measured and then Mum and I were shown into the garden for a meeting with one of the nurses, who spelled out exactly what was going to happen to me.

Rhodes Farm has an extremely strict policy whereby all patients must put on 1 kilo (2 lb) every week of their stay – not more and certainly not less. The clinic's success rate with this is remarkable and they boast that no child remains in their care not putting on weight. I'd spent months and months in various different units never putting on weight, and I was terrified about how they could be so sure they would achieve it with me.

Under the 1-kilo-a-week scheme, everyone who goes into Rhodes Farm is immediately given the date they will be discharged at their target weight. I went in on 9 January

1998 weighing 31.3 kilos (4 stone 13 lb) and was given a discharge date of 8 May, at which point, they calculated, I would be 45 kilos (7 stone 1lb). But when they revealed this target to me, I went mad. 'There's no way I'm going up to 45 kilos,' I stormed. 'I won't do it.' I flew into a tantrum and threw myself around the garden for the best part of an hour, screaming and thrashing my arms around.

I smashed Mum in the face, I was so mad at her for bringing me there, and the following day she had a terrible black eye.

What I didn't know then was that my every move was falling under the scrutiny of Dee Dawson, who was staring out of the kitchen window at my antics as the other girls quietly ate their lunch. 'It would appear,' she said to the girls in her very correct and considered manner, 'that the child from hell has arrived.'

When I finally calmed down enough to go inside, Dee came over and slowly looked me up and down, before saying, 'What a strange little thing you are.' She was probably right as what she must have seen that day in front of her was a scrawny little creature with tear stains down her face, pink hair, umpteen rings through her nose and ears and purple nail varnish.

Dee, by contrast, was a strong-looking woman in her 50s, her suit and brown bobbed hair reinforcing her no-nonsense appearance.

Standing face to face, maybe at that moment we both met our nemesis. We were poles apart but in some ways very similar, both being determined to succeed. This was going to be my greatest battle yet.

'No nonsense' pretty much summed up the philosophy of Rhodes Farm. The main focus was on feeding up dangerously ill girls so that they could enjoy some of the activities on offer there – dance, drama, trips to the theatre, sport – and then begin to actively engage with individual, group and family therapy.

Dee felt other institutions placed too much emphasis on therapy in the early stages and gave girls too much choice and involvement in meal planning. At Rhodes it was 'like it or lump it'.

Mum kissed me goodbye and Dee took me to the dining room, where the other kids were finishing their lunch.

Everyone in the room looked at me. I could see them assessing my weight, looking for the jagged edges of my bones jutting through my jeans and T-shirt. They'd heard about me already – how I'd been kicking around the anorexic circuit for seven years with no one yet able to sort me out.

I'm not sure what they were expecting me to do when I took my place in the empty chair at the table, but they weren't going to get any dramas. Not that day, anyway.

Instead I picked up my knife and fork and calmly ate the chicken Kiev and chips placed in front of me.

All new arrivals at Rhodes Farm are on 1,500 calories a day for the first three days, which I could just about cope with. But then my daily allowance was upped to 2,000 and after a week to 2,500 until it finally hit 3,700 because I had so much weight to gain. Not even the stories I'd been told by former Rhodes Farm patients could have prepared me for day after day of 3,700 calories.

At Huntercombe we had eaten generally very healthily from a menu devised individually for each patient by a qualified dietician. But at Rhodes Farm all you had was a number – your calorie intake for the day. And they didn't care if the food was healthy or unhealthy, as long as we got it down us.

In fact I thought at the time that I was on loads more than 3,700 calories a day because the portions were so huge. For breakfast I had 55 grams (2 oz) of high-calorie triple-choc muesli or maple pecan from Marks & Spencer mixed with 90 grams (3 oz) of Frosties, Golden Grahams or another sugary cereal soaked up with 0.15 litres (¼ pint) of full-cream milk – every morning. Thick globules of cream would float on top of the cereal. Disgusting. The milk alone was 68 calories but they didn't even count that. Or the 50 calories in my fruit juice.

Then to finish breakfast there was a 200-calorie muffin with so much butter on it that it would slide down my chin and arms as I ate it.

Lunches and dinners were often chicken Kiev and rice or similar, which they loved because the rice was good at mopping up the grease. They'd put maybe one carrot and a tomato on the plate but that was just to make it look pretty.

For pudding it would be something like a steamed sponge pudding with two scoops of ice cream. The pudding was 350 calories and the ice cream was supposed to be 150 but one day I had such a huge scoop – they'd put at least 300 calories of ice cream alone on my plate – that I called Dee in to complain. She went mad at the nurses. 'Who served this up?' she said. 'We'll never be able to calculate the girl's weight if we are confusing the portions like this. Take half that ice cream off her plate.'

It was a victory, but a very small one.

After every meal I could hardly move, I felt so full. I was lethargic and uncomfortable all the time.

Then we'd go into class but we would only just have sat down and started on our work when it was 'extras time'. They didn't even bother calling it snack time at Rhodes Farm. 'Extras' simply meant extra calories. Four boxes were laid out, labelled to show their contents: 50-calorie biscuits, 250-calorie biscuits, 300-calorie biscuits and king-size Mars Bars (450 calories). You had to select the right combination to meet your quota for the day. My 'extras' had to total 500 calories, so that was a king-size Mars and a 50-cal biscuit. And that was only an hour and a half after I'd finished an almighty great breakfast. For the first couple of weeks I complied, though eating those portions was agony.

I had a few mealtime tantrums but the staff weren't interested in my histrionics – they just told me to sit down and eat. A couple of times I was sedated with an injection but as the weeks rolled on even I realised that tantrums weren't getting me out of anything at Rhodes Farm.

Also, I think something in my mind had switched and deep down I was ready to cooperate and it was just habit which prevented me from doing so. Because for the first time in five years someone had offered me the chance to go home. To go back to my old bedroom, see my old friends and have a normal life again. Oh my God, I thought one morning. I could actually be going home in just 17 weeks' time.

There were two kitchens at Rhodes Farm. The brown kitchen was for the very severely anorexic kids and the blue kitchen was for those who were on the road to recovery and so were allowed to prepare their own food. In the brown kitchen sat the three anorexic 'pros', Janice, Sara and me. We would all sit in a line at the dinner table, Janice at the top because she had been there longest, then Sara and then me. I hadn't been there very long at all but my reputation as a 'special anorexic' won me a good position.

The meals would be handed by a member of staff to Janice, who would then hand them down the line. Janice, being first, would get first choice of whichever plate she thought looked smaller or lower in calories. Next it would be Sara's go, then mine. It was all-out war between the three of us as we were all so desperate to get the smallest portion, even though in reality there was probably almost no difference between them.

As each day passed I felt more and more sick at the thought of how much food they were going to serve up. I started trying to hide food at mealtimes and I got away for it for a few meals, but then one day Rachel, a really strict nurse, spotted me.

You could never get away with anything for very long at Rhodes Farm. They knew every trick in the book and watched you like hawks at dinner in case you were hiding or rubbing grease into your hair or clothes. Then there were regular room searches and spot checks on weight.

'OK – it's a cheese sandwich for you, Nikki,' said Rachel as she made me empty the food I'd just stashed down my knickers. They were the words everyone dreaded at Rhodes Farm. Cheese sandwiches were the punishment meals for breaking the rules. Each sandwich was about 500 calories, with chunky cubes of cheese put between two slices of bread lathered in butter so thick you could carve your name in it.

But if you refused the sandwich or spat it out you'd go on to a nasal tube feed. And this wasn't any namby-pamby milk feed like I'd had at Great Ormond Street. At Rhodes Farm they liquidised a mixture of mayonnaise, double cream and Mars Bars, then squirted it up your nose. It seemed utterly barbaric. I couldn't believe they would do that to people – but they did.

What I didn't realise then, though, was that they rarely tubed people at Rhodes Farm and kept it for the absolute last-resort cases. Because in many ways tubing makes it too easy for anorexics – it gives them the option of totally retreating from food, which is what had happened to me at Great Ormond Street. By using the gastrostomy for more than 14 months I was able to remove myself from any interaction with food at all. I didn't need to get better, I could just plod along, taking in the calories they pumped into me. That's why they avoided the tube wherever possible at Rhodes Farm. Instead their philosophy was 'just get on and eat it'.

It was only now that I was able to see how most of the units I'd been in up until this time had pussyfooted around me. I'd been allowed to select meals and persisted in my tantrums. But at Rhodes Farm I wasn't being asked, persuaded or bullied into feeding. I was simply being told to do it. And I did.

There was no time or attention for people who messed around or wanted to hog the limelight. And, more than anything, there was the idea that if you did follow the programme you would go home – and soon. That was an amazing thought for me after so long away.

That's not to say I didn't continue to fight the system. It was still to be a while before I could let my guard down and give in. Meanwhile I continued to leave the dinner table with as much food still crammed in my mouth as I could squeeze in without looking like a hamster. As soon as I was out of the room I spat the entire mouthful into any bin or toilet. But when a member of staff spotted me doing it one day, it was cheese sandwich time again.

I was also exercising at any opportunity I could find. Every lunchtime we were allowed out for an hour's walk, the idea being that a bit of fresh air would make us feel better. But as soon as I was out of eyesight of the building I would break into a brisk run, although that was risky because members of staff would often come out checking on us in their cars. In addition I was exercising every night that I could get away with it in my bedroom.

But my best trick was picking up my plate at the end of the meal and taking it over to the sink, where I would pretend to wash it up. Then, with my back to the room, I'd throw up my entire lunch into the sink and ram it down the plug hole with my fingers. I'd learned to do it totally silently so no one noticed a thing.

I could puke up a 1,000-calorie lunch in less than a minute. First up would be the ice cream, which would reappear like foam, and then the main course. When I started to get an acidic residue swilling around my mouth and teeth I knew I'd got the lot up. Then I'd feel good again – nice and empty.

A lot of trust was placed in us, but the staff were able to monitor exactly what we were up to through the weekly weigh-ins, at which we were supposed to have gained a kilo each time. If a fortnight went past and you hadn't hit your target, all your privileges, including the lunchtime walk, were taken away and you were placed on supervision.

Once I'd started throwing up, hiding and spitting out

food, my weight soon failed to make the weekly target and I was put on supervision. At first I was supervised for one hour after meals to ensure I wasn't being sick. This meant that for the hour after a meal I'd have to sit with all the other kids on supervision in the brown kitchen, unable to go out of sight of members of staff for even a moment. But, the minute my hour's supervision was up, I'd still run off and be sick.

But when my weight still didn't increase it became two hours post-meal supervision, then three and four. Even after four hours of post-meal supervision I'd still go off at night and puke up anything that might be left in my stomach. By that point I was only really bringing up stomach juices but I still did it. My teeth are destroyed now by the amount of acid I regurgitated.

Around that time Janice, Sara and I went down to Argos one lunch break for our walk and bought a pair of electronic scales. It meant we could calculate our weight perfectly before our official twice-weekly weigh-ins, so we knew how much we needed to waterload if necessary. Sometimes I'd drink 5 litres (9 pints) of water, which weighs around 5 kilos (11 lb), before a weigh-in to ensure I hit my target.

I also had another brilliant scam for adding a bit to my weight. One of the other girls had come up with the idea of sewing fishing weights into her hair scrunchy, so one weekend I went into a fishing tackle shop and bought myself some too. I cut a neat slit in the scrunchy, slipped the weights in, then sewed it up again. It may have added only half a kilo or so, but it all helped.

We hid the scales in a boiler cupboard beside the fire escape and only referred to them by the codeword 'hairdryer'. So Sara might say to me, 'Can I borrow your hairdryer?' and I'd reply, 'Janice is using it at the moment but you can be next.' It was a brilliant way of staying ahead of the game and the 'hairdryer' scam survived for a couple of years after I left Rhodes Farm before it was discovered.

There was one member of staff called Tony and I'm sure he knew something was going on but he didn't know what. On weigh-in days he'd always say to me, 'Isn't it amazing, Nikki, how your weight is always bang on target every week?'

'What do you mean?' I'd say in mock horror.

'Oh nothing,' he'd reply. 'It just seems quite incredible, that's all.'

Because I was able to stay on my target week after week, I was allowed evenings out with my parents and even some weekends at home. For my first 'meal out' Dad took me to a Beefeater but he'd been given strict instructions about what I had to eat – something with chips for a main course and then the pudding had to include pastry and cream. A sorbet or mousse was out of the question.

Afterwards, though, I got Dad to give me a game of badminton at a gym in London. He loves sport and I just loved the chance to exercise.

Staff at Rhodes Farm must have become increasingly suspicious that I was manipulating my weight on weigh-in days because late one night my little scam came to a sudden end. I'd been fast asleep when one of the nurses knocked sharply on my door and walked in. I opened my eyes slowly, blinking as the brightness from the corridor pricked my eyes.

'Hello, Nikki,' the nurse chirped as if she'd just popped

in for a chat. 'I'm just going to take you downstairs to weigh you.'

When they put me on the scales I was 4 kilos (9 lb) lighter than they had thought. After that I was back on those enormous meals, being watched so closely now that there wasn't a moment for me to exercise or vomit any more. I felt full to bursting with their disgusting food and it was unbearable. I felt I hadn't got any other choice – I had to run away. I waited for the perfect opportunity when I could slip away unnoticed.

It came shortly afterwards, on a Sunday morning. There was no one around, so I didn't pause for a moment but darted straight down the stairs and out of the front door without looking back. It was a chilly spring day and I was wearing a thin cotton purple dress and flip-flops, so I was soon absolutely freezing.

I ran to the tube station, desperately wondering where to go next. The only person I knew who lived anywhere nearby was Vicky, my old friend from Great Ormond Street, who was back home in North London. I ran into a phone box and dialled her number. 'Vicky, I've run away,' I told her. 'I'm coming round.'

My hands were numb with cold and my teeth were chattering by the time I knocked on her door. I'd been imagining us curled up on Vicky's bed, giggling and chatting the way we had at Great Ormond Street. But one look at her face as she opened the door told me it wasn't going to be like that.

'Come in for a minute, but I'm sorry, Nikki, you can't stay,' she said immediately. 'My Mum knows you're here and she's ringing Rhodes Farm. You're going to have to go back.'

We went into Vicky's bedroom and she dug out a pair of her trainers for me to put on my freezing feet as I warmed my hands on a radiator. I could see her mum hovering in the hallway. I knew she already hated me, seeing me as a 'bad influence' on Vicky.

Five minutes later I was back on the street again. I took the tube to Camden Town and wandered around for hours. It was so cold that my bones were aching and I couldn't stop crying.

After a couple of hours I looked through the steamed-up window of a café. Inside it looked warm and welcoming, so I popped in and asked to use their toilet and begged a cup of hot water. I sat at a table, cradling the mug in my hands and trying to get just a little bit of warmth back into my body.

I didn't know it then but when Dad got the call from Rhodes Farm saying that I was missing he thought I might go to Camden and spent hours driving around the streets there. He even went into the same café just five minutes after I'd left it.

I carried on wandering about aimlessly. Then I rang Mum's sister, Auntie Rita, and asked if I could come round, but she said no. So I carried on walking, getting colder and colder until my hands were turning blue and I felt more lonely than I could remember. I knew it was pointless, I had to go home. I caught a tube and was soon at Mum's doorstep, but I'd barely got inside the door before she had turned me round and bundled me back in the car for the return journey to Rhodes Farm.

There I was presented with a snack and told I'd have to wear my pyjamas for the next three days for running away. And I was put straight on total supervision, or 'total' as we called it. People in prison probably get more freedom than we did when punished in this way. All the girls on 'total' would have to sit in the brown kitchen all day long so they could be observed every minute by staff. We'd do schoolwork during the day, then watch television in the evening. And that was it.

The only time you were allowed out of that room was to go to the loo or take a shower. Even in the toilet a member of staff would come into the cubicle with you, shut the door and stand there with their back to you as you had a wee or a poo. It must have been horrible for them.

At night they would roll out lightweight mattresses on the floor of the kitchen and we would sleep on these next to one another. The lights would be kept on all night and a staff member would stay awake in an armchair watching us in case anyone tried any tricks.

I remained on 'total' for months and all that time my weight could only go up because there was just no chance of getting away with any of my dodges.

Running away, though, had reminded me what it was like outside of institutions, and gradually an idea was taking shape in my mind. I wanted to get out of there and places like it. I wanted to live a normal life, surrounded by normal people. I started wondering what Lena looked like now and if she and my other friends had boyfriends or were going out to discos. I'd like to go to discos, I thought. I'd like to have a boyfriend. I'd like to have a life.

For years at Great Ormond Street, Sedgemoor and Huntercombe going home had never really been an option and so my only means of having any control over my life had been to starve myself. But at Rhodes Farm they'd told me that very soon I would be back in the big, wide world again, like a normal person. And I craved that desperately.

But the amount of food being served up was still doing my head in. I felt bloated and sick all the time. As the weeks passed I felt I no longer needed help from Rhodes Farm. Because I didn't want to starve myself to death any more, I could cope on my own now.

And because I was in a hurry to get on with living, I was determined to run away again.

CHAPTER 18
I WANT TO LIVE

I eased myself through the tiny gap in the window of the telephone room and jumped down silently into the garden.

I'd done it. I'd escaped from Rhodes Farm – again. With a bit of planning it hadn't even been that difficult. When I was on 'total' the only time I had a moment to myself all week was during my Thursday evening phone call to Mum. So I persuaded Sara to come down to the telephone room while I was there, bringing with her my trainers and a jacket. Then, cutting short my conversation with Mum before the nurse was due to escort me back upstairs to the brown kitchen, I jumped out of the window and was away.

It was already dark outside and a chilly evening but I started running and headed for the end of the tree-lined garden. I knew from our lunchtime walks exactly which way I needed to go to get to the tube station without being spotted.

Rhodes Farm was next to a church and I had to run through the graveyard if I was going to keep away from the road. It was pitch-dark and really spooky and I kept tripping over every bit of uneven ground, but all I could think was that I had to keep going.

From the graveyard, I had to jog through a tunnel before I emerged on to Mill Hill Broadway, from where it was just a couple of hundred yards to the train station. I slipped through the ticket barrier when no one was noticing, then ran down to the platform and on to the first train that pulled in.

I'd already decided where I was going – Taunton. I knew I couldn't go home as Mum would take me straight back to Rhodes. And I couldn't think of anywhere else to go. Besides, I'd quite enjoyed my time at Sedgemoor and liked the idea of being a long way from London.

Once I was on the train at Paddington I went into the toilet and lay on the floor the whole way to avoid the ticket collector. It was filthy and stank but I didn't dare go outside in case I was caught and made to get off the train.

It was about one o'clock in the morning when the train finally pulled in at Taunton. I came out of the station and walked down to the centre of the town. I was still wearing the short black cotton flowery skirt and thin coat I'd had on when I left Rhodes Farm and it was perishing cold.

Now I was in Taunton I realised I had absolutely no idea where I was going next. I walked along a deserted street, rehearsing in my mind what I'd say if anyone asked me what I was doing. I'd decided to tell them I'd had an argument with my mum and run away from home, simple as that. Hopefully they wouldn't ask any further questions.

After half an hour I realised I was just going to have to find somewhere to sleep until the morning. I looked around and saw the recessed doorway of an estate agent. I found a box and wrapped it around me, like I'd seen tramps do. I knew I'd rather sleep on that than the filthy ground, and I told myself it would soon be morning anyway. I lay still and clamped my eyes shut but it was too cold to sleep. My body was aching with the biting cold and I felt utterly miserable.

Every minute seemed like an hour. I don't think I can do this, I thought. But I didn't know what else to do. I stared at my watch, following the minute hand with my eyes as it dragged itself around. Please, morning, hurry up and come.

I had a little money to buy food with later and I started to feel confident I could look after myself now. I'd been more compliant at Rhodes and knew how much I could eat to be healthy, so I felt I was never going to get really ill again. Meanwhile, if I could just get through this one night, everything would be OK.

But I'd been lying there for about an hour, every fibre of my body crying out from the cold, when I realised I just couldn't do it after all. A couple of minutes later I looked up and saw a bloke walking past. He looked quite respectable with his smart suit and neat hair, so I called out quietly, 'Excuse me.' It took him a couple of seconds to focus on me and I could tell he'd had a couple of drinks.

He looked me over slowly and I knew exactly what he was seeing – a skinny little girl with pink hair who was a long way from home and way out of her depth.

'Oh my God, what are you doing out at this hour?' he said.

229

I already had my well-rehearsed answer: 'I've had a row with my mum and I've run away from home. Do you know if there any hostels or anything around here I can stay at, because I've got nowhere to go?'

He stared at me for a while, obviously taking in the situation, and then said slowly, 'I want you to call your mum now. I want you to ring her and tell her that you're OK.'

It was before everyone had mobile phones, so we walked in awkward silence to the nearest phone box. He stood outside while I dialled the number. It rang just once before Mum picked up, so I knew she'd already been told I'd run away. 'Where are you, Nikki?' she said, the panic clear in her voice.

'I can't tell you, Mum,' I said. 'I just want you to know I'm OK.'

Before she had the chance to say anything else, I put down the phone, pushed open the heavy door and stepped outside.

What I didn't realise was that Mum had recognised the code that flashed up on her handset as the one for Taunton. She assumed I'd gone back to Sedgemoor, so that put her mind at rest a little bit.

Outside the phone box the man looked me up and down again. 'Right, come back to my hotel and you can stay there the night. There are two single beds in the room and you can have one of them.'

He could have been a rapist or an axe murderer but that didn't occur to me then. I was just desperate to be somewhere warm.

We walked further down the street to his hotel, through the deserted reception and up to his room.

'You take a shower and relax while I pop downstairs for a bit,' he said.

I had the most gorgeous long, hot shower and towelled myself dry before putting my clothes back on and climbing into bed.

Amazing, I thought. A free night in a hotel and no one here to make me eat. This is living it up!

I hadn't even closed my eyes when there was a sharp knock on the door. I climbed out of bed and opened it to find a policeman and a policewoman staring at me. 'Hello, we'd like to take you down to the police station,' they said.

My heart sank. It really had been too good to be true. My kind stranger must have gone straight downstairs and shopped me to the police. I can understand now why he did it, but at the time I was gutted.

It was 3am when we arrived at the police station. The policeman pointed me to a chair, then sat down opposite me.

'OK, love, you've got two hours and then at five o'clock we're going to sling you in a children's home, so why don't you just tell us where you're from and you can be on your way home?'

Hallelujah! I thought. A children's home is exactly where I want to be – I'll be able to eat what I want, no one hassling me. Don't wait till five, do it now.

But I didn't say that. I just sat there sullenly, kicking my feet backwards and forwards.

'Come on, then,' he said, pushing my chair leg with his foot. 'Where are you from?'

I gave him the same old bullshit about having an argument with my mum and running away from home. But I wouldn't tell him my name or where I was from.

231

'Skinny little cow, aren't you?' he went on. 'When did you last eat? And why aren't you wearing more clothes for the time of year?'

By this point I hated him and had made up my mind I wasn't telling him another thing.

Come on, five o'clock, I kept thinking. I really want to go to sleep now – I'm so tired.

At 5am they pushed me into a police car and took me to a children's home on the outskirts of the town.

The home was like a big family house. It was a bit shabby but warm and had a friendly feeling about it. A kind-looking woman helped me upstairs to a room with clean sheets and a rough but chunky blanket on the bed. What a result, I thought. I could stay here for years. I guess other kids would have been horrified by living somewhere like that but I'd been in and out of institutions for the past seven years and this seemed like a nice one.

I told them the same dodgy story about running away from home, and even if they didn't believe me they didn't give me a hard time about it. Then they gave me £50 to go into the town to buy some warmer clothes with some of the other girls who lived there. The girls were really nice and we chatted all the way there and back, but I was careful not to give too much information away to them either.

In the evening we sat around watching films and having a laugh. Some of the kids were total nutcases but I was used to that. I'd grown up with nutcases.

I stayed there for five nights. And I ate. I'd already made the decision at Rhodes Farm that I would eat because I wanted to live.

I called Mum a few times from the children's home. I

told her where I was and what was going on but said I still didn't feel ready to come back, not yet.

Then one afternoon I called her again.

'Hi, Mum,' I said. 'I want to come home – I want to get better.'

I could tell by the silence that followed that Mum wasn't sure whether it was another of my con tricks or if this time I was serious.

'But I don't want to go back to Rhodes,' I continued. 'I can do it on my own now.'

Mum offered to come straight down to collect me but said I had to go back to Rhodes Farm. We couldn't agree but the next day she turned up anyway.

We had a long wait before our train back to London, so we went into Debenhams department store for lunch. We sat at a table and I said, 'Mum, I'm going to prove to you that I am going to eat – that I can eat and that I am coming home for good. I'm going to do this if you promise not to take me back to Rhodes.'

I chose one of those little picnic boxes they have for children and I ate the lot – no fuss, no bother. Mum couldn't believe it. She didn't dare believe that our nightmare might be coming to an end. We spent the train journey home talking and laughing like the old days.

Mum had changed a lot too and it was good. For years she had been having counselling at the different units treating me but then she had met a therapist who helped her turn everything around. She taught Mum to be true to herself and to stop pleasing other people all the time and showed her she could be a good mother *and* look after herself.

I think when Mum really started to believe that, it was

the point she was transformed from a quivering mess into someone strong enough to keep her daughter alive.

So she had got a job as a radiographer's assistant. I hadn't liked it at first as it meant she wouldn't be there to attend to my every beck and call any more. But I got used to it.

And she had become firmer with me too. She was able to look at things more dispassionately and less emotionally. Sometimes she'd even get tough with me. 'For God's sake, Nikki. Just stop this behaviour,' she'd say when I started one of my fits.

She had kitted herself out with a whole new wardrobe – slinky dresses, high heels and pretty underwear. For the first time in ages she paid attention to the way she looked.

Maybe seeing Mum get stronger during the time I'd been at Huntercombe and Rhodes Farm made me feel safer deep down. Maybe it took away so much of the uncertainty in my life and had helped me on my road to recovery.

Back home from Somerset, Mum cooked me a plain piece of cod and some new potatoes, followed by a yoghurt and a piece of fruit. I ate the lot.

After dinner we sat down with Tony and watched telly. I felt normal. After all those years I was doing what normal people did on a Tuesday evening. And it was great.

For a week I lived at Tolcarne Drive and loved it; sleeping in my bedroom, going shopping with Mum, hanging out with Natalie and seeing my old school friends.

I'd begged Mum not to tell Rhodes Farm that she had seen me if they called, and she agreed. She wanted me home too.

One afternoon I went round to Carly's house as she was

back home and only living 20 minutes' walk away. Then the phone rang – it was Mum and she needed to speak to me urgently.

'You've got to come home straight away,' she said. 'I'm taking you back to Rhodes Farm.'

I felt like I had been kicked in the belly. 'No, Mum, no,' I begged down the phone. 'You promised, you promised.'

'I've got no choice, Nikki,' Mum said, her voice desperate. 'Social Services have been on the phone. They must have worked out you were home, and they've said if I don't take you back now they will take you away and section you. If they do that you could be locked up until you're 18.'

Mum was crying and I could tell there was going to be no way out of this one.

Within five minutes she was outside waiting to pick me up. I hugged Carly goodbye, dreading my return to Rhodes Farm.

Back there I was put straight on three days in pyjamas and total supervision again.

I've just got to get the hell out of here as quickly as possible, was all I could think.

I'd been out of there for a fortnight and it had really made me realise for the first time how much I was missing the outside world. I was now certain I wanted a life outside of hospitals and eating-disorders units. They say that if you spend years and years in prison you don't see a way out, you don't even want to get out because it has become your life. That is what had happened to me even before I went to Rhodes Farm. I was so institutionalised that for years I couldn't even think about going home – I didn't even know about the outside world any more. But the thought of being able to go home opened up a whole world of new possibilities for me.

However, while I'd been away my weight had fallen way below my target, so I had loads of catching up to do. I started bingeing in a bid to get my weight up so that I'd be discharged as quickly as possible.

I'd steal bottles of full-cream milk from the fridge and neck the whole lot while I was in the shower if I had a moment unsupervised.

Then one night we were allowed into the video room to watch a film as a special treat. On the way down I sneaked into the pantry and stole a loaf of bread. Once the film started I sat behind a sofa in the video room and ate the lot.

And one morning I stole some jam from the breakfast table and that night scooped great handfuls straight from the jar into my mouth.

I even got Mum to send me chocolate bars through the post. And she did it, because she thought it was great that I was eating. One evening I ate nine chocolate bars – 350 calories each! I couldn't sleep that night I felt so sick, but I kept them all down. I didn't even feel guilt about eating so much any more, I just wanted out. I wanted to make a go of life.

As my weight increased I was finally taken off 'total' and moved into the blue kitchen, where you could prepare your own food and sit without supervision. I was even allowed out to do work experience looking after children at a nursery in the hope it would help me get a job when I went home. I loved it, and I loved being part of the outside world – although it was still a pretty scary concept to grasp.

I admit I still waterloaded before weigh-ins to be on the safe side but apart from that I'd given up fighting. For the first time in eight years I handed myself over to the system and let them do what they wanted with me. And it was an incredible relief. I suddenly felt tired, utterly exhausted. For weeks, whenever I could I'd go and lie down on one of the sofas and sleep and sleep. It was as if the effort of all those years of battling had finally caught up with me and I was shattered.

I still didn't want to be 45 kilos and I was certain I would lose some of it when I got out of Rhodes Farm, but I was never again going to starve myself almost to death. I wanted to live too much for that.

On my last weigh-in on my last day at Rhodes Farm, on 19 June 1998, I was 46.7 kilos (7 stone 5 lb). It was the first time my weight had been within a normal range for years.

'I won't be back,' I said to Dee as I packed my bag that last morning.

'I hope not,' she said. 'But we will always be here for you if you need us.'

CHAPTER 19

A NEW STRUGGLE

Some of the institutions I had been in had been frightening, harsh and lonely. But living in the real world again was the hardest thing I'd had to face yet. Because, however bad it had been in a hospital or a specialist unit, at least I had felt secure there, safe from the challenges and disappointments of the outside world.

Now it was time to face reality.

I'd made the decision I wanted to get better, but that was just the start of the battle. Returning home to Tolcarne Drive that summer of 1998, I felt like a freak, a leper. I'd been away from normal life for most of the past eight years and had no idea how to behave, no dress sense, no social skills, no qualifications – nothing.

Now I was 16 I didn't have to go to school any more, so I started looking for a job. I tried loads of places but nowhere was interested in me. Even McDonald's wouldn't have me because I hadn't got a single GCSE after missing out on so much education.

I must have looked a total mess too. At that point I was a little plump by my standards and my hair was all frizzy and short like a baby's because I'd destroyed it with so much dye. I had no idea about make-up or what was cool or fashionable and was still wandering around in dungarees and Dr Martens when other girls my age were looking glamorous and trendy.

Natalie was away at Manchester Met University studying drama, so I was stuck at home with Mum and Tony. When Nat came home for holidays she would take me out with her mates but I was totally socially inept. I had missed out on so much growing up I had no idea what to say to people, and for years the only thing I had discussed with anyone was calories.

One of my first 'normal' nights out was for a drink with Natalie and a big group of her friends. We were in a beer garden and Nat was drinking a pint of lager. 'Oh, I feel a bit pissed,' she giggled.

'That's because Prozac doubles everything,' I said matter-of-factly. There was a moment of total silence. I looked at the shock and embarrassment on Nat's friends' faces and it slowly dawned on me that taking Prozac for depression was probably the sort of thing people in the outside world preferred to keep private. Everywhere I'd been for the past ten years almost everyone had been on Prozac or some kind of drug, and I didn't realise it was such a big deal.

Natalie glared at me while everyone else around the table all started chattering at once to fill the silence.

I was like that all the time, embarrassing poor old Natalie. Despite that, she stuck by me, letting me hang around whenever she was at home. When she was back at uni, though, it was horribly quiet. Old friends from school had moved on and obviously thought it was very uncool to be seen hanging around with a weirdo like me. I had no social life apart from a Christian friend of Natalie's called Sian who used to invite me out occasionally.

And I wasn't happy about the way I looked either. Although I'd made the decision not to starve myself ultra-skinny again, I still felt too big at just 44.5 kilos (7 stone). One day I went shopping with Mum and cried the entire time because everything I tried on looked so bad on me.

I joined a gym and spent my days exercising – it was the only thing I knew how to do. I'd walk to the gym in the morning, train, walk home again, then watch telly all evening with Mum and Tony. And that was my life.

But I was just about in control of my eating, and I was determined not to get really ill again. I wasn't out of the woods by any means, though. I was drinking high-calorie drinks rather than risk eating anything with fat in it. I couldn't even bring myself to touch fat.

I could tell Mum was terrified that with all the knocks I was getting I was about to relapse again. All those years I'd been lying dying in hospital, she had always said, 'You've got to fight, you've got to get well, because there's a world out there for you – a life.' But then here I was out in the world and there was no life at all – no job, no friends, nothing.

I'd been home about five months when Dad got me a job through a friend of his, serving breakfast to tramps at Watford YMCA for £3 an hour. The tramps were only allowed one slice of toast each but they used to try to distract me so they could nick another couple. Imagine anyone trying to pull that stunt on me – the expert at food cheating in communal dining halls!

I'd get up at six to be there for seven, then work a four-hour shift. But it was really hard because by then I'd developed a phobia about eating in front of anyone. I just couldn't do it and I would get starving hungry waiting for my shift to end before I could eat. After a couple of months I gave up the job.

My fear of eating in public was so bad that when I went shopping I'd take a sandwich with me and go into a public toilet and eat it. I had it in my head that everyone would be staring at me if they could see me eating, so I wouldn't do it.

After Rhodes Farm I also developed other obsessive-compulsive behaviour. It was a new thing to focus on rather than just calories. I became obsessed with cleanliness and hygiene. Experts would have described my fear of germs as morbid. When Mum set the table for dinner I would have to wash my knife, fork and plate three times before I could use them. Everything became a ritual, a routine. I guess it was another way of feeling in control in my life now that I'd stopped starving myself.

If Mum ever put my dinner on a plate I hadn't just washed I would go mental, shouting and screaming like the old days. I was the same about bad smells. I felt they were getting into my body and polluting me.

Then I got a place at Stanmore College to study for a Business & Technology Education Council qualification in the performing arts. But from my first day there I locked myself in a toilet cubicle to eat my lunch. I was marking myself out as different and as a teenage girl that is always dangerous.

Within a week the bullying had started. At first I was aware of the other girls staring at my body and whispering. Then they would snigger at the way I looked and the clothes I wore.

I only made matters worse when I started falling asleep in lectures. Because I wasn't sleeping well at night I always felt exhausted during the day. That only gave the other girls in my class something else to laugh at me about.

One day we were doing a performance and the girls said we all had to wear hotpants. I didn't have any with me so I went all the way home on the bus in my lunch break to get them. Then, when we all went on stage, everyone apart from me was wearing leggings. They just wanted me to feel different and uncomfortable – and they succeeded.

I became really miserable and dealt with it the only way I knew how – by cutting down on what I was eating. Looking back, at this point I should have asked Rhodes Farm for help again but I was terrified that as a returner they'd put me straight on 4,500 calories a day. They do a scheme there where you can return for weekends if you've lost just a little weight but I had refused to do that in the first few months after leaving and now my weight was falling fast and I was too scared to go back full time.

Within weeks I was living on sandwiches made from fat-free crumpets and fat-free soya cheese, Lucozade tablets and spoonfuls of sugar to at least get some calories inside me. I wouldn't eat anything containing fat.

After the first term I couldn't face going back to college, so I packed it in.

Then I got a job as a waitress at a private health club in Northwood. I loved the work at the Riverside Club, but soon I started to feel excluded again by the other members of staff. I think I must have just been a bit too weird, with my skinniness and my secret eating and my social inadequacies, for them to be comfortable with. I made myself an easy victim for people, although I didn't realise it then.

My only friend there was a guy called David, who I'd known since I was ten, from the church youth club, and we had such a laugh together. We'd chase each other down the corridors, waving mops at each other. Once we were in the men's toilets and I'd climbed up on a sink trying to get him with my mop when our manager walked in. That took some explaining!

The first Christmas I worked at the Riverside the staff party was at a nightclub in Watford called Destiny. I was so excited because I'd never been to a nightclub before. Mum and I spent hours traipsing around the shops looking for the perfect thing to wear before I found a little black Lycra dress and some black and white platform shoes.

I really fancied one of the chefs, and that night he and I got chatting. He knew I fancied him and I was just bowled over that he was showing me any attention at all.

He came home with me that night and stayed over. Mum was cool about it. I think she was just happy I was doing normal teenage things.

But pretty soon it was apparent things were very one-sided. I wanted to go on dates, to the cinema and nice restaurants. He just wanted to come round late at night after he'd finished work or been out with his mates. It was obvious he was using me. In the end I think he felt guilty about it and after about a month it fizzled out. That hit me really hard and I fell into a dark depression again. I'd spend hours lying face down on my bed crying. I'd lost the man I liked, I had no friends, I was a freak of society and couldn't see any future.

I'd worked so hard to get out of hospital and it was all for nothing. Everything in the outside world was so unreliable and scary. I didn't belong here.

Even in my misery I was aware I was entering a dangerous phase. I was beginning to think, I can block out all this misery now if I stop thinking about it and focus on not eating, because I'm good at that.

I knew I needed to go somewhere I'd feel safe and where I belonged – hospital.

Hospital was where I'd grown up, so I suppose it was just like other people wanting to go home when they're going through a rough patch.

I dismissed the idea of Rhodes Farm because I knew it would be mammoth amounts of calories and fat. So instead I rang Dr Lask and on 13 January 1999 I checked myself back into Huntercombe.

I'd lost 9 kilos (1 stone 6 lb) in the seven months since I'd left Rhodes Farm and was down to 36 kilos (5 stone 9 lb) and suffering from dehydration. I knew that at Huntercombe they would let me do things my way and I was keen to make it work. The dietician helped me draw up a meal plan and I stuck to it.

I requested therapy with one particular counsellor who was young and cool and they agreed. He was fun but gave me good advice on how to cope in situations I found stressful in the outside world and it really helped.

But it was while I was back there that my obsession with cleanliness really took hold. I started washing my plates and cutlery excessively and if anyone looked at me while I was washing a plate I'd have to wash it all over again. I wouldn't allow anyone to touch anything I ate or anything I ate my dinner off.

After staying at Huntercombe for just over three months I left weighing 39.2 kilos (6 stone 2 lb) and feeling ready to go home and back to my job at the Riverside Club.

I was still having to nip to the toilet to eat a sandwich halfway through my shift and I survived on cups of peppermint tea with four sugars, but I was better than before.

I avoided the chef and got on with my work. But then some of the girls I'd been friends with at school got jobs there. I was still too freaky and immature for them to hang around with and they did everything they could to make my life a misery. They'd go to nightclubs in Watford but say there was no way I'd get in because I looked so young. Eventually, though, they agreed I could go out with them one Saturday night.

Beforehand I spent days agonising over what I should wear. I remembered them showing me pictures of when they'd gone out while I was at Huntercombe and one of them was wearing a grey suit. That must be fashionable – I'll get one of those, I thought. On the day we were going out I went to Mark One and found a virtually identical suit. Later, after I'd spent two hours doing my hair and make-up, I got Mum to drop me at Northwood Hills station to meet the girls.

As I stepped out of the car I saw two of the girls – I'll call them Jill and Karen – staring at me, obviously trying to stifle giggles.

'Why are you dressed like that, Nikki?' one of them asked. 'We're only going round to Karen's house to watch a video.'

I was mortified.

When we got to Karen's we passed round a bottle of

vodka. They were saying, 'Go on, Nikki, neck it – get drunk and let yourself go.'

I was so immature and otherworldly that I did just that. Soon I was completely out of it and they had to almost carry me back home. On the way I collapsed on the street. All I remember is them falling about laughing as I lay there. They called an ambulance to check I wasn't dying and paramedics came and looked me over.

I was OK but once again I felt totally humiliated.

Not long after that I was desperate to go up to Leicester Square to see the crowds and the fireworks on the eve of the Millennium. I'd heard that the girls at work were all going, so I dashed up to one of them, and asked, 'Can I come with you for New Year's Eve?'

'Er, we don't know what we are doing yet,' she said.

Then I rang Jill and she didn't seem to know either.

Then I rang Karen and it was the same again.

Finally our mutual friend David had to tell me the truth: 'Sorry, Nikki, but I don't think they want you to go with them.' I was devastated.

I was really struggling with life on the outside and not attending my outpatient counselling sessions at Huntercombe as often as I should have done. My eating and exercising were both under control – but only just.

As well as being so socially immature and out of touch I also looked much younger than other girls. I may have been approaching 18, but I was still living inside the body of a young boy – no breasts and still no periods. So I decided to have a boob job. I knew it was too late for them to ever come naturally now because of the damage anorexia had done to my body. I went on an NHS waiting list before undergoing the operation to boost me from a pancake-flat AA to a more shapely B cup.

The operation was a bit of a disaster. They put far too much drainage tube inside me and my body rejected it. I had to stay in for six nights while they sorted it out. It really hurt but when the swelling eventually went down I was delighted.

I bought loads of new clothes and a fortnight after the op Lena agreed to take me out to celebrate my birthday. I was 18 and finally felt like a woman. For the first time I felt confident about the way I looked. My new boobs also won me kudos and respect from the girls at work.

In my spare time I had started doing dance classes at Pineapple Dance Studios in Covent Garden. Then I decided I wanted to do it full-time and enrolled on a course at the Gypsy Booth School of Ballet and Theatre Arts near Watford. It was clear that I had a degree of natural talent – like at gymnastics all those years earlier – and I was soon keeping up with girls who had been doing ballet since they were kids. I wasn't the best, but I was good at it – and that made me feel good.

And for the first time I made friends who made me feel comfortable and who I enjoyed going out with. That group of friends saved me. We'd go out most evenings and even went on holiday for two weeks to Ibiza.

For a year everything was brilliant but then history started repeating itself.

There were more exams and more shows at Gypsy Booth and I could feel pressure mounting on me. There was also a lot of competition for places at the big dance schools we hoped to get into after finishing our course. I dreamed of going to Laine Theatre Arts, in Epsom, one of the best schools in the country, but competition was fierce and that panicked me.

Meanwhile some of my friends were leaving and going to various colleges. Everything felt uncertain and difficult again and I tried to regain control the only way I knew how – by losing weight.

I realised that I was no longer dancing because I enjoyed it but because it was exercise and that, for me, was wrong. I would arrive at the college in the morning and do body conditioning for an hour, then ballet, then contemporary, then jazz, and stay until nine at night.

At the same time I was eating less and less. Gypsy Booth, who ran the school, called me over one afternoon. 'Nikki, I'm really sorry but I'm going to have to pull you out of some of the dances for the Christmas show,' she said. 'You're too weak.'

I told Gypsy I had an overactive thyroid and I was waiting for the doctor to sort it out but I don't think I fooled her for a moment. For some time I'd known I wasn't doing the jumps properly because I was so weak but I'd been trying to ignore it.

I was distraught at being dropped from the dances and that just made me more stressed. So I ate even less. And as the weight dropped off me and I spent day after day looking at myself in front of a dance mirror in a leotard, I got to like what I saw and wanted to get even thinner. I had tumbled back into that old vicious circle.

Mum was desperately worried too.

I knew perfectly well what was happening – I could tell from the haunted look in my own face. And I knew I had to do something if I wanted to avoid going back into hospital. I tried making myself eat things like Twix bars but then I'd be so racked with guilt afterwards that I'd make myself exercise like a freak again.

By the beginning of 2001 I was in a bad state and my weight had slid to 34.5 kilos (5 stone 6 lb). Then one afternoon Gypsy sat me down and said, 'I'm sorry, Nikki, but I'm going to have to bar you from the school until you put some weight on. If anything happened and you had an accident because you are so weak, it would be my fault, and I can't have that on my conscience.'

I was devastated. I'd been planning to make dancing my career and now the dream was being ripped away from me. I admitted to myself that I had to go back into hospital – I was too far down the road to pull myself back on my own. But now I was an adult there were more problems than ever securing funding from the local authority to get me a place in an eating-disorders unit.

My GP tried everywhere to get me help. By April the situation was critical and I lost a further 2 kilos (4½ lb) in four weeks. But, with the restrictions on funding, even Dr Lask and Huntercombe were unable to do anything. I was getting more and more angry and miserable that no one seemed to want to help me and my weight dropped further. I spent my days charging round the local streets, burning off calories. I'd gone past the point of being able to help myself.

Then in June they admitted me to the Adult Psychiatric Unit at Hillingdon Hospital. It was to be my first experience living with adults with severe mental problems and it was utterly terrifying.

CHAPTER 20
NEVER GOING BACK

At night, men would trail their bodies up and down the corridor outside my room. Sometimes they'd bang their heads on the wall in frustration, as if trying to rid themselves of whatever demons writhed inside. Other times they would rattle my door handle, terrifying me as I lay, not daring to breathe, under my duvet.

Schizophrenics, alcoholics and the homeless, unloved and unwanted, had washed up in the psychiatric unit, their minds disconnected and floating free of the outside world. I hated it and couldn't face leaving my room to be brought so close to the brutal sadness of others' tragedies.

Day after day I sat in my room and watched television. If I even went to the loo I had to take my valuables with me so they didn't get nicked.

Being in that place didn't help me one bit. It didn't make me eat – I was just given my meals and left alone, so it was little different from being at home. I'd been there about a week when one evening I was in the day room watching telly when I became conscious of an old man sitting in the chair opposite, staring at me. When I looked over at him, I glanced down and thought I was going to be sick. His eyes focused on me, he was masturbating.

I ran straight out of the room and to the phone, where I rang Mum's number, my hands shaking.

'You've got to get me out of here!' I screamed. 'Now.'

Mum was there within half an hour and as we accelerated away from Hillingdon Hospital I was shuddering with relief.

Almost immediately I was found a bed in the Eating Disorders Unit at the Bethlem Royal Hospital in Beckenham, Kent. The world's first psychiatric hospital, it is famous for being known originally as 'the Bedlam' and giving that frightening word to the English language. Nowadays it has staff expert in treating adult eating disorders. But the regime was horribly tough.

When I arrived I weighed in at 32.8 kilos (5 stone 2 lb) and was 155 centimetres (5 feet 1 inch) tall. And although I was a voluntary patient there was no messing around. If I didn't eat what they served up to make me put on weight, I'd be instantly tubed.

The meals were absolutely awful, and you had to eat it all, every time. For breakfast it was a cup of tea with two sugars, three Weetabix with 0.15 litres (¼ pint) of full-cream milk, then beans on toast plus two extra slices of buttered toast and orange juice.

Ten o'clock was snack time – a mug of full-cream milk with two sugars or a Nesquik milkshake and two digestive biscuits.

For lunch you were allowed to choose from a menu but

it was usually something like quiche and veg, followed by chocolate sponge with chocolate sauce.

The afternoon snack was a cup of milk and a doughnut. Dinner would be similar to lunch.

There was a 45-minute time limit for finishing every meal and if you refused food outright, or even just messed around with it, they would use the replacing rule that was so familiar to me.

The nurses didn't take any nonsense. Once, I said, 'Please, I really can't drink that milk with all that cream in it.'

'Deal with it,' the nurse snapped back.

They wouldn't even let me know how much I weighed, making me stand backwards on the scales so I couldn't see the reading.

There was no camaraderie between the patients either. Everyone was out for themselves and anorexic competitiveness and bitchiness was at its worst.

It was shocking to see how sick some of the adults were. There were women with really high-powered jobs being sick in paper bags and ex-junkies wandering around. Then there were other women in their 40s with kids, sitting sobbing as the nurses just walked past them. Other women had been banged up in there for years.

The whole place was vile but something there must have worked for me because I complied. There were no tantrums and I ate everything put in front of me.

The whole experience showed me how horrific those adult units are and made me determined not to spend the rest of my life yo-yoing in and out of them. I knew that mentally I'd left all that shit behind me and this was just a temporary relapse. I'd grown out of all this – I didn't need it any more.

253

And I hated being away from friends and family more than ever. I'd fought so hard to build myself a life in the outside world and I was in danger of losing it all over again.

But lurking at the back of my mind was another huge reason to comply. I knew that if I refused or acted up, they had the option of sectioning me – legally holding me against my will. And if they did that I'd be locked up in there for a minimum of six months and possibly for ever.

After two weeks at the Bethlem Royal I was eating sensibly again. I'd just needed a kick in the right direction. But I couldn't bear another moment in there and when my doctor appeared at the edge of my bed on ward round, I announced that I was discharging myself.

I knew I had made good progress, so they no longer had grounds for sectioning me, and on 9 July, a fortnight after I'd arrived, I walked out of the door.

As I sat in the back seat of a cab on the way home, I swore to myself: I am *never* going back into one of those places again.

And until now – touch wood – I haven't.

Back home I made some tough decisions. As much as I loved dancing I knew that for me it was too dangerous to pursue professionally, so I reduced it to a couple of evening classes and made it into a hobby instead.

Then I enrolled at college in Harrow to study for an NVQ in beauty therapy. I'd always loved beauty products and make-up and the course seemed perfect for me. At the same time I got a part-time job working on the Clarins counter at John Lewis in Watford.

I loved doing my NVQ – it felt like I was making up for all the school time I had missed out on. When I finished college I was able to make the Clarins job full-time. But I was always getting into trouble and had five disciplinaries against me for chatting on the phone at work, chewing gum, wearing the wrong shoes and even sleeping and putting on fake tan while on duty! At the same time I had the highest sales in the region, so they kept me.

I was out most nights with my old friends from dance college, drinking, going to nightclubs and snogging boys. It felt like this was what I had worked so hard to get out of hospital for – to have a job, have a laugh and be normal. My eating was fine and I could even eat in public, so I'd have my breakfast and lunch in the canteen at work.

It was around then that I applied to go on *Blind Date*. After everything that had happened in my life, I felt a desperate need to achieve something special to make up for all the bad times. London Weekend Television's hit show seemed to offer a chance to do just that.

When I got through the audition and was chosen as a 'selector' I was so delighted. I felt really special, and that was good. I bought myself a fab gold-sequinned butterfly top and new jeans and turned up at the studios really hoping I might be about to meet the man of my dreams. But it didn't work quite like that.

Out of the three blokes answering my questions one really did seem as if he could be 'The One'. He was from Hertfordshire, which was nice and close to my home, and he spoke very nicely.

The first bloke I rejected was Scottish and ginger, so that was a result. The second was shorter than me with a shaved head and I never go for bald guys, so it was going well. Then the screen went back on the boy from Hertfordshire and I just thought, Oh God! But not in a good way. There was no substance to him whatsoever and

I just didn't find him attractive. We went on our date to Portugal for three nights but there was absolutely no funny business.

Weirdly, Natalie was waiting for a train about a year later when he came and sat next to her.

'Were you on *Blind Date*?' she asked him.

'Yes, I was,' he replied, obviously loving the fact someone had recognised him.

'Mmm, my sister Nikki picked you,' Nat replied.

Then, even more bizarrely, I bumped into him on holiday in Malia, Crete. But there was never going to be a 'big hat' day for Cilla!

I did come pretty close to marriage fairly soon afterwards, though, when I met my first true love, Chris Jakes, at a John Lewis Christmas party. He was really good-looking but most importantly he was incredibly caring and warm. He was out that night with his colleagues from a different firm. Within days I was head over heels in love with him.

A fortnight after we met he went on holiday with his family to Dubai for Christmas. I couldn't cope without him and after two days I rang his Mum and said, 'I can't live without him over Christmas. I'm going to fly over to see him.' And I did.

A lot of people will think that is just bonkers but it was love. For six months I didn't tell Chris anything about my childhood or my anorexia – I needed him to think I was normal. But when I finally told him my whole story he couldn't have been more supportive.

One of the side effects of my anorexia is that I have deprived my body of oestrogen – the female sex hormone – and as a result I never have periods and don't find sex enjoyable. When I was with Chris I was taking hormone supplements, which meant I could even enjoy sleeping with him, and for the best part of a year everything was good.

But then I started feeling he was being too nice and I felt a bit suffocated. He wanted to marry me but I wasn't sure about that kind of commitment. I realised I was treating him like shit and he was letting me get away with it.

When I ended our relationship I broke his heart and I feel bad about that because he is such a nice guy. But we're still good mates now.

Eventually I got the push from John Lewis for being just too naughty but Clarins still wanted me, so they moved me to Debenhams and I loved it there too.

The only difficult area in my life was Mum's new boyfriend, Rory. She had split up with Tony soon after I came out of Rhodes Farm. Apparently they'd been growing apart for a while and it can't have been easy for him coping with me and Natalie. We'd both been pretty mean to Tony at times but deep down we were really fond of him and the separation came as a shock.

This new bloke, from Mum's work, was just awful. He was only 27 and I felt that he hated me and Natalie. Things got a bit tense at home and I went to live with Dad for a while. But then we had a fall-out and he kicked me out. It was a bit complicated really because Natalie was then working locally as a home carer and had been living with Dad when I turned up one day with all my bags in the back of a cab. There was no room for all of us, so Nat moved back to Mum's.

But after Dad kicked me out I couldn't turf Natalie out of a room again by moving back to Mum's and we were getting on so badly again I knew we wouldn't survive long under the same roof. One night we had a massive row after my friend wouldn't get off Natalie's computer and it ended up with us physically fighting. I got on top of her and was pulling her hair, then she kicked me and broke a rib.

My bones are very fragile because of my osteoporosis caused by anorexia but it didn't stop me getting into scraps with Natalie.

Another time we went to Lyme Regis with Mum, and Natalie threw my towel out of a window. It ended up with me chasing her with a kitchen knife.

There was still so much anger and jealousy between both of us and the merest incident brought it all tumbling out. Natalie was still mad that Mum had dedicated so much time and attention to me when I was ill and I was mad at her that she'd been at home with Mum while I was banged up year after year with a load of nutcases.

So all in all we decided it was best for me to find my own place and I went on the council list for accommodation. They found me a room in a hostel-type block with communal shower and kitchen areas. I was there for a year and a half and it was awful.

The shared areas were filthy. Sometimes I'd walk in the bathroom and there would be bloody sanitary towels stuffed behind the radiator and used razor blades lying on the floor. Some of the children even pooed in the back garden.

My bedroom was damp and at one point the whole place became infested with cockroaches – they were there for three days before the pest-control team turned up.

One night someone tried to force their way into my room. Terrified, I just lay there rigid under my duvet until they gave up and went away. Another time I had to lie and listen as a guy beat up his wife. I could her head being banged against the wall.

With all my OCD issues it was a nightmare and I ended up cooking most of my meals and taking showers at Mum's flat.

I signed on with an employment agency which got me work on beauty counters in all sort of different stores, including House of Fraser and Harrods. Working in the West End was brilliant – I loved the buzz of it.

Then I rented my own flat really near to Mum's and Carly moved in with me. We were both in control of our eating and things couldn't have been better. The two of us started going out in London virtually every single night. We had such good times. I'd go out straight from work and often carry on partying until it was time to go into work again the following morning.

There was a club circuit and I was definitely on it: Funky Buddha on a Tuesday, Chinawhite on a Wednesday, the Embassy on a Thursday, Faces on a Sunday and 195 in Epping on a Saturday.

Carly and I were living the teenage years we had both missed out on when we were behind the closed doors of institutions. Drinking and partying were a great release for us – when we were out we forgot about anything other than having fun. It became addictive and you felt that if you hadn't been out, you must have missed something.

It was a pretty tacky scene, though. All the clubs were swilling with cocaine, everyone was doing it and soon I was too. It was the only thing that could keep everyone partying all night after working all day and I was soon taking line after line, night after night.

But I never felt I was becoming addicted and I never bought it. I didn't need to, as there were so many sleazy blokes happy to offer it to me and my mates for free. And I was drinking obscene amounts of vodka (with a slimline mixer!) and champagne.

In the clubs I started hanging around with all the glamour model girls who were in there every night trying to bag themselves a footballer. I even managed to pull a couple myself! The only difference for me was that I was never interested in one-night stands because I'd stopped taking hormone pills and my sex drive was virtually non-existent.

The glamour girls opened up the whole modelling world to me and I decided to give it a try. I was travelling over an hour each way every day to Harrods to stand there holding a bottle of perfume for seven hours for £70. It was soul-destroying and I thought anything had to be better than that.

Loads of bosses of model agencies hung around in the clubs and when one guy gave me the chance to do a photo shoot I jumped at it. I really enjoyed the work and after spending years thinking I looked physically disgusting it was great to have people tell me I looked good.

But I was so naive. When photographers said things like, 'You should do topless, Nikki, it'll be good for your portfolio,' I believed them.

I would keep my knickers on for the shoots, but then they were airbrushed out afterwards. I always felt uncomfortable about those shoots but I went along with it anyway, hoping one day it might lead to the front cover of *Vogue*.

My pictures were used in men's mags like *Loaded*, *Nuts* and *Zoo* a few times and it was nice to think people liked the way I looked. But all in all the whole experience was pretty sleazy and depressing.

When you're a kid you think modelling is all about glamorous fashion shoots in Paris or Milan. But more often than not the reality was being leered at by a middle-aged sleazeball clutching a camera in his sweaty hands in a dingy room on an industrial estate in Hackney.

One glamour model was always running around Chinawhite on a Wednesday and one night she said to me, 'I've got you the best modelling job ever. It's £150 an hour and all you have to do is wear a pair of big knickers.'

It sounded too good to be true – and it was.

A couple of days later I trailed down to Kent with this girl for one of the worst days of my life. We arrived at this studio and the whole set-up was so sordid I felt sick. I had to wear big knickers and a school uniform, then pull my skirt up. Then I had to frolic around with this girl as if we were lesbians.

I hated myself for doing that and I hated myself for being so stupid. I was angry too, because I hadn't worked this hard to build myself a life out of hospital only to spend it doing porn shoots for dirty old men.

Fairly soon afterwards, in 2005, I was approached by another woman in a nightclub with another offer which seemed too good to be true. And yes, it was again. And yes, I still fell for it. 'I run an agency for high-powered businessmen who need bright young women to accompany them to corporate events and you would be just perfect,' she told me. 'You could earn £500 for just going along for an hour's lunch. And it would be brilliant for your modelling career.'

261

My mouth nearly hit the floor at the mention of all that money. I didn't have to be asked twice.

The first job she sent me on wasn't quite what I had been expecting. I was told to go to a party in a house in Shoreditch, in the East End, and ask for a man called Pete. It seemed fairly straightforward, but when I arrived it was total chaos. There was graffiti all over the walls, bloody needles on the floor, a filthy sofa and tables with legs missing. The kitchen was a bombsite and spaced-out people were wandering aimlessly from room to room.

In the middle of it all I saw the 'Pete' I was looking for – Kate Moss's then recent ex and Britain's most famous crack-cocaine user, Pete Doherty. He was wandering around the room heating up crack. I couldn't believe my eyes. I'd been a really big fan of his band, the Libertines, so I'd read all about his chaotic lifestyle, but being up close to it was truly shocking.

'Hi,' he said hazily when I introduced myself. 'Do you want to watch a film? It's my favourite – in French.'

'Er, do you speak French then?' I replied awkwardly.

'No.'

We both laughed. His teeth were covered in a yellow fur, his face was pale and there were massive dark bags around his eyes. His fingernails were caked in filth.

'Would you like any crack?' he said as if offering a cup of tea.

'No thanks,' I replied.

We talked for a bit and he told me how sometimes he got so depressed he couldn't leave his bedroom. He reminded me of myself years before – a lost soul.

After an hour spent chatting I said I had to leave and he

offered me a lift home. Outside he had two old Jags and a black London cab.

We tried to get in one of the Jags but he had the wrong key so we went back upstairs to look for the right one. But instead he got his guitar out and started strumming away. 'Seriously, I've got to go,' I said.

Finally, amid the chaos, he found his keys but still the engine wouldn't start. 'We'll take my cab,' he said. So it was back indoors to find the key – except this time he turned on the stereo and started dancing around to 'Penny Lane'.

'Honestly, I'll get the bus,' I said.

He wanted my phone number but I told him the woman from the agency had said I couldn't give it out under any circumstances. I said he could have my email address, though. He searched around everywhere for a pen but couldn't find one, so eventually he picked up one of his blood-stained needles and wrote it with that.

Then he kissed me on the lips – no tongues – and off I went.

By the time I got away I'd been there two hours – and earned £800. And I'd have paid someone to let me meet Pete Doherty!

My next job was at a big posh lunch with a middle-aged businessman. The meal was incredible and I got really pissed on the champagne. And at the end of it I was presented with £500. Happy days!

'I've found this most amazing job,' I told Carly one night. 'You've got to do it. I'll show you the website and you could join too.'

I hadn't looked at the agency's website before but I typed its name into Google and waited for the home page to open. But when it popped up on the screen, my excitement instantly turned to horror. There on the home page were pictures of me wearing a basque and suspenders and underneath was written: 'Bonnie – £1,000 a night.' I felt sick.

I'd given the woman some of my modelling shots because she said she wanted to see them – but I had no idea she would do this with them. Clearly she was lining me up as a hooker. There was no way that was going to happen. I could scarcely bring myself to have sex with boyfriends, let alone total strangers.

I rang the woman immediately. 'I don't want to do this any more,' I said. 'I couldn't have sex with strange men and if my mum and dad found out about your website it would be awful. Please take the pictures down immediately.'

And I went back to holding up bottles of perfume all day in Harrods for £70. It was still soul-destroying but at least it was safe. Besides, I already had a new plan to achieve my dream of doing something special – my application to appear on *Big Brother*.

CHAPTER 21
BIG BROTHER

I'd already applied to *Big Brother* once but hadn't been selected. On my application form I'd told them the whole grim story of my illness and the years away from home and they probably read it and dropped it like a hot potato.

So when I decided to apply again for the 2006 series I knew this time I had to hide everything about my anorexia if I was to stand any chance of getting selected. Open auditions were being held in Wembley towards the end of 2005 and I persuaded Carly to come along with me for moral support.

By the time we arrived, it was already mid-afternoon. We joined a queue which seemed to stretch for miles and waited our turn. I was supposed to be meeting another friend at five o'clock. She was dating a footballer and we were going up to Sheffield for the weekend to see him and his mate, who I really fancied.

As it got closer and closer to five o'clock and then

passed it, my friend kept ringing me, increasingly frantic that I hadn't shown up.

'I think I'd better just go,' I said to Carly. 'This guy in Sheffield is really fit and I'll never get chosen for *Big Brother* anyway.'

Another five minutes went by and my friend kept on ringing my mobile.

'That's it, I'm going,' I told Carly. 'I can't keep her waiting any longer.' And at that exact moment I was called in front of the judging panel.

'Right, you've got one minute to say why you should go into the *Big Brother* house,' a producer shouted in my direction.

And then my phone rang again. It was my friend going mad that I still hadn't shown up. So I spent the first 30 seconds of my precious minute on the phone to her, telling her to calm down and go without me.

By the time I came off the phone, all I had time to say was, 'My name's Nikki, I just love going out and I love money and I love Essex.'

I haven't got a clue what I was talking about and I don't even come from Essex but a woman from the production team stamped my hand and said, 'You're through.' I nearly collapsed!

Months later the Executive Producer, Phil Edgar-Jones, told me he'd decided I was through to the next round from the first moment I opened my mouth.

Next I had a minute in a mock diary room in which I had to talk about myself. I remember saying, 'I want to be rich and I want to never have to work again and I want to go out for lunch and get my nails done every day.'

I was totally superficial but to be honest that is

exactly what I was like at that stage. I was hanging around with all those awful people in those West End nightclubs and all I wanted was to marry a rich footballer and have that lifestyle.

That night I went home so excited. Deep down I had a feeling I was going to be accepted.

For weeks after that nothing happened at all. Then finally I got a phone call from Endemol, the production company which makes *Big Brother*, asking me to come and see them. At the meeting they asked me what kind of things I enjoyed doing and all about my family and my job. But any questions about my childhood I neatly avoided – or simply lied.

The audition process went on for six months. I had home visits, medical checks, reference checks and psychiatric checks. Luckily I was an old hand at telling psychiatrists what they wanted to hear.

As for the home visit, they came round when Mum was on holiday and so they just met Carly at my flat instead, and she already knew not to mention anything about anorexia. Then a couple of the producers came on one of my nights out at Chinawhite, to see what I was like in a group.

I hadn't told anyone in the world apart from Mum and Carly that I'd applied for *Big Brother*, so I had to tell my friends that the two blokes were a long-lost cousin and his mate. I didn't tell anyone else that I'd applied because once one person knew, everyone would know. And I wanted this to be my secret.

As well as face-to-face interviews there were endless phone calls asking me more questions about myself, but whatever they asked I never let anything slip about my anorexia. I was a reasonable weight at the time, so there was no reason why they would have guessed.

The night before my twenty-fourth birthday I went on a big night out with a group of friends. Somehow we got separated and I lost them. They had my door keys, so when I got home to my flat in the early hours I couldn't get in and had to go round to Mum's.

The next day I was tired, hung-over and still in my clothes from the night before when my phone rang.

'Hi, Nikki,' said the woman on the other end. 'I'm Claire O'Donohue, Executive Producer at *Big Brother*.'

By then I knew enough about how things worked to take a big gasp when I heard the words 'Executive Producer'. I certainly knew one of those wouldn't be bothering to ring me if it was just another umpteen questions about my favourite colours and star sign. I sat down slowly on the edge of the chair, my hands beginning to tremble.

'I'm delighted to tell you,' she went on, 'you've been selected as a housemate.'

I screamed. And screamed. And screamed. It was the best news I'd ever had – ever.

'What, do you mean an actual housemate? Not just a standby?' I asked when I finally came back to my senses.

'Yes, an actual housemate,' she laughed. 'We need you to meet a chaperone at Sloane Square station at eight o'clock on Monday morning. And bring plenty of clothes – you'll be away from home for a while.'

When I put the phone down I could feel charges of electricity pulsing through my body. Mum and I hugged and screamed and hugged some more. At last I was going to achieve something special after all the awful things I'd been through. And something that would stick two fingers up at all the people who'd made fun of me in the past and thought I'd never amount to anything.

I also hoped it would help me challenge some of my demons, particularly my OCD problems. By throwing myself into an incredibly difficult situation I might emerge stronger.

In the heat of all that excitement and hope, I was thinking, This is the moment my life changes. And it was.

That evening Mum and I were due to meet all my friends for a curry. They were all late as they were still hung-over from the previous evening. Mum and I sat in the restaurant waiting for them, squeezing each other's leg in excitement, barely able to believe the adventure I was embarking upon.

That was a Friday, which meant I had just two days to prepare to meet the chaperone who would be minding me for the fortnight until filming began. I spent the whole weekend shopping, looking for an entire new wardrobe to take with me into the house – including my arrival and eviction outfits.

I had the idea of going into the house dressed as a Playboy Bunny – I was determined to make an instant impression and that seemed the perfect way. I bought myself a pink corset and fishnet stockings from La Senza and some bunny ears from Clare's Accessories. I couldn't help but grin when I thought how it would look in the newspaper pictures.

On the Sunday evening Mum came round to my flat to say goodbye.

'The next time you see me, Mum, I'll be coming down

the stairs at the *Big Brother* house,' I said as we stood hugging in my hall. We were both crying.

Next morning I felt like a spy on a secret mission as I stood outside Sloane Square tube station looking for a woman called Anna Dunkley, a *Big Brother* researcher. When she came up to me and introduced herself, we got into a car and went straight to a nearby Holiday Inn, where we spent the rest of the day.

First there was a photo shoot for our official *Big Brother* pictures, then I had to fill in a mammoth questionnaire about everything you could imagine. What would my epitaph be? What was the most recent argument I'd had? The most upsetting moment I'd ever had? The happiest moment I'd ever had?

Then we spent the rest of the day eating, sleeping and just hanging around.

There was no phone in the room and Anna took my mobile from me too. The production team were terrified about the press finding out where we were, so security was paramount. And I wasn't allowed magazines, newspapers or even a television because they didn't want us to know anything about what was going on in the outside world.

I wasn't even permitted to step outside the room as other housemates were staying in the same hotel and we couldn't be allowed to meet before arriving in the house.

It all felt really weird, but I was used to weird environments and I'd spent years sitting around doing nothing in particular.

The next morning we got into Anna's car and headed south to Dover. We were off to Belgium. I guess it was a strange place to take me but if they were looking for somewhere remote where there was no chance I would bump into anyone I knew or be found by the press, then the Belgian countryside was the place.

Anna and I had a wicked time. We stayed in a really remote three-bedroom farmhouse which was part of an old castle. Cows were grazing in the fields outside but there was nothing else for miles all around.

We joined a gym and a video shop in the nearest town and hired videos every night as I wasn't allowed to watch television. We went to theme parks, hired bikes for the day and went shopping in Brussels and Bruges.

One day there was a carnival in the local town and we had a brilliant time watching everyone singing and dancing. And one night we went to see a band play there and we got really drunk on cherry beer.

It was one of the best holidays I'd ever had. Although it was like a girlie trip, I was still aware that at no time could I let my guard down to Anna, and I never let slip anything about my anorexia and childhood.

We took it in turns to cook and I ate quite well, although after just a day my OCD became apparent when I kept having to wash my plate before every meal.

'Do you think you'll be OK in the house if you get like that,' Anna asked me seriously. 'Oh, I'll be fine,' I breezed. 'You'd be amazed what I could cope with.' She would have been amazed too!

Towards the end of our two-week stay we both got a bit bored and began bickering. I really missed Mum and was desperate to speak to her. Although I'd been away from home for most of my childhood and teens, I'd never gone a fortnight without speaking to her and it was killing me.

Sometimes I'd look at Anna's phone lying on the table while she was in the shower. A quick phone call to Mum wouldn't hurt, I'd think. *Big Brother* would never find out. But if anyone had discovered where I was then, I would be instantly thrown off the show and I wouldn't risk that, so I never picked up the phone.

Every day we had to film clips for the show reel about each housemate which is screened just before their arrival. But I was rarely in the mood for filming and would throw a tantrum at the thought of having to put make-up on and get ready. I must have driven poor Anna mad.

Another problem was that my right eye became seriously inflamed and I had to go to hospital. I'd cut it months earlier on a sheet of paper when I was working in Harrods. Whenever I got stressed, it flared up and in Belgium it became so bad it became incredibly swollen. By the time we returned to Britain it was going down but I was still terrified about entering the house with a massive swollen eye.

As the ferry docked at Dover and we drove off the ramp on to the terminal, Anna made me lie on the back seat of the car with a blanket over my head. And as we approached London I stayed hidden in case any photographers spotted me. It sounds like something out of a spy film, but every single newspaper was desperate to discover the identities of the housemates and the show's producers weren't prepared to take any risks.

What I didn't realise was that my name had already been in the newspapers in Britain as someone thought to be going into the *Big Brother* house.

I'd left Mum with instructions to tell anyone who wondered where I was that I had gone on holiday to Tunisia. But it didn't fool everyone. At that time I was on guest lists for different clubs every night of the week and saw the same people all the time. So when I disappeared off the face of the earth a lot of people noticed. I think a couple of them must have put two and two together and rung the newspapers.

When Mum opened her paper one morning and saw my name printed there she nearly collapsed from shock. Then she had to lie her teeth off as she knew if she gave the game away I'd be pulled from the show.

Mum even lied to Dad and Natalie, saying I'd gone to Tunisia on a late holiday deal with some of my dancing friends.

Dad says he was never convinced because he'd known Mum long enough to know when she was lying. And he knew that going on *Big Brother* would be my dream come true. But Natalie believed her. I don't think she thought Mum would lie to her like that. Dad took Nat to one side and told her what he had guessed, but I think she chose to believe he had got it wrong. For her it was too horrific to contemplate that I might really be going on *Big Brother* and creating even more disruption for our family just as things were getting back on an even keel.

Back in London, Anna drove me to a Holiday Inn at Brent Cross. There I had another medical check but it was pretty routine and they didn't pick up on any of my former problems. I saw the psychiatrist again too, but again I sailed through it. I had all my answers off pat.

The next morning I was woken up at 6am and driven to Elstree Studios, just north of London. There I was shown into a dressing room and told to change into a dressing gown while my suitcase was taken away to be delivered to the *Big Brother* house. The case was checked over and over again just to ensure I hadn't tried to smuggle in anything that was forbidden in the house.

Apart from clothes and toiletries, you could take in five photographs and I had included my favourite snaps of Mum, Dad, Natalie, Carly and another friend at the time. Those pictures were such a comfort to me on bad days inside the house.

That day before we entered the house was so strange. I was exhausted because I hadn't slept the night before and I lay down a couple of times to get a few minutes' rest but then my mind would start whirring again and I'd be unable to drift off.

The production crew were popping in and out all day too, filming segments for *Big Brother's Little Brother*.

As the hours rolled by before we would enter the house at 9pm, every second dragged. For the first time I sat there feeling utterly terrified about what I'd let myself in for.

I knew loads of stuff was likely to come out in the newspapers – all about my anorexia, ex-boyfriends and probably even my modelling career. But that didn't really bother me. This was my chance to turn my life around. To seize it back after all that time stuck in the gutter and transform it into something amazing.

I had to have the stereo in my dressing room turned up really loud so that I couldn't hear any of the other housemates who were in other dressing rooms down the corridor. And if I even wanted to leave the dressing room to use the loo, I had to go with a member of staff and wear a plain white mask in case I bumped into any of the other housemates.

At about six o'clock I started getting ready and climbed into my pink corset, fishnet tights, black, peep-toe stilettos and pink bunny ears, then I carefully did my hair and put on my make-up.

As the time crept closer to 9pm I was finally allowed out of the dressing room and into the limo which was going to drive me on the 30-second trip to the official entrance to the *Big Brother* house.

When the car drew to a halt, one of the *Big Brother* minders opened the door and I stepped out of the car to the loudest barrage of screaming and shouting I'd ever heard. 'Nikki, Nikki,' people all around me were yelling. I kept looking, thinking they must be people I knew, but they were total strangers. I couldn't work out how they knew my name as I hadn't realised Davina McCall had just announced my arrival as last housemate of the night.

I felt like Angelina Jolie at a film premiere. It was so overwhelming seeing all those people looking at me and screaming my name. I waved and stared, totally overcome by it all, and gradually I made my way up the red carpet to Davina, who took my hand and guided me up the stairs to the doors of the house.

For a couple of seconds I stood there, breathless with excitement, before the doors swung back and I stepped into my new life.

Then the doors slammed shut behind me. So here I was. Finally, inside the *Big Brother* house, being watched by five million people from every imaginable angle.

A couple of minutes earlier, 15 miles away at home, Natalie had been curled up on the sofa watching a Jimmy McGovern drama on BBC1. Then the phone rang.

It was Natalie's godmother, Julie. 'Are you watching it?' she asked urgently.

'Watching what?' replied Natalie.

'Oh,' said Julie, suddenly realising Natalie had no idea what was unfolding. 'I think you should turn over to Channel 4 – your sister has just walked into the *Big Brother* house.'

Lunging across the room for the remote control, Natalie changed channels just in time to see me standing at the top of the stairs waving at the thousands of people who had gathered below. She said afterwards that all she felt at that moment was pure horror.

Natalie hated *Big Brother* anyway and loathed the idea of all the public scrutiny of our family which would inevitably follow my appearance.

But nothing could have been further from my mind. Inside the house I tiptoed down the stairs and into the kitchen, where all the other housemates were already standing chatting.

At first it was a horrible feeling, like arriving stone-cold sober at a party where you don't know anyone at all. I looked around the room and couldn't see anyone I fancied – or even anyone I could imagine being friends with.

But I guess everyone else must have been equally nervous because we all chatted manically for hours through a mixture of excitement and terror.

The most commonly asked question about *Big Brother* is, 'Are you aware of the cameras all the time?' For the first two or three hours I was and felt I had to be on my best behaviour, but after that I totally forgot about them for the rest of my stay. If you didn't forget about them and tried to think about everything you said and didin advance to make sure you always looked good, you'd go utterly demented.

And it didn't bother me being watched all the time at all. I was used to it after spending months and months on total supervision, so having no privacy wasn't a problem for me.

I did find claustrophobia a struggle in the first few days, though. At that time I was used to going out every single night, so being stuck in one place day and night for days on end was really tough.

But after the first week I became institutionalised all over again – and I didn't miss the outside world one bit.

Back at home things weren't so jolly. When Mum returned from Elstree Studios that first night, Natalie wouldn't even let her in the house because she was so mad she hadn't told her I was going on *Big Brother*.

And already, stretching all down the road, there was a line of cars full of reporters and photographers trying to find out any nugget of information about me. *Big Brother* had sent an advice pack to families about how to deal with press enquiries but it was still daunting for Mum, and Natalie even more, to find themselves thrust into the spotlight like that.

It took Natalie weeks to adjust to my being in the *Big Brother* house. For her it was bad history repeating itself. After years of working to gain her own identity she was back to being 'Nikki Grahame's sister'. Everywhere she went people only wanted to talk about me and she felt Mum was focusing all her attention on me again, dropping everything to make sure she was around on eviction nights and spending all her spare time glued to the live feeds on E4.

It nearly pushed Natalie over the edge and she went a bit off the rails until finally she got the sack from her job as a receptionist.

But I was unaware of any of that. Once you're in the *Big Brother* house you could be on the moon, you are so disconnected from the rest of the world.

For me it was just like those years in hospitals and eating-disorders units all over again.

I was certainly used to sitting around isolated from the rest of the world with nothing to do. I'd done that for years in different institutions. And I was used to living in communal groups, so I never felt bothered by the lack of privacy.

There was always someone to talk to in the house, or a conversation that you could join in with. The tasks were fun and every night was a party. I absolutely loved it.

On top of that there were none of the stresses of the outside world to deal with. They provided all the food, there were no bills and no job to turn up for every morning. It was like a holiday camp and I could have lived there for ever.

The only downside was how nasty and bitchy people could be to one another. I quickly realised it was a very false environment and that people could be acting as your friend one moment, then nominating you for eviction the next. I could always tell if someone had nominated me because they couldn't look me in the eye. But it was still tough to come to terms with. I'd struggled for years with low self-esteem and having people explain publicly what they thought was wrong with me was never easy.

Most of what they said, though, I only discovered after I came out of the house and saw some of the recorded clips. Perhaps it was for the best that I didn't know when I was in there.

At first I stuck with Leah, a model and mother figure, Richard, a gay Canadian, and Glynn, a slightly gormless kid from Wales. The four of us really clicked and would laugh at the silliest things for hours on end.

Then, about halfway through my first week, it hit me out of the blue – I'd fallen in love.

CHAPTER 22
THE MAGIC AND THE MISERY

Pete Bennett was warm and gentle, with a spiritual side to him. I could tell he had been one of life's underdogs and outsiders because I had too. He suffered from Tourette's Syndrome – a disorder which meant he had uncontrollable tics and verbal outbursts – and I'd had anorexia. Because of this, of all the housemates in *Big Brother*, I could relate best to him. I felt close to him from the very beginning.

One day we were sitting in the house and Pete told me that he had seen his friend die when he was electrocuted on a railway line. It had clearly had a terrible impact on him and I thought, This guy is special, he really is. From then on we spent loads of time together and I totally fell for him.

Nothing ever happened between us before I was evicted from the house but it was clear to everyone that we really liked each other as we'd spend hours talking about our lives and thoughts.

I even told Pete a little about my anorexia, although I didn't mention it to anyone else in the house. My eating in there was fine so long as I was able to carry on exercising, which I did by pacing up and down on a step in the house.

But my OCD remained an issue. I had to wash my own plate and cutlery before eating and I wrote my name on a mug in nail varnish so no one else would use it.

'I'm just a bit funny about germs,' I explained to the other housemates one morning. I didn't want to tell them everything about my life but I needed them to be aware of my problems as we were all living together so closely.

My tantrums and histrionics, which Mum and Natalie had been subjected to week in week out at home, quickly became a national entertainment. I became the most talked-about contestant in *Big Brother* history.

My diary-room outbursts, shouting, crying and throwing my arms and body around in that huge, gold padded chair, were getting record viewing figures for the show. I was being discussed in newspapers and on radio shows even though I was only behaving the same as I always did.

We'd been in the house four weeks when a new arrival, Susie Verrico, nominated me for eviction. I was furious and went into the diary room to vent my anger. 'Who is she?' I kept yelling at the camera, flinging my arms around in outrage. 'Who is she?' Even now people come up to me in the street and say how funny it was.

Another time we had to do a task where we had to dance for as long as we possibly could wearing masks and mp3 players – except mine wouldn't work. I went mad about it and when they called to the diary room I became hysterical because I thought I was being disqualified.

People who watched it tell me it was hilarious – but that is really just the way I am when things are going wrong for me.

For another task we had to pretend to run a recruitment agency and I was the PA. I couldn't work out how to use the typewriter and that whole episode was pretty funny too.

But at other times in the diary room I was very low. When things were going wrong or I was feeling lonely or isolated in the house, my face would crumple and I'd start to cry, gasping for breath between each sob.

One day, I got into a rage when the air-conditioning kept getting turned down because I'm very susceptible to cold and I was absolutely freezing. I was crying and really upset because being that cold is really painful for me.

A lot of people watching must have thought I was a total prima donna making such a fuss about air-conditioning, but things like that can really get to me and when I start to feel down, my mood spirals out of control.

People that I've spoken to since my time in the house have said that watching my outbursts on screen were a weird mixture of hugely entertaining and frightening. They were able to see I had an anger and frustration inside me which could build up to such a pitch that I would be unable to control it and it would physically overtake my body.

But then soon after I'd be laughing, dancing and singing all around the house again. One minute I could be acting like a petulant child and the next I was showing genuine feeling for Pete. And one minute I'd be dancing and laughing my head off and the next I would be screaming and throwing myself around the house. Or worse, sobbing silently in the diary room.

I think that is what the viewers found extraordinary about me – that I could change so much and there were such extremes of emotion which could spill out in such a violent fashion at the slightest provocation. They also responded to the parts of my personality which are still quite childlike. I'm aware of that but it's just the way I am, probably because I was deprived of the opportunity to grow up naturally like other kids and so bits of my character are still stuck at the point before I got sick.

While we were in the house we had to come up with one word which we thought described ourselves. 'Special,' I said, and that label stuck with me. The weird thing is that I'd never felt special in my whole life before *Big Brother*. I'd never felt I fitted in or belonged anywhere really until then. But finally I did.

And I think 'special' is a pretty accurate description of me really – I'm certainly unique.

I'm sure some people think I faked those tantrums and hysterical outbursts for the cameras, but that really was me. Mum and Natalie (who calmed down after a couple of weeks and agreed to watch it) say they could always see one of my fits of temper or crying coming on screen long before the other housemates had realised what was about to be unleashed. And although they found it entertaining on the good days, it was deeply distressing for them on the days when I was obviously low.

I was nominated for eviction five times and each time was a huge blow to my confidence and took me longer and longer to bounce back from. It was just so hard knowing that people I had thought of as friends actually wanted me out of there.

When stories came out in the press about my anorexia

there was criticism of Endemol, the production company, for selecting me and endangering my 'fragile mental state'. But it wasn't their fault – I'd lied to them about my past. Besides, I didn't feel mentally fragile at all – I was having the time of my life.

Mum also came under attack in the media for letting me go into the house, but there was never anything she could have done to stop me. From the moment I applied it was my dream to be selected and there is no way I would have let her stand in the way of that.

Being in the house was everything I had ever dreamed of – and more. There were parties and tasks and fun. And, of course, I loved being with Pete.

Then, around the seventh week, my ankle and foot became so swollen from doing my daily stepping exercise that I was walking around limping. I had to go to the diary room to see a doctor and he advised me I had to rest my foot. And as soon as I stopped exercising I rapidly felt I was losing control of the entire situation and began feeling very oppressed by the house. It got me down and I became preoccupied and withdrawn, unable to interact with the other housemates. I started eating less and less at mealtimes and could feel things sliding away from me.

After a few days I went into the diary room and begged them to let me have a cross-trainer so I could exercise. At first they wouldn't do it but by then I was crying and begging for any means to exercise. 'If you don't let me exercise, I'll leave,' I cried. 'I'll have to walk out.'

Then I told the *Big Brother* people everything – all about my life and the anorexia and the obsessive need to exercise. I didn't know whether Endemol would go mad at me for not having told them earlier, but I was beyond caring. I just desperately needed to exercise.

They listened to everything I had to say and were really supportive and promised to sort things out for me. There wasn't a single word of reprimand for not having been honest with them. And they didn't televise that diary-room conversation either, which was a huge relief.

Each time I was up for eviction Mum would travel to the house and wait outside with all the thousands of fans. She was really missing me and although she wanted me to stay in there for as long as possible, she was desperate to see me again too. I missed Mum badly as well.

On Day 58, when I was nominated for eviction for the fifth time, I was finally voted out of the house with 37.2 per cent of the public vote.

'And the seventh housemate to be evicted,' Davina said in her most dramatic voice, 'is...' – and then there was a pause that seemed to last a lifetime – '...Nikki.'

At first I couldn't believe it. I'd known for weeks that it was a possibility but now my dream was over it came as a horrible shock. I desperately hadn't wanted it all to end. And the thought of leaving Pete was agony.

None of the other housemates could believe it either and they all gathered around me, hugging me and saying how shocked they were.

I changed into my eviction outfit – denim hotpants and a white blouse – and prepared to leave the house. Then, shortly before I had to walk out of the door, I suffered a panic attack, hyperventilating and crying uncontrollably. I'd heard the crowd booing when other housemates had been evicted before and I was terrified they would do that to me. What if they throw things at me? I thought. And what if Mum isn't there to meet me?

Again, just like at the point of leaving all those other institutions and hospitals I'd endured earlier in my life, suddenly the thought of facing the outside world was terrifying.

I kissed everyone goodbye, before a final hug with Pete which I never wanted to end. It was so sad leaving him there in the house and not knowing when I would see him again.

Finally I summoned up all my strength and climbed the stairs out of the house and waited for the double doors to shoot open to reveal the outside world once more. When they opened I was nearly knocked sideways by the noise. On my way into the house the screaming and shouting had been loud but this time it was utterly overwhelming.

I stood paralysed at the top of the stairs, initially unable to work out if they were booing or cheering me. Too scared to walk down the steps towards that throng of people, I just wanted to go back into the house, where I knew everyone and where I felt I belonged now.

But in front of me were thousands of people shouting, 'Nik-ki, Nik-ki,' and everywhere I looked they were waving and holding placards with my picture on them. I just couldn't understand what all these people were doing and why they were screaming for me.

Then I saw a banner which said, 'Nikki to win,' and I thought, I've blown it. Winning *Big Brother* would have been my chance to change my life but I've blown it and I'm going home.

I started crying from all the extremes of emotion and really didn't know what to do. I put my hands over my face, wanting to hide myself from the madness in front of me.

In the end Davina had to come up the stairs and pull me out of the doorway and down the steps away from the house. All the way I was desperately scanning the crowd, searching for a glance of Mum, but I couldn't see her anywhere.

At the bottom of the steps we walked through the *Big Brother* fans and the throng of photographers all trying to get a snap of me for the next morning's papers.

Then we reached the stage and I sat down opposite Davina to be interviewed about my time in the house. At the end of our chat they flashed up my 'best bits' on a huge screen behind me. I was overwhelmed as I saw myself in the house. Wow, I thought, this is what I have finally achieved. I've done all this and millions of people have watched it.

From the studios I was driven straight to Sopwell House, a beautiful hotel in St Albans, where I was told I'd meet my family, Carly and my other best friend, Alana.

It was a warm, mid-July night and when I jumped out of the car and knocked on the door of our apartment in the grounds of the hotel, I felt invincible. As if things could never get any better than this.

Mum opened the door and for a second we just stood there grinning at each other. Then we hugged and it felt like we would never, ever let go.

'I'm so proud of you,' Mum said.

And that is all I had ever wanted to hear. I had finally achieved something Mum could be proud of. Yes, I thought. I've done it.

Inside the apartment, Mum, Dad, Natalie and I all hugged each other so tight. It was incredible, all of us together again like that. For a moment it was as if the past 16 years and all that bad stuff had never happened.

288

Even Natalie had got over all her concerns about *Big Brother* and was delighted for me. She knew it had been my dream to do something special, and I'd turned it into a reality.

We sat up all night, chatting, drinking champagne and eating cakes and crisps. I finally fell asleep at 6.40 in the morning. Then Mum woke me at seven, telling me there had been a phone call and I had to get back to London for a meeting with my new agent. Agent? Me? I'd never felt so special in my life.

John Noel Management, a really well-respected agency which represents people like Davina McCall and Tess Daly, wanted to take me on.

When I turned up in their smart London offices a couple of hours later, they had a pile of interview requests from newspapers and magazines on the desk as well as offers of work and sponsorship opportunities.

It was while I was at the agent's offices that my phone started ringing again and again with a woman asking to speak to me 'urgently'. Mum finally took the call and when she came back in the room she was grim-faced.

'There has been a woman on the phone saying a story is about to come out in the papers saying you worked as a vice girl,' Mum said.

I tried to swallow but my throat suddenly felt totally dry.

'I've told her she must have got it wrong but she said I ought to speak to you. She is going to ring back. What is she talking about, Nikki?'

I put my head in my hands. Everything had been so magical, so perfect, surely someone wasn't about to ruin it all for me? Not when I hadn't even done anything wrong.

I knew the only thing that would save me was to tell

Mum everything. I told her all about the date with Pete Doherty and lunch with the businessman. Then, with my voice dropping, I told her about the day I'd found the pictures of myself in a basque on the agency's website.

When I'd finished the story, Mum just looked at me. Then she smiled. And then she hugged me. And I knew everything was going to be all right.

Mum said this woman was probably after money, trying to blackmail me, but we couldn't get involved with anything like that. She said we had to tell John Noel everything and he would know how best to manage the situation.

John's advice was simple: 'When you do your big newspaper interview just tell the truth. If you do that, it'll get the story out there and stop this woman and anyone else trying to sell stories about you.'

A couple of hours later I was sitting in a trendy, bright photographic studio for a shoot and interview with the *Sun* newspaper. They treated me like royalty, with champagne and chocolate waiting for me when I arrived.

I did exactly what John had told me and explained to the reporter all about my past – the anorexia, working for the agency and my modelling. It was a real relief to get all that stuff out in the open, because that way it could never hurt me in the future. And I loved the photo shoot – it was so exciting trying on all those lovely clothes and posing for the camera.

On the Monday morning I was staying in a hotel with Carly when our copy of the *Sun* arrived in our room. I picked it up and saw my picture all over the front page. It was like a dream.

The next couple of days I spent doing back-to-back

interviews and photographs with magazines, radio stations and televisions channels. I'd get up at 5am to do a radio interview, then the rest of the day it would be meetings about work projects or photo shoots.

The best shoot I did was for the cover of *Pop* magazine. A really high-fashion affair by candlelight at the Café Royal, it was amazing. No other *Big Brother* contestant had ever done that magazine before, so it was a great honour to be asked. I also did front covers for *New Woman* and *You* magazines, and they turned out wonderfully too.

In the evenings I was getting invited to functions with celebrities at nightclubs and posh restaurants. I went to the Cartier Polo tournament at Windsor Great Park and even the film premiere of *Miami Vice*, where I walked down the red carpet. People in the crowd were calling out, 'Nikki, Nikki,' and trying to take pictures of me like I was a movie star or something.

I had gone from feeling I didn't belong anywhere on earth and was a totally unimportant object to people stopping me in the street to tell me they loved me. It was beyond incredible.

One day I had to do an autograph-signing event at Carphone Warehouse's head office. When I stepped out of the car I was mobbed by three thousand people all taking pictures of me and trying to get my autograph. I couldn't handle it and freaked out. I'm sure some people thought I was turning into some kind of prima donna, but at times I really did find the attention overwhelming. For so long I'd felt so shit about myself that it was very difficult to get my head around the idea that this was for real and all these people weren't playing some huge joke at my expense.

And my phone never stopped ringing. I had to change my number six times because all sorts of people I hadn't seen for years or barely met came out of the woodwork. All of a sudden everyone wanted to be my best friend. But I wasn't totally naive and I knew what they were after – invitations to smart parties, new nightclubs and premieres. No, I knew my real friends were still the ones who had got on a bus and come round to visit me on the days when I'd been feeling low or sick.

I did 40 personal appearances in a row all over the country, from Scotland to Northern Ireland to Manchester and then on and on to other towns and cities. I lived in a car, going from one nightclub or shopping centre to the next. I'd be driven five and a half hours to somewhere like Aberystwyth, go to a hotel, fall asleep on the bed and then have to be woken up to go out to a nightclub where I'd have to do signings, have my picture taken with people and answer endless questions about *Big Brother*.

I was constantly having to get myself dolled up and step out with a smile on my face, even when I was exhausted.

Any spare moments I had, I'd be glued to watching the live feed of *Big Brother* on E4. I was desperately missing Pete and seeing him on television was the only way I could feel close to him again.

One night he was shown on screen pining for me. Thinking that he might just feel about me the same way I'd felt about him for weeks made me love him even more.

I'd been out of the *Big Brother* house four weeks when I got a phone call out of the blue from Endemol. Would I be interested in returning? They'd had an idea to give the closing stages of the series a twist by allowing the public the chance to vote four evicted housemates back into the 'house next door', a smaller new house adjoining the existing one. Then, after a week, one of the four would be selected to return to the main house.

I didn't have to be asked twice. I'd loved my time in the house so much I was desperate to get back in there. I was also delighted at the thought that I could be there on final night and even still in with a chance of winning the £100,000 prize. And of course there was the hope of seeing Pete again.

I had just one day to get myself ready and ran round in a flurry of excitement, packing clothes and saying my goodbyes before the public vote.

Sixty-three per cent of the voting public voted me back into the 'house next door' and I was utterly delighted. But it proved hard living there as it was even more suffocating than the original house, smaller, with no windows and absolutely nothing to do all day.

At the end of the week the remaining housemates in the main house had to decide which of the four of us in the 'house next door' they would select to join them. They all knew how much Pete had been missing me and so they chose me so that we could be together again.

As I stepped back into the main house six weeks after leaving it, I was walking on air at being given this incredible opportunity all over again.

Pete came up to me, wrapped his arms around me and for the first time kissed me full on the lips. It was the first time I could be sure that he really liked me and I knew then we were going to be together. I was so happy.

Back in the house, I was blissfully ignorant of the fact that *Big Brother* had been inundated with viewers complaining because they had changed the rules to let evicted housemates back onto the show.

Pete and I spent that week lying on his bed, cuddling and talking. I knew I'd fallen for him deeply. Some people think the producers were so worried that I might win, causing a public outcry about rule changing, that they deliberately put me in situations that caused me to have tantrums in that last week to annoy voters.

The atmosphere was electric inside the house on the final night. And outside more than eight million people across Britain were tuning in to watch what happened. When Davina called out my name I was really disappointed to be leaving again but at least this time I knew I'd be reunited with Pete within a couple of hours. When he did emerge – as winner of the show – I was delighted for him and so proud of him. The next few days were a whirlwind of interviews and public appearances for both of us.

Then, around that time, I started filming *Princess Nikki*, a series of programmes for Channel 4 in which I had to take on a string of really horrid jobs. The *Big Brother* producers had come up with the idea for the six-week series while I was still in the house. Apparently they'd been inspired by my working as a PA in the temping agency task in the house.

They knew from the way I reacted in there that I would find it really hard doing disgusting jobs and would inevitably throw tantrums when things got difficult. But that's what they wanted, as they knew it would make good TV.

Because of my OCD, *Princess Nikki* was very difficult for me. The jobs I had to do included working on a sewage farm, cleaning out an abandoned council house which was infested with rats and maggots and back-flowing sewage in the bath, cleaning up shit at a dog kennel, mucking out at a zoo, being a dustman and mucking out pigs on a farm.

I can understand that they thought it would be funny for viewers to watch me have a screaming fit every time I had to do these awful jobs, but I hated it. I put my head down and got on with it, though, because the money was good and I was excited at the idea of working in television. The production team were really nice but I don't think any of them realised quite how hard I found filming in those places and how real my problems with germs and dirt were. Even at the wrap party the crew bought me a cake in the shape of a turd. It wasn't funny.

Then, just at the time I was struggling with the demands of *Princess Nikki*, things were going wrong between me and Pete.

When he first came out of the house I really believed we were going to be a proper couple and he could even be 'The One'. He and his mum came round to visit me and my mum and we all got on really well. But within days things were becoming strained. Inside the house Pete had been gentle and spiritual but outside he could be self-centred and I felt squeezed out of his life.

His friends didn't like me at all and he was really influenced by his Mum too. We spent a few nights together at the Covent Garden Hotel but everywhere we went she came too.

One morning I said to her, 'Can you please give us some time together tonight on our own? We really need it.'

Then Pete and I went out but when we returned that night his mum was fast asleep in our bed. So much for time on our own! In the end I had to get into bed next to her while Pete slept on the floor.

Things came to a horrible end two weeks after we left the house when we had an all-day photo shoot with *OK!* magazine, followed by an appearance on *Friday Night with Jonathan Ross*. You would think it would have been one of the best days of my life. But it became one of the most miserable. Pete ignored me throughout the photo shoot, preferring to talk to the photographer and the make-up girl instead.

So by the time we arrived at the television studios to film *Jonathan Ross*, things were already tense. It was OK at first and I was answering all Jonathan's questions but then Pete lay down on the sofa with his fingers in his ears like a child so he couldn't hear anything I was saying.

It was utterly humiliating. He was making a fool out of me in front of millions of people on live television. That was the final straw. We returned to our hotel that night in silence.

The next morning I went home and that was pretty much it. We spoke a couple of times on the phone over the next few days and then one day Pete told me he didn't want to see me any more. It was all over. I was devastated. I really had been madly in love with him. For me it was never a publicity stunt or to win votes in the house. I'd genuinely thought we could be together in the outside world.

All I wanted to do was lie down in a dark room. The newspapers were all reporting that we had split up and that I was heartbroken – and they were right. It was all so public and embarrassing.

It wasn't helped by reports in the papers about Pete

discussing our sex life and saying that he'd found himself a new girlfriend within two days of our splitting up!

For two weeks I couldn't face leaving the house just at the time that all my offers of work were pouring in.

I was sacked from presenting *Celebrity Soup*, E! Entertainment's show based on reality-TV clips, with Ian Lee because I didn't turn up for work. And one day when I'd made it in to film *Princess Nikki*, I locked myself in a toilet and wouldn't come out. I was too upset.

Perhaps I'm oversensitive and feel pain terribly deeply when things go wrong. And maybe that's because of all the things I've been through in the past. But whatever the reason, it made that period, which should have been one of the best of my life, particularly hard.

The only good thing was that I managed to keep control of my eating, and although I was still thin, I'd gained far too much by then to throw it all away by starving myself again.

Then, at the beginning of October, came news which gave me a real boost. I'd been nominated for a National Television Award in the category of Most Popular TV Contender. This was a new category, so it was a real honour. But I was up against four other reality-TV contestants and didn't really believe I had much chance of winning. I thought Pete would get it. But it was exciting just to be nominated and invited to the ceremony at the Royal Albert Hall.

Mum and I spent ages wandering around London searching for the perfect dress until we finally spotted it hanging on a rail in the beautiful Betsey Johnson shop in Covent Garden. I'd never spent that much on an outfit before but this felt like such a special occasion that I had to go for it.

As soon as I stepped out of the limousine at the Albert Hall that evening, 31 October 2006, I knew it was going to be a very special night.

I was interviewed by Kelly and Jack Osbourne on the red carpet – *them* interviewing *me*!

And inside, the hall was packed wall to wall with celebrities. Everywhere I turned, someone wanted to talk to me, and because so many people had been following me on *Big Brother* they all felt like they knew me personally.

Matt Lucas – I've always loved him and think he's so funny – came up to me. Hardly able to speak to him, I blurted out, 'I can't believe it's you.' He gave me a huge smile and replied, 'I feel like that about you! You're going to put me out of a job.'

Then we all took our seats and the awards ceremony started. When it came to our category, Michael Barrymore appeared on stage to present it.

He read out the award – Most Popular TV Contender – and then they showed a clip of me doing my 'Who is she?' rant on *Big Brother*. I remember Michael saying, 'And the winner is...' and then everything goes a bit blurry. He must have said my name, because I turned to my agent, who was sitting next to me, and asked, 'Has he made a mistake? Are you sure?'

I was so gobsmacked I practically stumbled up on to the stage. There I was handed the award and as I turned to look at all those people, all cheering and clapping, it felt unbelievable. And then a voice from the back of the hall shouted, 'You deserve it, Nikki.' I hadn't prepared a speech because I'd never thought I would win, so I just kept thanking everyone who had voted for me and then went to walk off the stage – but went completely the wrong way!

When I got back to my seat there was so much adrenalin running through my body that my hands and legs were visibly shaking.

Later on, *Big Brother* won an award for Most Popular Reality Show, so it was a magical night.

Afterwards we went to the show party with all the team from Endemol and then on to the Met Bar, drinking and dancing.

Mum was then working at the sorting office in Pinner and started her shift at five in the morning. An hour later I was just returning from central London and I got the cab driver to drop me off there. It was a cold, sharp night and I was still just wearing my flimsy silk dress when I teetered up the ramp into the sorting office, holding my award behind my back.

I spotted Mum across the other side of the building in her uniform and I quietly tiptoed up behind her.

'Guess what's happened,' I laughed as she heard me and turned round. I whipped out the award from behind my back and watched as her face filled with delight.

Mum picked me up and spun me round and round, shouting at her colleagues, 'Everyone, look, she's won. My little girl has won.'

Now I keep that award – engraved with the words 'Most Popular TV Contender 2006 – Nikki Grahame' – on my coffee table at home. It's always there to remind me of that night and the most amazing time of my life on *Big Brother*.

According to a poll by Channel 4, I was the twelfth most written-about person in the newspapers in 2006. But I'm under no illusion that everyone loved me! I was also voted the Second Most Annoying Person of 2006 in a BBC3 poll.

But the fact that I was appearing in TV polls at all was still pretty mind-blowing for me.

Towards the end of that year I finished filming *Princess Nikki* and after six months' non-stop activity and work, Mum and I finally escaped for a holiday to Dubai. The trip was a huge treat, but I'd been working so hard and earning good money and hadn't had a chance to enjoy any of it until then.

When we arrived in Dubai I turned off my mobile phone and slept on and off for days. I was so exhausted. In the evenings Mum and I would go for a cocktail at a bar overlooking the beach and talk about everything that had happened over the past year and how much my life had changed.

The *bad* part of my life had already ended well before I went into *Big Brother* and I'd been fit and well for several years. But *Big Brother* was still the defining point in my life. Entering the house was the moment when life became *good*.

CHAPTER 23
A LIFE WORTH LIVING

It's more than two years now since I stepped out of the *Big Brother* house and every day I'm grateful for the opportunities it has given me.

I now write a weekly showbiz column for *OK!* and am regularly filming for television.

During the last two series of *Big Brother* I've been a roving reporter on *Big Brother's Little Brother*, the magazine show about the series which goes out on Channel 4 and E4. I've interviewed Dustin Hoffman on the red carpet, acted out comedy sketches and done background reports on housemates.

And I'm often a guest on all sort of TV shows. I was on *8 Out Of 10 Cats*, *The Friday Night Project*, the quiz shows *The Weakest Link* and *Celebrity Juice*.

I've even starred in a TV ad for Domino's Pizza.

And, according to something I read recently, I'm the fifty-second most Googled woman in the world. I love the celebrity and television life and all the interesting people that you get to meet through it.

But I love my quiet life at home too. It is as if getting that taste of stardom has made me appreciate more than ever the simple things, like walking my dogs in the fields near my flat, popping round for a coffee and a chat with Mum, or going for a quiet drink with a close friend.

I do still go clubbing every now and again but I'm not at it every night any more – I haven't got the stamina and I think I've grown out of that lifestyle. So much of it was very superficial and all about being seen with the right people in the right places. Now, I'd far rather spend time with people that I feel comfortable with and really care about rather than being at some super-trendy bar with people who deep down don't care a jot about me and vice versa.

Having a celebrity profile has also allowed me to help other people. I've worked with Macmillan Cancer Support and the Stroke Association and I was privileged to travel to Scotland to spend a day with a little girl who'd asked to meet me as a wish through the Rays of Sunshine Charity for kids with cystic fibrosis. We went shopping and had a McDonald's together but she died shortly afterwards, which was a shocking reminder of how precious and fragile life is.

I live alone with my two chihuahuas, Thumbelina and Baby, and I'm just five minutes from Mum and Natalie's flat. I see them every day and we are still as close as it is possible to be. We also speak on the phone a lot and all go on holiday together.

Mum and I have been through so much together, both good and bad, that we are bound very tightly by it. Those experiences have made us stronger both individually and together. I don't know how I would cope without her around – she still looks after me a huge amount and is the rock on which my life is built.

Natalie and I still drive each other mad at times and still fight for Mum's attention, but we get on better now than we have ever done. Nat says ever since *Big Brother* she has found a respect for me that wasn't there before. She says seeing me pull myself up from the gutter, from having nothing when I came out of Rhodes Farm to winning a National Television Award, made her think about her life differently too.

After she was sacked from her receptionist's job while I was in *Big Brother* Natalie started thinking about what she really wanted to do, which was to become a scriptwriter. She'd loved writing stories since we were kids. So she enrolled on an MA course, which she has just completed, and now she is writing scripts for films and plays, hoping one of them will get commissioned.

I really respect her for following her dream too and I hope so much that she achieves it. I'm sure she will.

Dad lives a couple of minutes away and I see him about once a week. I still blame him a lot for my parents' divorce and ending my perfect childhood. But writing this book has made me see that things may not always have been easy for him either and perhaps he too was just someone muddling through life as best he could.

Now we get on pretty well and sometimes he'll pop around for a cup of tea with me and Natalie and we'll take the mickey out of him and he'll tease us like when we were kids. Just a few years ago I could never, ever have imagined that happening again. But it has because he's my dad and I love him. And I'll always love him.

I often think back to our house in Stanley Road where we all lived together before I was eight and everything seemed so good, so happy. Three times I've knocked on the door of that house and asked the people who live there now to show me around because I've felt so desperate to return there and to try to reclaim that life.

But I'm learning to accept that that life has gone for ever and isn't coming back. Instead I've got to focus my energy on this life, right now, and look to the future and all the opportunities it can bring.

At the moment I'm single and meeting Mr Right isn't easy. In fact I think becoming a recognised face from television has probably made finding a bloke harder than ever. Nowadays I tend to attract men who just like the idea of dating someone who has been on telly and writes a magazine column. I always fall for good-looking blokes with all the patter, but I've discovered they are generally not the ones to trust. I've been cheated on and mucked around by enough blokes to make me suspicious of their motives, but I keep on hoping I'll find my perfect man soon.

I'd love to settle down one day and have kids, but that is quite a lot for me to hope for. I'm 27 and I've still never had a natural period, which means I have virtually no chance of ever falling pregnant naturally. For a while I was taking oestrogen pills, which gave me 'fake periods', but as they also made me tearful and depressed I gave up taking them. The prospect of never having children is probably the worst thing anorexia has left me with.

But another of its legacies is osteoporosis, a bone disease in which your bones become thinner and thinner, making them hugely susceptible to fractures. Osteoporosis can be caused by low oestrogen levels, which is a side effect of anorexia's preventing the body going through puberty.

Missing out on calcium in my food when I was younger has only made the problem worse. Women of my age can expect to have bone density of between 0 and −1. When it gets to −2.5 you're classed as having osteoporosis. A scan last year showed my spine is −2.9. My bone density is like that of a 68-year-old. There is little I can do to reverse the damage I've already done, but I take a calcium supplement and eat as much dairy food as I can to prevent it getting worse.

I've had two fractured ribs (one from just a strong hug), fractured toes (when a television fell on me in a nightclub) and a fractured elbow (from falling over). I'm constantly in danger of fracturing myself again, which means I have to be incredibly careful never to slip or hurt myself. The main concern is what it'll be like when I get older. In extreme cases of osteoporosis, even sneezing can cause a fracture and it can be incredibly painful.

My OCD remains with me too. I'm still obsessive about cleanliness and hygiene and I don't like other people touching things that I am about to eat or drink. Recently I was doing interviews at a radio station and a woman offered me a cup of tea. 'Thanks very much,' I said, 'but can I make it?'

She thought I was joking – but I was serious.

'No, you sit there, I'm making it,' I barked at the poor woman when she still hadn't got the message after a couple of minutes.

And while I might let a friend make me a sandwich I still have to stand over them to supervise everything they do.

If I eat in a restaurant, as soon as the knife and fork are

put on the table I wrap them in tissue so they can't get contaminated by anyone touching them or breathing on them. Minutes earlier the waiter or waitress may have had their hands all over them, but if I haven't seen it I can cope with. But if someone were to touch my cutlery in front of me, I'd freak out.

At home I still have just a couple of plates, knives, forks and spoons that I will use over and over again. And I love that pre-packed plastic cutlery they give away in shops. Even though logically I know it hasn't just magicked itself into that packet and someone, somewhere, has touched it, for me the thought of it being wrapped in cellophane makes it clean and safe. Every time I go into Marks & Spencer I take away massive handfuls of the stuff.

My OCD is gradually getting better but it's still very tough if I'm feeling low or if I've been out all day and been unable to wash my hands.

And I have to work hard not to become compulsive about exercise too. I limit myself to three trips to the gym a week and have a very structured routine while I'm there: 22–3 minutes on the cross-trainer, a set of 23 chin-ups, then a second set of 19.

In my view you never fully get over anorexia but you can learn to live with it. You can keep it in check and be aware of the danger signs if it is threatening to overcome you again. I still know the calories in virtually any food you can mention and it is hard for me to decide on what to eat for a meal without those numbers bouncing around my head. And I still weigh foods like pasta just to make sure that I don't have more than I feel comfortable with – 45 grams (1½ oz) and no more.

But I no longer feel those issues are putting my health in

danger and I'm getting better all the time. Until fairly recently I was still mopping up grease on my food with a tissue but I've stopped that now. And this summer I ate a plate of chips when I was at a festival with my friends. It was the first time in ten years, since I was at Rhodes Farm.

I'm still reluctant to let my weight go above 40 kilos (6 stone 4 lb). To most people that will seem very thin but it is a weight I'm comfortable with.

So yes, there is still a lot of control in my relationship with food and my body. But so long as I can retain that control and exercise regularly I know I won't make myself sick again. The only danger is if for some reason I can't train as often as I want. It is then that I'll start to eat less and I have to be careful not to slip back into one of those dangerous cycles where I start enjoying the idea of not eating.

Last year I had a second boob job to correct some of the mistakes made during my first op when I was 18. After the surgery I couldn't exercise for a month and I did struggle with my food for a while and was becoming very conscious of how much I was eating every day. But once I was able to start exercising again it was fine.

I'll never return to the person I was before I was eight – I'll never have that carefree attitude to life and my body and food. But I know I will never slip back into full-on anorexia again either. There is no way I'll ever starve myself to death now as I enjoy life too much. I've seen how much there is for me out here and I want to remain a part of it.

In the past couple of years I have met lots of young people – boys and girls – through B-eat, a charity which supports people with eating disorders.

I've also visited hospitals and gone to Rhodes Farm to speak to patients.

When I meet kids still fighting anorexia it is an in-your-face reminder of how far I have come. Because when I see girls with their twig-like legs and bones jutting out from their clothes I think, That's how I was – but probably worse. It makes me feel incredibly sad because I know they have a huge struggle ahead of them. But I also know the struggle is so worthwhile. And that is what I try to explain when I talk to them. All I can do is attempt to give them hope that they can get better and there is a life outside for them.

Every day I look at the scar across my stomach where my gastrostomy tube once was. It is a permanent reminder of the two-inch piece of plastic that stood between me and certain death.

Thinking back on those years to write this book has been at times excruciatingly painful and led to many nights of broken sleep and silent tears as I've relived those times.

I had some good times and made amazing friendships in the hospitals and units where I stayed, but in general the years from eight to 16 were marked by sadness, loneliness and anger. They were certainly not a childhood.

Sometimes I just can't believe it all happened – being pinned down by six nurses while a tube was shoved up my nose, being drugged up for weeks on end to stop me screaming and fighting like a demon, falling into a coma one Boxing Day night, crawling up stairs because I was too weak to walk, cramming paracetamol down my throat because I'd had enough of living, sleeping in a shop doorway.

The only reason I know it is all true is because when I do think over all that stuff, I can still feel the pain inside me. Because, despite all the good things that have happened since, that ball of hurt and sadness of a little girl so incredibly alone remains buried inside me. And I think it will probably always be there. It is part of who I am.

Dr Dee Dawson, who runs Rhodes Farm, told me recently that when she accepted me there she was told, 'Do what you can with her but it doesn't really matter – she is going to die anyway.'

It is stories like that that make me feel so incredibly lucky to be alive. And even more lucky to have had the opportunities and experiences that getting selected for *Big Brother* brought with it.

I have vowed I will never take this life for granted. It is all too much of a miracle.

For so long I cared about no one and nothing apart from starving myself. Anorexia was my best friend, my only friend. Thoughts of not eating dominated my every waking moment and gave me a superhuman strength to fight off anyone who tried to stop me pursuing my mission.

As for why I did it? I think maybe it was something I was born with and that I would have become anorexic at some point in my life, but my parents' divorce, Grandad's death and then my competitiveness at gymnastics were triggers when I was eight.

Add to that my ultra-competitive nature in general, which meant I didn't just want to be any old anorexic, I wanted to be the best.

And what was it that brought me back out of it? I believe it was purely my own decision that I wanted to live

– I wanted to give the outside world a try after being away from it for so long.

I know I was very lucky to have stayed alive long enough to make that decision. Others were not so lucky. Sara, one of the 'hairdryer gang' at Rhodes Farm, died three years ago at 23 from heart failure brought on by anorexia. She was the same age as me.

But many others who I lived with at those clinics and specialist units have managed to go on to live amazing, fulfilled lives with great jobs, loving relationships and families of their own.

Because there is hope for anyone who has an eating disorder. And so there is hope for their parents, brothers, sisters, husbands and children. That's why I have written this book. Not to say, 'Hey, look at me and what a great time I had in *Big Brother*' or, 'Check out all the trendy nightclubs I hang out at with my celebrity mates.' But to say to anyone who is now in the pit of despair that I once was in: There is a life out there for you. And it is worth living.

I guess it is pretty unlikely many other people with anorexia will end up getting selected for *Big Brother* and land their own TV show cleaning out pig shit! But there will be other things in their future that bring them the happiness and security that I know deep down they are desperately craving. Writing this has made me realise how much of my life I wasted before I got on with living and how much I want to prevent other girls making that same mistake.

So my advice to kids with anorexia now?

First, make the most of whatever help you are already receiving, because as you get older it gets harder and harder to get that specialist help and the places you will be sent will become more harsh and more uncaring.

Second, *you* have to make the decision that you want to get better. To do that, try thinking about how different your life could be if you weren't stuck in this battle to be thin. Because your life in the future will be better than what you are going through now, I promise.

And my advice to mums and dads worried that their kids are developing anorexia or an eating disorder? Get professional help as quickly as you can in the hope you can nip it in the bud, before it becomes more difficult to reverse patterns of thinking.

And please, please, don't be dissuaded by doctors or friends who think your child is 'being faddy' or 'just in a phase'. Trust your instincts and don't stop fighting until someone helps you. Because I know only too well that is what your child is screaming out for you to do, even if they are saying the total opposite.

But most of all never stop believing that things can get better. I am living proof of that. However much someone with anorexia might doubt it now, there is a fulfilling and happy life out there waiting for them, once they choose to live it.

I never, ever thought I would find such a special life and it took me almost 11 years of fighting to reach it, but now that I have, I know it has been worth every little bit of effort along the way. Because, as I have discovered, there is an amazing, special life out here for everyone.

It has been a horrible, long and painful journey, sodden with so many tears and bruised by so many knocks and setbacks. But I'm here – and it is good.

I'm happy in my life and in myself now. I love my job

working on the magazine column and in TV reporting and I am so grateful for the chances I've been given.

In fact there's probably only one place I'd rather be – back in the *Big Brother* house. I loved it in there so much. It was such fun and so safe. I could have stayed there for ever. *Big Brother* was the point in my life where everything changed, everything became good.

Since then I've learned that the outside world doesn't have to be scary. Yes, it can be tough and there are pitfalls and people who want you to fail. But there are also people who will stand by you however bad everything gets. However much sadness and pain fill your life, they are still there beneath it all, next to you.

And those are the people who make your life worth living. So for them – Mum, Dad, Natalie and Carly – thanks for showing me my life *was* worth fighting for.

FURTHER READING AND RESOURCES

Anorexia and Bulimia: A Parent's Guide to Recognising Eating Disorders and Taking Control by Dee Dawson. Vermilion (2001)

Eating Disorders: A Parents' Guide by Rachel Bryant-Waugh and Dr Brian Lask. Routledge (2004)

Eating Disorders: The Path to Recovery by Dr Kate Middleton. Lion Hudson plc (2007)

Coping with Eating Disorders and Body Image (overcoming common problems) by Christine Craggs-Hinton. Sheldon Press (2006)

b-eat – leading UK charity for people with eating disorders
www.b-eat.co.uk

Another day of tears and pain
Lying here I'm going insane,
Fighting hard not to be fed,
Trapped in my body lost in my head

Feeling fat and looking thin
Rejecting life my gravest sin,
Leave me upon my bed,
Trapped in my body lost in my head.

I want to be free and seal my fate
Why is my life all about weight?
Hope is gone though it's never said,
Trapped in my body lost in my head.

Nikki Grahame

RONNIE

Titles available in this series

Yannis
Anna
Giovanni
Joseph
Christabelle
Saffron
Manolis
Cathy
Nicola
Vasi
Alecos
John
Tassos
Ronnie

Greek Translations

Anna
published by Livanis 2011

RONNIE

Beryl Darby

ISBN 978-0-9574532-4-1

Printed and bound in the UK by
CPI Antony Rowe, Chippenham

First published in the UK in 2014 by

JACH Publishing
92 Upper North Street, Brighton, East Sussex, England BN1 3FJ

website: www.beryldarby.co.uk

For my brother, Philip and
his wife Philippa with love

Family Tree

Veronica Vandersham

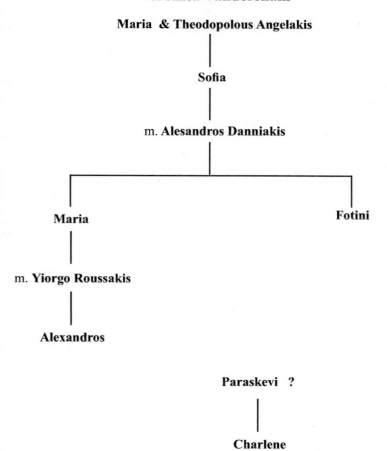

Maria & Theodopolous Angelakis

Sofia

m. **Alesandros Danniakis**

Maria   **Fotini**

m. **Yiorgo Roussakis**

Alexandros

Paraskevi ?

Charlene

Veronica (Ronnie)

Acknowledgements

My thanks to

Ronald Smith (once supplier to many prestigious establishments in England and America and many private clients) for the information he gave me about the techniques for painting on enamel, the subsequent firing and mounting of his work.

Author's Note

I have used the pretty village of Kastelli for much of the setting for this book.

There is a large, stone built house there that has been allowed to fall into total ruin.

I have taken the liberty to weave, what I hope, is a plausible reason for the sad and desolate condition of this once beautiful building.

I have no knowledge of the history of the house or the owners, past or present.

Everything, except for the description of the exterior, is a product of my imagination and any resemblance to the true history or any of the people who ever lived there is entirely coincidental.

May 2010

Ronnie opened the door of her apartment and moved to one side to allow Mark to take their cases in. They had hardly spoken since Mark had accused her of having an affair with John. During their flight she had feigned sleep or sat and talked quietly to Teri about her decision.

'I'll put the kettle on,' she announced, 'unless you'd like something stronger? Then we need to sit and talk.'

'That will make a change after hardly speaking to me for the last few days.'

Ronnie ignored the jibe. She was not prepared to start a row. She knew the acrimonious accusations would start as soon as she told Mark she had decided to accept Saffron's offer and planned to return to Crete.

She walked back into their tiny lounge carrying two glasses and a bottle of wine. 'I forgot we wouldn't have any fresh milk. We'll have to make do with this or water.'

Mark poured a glass for each of them. 'I've had enough water recently.'

Ronnie sat across the room from him and took a mouthful from her glass. 'I've changed my mind, Mark.'

Mark smirked. 'I thought you would see sense.'

Ronnie looked at him levelly. 'You don't have to pack your belongings. I will be packing mine. You can stay here and take over the agreement for the apartment if you want. I will tell the agency tomorrow that I'm cancelling my part of the contract as from the end of the month.'

'You can't do that!'

Ronnie shrugged. 'I can. I have to give them a month's notice of cancellation so I won't be staying here after the end of the month. I'll leave it up to you if you want to go to the agency. If you decide to move on you will have to be out by the end of May, the same as me.'

'I can't afford this apartment on my own,' protested Mark.

'That is your problem. I've subsidised you long enough. I've been paying three quarters of the rent, remember, and most of the utility bills. You'll either have to find someone to share it with you or ask your parents for a loan. You could always go back home to live for your final year at Uni. The choice is yours.'

'Where are you going?'

'I've decided I'll take Saffron up on her offer. I'm going back to Crete to work as an artist.'

'You're going back to be with John, aren't you? I was right,' declared Mark triumphantly, 'you are having an affair with him.'

'I have no plans at all with John. I've always wanted to be an artist and this is my opportunity.'

'I won't let you. It's a ridiculous idea.'

'You won't let me?' Ronnie raised her eyebrows. 'You are not my keeper. I will do as I please.'

'You'll never make enough as an artist to live on. Then what will you do when you're destitute?'

'If it doesn't work out I can always come back to the States. At least I will have taken the opportunity rather than spend the rest of my life working in a mundane job and regretting that I didn't have enough courage to take a chance.'

'You're talking a load of rubbish. Do you really think tourists are going to buy your daubing of sunsets?'

'Saffron seems to think they will. I won't know until I've tried.' Ronnie finished the last of her wine. 'I'm going to start packing up. I'll pass you out a blanket and pillow and you can bed down on the sofa.'

'Ronnie, I can't sleep here. I'm too tall to sleep on the sofa.'

'Then you'll just have to bend your knees.'

'Hi, Mom, only me,' called Ronnie as she opened the door and entered her mother's house.

'In the kitchen,' called back Charlene.

'What are you doing?' asked Ronnie

'Ironing – what do you think I'm doing?'

'Ironing sheets! What are you ironing sheets for?'

'I like them to look good when I change the bed.'

'As soon as you get into bed they're creased. Here, let me finish them for you.'

'No, I'm nearly there. You put the kettle on. I'm longing to hear all your news of your holiday. Did you enjoy the parties?'

Ronnie threw her purse onto the chair and filled the kettle. 'The parties were magnificent. I thoroughly enjoyed them. We had some good walks and I thought parts of Crete were beautiful. I've brought a disc with me that we can put into the computer so you can see them properly.'

'Did Mark enjoy himself?'

Ronnie frowned. 'Yes, most of the time. That's something else I want to talk to you about.'

'You two are getting married?'

Ronnie shook her head. 'No way. We've parted.'

Charlene raised her eyebrows. 'What brought that about?'

'Well,' Ronnie poured the boiling water onto the tea bags and took the milk from the fridge. 'It's a bit of a long story. Everything went well as far as the travel and accommodation arrangements, Mark had done a really good job at organising everything. The family were so welcoming. They took us out to dinner at a local taverna the first evening so we could get to know them and not feel like strangers at the parties. There wasn't much opportunity to talk at the old lady's birthday party. Everyone was making such a fuss of her. We went out for a walk on the Sunday morning before the party that had been arranged for the twin girls and bumped into Mark's mother and father. She was insistent that the boys stopped for a drink with them. She didn't even speak to Teri or me. We were so obviously not included that we went off on our own.'

Charlene raised her eyebrows. 'Didn't she even say hello?'

Ronnie shook her head. 'Nothing. Teri and I walked over what they call the Causeway and found an interesting taverna. I've some photos and I'll show you in a minute. Anyway, the boys arranged to spend some time with their parents and that was fine by us girls, but Mark seemed to think he was obliged to spend every waking hour with his mother. She tried to invite herself to Knossos with us, but luckily Paul was firm there and didn't agree to hire an extra car or anything. Then when the ash cloud affected their travel plans they went up to Heraklion and she wanted Mark and Paul to go up there and stay with them. Teri and I dug our heels in and insisted we followed the itinerary we had planned. We decided to go up to Rethymnon and do the walks there in our second week and return to Elounda and walk locally in the third. Teri and I were willing to compromise and call in at the hotel for the boys to say goodbye to their parents as we drove through Heraklion.' Ronnie grinned and took a mouthful of her tea.

'They were out and Mark couldn't contact either of them on their mobiles. We agreed to wait for an hour and then insisted that we drove on and had lunch. Mark's mother phoned later and tried to persuade us to drive back to Heraklion. She'd had one of those fish pedicures and been to the hairdresser in preparation for flying back to New Orleans.' Ronnie rolled her eyes. 'You're not exactly going to look your best after hours on an aeroplane so why bother to have your beauty treatments before you get home.'

Charlene smiled sympathetically as Ronnie continued. 'I enjoyed Rethymnon; the waterfront there is beautiful, particularly at night when all the restaurants are lit up. Whilst we were there we visited a man who makes lyra. He is amazing. From a rough piece of wood he makes the most beautiful musical instrument. Fortunately Giovanni had told us where to find him; we would never have found his little workshop otherwise. We did some lovely walks and went to a rather special memorial. I'll tell you about that when I show you the photos. One of our walks was through Mili Gorge and we stopped at the taverna there and I took some photos, of course.'

Ronnie finished her tea and leaned her elbows on the table. 'This is where it becomes interesting,' she assured her mother. 'We returned to Elounda and went down to Kritsa to walk the gorge there. It was quite a climb in places and Mark made a very uncalled for remark that was really hurtful.' Ronnie waved her hand as she saw her mother was about to ask for clarification.

'It's not important and he did apologise afterwards. Anyway, the following day the others thought they'd have a lazy day at the apartment and I went over to the family house and did some painting. You have to see the view from there to believe it. I've masses of photos to show you. Anyway, John saw my paintings and thought Saffron might like to purchase them to sell in her shop. I'll get to that later as well. John is a very talented photographer and I gave him my disc of photos to look at. I wanted him to go away, actually, so I could continue to paint,' she smiled guiltily.

'John had been trying to track down a man who'd escaped from the local island years and years ago. There was an old man at the taverna at Mili and he's in one of my photos. John asked who he was and I said I had no idea, but that he had given me a shock when he waved goodbye as instead of a hand he had a hook.'

Charlene raised her eyebrows.

'John was so excited. The man he'd been looking for had lost his arm during the war apparently. John drove up to Mili the following day and met him. Would you believe it; he was the man and I'd taken a photo of him by pure chance. When I went out to the car the next morning John threw his arms round me, kissed me and told me all about their meeting. Mark saw us and jumped to the stupid conclusion that we were having an affair. It was the final straw. Our relationship has been somewhat rocky for months now. I told Mark that when we arrived home he could pack his bags, but I've changed my mind. He can have the apartment. I'm leaving.'

'Are you planning to come back here to live? You're welcome, you know that.'

Ronnie shook her head. 'No, but I'd like to stay for a few weeks, just whilst everything gets sorted out. I don't really want to be in the apartment with Mark. Then I'll ask you to store some of my belongings, please; my books, ornaments, some of my clothes. This is something else I want to tell you. I talked to Saffron about my paintings and she offered to buy all I could do. I thought about it and decided that I'd go back out and live there for the season. I'll be able to paint all day every day.'

Charlene held up her hand. 'Now, slow down, Ronnie. It's one thing leaving Mark, but what about your job here?'

Ronnie waved an envelope at her mother. 'My resignation is in there. I plan to leave at the end of the month.'

Charlene frowned. 'Are you sure about this, Ronnie? It's a big step to take with no guarantee of success.'

'I know, Mom, but I've always wanted to be an artist, you know that. I plan to go over to Elounda and stay in one of the self catering apartments until the end of the season. Giovanni's agreed to let to me for a decent price. If my paintings don't sell I have enough savings to live on for five months and then I'll return to the States. I'm sure I'll be able to find another apartment here and I can always temp until I find a permanent job.'

'Who are these people? How well do you know them?'

'Giovanni is married to Mark's aunt. She's totally different from his mother, although they're twins apparently. The whole extended family live together in a great big house. They also have the self catering apartments. John is their son and Saffron is a cousin, I think. She has just opened a gift shop and wants to stock items that are a bit different from the other shops in the area.'

'This John – are you truly not having an affair and going back because of him? Is this the real reason why you and Mark have split up?'

Ronnie laughed. 'No way. John is married and has twin daughters of a year old. He's a nice man, but nothing more. I've really thought about it, Mom. It only takes me about half an hour to paint each of the little water colours that Saffron wants. I can do those standing on my head. She also wants me to paint some pictures of Spinalonga and decorate the top of some wooden boxes with a painting of the island. Those will take a good bit longer. I can sit down by the quay and the tourists will see me painting. I'll arrange with Saffron to sell my work at the same price as she sells in her shop if the tourists want to buy directly from me.'

'Are you sure you'll make enough to live on?'

Ronnie shrugged. 'I don't know. My idea is to give it a try this season. Ideally I'd like to make enough to pay my living expenses without touching my savings. If I work hard and the venture is a success I might even recoup my air fare. If the whole project falls flat then I'll put those months down to experience and accept that my art is not good enough to be considered commercially viable.'

Charlene smiled at her enthusiastic daughter. 'You have it all worked out, haven't you?'

Ronnie nodded. 'If I'm successful I thought you and Uncle Alex might like to come over at the end of the season. I could leave some paintings for Saffron so it would only be my own sales that I was losing and you could see for yourself that I wasn't starving in a garret.'

'Maybe your uncle wouldn't want to visit Crete. He's never been back since he was a child.'

'Uncle Alex comes from Crete? I never knew that. I always thought he and Grandma had been born over here. Whereabouts did he live?'

'I'm not sure. Castle something I think.'

'He lived in a castle?' Ronnie's eyes opened wide.

Charlene laughed and shook her head. 'That was the name of the place. I doubt if he really remembers, he was only a little boy when the family came to America.'

'I'll visit him next week and tell him my plans. I can ask him the name of the town at the same time, then I can look it up on the map and if it's reasonably close we could visit and see what it looks like now. You'd come, wouldn't you, even if Uncle refused?'

'We'll see. No promises. You could hate living out there and be back within a month.'

'I might decide not to return the following year, but it's only sensible to stay for the complete season. I have to give myself a reasonable amount of time to find out if I can be a success. Now, do you want to put my disc of photos on the computer or just look at those I've printed off?'

Giovanni sat in the office with Marianne whilst she checked their computer bookings for the following weeks.

'Considering the ash problem that affected Europe we've only had three cancellations. It could have been far worse, particularly if it had lasted longer.'

'I just wish we had some more bookings. We're well down on this time last year. At this rate we'll be lucky if we manage to cover our overheads,' remarked Giovanni gloomily. 'If there are any more riots in Athens they could spread to the islands and the coach drivers are talking about going on strike again.'

'Now our families have finally gone home, I'll contact the travel companies and see if I can drum up some more business. It could be worth our while to offer seven nights for the price of six until the end of June. If that is successful we can increase the prices a little in July for new bookings to cover the loss. What do you think, Giovanni?'

'I leave you in charge of bookings. You do whatever you think is best.'

'We'll give it another week before we start offering any deals. It's often slow at the start of the season. People haven't always got their holiday dates arranged at work or made up their mind where they want to go. Oh, I think this must be a personal mail come through on the business address. It's from Ronnie. I don't know what happened between her and Mark, but they must have had a terrible row. I don't think they were speaking to each other when they left.'

'Apparently Ronnie is planning to come back over here. She's going to work as an artist on commission for Saffron. She's asked me if I'll give her a special rate at one of the apartments for the season.'

'And will you? You didn't mention it to me.'

Giovanni shrugged. 'It won't surprise me if she changes her mind and cancels. If she does come she'll pay the same rate as everyone else, but I'll tell her it includes her water and electricity. That way she'll think she's getting a good deal and it would mean a guaranteed booking until the end of October.'

'What will she do then? Go back to the States?'

'I don't know her long term plans. They would probably depend upon the success of Saffron's shop.'

'With the number of visitors who are coming to this area whilst that film is being made Saffie should be successful.'

'I hope so. I just wish the tourists would stay down here and not just visit for the day.'

Giovanni began to open his post. He read the letter through a second time and threw it to one side in disgust.

'The bank says they're increasing the interest charged on loans by twenty per cent with immediate effect and they've already increased the business tax. The cost of electricity and oil has already doubled this season. We might as well close down now.'

Marianne patted her husband's shoulder. 'Don't worry so much, Giovanni. We've always managed to come through somehow. I'll see if Grandma is ready to get up, then I'll make some coffee and get on to the travel firms.'

Marianne entered her grandmother's room and stopped in horror. It was obvious that her grandmother was no longer with them.

'Giovanni, Giovanni, come quick. 'Phone the doctor. Grandma ....' Marianne's voice broke and Giovanni placed his arms around his wife and held her tightly.

'You can't possibly expect us to drop everything and come rushing back to Crete whenever you call. We haven't got that kind of money, you know.'

Marianne did not remind her sister that they only needed their air fare and they would be accommodated free in the self catering apartments.

'We could get stuck over there again with another ash cloud or something. That was terribly inconvenient, and after John's disgusting behaviour I'm sure the boys won't want to come.'

'What do you mean? What did John do?'

Helena snorted. 'Don't tell me you don't know. He and Ronnie are having an affair. Mark saw them together. He's thrown her out, of course.'

'Oh, no, now wait a moment, Helena. John is certainly not having an affair with anyone. Saffron offered Ronnie a job as an artist, painting pictures of the area for her to sell in her shop. Ronnie has taken her up on her offer and before she left she arranged with Giovanni to rent a self catering apartment for the rest of the season.'

'Very convenient for them, I'm sure,' scoffed Helena. 'If you hadn't decided to give grandmother that party and get her over excited and over tired she'd probably still be alive now.'

Marianne felt the tears coming into her eyes. Surely no one could blame Annita's death on a party that had been held three weeks earlier.

'And don't expect mother to come over,' continued Helena, 'and I'm sure Uncle Andreas won't come either. I suggest you just go ahead with whatever arrangements you need to make and get grandmother's funeral over and done with.'

'Mother has already arranged to meet Uncle Andreas in New York and fly out with him.' Marianne replied, somewhat smugly.

'What! How dare you speak to her before talking to me?'

'I don't have to ask your permission to speak to our mother. She had every right to know before you. I called her and Uncle Andreas before anyone else and it was her decision. I tried to 'phone you yesterday but you were out and I left a message asking you to call me back.'

'I was busy yesterday. I had a nail appointment and then spent some time with Mark. He needs my support. I'll speak to mother and tell her it's out of the question for her to come over. She's too old to be gallivanting around like that.'

'Helena, she's only in her seventies. Grandma was her mother and if she wants to come over to be at her funeral she has every right. Uncle Andreas will look after her.'

'He's hardly any younger than she is. I'll hold you directly responsible if anything happens to her,' threatened Helena.

'There's no reason why anything untoward should happen to her. What's wrong with you? You never used to be like this.'

'There's nothing wrong with me. If you hadn't gone off to Crete, got yourself pregnant and then married that Giovanni man, you'd be over here helping me to look after mother. You've managed to evade your responsibilities very nicely.'

Marianne took a deep breath. 'I think we ought to end this conversation right now, before either of us says anything more hurtful to each other. Goodbye.'

Marianne dropped her head into her hands. Had she evaded her responsibilities? She didn't think so. She had taken care of Giovanni's Aunt Anna and Uncle Yiorgo, then her grandmother. She now had Giovanni's mother living there along with Uncle Yannis and Aunt Ourania. She knew that eventually she would be responsible for caring for all of them as they became older and incapable of looking after themselves. Helena did not look after their mother; Elena was quite capable of living alone and looking after herself.

Helena's words niggled at her for the remainder of the morning and despite being convinced that John was not having an affair she would have to drive up to the taverna and ask him for clarification of his aunt's accusation. Surely Helena had not invented the story from spite?

'John, I have to ask you this for my own peace of mind. Are you having an affair with Ronnie?'

John looked at his mother in amazement. 'Whatever gave you that daft idea?'

'Your Aunt Helena said Ronnie and Mark have parted and it was due to you. Ronnie told me she was coming back here to work as an artist on commission from Saffron. Is that an excuse to be here near you?'

'If it is, it's news to me. I am definitely not having an affair with Ronnie or anyone else. Why would I even consider such foolishness when I have Nick and the girls?'

'Helena said Mark saw you and Ronnie together. He wouldn't have made that up surely.'

'Mark's an idiot. When I came back from speaking to Tassos I threw my arms around Ronnie and kissed her. Had Mark found Tassos I would probably have kissed him!' John squeezed his mother's shoulders. 'I'll be interested to hear Ronnie's version of events when she does come. I bet it doesn't tally with Aunt Helena's and I'm sure Aunt Helena is only too pleased they're no longer together. I heard that she was really rude to both the girls. I think Teri is a little more acceptable to her, but no girl will be good enough for her precious little Mark.'

Marianne let out the breath she had been unconsciously holding. 'I'm sorry, John. I should know better than to doubt you. It's just, oh, everything seems to be on top of me right now.'

'Come on, Mum. This isn't like you. Sit down. I'll bring you a drink and you can tell me everything that's on your mind.'

'So,' John placed a glass of wine on the table in front of his mother. 'Tell me your troubles.'

Marianne smiled shakily. 'I suppose it's really due to Grandma dying so suddenly. We all knew she would go one day, but it was rather a shock to walk in and find her. Helena said that if we hadn't given Grandma that party she would still be alive.'

'Utter rubbish. Grandma loved her party and being the centre of attention that day. She was delighted that her children and grandchildren bothered to come over.'

'When I spoke to Helena about the funeral she said they wouldn't be coming and nor would the boys or our mother. I told her I had already spoken to your grandmother and she was meeting Uncle Andreas and they were travelling together. She said I had evaded my responsibilities by marrying your father and staying out here, rather than being in New Orleans to help look after your grandmother. I haven't, have I, John?' Marianne's brow creased in a worried frown.

John looked at his mother in amazement. 'Evaded your responsibilities? What is she talking about? She must live in cloud cuckoo land. You had Aunt Anna and Uncle Yiorgo to look after for years; then you offered a home to Grandma and looked after her. Did she bother to find out what was happening to Grandma when Hurricane Katrina struck? No, she was quite safe somewhere else. I remember how frantic you were, thinking something awful must have happened when you couldn't contact her.'

John poured his mother another glass of wine. 'I didn't like Aunt Helena when she visited with the boys when they were small. Uncle Greg seems easy going and Paul isn't too bad now, but Mark is a pain. He puts on a big act of being in charge and organising everything but I think it's a cover for his basic insecurity. I'm not surprised Ronnie has left him. It's a wonder he doesn't still hold his mother's hand to cross the road,' ended John in disgust and Marianne could not help smiling at his vehemence. 'If it's only Aunt Helena being spiteful that is making you feel down, forget her.'

Marianne sighed. 'I think I'm tired. It's only the start of the season and I feel ready for a break.'

'You went to tremendous trouble to organise the parties and everything. I'm not surprised you feel tired. Couldn't you and Dad have a few days away somewhere before the season really takes off?'

Marianne shook her head. 'There's Grandma's funeral to organise now and I don't think we could afford to go away. The bank's increased the interest on Dad's loans, put up the cost of the utilities and almost doubled taxes. I know he's worried about the bookings. We've only had three cancellations, but very few enquiries and only fifteen new bookings for the season so far.'

'It's early days yet. Once people have forgotten about the ash cloud they'll come flocking over as usual,' John tried to reassure her. 'If you and Dad can't go away why don't you have a few days relaxing with your mother and uncle after Grandma's funeral? Ask Saffron where she thinks they might like to go and take them out for the day.'

'I suppose I could,' answered Marianne doubtfully.

'Of course you could. Now, shall I top your glass up?' John held up the bottle and Marianne shook her head.

'I mustn't have any more, I'm driving remember.'

'You are only going down the road.'

'And I don't want to end up in the ditch. I am sorry I had to ask you, John.'

'Provided it has put your mind at rest I don't mind a bit.' John squeezed her hand. 'I'm here, Mum, if you need to talk.'

Marianne shook her head. 'I just wish you had talked to us last year when you had so much on your mind.'

Bryony wandered disconsolately into the kitchen, poured a glass of mango juice and sat down heavily in a chair. 'What can I do, Marianne?'

'There's nothing really to do. The vegetables are prepared for this evening's meal. I thought I'd put some chicken pieces in the oven and make a sauce to go over them.'

Bryony shook her head. 'No, I mean, what can I do with myself. I'm always willing to help with any of the household chores or cooking, but they won't keep me occupied all day. The taverna and shop are not that busy yet, so I'm not needed up there.' Bryony sighed deeply. 'I do miss Grandma. Once she was up and you'd helped her to dress I used to spend the remainder of the morning with her.'

'Nicola would probably appreciate some extra help with the girls.'

'I'm always willing, she knows that, but they're her children. She wants to spend time with them herself. Now the weather's warmer she walks up to the taverna with them each morning, and after their lunch they still have a nap. When John comes home he wants to play with them, of course, and most nights he helps Nicola with bathing them, besides, giving them a bath wouldn't keep me occupied all day.'

'Nicola might appreciate an hour to herself in the afternoons if you were willing to keep the girls occupied,' suggested Marianne.

Bryony nodded. 'I'd be happy to do that, but what do I do with the rest of my time? I didn't realise what a large chunk of my day Grandma took up, just talking to her and fetching something she wanted from her room or a drink.'

Marianne smiled sympathetically at her cousin. 'You were so good with her. I would never have had the patience to sit with her each day and listen to her telling me stories about when she was a girl over here or first lived in America.'

Bryony's eyes filled with tears. 'I miss her so much.'

Marianne placed her arm around Bryony's shoulders. 'Of course you do. You were the only one in New Orleans who really cared about her.'

'She and Grandpa were so good to me. Grandma was more of

a mother to me than my own mother had been.'

Marianne nodded. 'We're all feeling the loss, but it must be hardest for you. Would you feel capable of helping me go through Grandma's belongings? I'll certainly need some help with that.'

Bryony frowned. 'What is there to go through?'

'That's part of the problem. I don't really know. You brought a box of her belongings back from the Care Home and she took the photographs out. I don't think she ever looked at anything else that was in there, but whatever there is must have been precious to her or she would not have bothered to take it with her.'

'Let me know when it's convenient for you.'

'After the funeral is over and my mother and Uncle Andreas have gone home. I'll need you to help me whilst they're here. John suggested that I took them out on day trips. I can't do that and prepare meals.'

'Is Helena coming?'

Marianne shook her head. 'She said it was impossible to return to Crete so soon for any of them. She was even going to tell our mother that she was not to come. It's a good job I spoke to mother and Uncle Andreas first.'

'Why didn't she want your mother to come?'

'She said it would be too much for her at her age. For goodness sake she's only in her early seventies. By the way Helena spoke you would think she was twenty years older and senile.'

Giovanni heard the door bell ring and ignored it. Marianne or Bryony would answer. It was probably someone from Elounda coming to offer their sympathy having heard that Annita had died. He would have to speak to them and thank them for calling. He pushed back his chair and opened the door of the office. Bryony had asked the visitor in, but Giovanni did not recognise him as a local resident.

'Can I help you?'

The man walked towards Giovanni and held out his hand. 'I

am film maker. You have hear?'

Giovanni frowned. 'Do you speak Greek?'

'Greek, no. I Italian.'

'I am also Italian, so it could be easier if we speak in that language. How can I help you?'

The man smiled in relief. 'I am finding communication over here rather difficult. Some people have a few words of Italian, but they seem mainly to speak English. My English is very limited. I told my producer he should come to see you. He speaks Greek, but he said it was my job as I am a camera man and it would be my responsibility to iron out any technical difficulties.'

'I really have no idea how I can help you. Maybe it's my son you need to speak to? He is the photographer in the family.'

'No, no, it is the head of the house that I need.'

Giovanni shrugged. 'In that case you need to speak to Uncle Yannis. He only speaks Greek.'

'Then maybe I can explain to you and you can then speak to him? Firstly I understand your family has suffered a bereavement recently and I would like to offer my condolences at this sad time. May I know when the funeral will take place?'

'Why?'

'As you know we are making a film about the island of Spinalonga. Sadly many deaths occurred over there. We would like to film the funeral of your relative. It would appear more authentic if it was a real funeral we recorded rather than a staged one.'

Giovanni clenched his fists. How dare the man even suggest such a thing? 'My grandmother's funeral is a private family occasion. Some of the villagers who knew her might attend, but a funeral is not a public spectacle for you to film.'

'We would not be intrusive, no close up shots of the mourners or family, I assure you. It would just be for us to show an authentic Greek funeral.'

'Then you are out of luck. Our grandmother, although a Cretan, had lived in America for most of her life. The Church service will be traditional, but her progress to the church will not be in a black draped coffin carried by members of the family. She will have a funeral cortege of cars.'

'The service, if it is traditional, maybe we could film and use that?'

'There will be no filming at all. Do you understand? I am reporting your request to Mr Christos, our chief of police for this area. I will request he places a restraining order on your company to prevent you from taking any photos or film of any sort of my grandmother's funeral.'

'It would be done very tastefully. You would not even notice that we were there.'

'If I see you or anyone from your film company with a camera I will report you to the police and press charges against you for intrusion of privacy. Now I suggest you leave.' Giovanni strode towards the door and opened it wide. 'Good bye and do not call again.'

Giovanni watched as the man returned to his car where he shrugged at the man who was waiting in the passenger seat. He closed the door and watched from the window as a conversation took place between the men. Finally the passenger climbed out of the car and approached the house. Giovanni pulled his mobile from his belt and pressed the numbers for the police station in Aghios Nikolaos. This film company would be made to understand that he was serious when he said they could not record Annita's funeral.

The door bell rang again and Bryony walked through to answer it. Giovanni shook his head and laid a restraining hand on her arm. 'Ignore it. That man had the audacity to ask if the film company could record Grandma's funeral and use it as footage in the programme they're making. I'm phoning the police.'

Inspector Christos sounded sympathetic as Giovanni complained vociferously to him about the suggestion made by the film company.

'I understand, Mr Giovanni. Of course they may not film the lady's funeral. I will visit the company myself, now, immediately, and tell them that it is completely forbidden by Greek law to do such a thing. I will make sure they understand. I will be along to visit you after I have spoken to them.'

Giovanni was forced to chuckle. He had not expected Inspector Christos to take his complaint so seriously. He knew Christos would expect something for himself as a mark of the family's appreciation. Was it truly against the law to photograph a funeral?

Ronnie sat comfortably in her great uncle's lounge. 'I've so much to tell you, Uncle Alex. I've decided to take a chance and go back to Crete for the season. I'm doing some paintings for a local gift shop.'

Alexandros raised his eyebrows. 'That's a long way to go to do some painting. Couldn't you have decided to try your luck over here?'

Ronnie shook her head. 'It's not the same here. There's so much competition and unless you have a sponsor you'll never get noticed. I'll never be famous, I realise that, but at least I'll be enjoying myself. At the moment I spend all day answering the 'phone or typing contracts. It pays the rent, but it isn't exactly exciting and I get very little time to paint. You see, where we stayed is absolutely beautiful. An artist's paradise. I'll show you some photos and tell you how the opportunity arose.'

Ronnie took her photographs from her purse and spread them out on the occasional table in front of them. 'You see what I mean?'

Alexandros nodded. 'Whereabouts is this?'

'Elounda is a large village down that way and Plaka is a small village at the other end of the bay. The island is Spinalonga. Most of the paintings I did were of the hills and the sun either rising or setting. The colours are quite amazing and different each day.'

Alexandros looked at the photographs. 'It's certainly beautiful. I can see why you would want to sit there and paint.'

'Mum told me last week that you had been born over there. I always thought you'd been born in the States.'

Alexandros shook his head. 'I was born in Crete, so was your grandmother. I know we lived in a big house in a small village, but that's about all I remember.'

'So why did your parents decide to come to the States?'

Alexandros shrugged. 'Probably because they thought they could have a better life over here. Besides, at that time the war was spreading across Europe.'

'Didn't you ever ask them?'

'It never occurred to me. There were a number of Greek families who had uprooted themselves to make a new life over here. We considered ourselves American. I even changed my name to an Americanised version. You call me Alex, along with everyone else who knows me. It is not my name. My Greek name is Alexandros.'

'Alexandros.' Ronnie stumbled over the unfamiliar name.

'Exactly,' smiled her uncle, 'It was simpler to call myself Alex. No one here could get their tongue around Alexandros.'

'Grandmother was known as Vivi. What was her name?'

'Paraskevi. It means Friday.'

'So she was called after the day she was born on?'

'Possibly, but it may also have been a family name. When you were born your godparents chose your name and it was usually that of a relative.'

Ronnie looked at her great uncle in surprise. 'Really? Suppose the parents didn't like the name their child was given?'

'There was usually a second name that could be used.'

'I wish I'd been given a second name,' grumbled Ronnie. 'When I say my name is Ronnie people think I'm a man.'

'Why don't you stick with Veronica? It's a pretty name.'

Ronnie pulled a face. 'It's cumbersome. Too many syllables. Ann would have been far easier.'

Alexandros smiled. 'And you would have had to add your

surname each time so people knew which Ann they were talking to.' He shook his head. 'No, Veronica makes you individual, even if you do shorten it to Ronnie.'

'It could have been if Mum hadn't changed my name when she remarried. Veronica Milton was manageable, but Veronica Vandersham!' Ronnie shook her head. 'Anyway, tell me more about your parents and where you lived in Crete.'

'There isn't much to tell. I have very vague memories of Crete. I was only six, coming up for seven when we settled in Dallas and father worked for a flooring manufacturer. He must have been good at his job and thought highly of because he had fifty men working under him when he died. My mother never really coped with life after that. She had depended upon him to make decisions, pay the bills and everything. I looked after her the best I could, but I couldn't expect Millie to have her come to live with us. She was struggling with her own health at the time, so it had to be a Care Home.'

Ronnie nodded. She knew her great aunt had died from cancer. 'When did you decide to move down to New Orleans?'

Alexandros shook his head. 'Had your grandfather not been killed in Vietnam I doubt if I would have moved. Millie had died, my parents were both dead, and now my sister was widowed with a young daughter. I felt I should come down here to live so I could give her whatever support I could.'

'That was good of you, Uncle Alex, leaving your home and memories to come down to help her.'

'It was the right time for me to make a move. All I had in Dallas were memories of Millie. Time to make a fresh start.'

'You didn't think about going back to Crete?'

'Whatever for? I don't know anyone there and I don't remember the language. I doubt if Vivi would have wanted to return. No, it never crossed my mind. We're Americans.'

Ronnie smiled. 'I'm glad you moved down here. I felt awful when Mom told me my father had been sent to prison. I was so ashamed. I felt that everyone I passed in the street was looking at me and knew about him. I loved it on the days when you met me from school. I hoped the children would think you were my father.'

'A bit old for that. They probably thought I was your grandfather.'

'What about your grandparents, Uncle Alex? Do you remember them?'

Alexandros shook his head. 'Not really. I know we lived with them, but I can't say that I truly remember them. There are some photographs packed away somewhere. I'll have to get them out to show you.'

'I'd love to see them. Can you get them now?'

'Not today. I'm not sure if they're in the cupboard under the stairs or up in the roof space. They could even be in one of the boxes under my bed. I'll need some time to track them down.'

Ronnie's face fell. 'I'm leaving in another couple of weeks.'

'Well, they're not important. You won't know anyone who is in them. You can always have a look at them when you come home in the Fall.'

'I suggested to Mom that you both came out to visit me at the end of the season. Mom thought you might not want to. I know Mom wouldn't want to travel that far on her own, but if you were with her I'm sure she'd be willing to make the journey. I really would like you both to come.'

June - July 2010

Ronnie landed at Heraklion airport, not sure whether the churning in her stomach was due to the turbulence of the flight over the Dolomites or the final realisation that she had made a life changing decision. It had all seemed so exciting when she was in New Orleans discussing her plans with her friends; now it was reality. Had she made big mistake? She only knew a few people and they could only be called acquaintances, not friends.

She watched her cases go round twice on the carousel before she realised they disappeared into a chute before re-emerging at the other end and she realised she would have to move further along to claim them. Saffron had mailed her a photograph of Vasi and assured her he would be there to meet her and drive her to Elounda. She hoped they would recognise each other, having only met briefly during the parties.

Ronnie showed her passport and was waved through. There were people everywhere, some holding up placards with travel company details or individual names. She wished she had asked Saffron to arrange for Vasi to hold up her name. She stood still, scanning the faces of the men who were waiting patiently and felt a tap on her shoulder.

'It is Ronnie, isn't it?' Vasi asked anxiously.

Ronnie smiled in relief and held out her hand. 'Hello, Vasi. Thank you for meeting me.'

'No problem. I was in Heraklion and I have to drive home to Elounda. Let me take your cases.'

Ronnie relinquished them thankfully and followed Vasi through the milling people and out into the sunshine. She drew a deep breath.

'Fresh air at last. I've spent far too long breathing recycled oxygen.'

'I'm afraid you will have to suffer it for a while longer. It will be necessary to have the air con working in the car as it is too noisy as we drive to have the windows open,' apologised Vasi.

'I'll survive. Hopefully I won't have to board another 'plane for a few months.'

'Saffie is relying on you to spend the season here. I will drive to Giovanni's and collect the key for your apartment. I will return later with Saffie and we will go to a taverna at Plaka for a meal. You and Saffie can discuss your work programme and sort out the necessary details whilst we eat.'

Ronnie nodded. Vasi's words sent a tremor of apprehension through her. She had planned to work whatever hours she pleased and he was making it sound as if she were to be treated as an employee with set times to start and finish.

As they drove along the highway Vasi pointed out various locations to her. 'Here is Malia. There is an archaeological site just outside of the town if you wanted to make a visit.'

'We didn't stop there when I was here before. In fact there are a number of places that looked interesting and we just didn't have the time to stop and explore. I thought I could hire a car occasionally so I can see more of the area.'

'Saffie will be able to tell you the most interesting villages.'

'I'd like to go back to Mili and see that old man that John found.'

Vasi smiled at her. 'As I understand it, you found him. I'm sure John would be delighted to go up there with you and talk to him again. It is a long drive to make alone.'

'Provided Nicola won't mind him coming with me.'

'Why should she? She might even decide to accompany you

if Bryony will look after their girls for the day.'

Ronnie nodded. After Mark's unfounded accusation regarding her and John she felt a little uncomfortable about being alone with him. She would certainly not want Nicola to jump to the same conclusion.

As Vasi drove around the corner and the view of Mirabello Bay and Spinalonga appeared before, Ronnie felt her earlier fears evaporating. It was just as beautiful as she remembered. She hadn't made a mistake to come here to paint.

Vasi carried Ronnie's cases into the apartment she planned to rent for the season. 'If you are not happy here you should speak to Giovanni. He will arrange for you to move.'

'Why shouldn't I be happy here?'

'It is close to the entrance. You could be disturbed by the visitors coming home late at night.'

Ronnie frowned. 'I'll see how it goes. I'd rather be on the ground floor, saves me hauling my easel up and down. If I do find it too noisy I'll ask Giovanni if I can move to a top floor apartment when one is free.'

Vasi smiled, but did not enlighten Ronnie that there were plenty of other apartments free. Giovanni was suffering the same as all the hotels. Most of them were no more than half full for the duration of the season. The ash cloud that had disrupted travel had caused some prospective visitors to cancel and the European news coverage of the financial situation that Greece was facing was making tourists look elsewhere for their holidays this year. The riots and strikes that had taken place had done nothing to encourage new visitors to the area.

'I will leave you to unpack and settle. The shop is open and you will be able to buy some basic goods there, but you know that, of course, from your earlier stay. I will return with Saffron at seven and we will go for a meal locally. It is early for us to eat, but no doubt you are tired from your journey and would not want to be out until the early hours.'

Vasi did not mention that Saffron would also be tired from her day at the shop and would not want to be out too late. Ronnie smiled gratefully. She felt wide awake at the moment, but she had a nasty feeling that her travelling and the various time changes she had passed through would catch up with her during the evening.

Saffron greeted her warmly and they walked to a taverna on the main road a short distance from the shop. 'Kyriakos knows us and the food is good. Whilst we eat you can tell me your schedule. I've sold all the paintings you did when you were here before. They were very popular so I'd like some more as soon as possible.'

Ronnie shrugged. 'If you're talking about the views of the bay they are easy enough. I could probably manage about thirty this week to stock you up again and then paint a few more each week to keep you going. How much do you plan to pay me?'

'I thought five Euros each.'

Ronnie nodded. 'How much do you sell them for?'

Saffron hesitated. 'Ten Euros,' she said finally.

Ronnie leaned forward. 'I'm planning to sit down by the harbour and paint. If you sell my paintings for ten Euros then I'll charge any tourist who wants to buy directly from me the same. Does that sound fair?'

'Will they be the same as those you sell me?'

'Exactly. I may paint some larger ones and some different scenes. We'd have to negotiate a price for those. You know the market and how much the tourists are willing to pay.'

'Suppose some of the other gift shops ask you to work for them?'

Ronnie smiled. 'If your sales are as good as you imply I won't have time to supply other shops. I'm not prepared to spend every minute of every day painting. At the moment painting is a pleasure, I don't want it to become a chore and lose the incentive. I need to make enough to cover my expenses each week, but also have time to myself to paint anything that appeals to me. Just doing pictures of the bay can become rather mundane and boring.'

'What about the boxes I asked you to paint?'

'I'd like a couple of rejects to experiment on. If you're satisfied with the result then we'll discuss a price. I only brought my watercolour paints with me and I'm not sure what paint I should use. Do you know what kind of paint they use on the icons?' asked Ronnie. 'They are painted on wood and the colours are so brilliant.'

Saffron shook her head. 'They used to be painted on wood. Now they use a transfer. Very few are truly hand painted examples and those are very expensive.'

'Is there an art shop in Elounda?'

Saffron shook her head. 'You'd need to go into Aghios Nikolaos or maybe even up to Heraklion. Do you know anywhere, Vasi?'

Vasi shrugged. 'I can make enquiries. I can drive you into Aghios Nikolaos if there is a shop there and you can catch the bus back to Elounda. If you need to go to Heraklion I can also drive you there. You would need to wait until I was ready to return or, again, you could return by bus.'

'Yiorgo might be able to let you have some paint to experiment with,' suggested Saffron.

'Yiorgo?' Vasi looked at her in surprise.

'His father and brother are in the building trade. They must have some small left over amounts of paint when they have decorated. They probably throw them away.'

'I don't want litre cans,' Ronnie protested hurriedly. 'Little pots will last forever.'

Vasi struck his forehead with his hand. 'I am a simpleton. Of course I know where to buy little pots of paint. I used to make model aeroplanes and paint them. The shop where they sold the models in Aghios Nikolaos also sold the paints.'

'That's the answer, then. I'll spend some time stocking Saffron up with water colours of the bay. I also want to move around and find some different views of Spinalonga. I'd like to leave the boxes for a while until I'm properly organised.'

Vasi nodded. 'No problem. In the meantime I can ask Yiorgo if his father has some old paint.'

'Would he have some small pieces of wood? I'm not sure that the paint you use for house decorating is suitable and I don't want to ruin box after box whilst I experiment.'

'I am sure he will be able to find something suitable.'

'If you're going to sit down by the harbour and paint will you need a table and chair?' asked Saffron.

Ronnie shook her head and smiled rather sheepishly. 'I brought my easel and folding chair with me. That way I can move around to wherever I fancy. They're not heavy and I simply strap them together on the wheels I use for my case or remove the legs from the easel and take just the flat area.'

'You could always store them at the back of the gift shop,' offered Saffron.

'Thanks, but I'd rather not. I may want them very early in the morning or back at the apartment. It's better for me to be independent of you. I'm self employed so I can move around however I wish. You may not see me for two or three days if I decide to go up to Elounda and paint or take a day off. I'm not prepared to sit in the same place every day. If I became known as a tourist attraction I would feel obliged to be there. You have my mobile number and if your stock gets low just call me.'

Ronnie hoped she had made her working conditions clear without offending Saffron. She was not prepared to be tied down to a five day week and regular hours. 'I'm hoping my mother and great uncle will come over for a visit at the end of the season and I'll want to spend time with them.'

Saffron nodded. She really did not mind how or where Ronnie spent her time provided she had enough of the popular water colours in stock and possibly some attractive boxes with pictures of Spinalonga on their lids.

When Ronnie had set up her easel by the harbour at Plaka the boatmen had eyed her curiously, one or two wandering over to have a look at her painting before losing interest. During her first two weeks she concentrated on reproducing the view of the bay time and again so she could provide Saffron with the stock she had requested. During the evening she worked at copying the pictures she had completed earlier in the day and filed them carefully. Once she had sufficient stock on hand she would be able to concentrate on Spinalonga itself and any other views she felt she could reproduce successfully.

When the tourists returned from their visit to the island they would mill around in the small square and usually walked over to inspect her art. She was always ready to smile and chat with them inevitably making a sale, keeping to her agreement with Saffron to sell at the same price as in the gift shop.

She signed each completed painting "Ve-Va" and on the reverse she signed her full name - Veronica Vandersham. When the purchaser commented she would explain that her name was far too long to put on the front.

After three weeks Ronnie decided it was time to become more adventurous. She was bored with reproducing the same picture time and again, despite trying to make each one slightly different by adding a fishing or sailing boat somewhere on the sea, or changing the cloud formation.

She caught the bus down to Elounda, struggling on and off with her bag of art materials and the cumbersome easel that she had collapsed. The new location gave her a different perspective of the bay and she was able to incorporate the Causeway and edge of the salt pans if she faced that way. When she turned she was able to paint the land on both sides of the bay with Spinalonga in the distance, but after half a dozen attempts during the course of the week she was not satisfied. Spinalonga no longer looked like an island, more like part of the mainland.

The tourists who thronged the water front seemed uninterested in her work, and after a cursory glance walked away. In the week that she spent in the location she sold no more than a dozen of her pictures and decided the journey she had to make was not worth the effort involved and returned to the harbour at Plaka. She could always experiment later by copying a photograph of the Causeway.

Saffron was pleased to see her return. A tourist, having seen Ronnie at work, would nearly always choose a painting from the selection she had in the shop. Occasionally they would shake their head and return to purchase directly from Ronnie, obviously not convinced that each of those that Saffron stocked was an original and not a photocopy.

Ronnie turned her back on the sea and painted both sides of the small square. On one side was a taverna with tables and chairs outside and on the other were the row of shops, all of them displaying their goods outside except for Yannis.

Saffron accepted the additions to the views with alacrity. 'I'm sure they'll sell as fast as the others. They're so popular that I thought I might increase the price slightly, put them up to twelve Euros. I'd give you six, of course. If I find the customers are unwilling to pay that I can always drop the price back down.'

Ronnie shrugged. 'You're the business woman. I'm just the artist starving in a garret.'

'Hardly starving,' smiled Saffron, knowing how much she had paid Ronnie over the past month.

'I'm not complaining. I'm covering my rent and my food. I'll stock you up with some of these and some more views. I thought I'd go over to Spinalonga next week and do a selection of paintings from there. I saw a number of possibilities when I visited earlier.'

'I'm sure they'd prove popular. The tourists seem to find anything to do with Spinalonga irresistible.'

Ronnie climbed aboard the first boat of the morning that left for Spinalonga carrying the visitors. She waited patiently until they had gone ashore before she handed her easel to the boatman who held it whilst she stepped onto the quay. She walked up to the kiosk where they sold the entrance tickets and took her place in the queue before following the dozen or more tourists who were making their way to the tunnel entrance.

Once in the square she set up her easel, adjusting her position until she decided the aspect was the most advantageous.

'Sorry,' said a man as he backed into her. He had been so intent on taking a photograph that he had not noticed her.

'No problem,' answered Ronnie, glad that she had not started painting. She waited until the group had moved forwards and made a start on the house opposite with its arched doorway and grilled window openings. Ten minutes later another, larger group emerged from the tunnel. They glanced cursorily at Ronnie and then proceeded to fan out, standing directly in her line of vision. She waited for individuals to move to one side so she could check a detail before continuing to paint, giving a sigh of relief as they moved further away.

It took her almost an hour to complete her picture, as she had to wait for the tourists who blocked her view to move. There seemed to be a continual stream of people coming through the tunnel now, gathering together to listen to their guide, jostling her easel or chair without regard as they passed her. With a sigh of frustration and despair, Ronnie packed away her paints, released the clips on her easel and folded it down. It was impossible to paint with so many people around.

She decided she would speak to John and ask if he would be able to negotiate for her to go over on the early boat with the locals who worked on the island. She could return on the first boat after it had deposited the early tourists from Plaka. That should give her at least an hour when she would be able to work peacefully.

Ronnie deposited her materials back at her apartment and walked up to the taverna. John looked at her in surprise when she arrived.

'You're early. Run out of paint?'

Ronnie shook her head. 'I've been to Spinalonga. I wanted to paint some of the views over there, but it was impossible with all the tourists. I wondered if you could arrange for me to go over on the early boat with the workers? That way I should have about an hour to myself before the tourists begin arriving.'

'Is an hour enough?'

'Not really, but better than nothing.'

'If you're prepared to be up early I'll take you over. I can borrow a key to the gate to the old port. I'd have to lock it after you, but you could have at least two hours, maybe a bit more.'

'Would you? I'd really appreciate it.'

'I'll speak to the boatmen when I've closed up here and tell them you'll be over there next week. How about that?'

'That would be perfect.' Ronnie smiled at John gratefully.

'The least I can do for you after you found Tassos for me.'

'Have you been back to visit him again?'

John shook his head. 'I've not had the opportunity. I want to go up there with Nick so she can meet him. It's rather a long drive for the girls and they're a real handful now they're walking around everywhere. It isn't really practical to take them. We'd have to carry them or take their stroller and I'm not sure we could get that up and down the path. I need to be able to persuade Mum and Bryony that they would love to look after them for a day.'

'Rather them than me. I'd be petrified. One small child for a day would be bad enough, but two! If you do arrange to go to Mili would I be able to come with you?' asked Ronnie tentatively. 'I'd love to meet that old man and see the gorge again, but I'd be a bit nervous about going alone.'

'No problem. You're no trouble, are you, Skele? You'd enjoy a walk in the gorge.' John tickled the dog's ears.

'Does he live up here?'

John shook his head. 'Dad doesn't really like him being over by the taverna, but when I'm working here he sits outside. He

42

never goes around the tables to cadge for food. He knows he'll get the scraps later.'

'I've seen him around, but I didn't realise he was your dog.'

'I found him on the beach. Aunt Ourania is frightened of dogs and she has her precious cat so he can't live at home. He's allowed to go in to the house to see Nick and the girls but he lives down at my friend Dimitris's house. He's doing his National Service at the moment so I collect him each morning and walk him back in the evening. He'd love a run through Mili Gorge.'

'What breed is he?'

'He's unique.' John smiled down at Skele who wagged his tail. 'He's a complete mix up, but he has the most wonderful temperament and is incredibly intelligent.'

Skele sat up straighter at John's words and looked up at him adoringly. Ronnie laughed. 'You'd think he understood what you said about him.'

John nodded. 'Of course. He's completely bilingual,' he said seriously and grinned at the look of disbelief on Ronnie's face. 'I'm sure it's the tone of voice he understands, not the words. I can give him a command in Greek or English and he obeys. He's very special. He saved my life when the chalets were on fire and then he stopped the man who had done it from running away.'

'Really?'

'Absolute truth, isn't it Skele?'

The dog made a low noise in his throat as if agreeing with John and Ronnie laughed delightedly. 'He's amazing.'

Skele looked at her, his head on one side and his mouth just open as if he were smiling.

'He likes a compliment.'

John arranged for Ronnie to meet him on the quay at Plaka at six in the morning. He had spoken to the boatmen and they had agreed to bring her back to Plaka whenever it suited her during the day. Now she felt quite excited. There were various locations that she felt she would be able to reproduce as paintings to add to the variety of stock in Saffron's shop, but it would be frustrating only being able to work until the tourists arrived and blocked her view.

She had planned her work carefully. She would start with the Church of St Panteleimon. When she had completed a couple of pictures it would be a simple matter of turning her easel around and she could paint a view of the road leading down to the square. By the end of a week she hoped to have a selection of pictures covering the view of Plaka and Elounda from the hill top, along with others of the main street, the square and Church to show to Saffron.

Ronnie had almost completed her second picture of the Church when she felt her skin prickling. She looked around to see who was watching her and was surprised when there was no one in sight.

'Imagination,' she told herself. 'I'm alone over here at the moment. The workers don't begin to arrive until eight thirty.'

For three days Ronnie moved to different locations until she finally set up her easel in the square. She began to paint the main street, showing the houses on each side with the giant palm hanging across the road that gave shade during the day. Later she would change her position slightly so she could paint the steps leading up the hill where a tree had taken root and was flourishing.

Once again she had the feeling that someone was watching her. She ignored the uncomfortable sensation and completed six paintings to add to her growing portfolio. It was almost a relief to pack her artist's materials away and know that she only planned to make one more early morning visit to the island. If Saffron liked her pictures she would copy those she had completed and no one would know when they had been painted.

The following morning she erected her easel in the centre of the square and began to paint the old buildings that still stood on either side of the tall palm before turning her attention to a view of the houses opposite. On two occasions she was sure she could feel eyes on her and she scanned the ruined houses behind her.

Had anyone been hiding in there they would have been clearly visible to her. She looked along the main street and the only sign of life was a sparrow pecking at a crack in the ground for an insect.

Absorbed again in her work she started in surprise when she felt a hand on her shoulder, leaving a streak of green paint on the sky. She turned to see who had disturbed her and could not believe there was no one standing there. The sun was shining into her eyes making her squint and she thought she caught a glimpse of movement in the house opposite. She was sure there was someone else on the island with her.

Ronnie walked across and peered into the open doorway. The house had been renovated and made safe, only the walls were standing and there was a clear view from where she was standing through to the house beyond. A narrow path ran between the buildings and she swiftly crossed the threshold and looked into the house opposite and then walked along the pathway to where it turned and met a wall. There was no one.

'You really are letting your imagination run away with you,' she admonished herself. 'It was probably one of the large palm fronds moving in the breeze that caused a shadow. Stop being so paranoid.'

Ronnie returned to her easel and added an extra palm frond to the tree to cover the streak of paint. She glanced at her watch. She had obviously spent longer than she had realised looking around the ruined buildings. It was unlikely now that she would have time now to paint the other houses as she had intended. Carefully she packed her paints away, checked her paintings were completely dry before placing them inside a protective folder and collapsed her easel.

As she walked through the tunnel to where the boats would arrive she shuddered. It was cold and claustrophobic. For the lepers who had been forced to shelter from the elements in there it must have been a thoroughly miserable experience.

To her surprise she found the gate was still locked and there

45

was no sign of anyone having arrived from the mainland. She shivered and walked back to the square. She looked at her watch again and frowned. It was only seven thirty. She was convinced that when she had looked at it earlier it had been eight forty.

'You really are losing it,' she muttered to herself.

Ronnie walked along to the old port entrance, climbed up above the laundry troughs and erected her easel. She would paint the view of Plaka from Spinalonga, although no doubt it had looked very different when the lepers had lived on the island. She felt quite relieved when she could see the workmen's boat approaching and she packed away her equipment and walked back to the square. When she heard the gate being unlocked she walked through the tunnel and waited beside the boat until the boatman was ready to leave.

As the days had become warmer Ronnie had changed her routine. It was impossible to sit outside and paint all day unless she was prepared to have sunstroke. She would be down at the square in Plaka by seven each morning and paint until ten. She would then return to her apartment and sit on her small balcony in the shade to examine the art work she had completed and add any finishing touches that she thought was necessary. When the sun moved round so that her balcony received the full force of the sun's rays she went down to the beach for a swim before her lunch. Once the direct sun had moved from her balcony she would return to her painting until the light began to fade.

Her experience on Spinalonga had unnerved her and she had no inclination to look at the pictures she had executed. Instead she hurried back to her apartment and changed into her bikini and slipped a sun dress over the top. She would go for an early swim and look at them later. Tomorrow she would make one more trip to Spinalonga to complete her portfolio and then take her work to show to Saffron.

Her swim in the sea was refreshing, although she noticed that the breeze she had noticed on Spinalonga seemed to have dropped completely. She looked towards the island and could see the myriads of people swarming everywhere. Thank goodness they had placed gates at the entrance to the tunnel and the old port or tourists would have been tempted to swim over and party on the island at night unchecked. She wondered what it would be like to be over on the island in the darkness. She certainly would not want to be stranded there alone after her unnerving experience that morning.

She swam leisurely back to the shore, slipped her feet into her flip-flops and rubbed her body free of excess water before donning her dress again. She checked that the key to her apartment was still safely in the pocket and walked back up to the road. A quick shower, then she would go to the taverna in the hope that John would be there and she could ask him to take her over to Spinalonga the following morning for her to complete the series of paintings she had planned.

John greeted her with a smile. 'You usual?' and Ronnie nodded. She had found that a small beer was the most thirst quenching drink apart from water, and she had already drunk two bottles and placed two more in her tiny fridge ready for later.

'Did you finish all your paintings?' asked John.

'Not quite. I need to go over once more.'

'No problem. I'll take you tomorrow if that suits you.'

'Would you be able to stay over there with me?' Ronnie blushed as she made the request. 'I shouldn't be more than an hour and it would save me from having to hang around for the boat.'

'You could always paint something else. Have you been round to St George's Church and painted that? It was more attractive when the trees were still growing there, but you could always look at an old photo and add them in.'

Ronnie shook her head. 'I just don't really want to be over there on my own again. You'll think I'm stupid, but I kept thinking someone was watching me and then it felt like a hand being placed on my shoulder. I looked around and couldn't see any sign of anyone.'

John smiled at her. 'You can feel the ghosts over there.'

'I don't believe in ghosts.'

'They're all very friendly,' John assured her.

'Don't be silly.' Despite her words Ronnie felt a tingle run down her spine. 'I was so sure that someone had touched my shoulder that I went looking for them. I only wandered in and out of the houses in the square, but when I looked at my watch I'm certain it said eight forty. I reckoned I must have spent longer searching than I had realised so I packed up ready to meet the boat. When I reached the end of the tunnel there was no sign of anyone and the gate was locked. I thought I'd go back up and wait in the sunshine and when I looked at my watch again it said seven thirty.'

'That was probably just your mind playing tricks or the sun on the face of your watch made you misread the time. I'll stay over if you really are nervous about being on your own. I can always take some photographs.'

Ronnie smiled at him gratefully. 'I'm sure it was just the wind playing tricks with me, but I'd be happier to know you were there with me.'

Ronnie slept fitfully that night. She kept waking up from a recurring dream. She was painting on Spinalonga and kept finding the paint palette was empty and the blocks of colour sitting on the ground at her feet. As fast as she tried to pick them up they moved just out of reach of her fingers.

At four thirty she gave up the unequal struggle and climbed out of bed. She was hot and sticky, despite having slept with her window open. She leaned her head against the cool glass and looked across the dark sea towards Spinalonga. The sun was just beginning to rise behind the hills, but most of the island was still in complete darkness.

As she stood there a solitary light showed half way up the dark mound. Ronnie closed her eyes and opened them again. It was still there in the same place. She shivered, relieved that John would be on the island with her that morning. Reluctantly she drew her eyes away from the light and made some coffee, returning to sit on her balcony to drink it, hoping the light would have disappeared.

The sky began to turn a vivid red, gradually paling to orange, pink and finally gold, as the sun rose. She must get dressed and go to meet John. If he was good enough to take her over to the island and stay there with her she must not be late meeting him. She looked for the light again and saw a small boat anchored a short distance from the island, the fisherman hauling in his early morning catch. Ronnie shook her head. How foolish she had been to imagine the light was on Spinalonga.

John was waiting for her, his camera slung around his neck in a waterproof cover. He took Ronnie's easel and bag from her and stowed them under the seat whilst she climbed aboard. 'I'm glad I'm a photographer, not an artist. I'd hate to haul that lot around with me all the time.'

'You get used to it,' Ronnie smiled. 'The easel isn't heavy now they make them from aluminium. The old wooden ones were a nightmare. What are you planning to photograph?'

'Anything that moves,' grinned John. 'I'll keep my distance from you. I don't want you having hysterics thinking a ghost has touched your foot when it's a beetle I'm pursuing.'

'It certainly wasn't a beetle that touched me yesterday.'

John raised his eyebrows. 'Well if it touches you again today let me know. I'd love to make a ghost's acquaintance.'

Ronnie dropped her eyes. John obviously did not take her experience of the previous day seriously. She was thankful that she had decided the light was from a fishing boat and not told John it had been on Spinalonga.

The journey across the water took no longer than fifteen

minutes in John's small motor boat. He moored it securely at the old port entrance and Ronnie picked up bag and waited for John to pass out her easel. He slung it over his arm and began to walk towards the gate.

'I'll carry it; it isn't heavy.' He fumbled in his pocket and drew out the key to unlock the gate, holding it for Ronnie to pass through before locking it securely again after them.

'Why do they have gates on the island? Were they to keep the lepers confined?' asked Ronnie.

John shook his head. 'They're a modern addition. They said it was to stop people coming over here when there was no one around to ensure they didn't do any damage. The church was broken into once. The silly thing is that if you know the island you can simply walk around past the graveyard and you eventually arrive in the square. The gates can't really keep anyone out.'

'I imagine you'd panic if you were a tourist and found the gate at the end of the tunnel was locked.'

'The last boats always sound hooters and the visitors are told to come straight back when they hear them. Occasionally youngsters think they are being clever and plan to camp out over here for the night. Once it becomes really dark they lose their nerve and begin to phone for help.'

Ronnie considered the information. Did they really lose their nerve because it was dark or did they have an experience similar to hers that made them want to leave the island?

'Where do you want to sit?' asked John.

'In the square. I want to paint the steps where that lovely tree has grown. Where will you be?'

'Just up there.' John pointed to where the facade of a house had been completely renovated years earlier. 'There's plenty of grass and weed around for insects to hide in. If you turn round you'll be able to see me.'

'Thanks. I doubt I'll be more than an hour.'

'Take your time. Provided I'm back to open up the shop at

about eight there's no rush.'

Ronnie clipped her paper firmly to the easel, although there was no wind at all. It was going to be another hot day. She tipped a small amount of water into a plastic beaker and placed it in the compartment to hold it safely in place. She moistened her paintbrush and covered it with blue paint that she then placed in one of the shallow depressions in her palette. She added a little white to tone it down, mixed the colours together thoroughly and made a start on the sky.

Once she had completed the picture she scrutinized it carefully. One wall needed to be a little higher and the tree was a little too central. She placed a number 'one' on the reverse of the paper and took a fresh sheet. She had almost finished the tree to her satisfaction when she heard a deep sigh. She looked around, expecting to see John standing behind her. There was no sign of him.

'John,' she called in panic and he straightened up from behind a wall up by the house.

'What's wrong?'

Ronnie gulped. 'I'm sure someone was standing behind me. I thought it was you. I heard a deep sigh, but when I turned around there was no one there.'

'It was probably the wind coming up through the tunnel.'

Ronnie shook her head. 'There isn't any wind at all. Yesterday there was a breeze over here and I thought it must have been the shadow of a palm branch that I had seen, but I'm *certain* I heard someone sigh.'

'You really do have the jitters. I'm just photographing a centipede, then I'll come and sit down here on the steps until you've finished. Maybe your ghost will come and sit beside me. I don't mind.' John smiled at her. 'I promise not to sigh.'

'You must think me so stupid. I'll be as quick as I can.' Ronnie picked up her paintbrush and began to shade the trunk of the tree as John mounted the steps hoping to find the centipede still there.

He returned a few minutes later and sat on the low wall patiently until Ronnie announced she was finished, packed up her paints and folded her easel.

'Fancy a breakfast when we get back?' he asked as he led the way towards the old port entrance. He patted his pockets. 'I've left my waterproof camera cover up by the house. I won't be a minute. I'll run up and get it.'

Ronnie nodded and stood on the path waiting for him. She looked at the buildings opposite, wondering whether they would make an interesting picture. She dropped her bag and her hand flew to her mouth. At a window towards the top of the house there was someone leaning on the sill looking down at her. Stifling a scream she forced herself to look again and then felt embarrassed. The window was blocked with stones; they made the opening look like a person due to their colouring. Thank goodness she had not shouted in panic for John.

She smiled a little self consciously as she saw John walking along the path towards her and then she heard it again. The colour drained from her face and she leaned back against the wall to steady herself.

'What's wrong?'

'I heard it again. A deep sigh. She sounded so sad.'

'She? What makes you think it was a woman?'

Ronnie frowned. 'I don't know, but I'm sure it was a woman.'

'It was probably just the sea. It can make strange noises when it flows in between the rocks.'

'It wasn't the sea, John. It was the kind of sound that someone makes when they are deeply unhappy.' Ronnie looked at him with distressed eyes.

'Alright, Ron, I believe you heard something. Whatever it was you have no need to be afraid. I'm certain of that.'

'You mean you *do* believe there are ghosts over here?'

'It's a long story. I'll tell you whilst we're eating breakfast. What would you like? I can do bacon, egg, sausage, beans and toast. How does that sound?' He took the key of the gate from his pocket and lifted Ronnie's easel.

John placed sausages and bacon into the frying pan. 'Do you want to talk about ghosts?' he asked.

'I'm not superstitious. I don't believe in ghosts or the paranormal or whatever, but I am convinced there is something strange over on Spinalonga.'

'Come and look, then tell me you don't believe in ghosts.'

John led the way from the kitchen area across to the side wall of the taverna. Hanging there was an enlarged photograph of a girl in a white dress. Her features were indistinct, but she gave the impression that she was curious about whatever was happening. Ronnie had seen the photograph on many previous occasions and taken no particular notice. Now as she looked at it she realised it was slightly blurred and out of focus and she was puzzled why they had bothered to have it enlarged and displayed prominently.

'That's Anna,' announced John.

'Anna? Oh, you mean your old Aunt Anna that you've told me about?'

John shook his head. 'It certainly isn't Aunt Anna. My mother took the photograph years ago. She and Nick's mother were here on holiday and Mamma left Elizabeth's camera on the island. She went off early the next morning as she was certain she knew where it was. A storm blew up and the boats were told to stay in the harbour. Despite the weather my father insisted a boatman had to take him over so he could find her. Whilst she was waiting for a boat to come she took some more photos and that was one of them. After it was developed both Flora and Manolis confirmed that it was Anna, old Uncle Yannis's daughter who had died over there.'

The colour had drained from Ronnie's face. 'You're kidding me.'

'I swear I'm not. Ask my Mamma or Pappa.'

Ronnie followed John back into the kitchen area where he turned his attention back to his cooking.

'The people who said the photo was of this girl Anna; did they actually know her?'

'Of course. Manolis took her over to Spinalonga and Flora was living on the island at the time. I'll have to ask Uncle Yannis if I can show you the rest of Anna's art work. It's very different from yours, but I'm sure you'd be interested. The pictures were copied and published in his book. The prints Uncle Yannis sells were done by her.' John placed slices of bread into the toaster and opened a tin of baked beans.

Ronnie shivered. 'So there really are ghosts on the island?'

'I've never actually seen one,' admitted John, 'But you can feel them when you're over there on your own. I think they're sensible enough to stay hidden when the tourists descend on them.'

'Have you ever had anything strange happen to you whilst you were over there?' asked Ronnie tentatively.

John shook his head. 'I think they accept me. I'm family. Why?'

'Do you think they resent me being there as I'm not family?'

'Why should they? You're not doing any harm.'

'What about the photo?'

John shrugged. 'I told you, that was taken years ago. Anna has never put in an appearance since and nor has anyone else that I know of. Mamma is convinced she was trying to tell her she had to stay in Elounda with my father.' John removed the sausages and bacon from the heat, placed them on the hot plate to keep warm and broke the eggs into the pan.

'Tell me more.'

John grinned. 'I was conceived on Spinalonga that day. That night Mamma had a phone call from her sister to say that her father had been taken into hospital with a stroke. She returned immediately to New Orleans and it wasn't until later that she realised she was pregnant. She didn't tell my Pappa. There was a robbery at the hotel in Athens where my Pappa and Nick's father worked and they were both shot. Mamma came back over to Athens to be with Nick's mum and brought me with her. The truth came out, of course, Mamma and Pappa were married and she stayed here as Anna had tried to tell her she should.'

'Do you truly believe that, John?'

John nodded seriously. 'I believe the photograph is of Anna who lived on the island and she was trying to communicate to my Mamma.'

'So why would anyone want to communicate with me? I'm not family. I have no connection with the island.'

John shrugged. 'I'm sure a number of people who lived over there were desperately unhappy. Maybe they sense you are a sympathetic soul; on the other hand you could be letting your imagination run away with you. Pass me the plates. Breakfast is ready.'

'Maybe I have been concentrating too much on my painting. It would probably do me good to take a couple of days off. I've been planning to hire a car and explore some of the surrounding area. I've only been as far as Aghios Nikolaos on the bus.'

'There are plenty of pretty villages around. You might want to paint some of the houses in those. You never know, you might run into a ghost somewhere else.' John grinned at her as he picked up the plates and led the way to the tables outside.

Ronnie felt unsettled during the remainder of the day. Whilst putting the finishing touches to her paintings she kept thinking about the photograph that hung in the taverna. John obviously believed the photograph was that of a ghost. Despite her own scepticism regarding ghosts she was sure she had experienced something very strange whilst on Spinalonga. She tried to convince herself that it had only been her imagination and she just needed to have some time away from the area doing something other than painting.

She took her portfolio of island pictures down to Saffron's shop and Saffron immediately enthused over them.

'I'm sure these will sell. When are you going back over to do some more?'

Ronnie shook her head. 'I'm not planning to go to Spinalonga to paint any more at the moment. I can always copy these. Today I'm going to have a lazy day on the beach and I plan to hire a car tomorrow. My mother and great uncle are coming out at the end of the season and I'd like to know a few places of interest to take them. I thought I'd drive up to Kritsa and look round the village. We only walked the Gorge when I was here earlier with the others.'

'It's very pretty. Well worth a visit. Stop at Panagia Kera. It's a small church where the walls and ceiling are completely covered with Byzantine frescos. It's just after Mardati and before you get to Kritsa.'

'Anywhere else you can recommend?' asked Ronnie.

'Well, you could have some lunch in Kritsa and from there you could return to the main road and drive to Neapoli, detour down to Kastelli, and join the road that leads down to Elounda and Plaka. Neapoli is nice, but you need a considerable amount of time there to look around properly. It's quite a large town.'

Saffron watched Ronnie walk up the hill back towards her apartment and felt envious. She had not realised just how time consuming and tiring it would be to have a gift shop. Since opening she had not been able to take any time off as the tourists visited the area every day. She had thought it would be something that would occupy her days and she could talk about with Vasi, but her evenings seemed to be spent ordering stock or working on her accounts whilst Vasi sat and read or watched the television. She really could do with an assistant so she had more time to herself and also time to spend with Vasi.

August 2010

Ronnie drove along the coast road towards Aghios Nikolaos, stopping wherever there was a space to pull off the road to enable her to take a photograph of the bay. A stiff breeze was blowing, creating white flecks of foam on the sea and she could see that the boats crossing over to Spinalonga were being tossed around. She had walked down to the beach, thinking she would try to reproduce the rough sea, but the wind had blown her hair into her eyes and tried to tear the paper from her hand so she had given in to the elements. It was no day for sitting down by the quay and painting.

Before leaving Elounda she had studied the map. The drive to Mardati and on to Panagia Kera should take her no more than three quarters of an hour and from there it was only a short way further up the hill to Kritsa. She would decide later whether to have lunch in the village or drive on to Neapoli.

On reaching the large roundabout she took the turn indicating Kritsa and began to drive carefully along the winding country road. The car hire proprietor had assured her that the roads were not particularly steep or narrow. If she did run into any difficulties she could telephone him and he would arrange for someone to come out and help her.

Ronnie followed the sign posted directions for Kritsa until she passed Mardati and drew up on some waste ground outside the church. The doors were open and sitting beside them was an elderly woman who waved and beckoned to her. Ronnie handed the woman three Euros, draped a scarf around her shoulders and walked inside where she stopped and gazed in awe. Every square inch was covered in paintings. As she moved from aisle to aisle she realised each aisle told its own story. There was the birth of Mary, the Nativity, events from the life of Jesus as related in the Bible, and the Last Supper. In the third section there was the Resurrection and everywhere the Apostles were depicted looking on. She craned her neck and studied the ceiling. Despite the corbelling of the roof the paintings looked in perfect proportion. Rubbing her stiff neck she began to examine the walls more slowly, moving from one life size fresco to another.

As she looked at them she realised that each face was almost identical; she studied their hands and feet, again they all showed similar brushwork and detail, it was only the colour of their robes and the artefacts they were holding that differentiated between the Apostles. She decided the work had been completed by a team of artists, each one specialising in a particular aspect, and wondered if the woman sitting by the door would know the answer.

Ronnie placed some coins in the donation box and lit a candle before returning to the doorway. She smiled at the woman and waved her hand towards the interior.

'Are you able to tell me about the frescoes?' she asked.

'Apostles.'

Ronnie nodded. She knew they depicted the Apostles. 'Who painted them? When were they completed?'

The woman frowned. 'Very old. Apostles.'

'Who were the artists? Did they decorate other churches?'

'Very old,' she repeated and Ronnie gave up. She would have a look in Kritsa to see if she could purchase a guide book with the information.

She returned to her car and continued up the hill and into Kritsa, following the signs directing her to the car park. It had been far more nerve wracking driving through the narrow streets of the village than it had been on the mountain road. Although the gradient had risen quite steeply in parts there were no deep drops on either side to alarm her.

Ronnie locked the car, checked she had her bottle of water, slung her bag over her shoulder and followed the arrow directing her to the village square. She walked up the hill, glad that she had decided to bring her hat. The sun was hot and the wind seemed to have dropped now she was away from the coast. Most of the shops appeared to be selling handcrafted goods, beautifully embroidered table cloths, runners, cushion covers and handmade lace. They were interspersed with gift shops offering onyx, marble and bronze statuettes along with pottery replicas of the finds on the archaeological sites and a miscellaneous collection of bottle openers, key rings, ash trays and dolls.

Ronnie took her time browsing, shaking her head as she was invited to enter and inspect the items more closely. She wished the shop keepers would return inside so that she was able to take some photographs to send to her mother and Uncle Alex. She would certainly bring them here to see the village when they visited.

She chose a table in the shade at a taverna in the square and ordered courgette balls followed by a mushroom omelette and salad. Despite the number of customers the service was good and when her courgette balls arrived she saw to her delight they were being served with tzatsiki and pita bread. She wished she had ordered a double portion rather than an omelette, but when that arrived, overflowing with wild mushrooms she decided she had made a good choice and ate with relish.

By the time she had finished her meal it was far later than she had realised. It was doubtful that she would have time to look around the town of Neapoli and decided she would wander a little more in Kritsa and save Neapoli for another day. The narrow streets seemed to merge into each other, taking unexpected turns or ending abruptly with a wall. She was offered nuts by an old lady who was sitting in her doorway and gave her a Euro for the dozen or so that were contained in a screw of paper. As she turned to go she was handed a tiny bunch of small grapes and she smiled her thanks.

Many of the roads had a tap set into the wall above a stone basin and she noticed people filled a bottle or container before making their way back to their house. Her own water bottle was nearly empty and she was not sure how long it would take her to return to the square where she would be able to buy another. She waited until a woman had filled a large polythene container and then held out her bottle.

The woman nodded. 'Drink. Is good. From mountain.'

Ronnie allowed a small amount to dribble into her bottle and then raised it to her lips. It was ice cold and lacking any discernible smell or taste. Trusting the information the woman had given her she filled her bottle and took a mouthful. It tasted pure and fresh. She glanced at her watch again. She really would have to curtail her wandering and return to the car. She had no idea how long it would take her to drive to Neapoli and she did not want to find she was driving down an unknown mountain road in the dark.

She walked along the first narrow road that led down the hill. Provided she went down the hill she should end up on the outskirts of the village eventually. Unsure how she had reached the area she found she was back on the main road and stopped to get her bearings. Just below her on the right was a small garden with a statue in the centre. She had been so busy following the sign for the car park that she had missed this completely as she had driven past earlier.

The statue, when she reached it, was a bronze bust of a woman and she wondered about its significance. There was an inscription in Greek on a plaque, but nothing in English to explain the reason for the commemoration. Frustrated, Ronnie turned back and walked up to the car park. She had asked in a number of shops if there was a guide book to the area available and had been greeted with a puzzled look and shake of the head.

Ronnie consulted her map and decided she would take the road to Neapoli, on to Kastelli and join the road leading to Elounda. It would probably take her about the same amount of time whichever way she went.

It was nearly five when Ronnie reached Neapoli and she decided it would be foolish to stop and attempt to look around the town. She took the turn off that was signed as leading to Kastelli and immediately the road became narrower, flanked by grassy banks and everywhere looked deserted. After driving for fifteen minutes she wondered if she had turned onto a farm track by mistake, although the surface was tarmac. She was sure the signpost had indicated that the road led to Kastelli. If she did see anyone approaching she would stop them and check that she was on the right road. She continued, driving carefully, finally deciding that it would be sensible to find somewhere to turn around and drive back to Neapoli before she ended up completely lost.

Ronnie was relieved when the grassy banks gave way to flatter ground and she could see chickens strutting around and wooden enclosures behind the wire fencing. She must be nearing somewhere, if only a farm. As she continued the first small house came into view and also a familiar bumping from the rear wheel. Surely she hadn't picked up a puncture!

Slowly, hoping not to do any further damage, she crawled along the road looking for somewhere she could safely stop and inspect the wheel. The road widened as she rounded the bend and there was a large space where she could pull in between the War Memorial and a large circular structure.

Ronnie climbed out of her car and inspected the tyre on the rear wheel. She was correct in her assumption that she had a puncture. She sighed. It would mean having to call the hire company and ask for someone to come out and change it for her. From the glove compartment she took the papers she had been given and searched for the telephone number.

As she pressed the numbers in to her mobile she realised she was being watched by a group of men who were sitting across the road. She could hear a telephone ringing and she waited impatiently for it to be answered. Finally it disconnected and the line went dead. Sighing in exasperation she dialled the number again and once more she could hear the ringing tone, but no one answered.

Ronnie looked at the men across the road. They were watching her curiously. She wondered if one of them would understand if she asked him to change the wheel and opened the boot. At least there was a spare wheel in there, although no jack or wrench to remove the nuts. She had no choice. She would have to 'phone Saffron and see if Vasi was able to come and rescue her.

She waited whilst Saffron's phone rang and then went to voice mail. Deciding it was pointless to leave a message; she scrolled down her list of 'phone numbers and looked for Giovanni's. As she began to press in the area code a man who had been sitting across the road strolled over.

'Problem?'

'I have a flat tyre and I can't get through to the hire company. I'm trying to contact some friends to ask them for help.'

'Spastico lastico,' The man observed and walked back across the road and into a workshop. Ronnie bit her lip. He had obviously not understood a word she had said. She debated the wisdom of approaching any of the other men who were sitting there in the hope that one of them would speak enough English to understand her.

Before Ronnie had a chance to enter Giovanni's 'phone number fully the man returned carrying a jack and a wrench. He waved Ronnie away from the car and placed the jack underneath.

'Oh, thank you. I'll be terribly grateful if you can get me on my way again.'

He made no reply, simply waved her away again, as he placed the jack in position and began to pump the handle to raise the wheel from the ground.

Ronnie took the hint. She was not wanted. She wandered over to the War Memorial and looked at the names inscribed; as usual many of them appeared to have the same surname, indicating that whole families had lost their lives. She looked at the large circular structure which was half full of water and had stone steps down one side. It was obviously not a conventional well as there was no winding gear for a bucket. Surely people did not have to climb up and down the treacherous looking steps for their water? She wished she could ask and looked back at the man who was dealing with her flat tyre. He was struggling to remove the nuts that held the wheel in place, finally he put the wrench to one side and walked back to the workshop returning with a hammer.

Ronnie decided that rather than stand and watch she would walk down the road a short distance and see what else the village had to offer. Side roads led off, but she did not feel she should venture down any of them. She could see the houses were old, some of them well maintained and others neglected. As she looked up a turning there was a house that was almost covered in a riot of colour from the plants that were growing outside. Unable to resist, Ronnie took out her camera and began to take photographs, moving closer. Finally satisfied she turned to retrace her steps to the main road and her attention was caught by the large house standing on the corner.

She drew in her breath. It must have been magnificent when it had been occupied. It was two storeys and double fronted, with a large wooden door that was chained and padlocked, the windows had decorative wrought iron at each window, although the glass was missing. She crossed the road and peered inside. On the far side of the room she could see a large bed and, dishes and plates were on an old dresser, whilst discoloured curling photographs still adorned the walls.

'Oh, you poor house. How could anyone bear to leave you to get into that state?' On impulse she photographed the front and side before she began to walk back to her car.

The man was carrying his tools back to the workshop and Ronnie hurried forward. 'Thank you so much.' She opened her purse and began to extract some notes, but the man waved them away.

'No problem.'

'But I must pay you for your time. It was so good of you. I was completely stuck.'

He waved his hand again and Ronnie felt helpless. 'Please, let me give you something to say thank you.' She pushed twenty Euros into his hand and mimed having a drink.

This time he smiled and did not refuse the money. 'No problem,' he said again.

Ronnie climbed into her car and started the engine. What was the difference between charging her for changing the wheel and accepting money for a drink? Then she realised. How naive she was. A garage would have charged her no more than ten Euros and she had given him twenty. She looked in her rear view mirror and saw him showing the notes to his friends, a pleased smile on his face. She had to smile to herself. Had he asked her for that amount she would have paid it without demur, anything to have the tyre changed so that she could drive on to Elounda. Once there she would have a few choice words to say to the car hire proprietor for not answering his telephone.

Ronnie drew onto the forecourt in front of the car hire premises. It appeared deserted. She wrapped the keys inside the papers she had been given earlier and pushed them through the letter box. She would return tomorrow and ask for a twenty Euro refund.

As she placed her bag over her shoulder and was about to start her walk back to the apartments she saw the car hire owner sitting in the cafe next door. She would confront him now, rather than wait until the following day. She strode forwards and sat down at the table in front of him.

'I would like a twenty Euro refund from you. I had to pay to have a wheel changed when I picked up a puncture.'

The man looked at her. 'You have telephone number. Call me. I come. No refund.'

'I tried calling you. There was no answer. I was stuck in a village and luckily a local man had a jack and wrench so he was able to help me. I had to pay him so I would like a refund.'

'Receipt?'

'I don't have a receipt. He was just a villager doing me a good turn.'

'No refund.'

'Look, the damaged wheel is in the boot. You can check for yourself that it has a puncture. You'll need to repair it before you hire the car out again.'

'No refund,' he repeated. 'Need keys and papers to sign for return.'

'I have put the keys through the letterbox and the car is outside.' She turned to go.

'Need here.'

'They are next door.'

'Closed now.'

Ronnie took a deep breath. 'You can see the car. The papers and keys I put through your letterbox. It won't take you a minute to unlock the door and pick them up.'

'Closed now. Collect tomorrow. Pay for extra day's hire.'

'No way.' Ronnie had a desire to push the man backwards off his chair as she walked away. She would speak to Giovanni. Even if she was not entitled to a refund she was certainly not liable for an extra day's car hire. Feeling thoroughly annoyed she began to walk back towards the apartments.

She had nearly reached Yannis's house when he saw John approaching with Skele. He waved his hand to her and she bent to tickle Skele's ears as he butted her legs with his head.

'Good day?' asked John.

Ronnie pulled a face. 'Most of it was. I was just on my way to speak to your father about the man at the car hire. He wants to charge me for an extra day.'

'How come?' John frowned.

'I had a puncture as I was driving back. I tried to 'phone him and there was no answer. Luckily a villager came and changed the wheel for me otherwise I would have been stuck.' Ronnie fell into step beside him.

'You should have 'phoned Dad.'

'I tried calling Saffie and it went to voice mail. I was just looking for your Dad's number when the man came over. Fortunately he had a jack and a wrench as there weren't any tools in the car. He refused to take any payment from me, but I insisted he took twenty Euros for a drink.'

'You should have called me. I'd have only charged you ten Euros.' John grinned at her. 'Never underestimate the Cretans. They realised you were unable to get help and took advantage.'

'Suppose I hadn't insisted on giving him some money?'

'He would have accepted the situation. He was no doubt happy to help you, but he hoped he would get a reward for his trouble.'

'If the hire company had answered their 'phone I wouldn't have had to pay anything,' grumbled Ronnie. 'When I returned the car everywhere was locked up so I put the keys and papers through the letterbox; then I saw the owner in the cafe next door. I asked him for a refund to cover the cost of changing the wheel and he said I should have called him. He then said that as I had put the papers through the letterbox he would not accept the car back until tomorrow and I would have to pay for an extra day's hire. He's a crook.'

John looked at Ronnie in disbelief. 'How can he charge you for an extra day when you have returned it?'

'That's what he said.'

'We'll go and have a word with him. He obviously thinks you're a tourist and he can take advantage of you as you don't speak Greek. Come on, Skele, we'll sort him out, won't we.'

Ronnie stood to one side whilst John spoke to the truculent car hire proprietor. He continually shook his head until he finally drew a dirty twenty Euros from the wad of notes in his wallet and waved it at Ronnie.

'Not understand. Car returned. All okay now.'

'Thank you.' Ronnie took the note and pushed it into her purse. 'Did he truly not understand before, John?'

John looked at her scornfully. 'He understood perfectly well. I'm sure when you hired the car from him his English was considerably better. He tried to tell me that you must have gone into a ditch to get the puncture and he wanted to charge you for damage.'

'The men in the village know that I did no such thing, besides you can see there isn't a scratch on the car. How did you manage to change his mind and get my money back?'

'I said I would be speaking to Mr Christos and telling him that the cars that were being rented out weren't roadworthy.'

Ronnie looked at John in alarm. 'Are they not safe?'

John shrugged. 'I expect they are, but Mr Christos would have to close him down until they had all been examined. That could take a week or more.'

'Who's Mr Christos?'

'Mr Christos is the chief of police in Aghios Nikolaos. His full name is Christos Christostofferakis.'

'What? Say that again.'

John repeated the name and grinned at Ronnie. 'His father had a stutter. When he went to register his son for his identity papers he was asked for the boy's name. The clerk wrote it down thinking Christos was to be his given name and Christostofferakis was his surname.'

'Didn't his father check and realise it was wrong?'

'His father couldn't read.'

'So what should his name have been?' frowned Ronnie.

'Christos Tofferakis.' John left a break between the two names. 'He's always been known as Mr Christos. Makes it easier for everyone. I'll just drop Skele off and then I'll walk back with you.' He opened the door to a small house and Skele trotted happily inside.

'So where did you drive to?' asked John.

'Kritsa. I stopped off to have a look at the frescos at Panagia Kera. I wanted to know more about them, but the old lady who took my money didn't speak English. I looked for a guide book when I was in Kritsa, but couldn't find one. I walked around the village and had some lunch there before I spent some more time wandering. I had thought I would stop and have a look at Neapoli but the time was getting on and I didn't want to be driving on mountain roads once it became dark. I turned off the main road to Kastelli, planning to pick up the road that comes down to Elounda. It seemed like a good idea, but it was somewhere on that road that I picked up the puncture.'

'That could have happened anywhere.'

'I'm just glad it happened so I could stop in the village. I don't know what I would have done if I had been in the middle of nowhere.'

'Been sensible, I hope, and stayed with the car. You had your mobile and it would have been a question of keep calling people until someone answered you and sent out some help.'

'That car hire man should have answered his 'phone.' Ronnie was still feeling aggrieved.

'He probably didn't hear it if he was next door.'

'He should have been in his office.'

John shook his head in amusement. 'Why sit in your office, bored out of your mind, when you can go next door, have a drink and play cards with your friends?'

Ronnie glared at him. 'You do that *after* you have finished work,' she stated.

'Not in Elounda. If business is slow you go next door to chat with your friends. If a shop is closed always look next door for the owner or in a cafe or taverna. He won't be far away.'

'I can hardly do that when I am stuck in the middle of another village,' replied Ronnie acidly.

John grinned cheerfully at her. 'When you decide you want to hire a car again let me know. I'll come with you. I'll insist you are given the owner's mobile number so you can contact him if necessary.'

'I thought I'd like to hire on one day a week. I know it's expensive hiring daily, but I really do not need a car all the time. I want to get to know some of the local area ready for when my Mom and Uncle Alex come out. I can't expect them to want to sit on the beach all day and they wouldn't want to go walking in the gorges.'

'Where do you plan to take them?'

'Well Spinalonga, of course; up to Heraklion for Knossos and the museum and also Rethymnon. I've heard that the Lassithi Plain is well worth a visit with all the windmills and I want to have a look further down the coast. I thought I might drive down to Sitia and Ierapetra and see if there's anything there that would interest them.'

'Sitia is quite a long drive over a mountain road. Ierapetra would probably be better, particularly if you are on your own. If your relatives are interested in museums and a Venetian fortress they have both of those there and the waterfront is attractive. Why don't you ask Saff? She drove just about everywhere last year.'

Ronnie smiled. 'I know. She was terribly helpful when we were over here on our walking holiday. I just don't like to bother her. She seems to be so busy during the day and I'm sure she wouldn't want to spend her time talking to me when she's closed. She probably can't wait to get home.'

Not having painted for almost two days Ronnie felt unsettled. She had no inclination to copy any of the pictures she had completed of Spinalonga and it was still too windy to sit down by the quay and paint the view. She looked at the pieces of wood and the paint that Vasi had procured for her. It would be sensible and also make a change if she tried her hand at reproducing the island in a format that Saffron would be able to use as a lid for a box.

She sanded a piece of wood carefully and placed a thin layer of white undercoat over it. She was not sure if she would be able to mix and blend the paints as she did her watercolours. It was experimental, she told herself. If this technique did not work she would have to invest in some artists' oil paints. Many of the old masters had been painted on wood, but never having tried to work in oils she was loath to spend money on paint she might never use again.

Whilst waiting for the undercoat to dry she examined her food cupboard and fridge. She was low on both coffee and tea, her lettuce looked brown and slimy and she wrinkled her nose in disgust. She would walk over to the shop, make some necessary purchases and if the pieces of wood were still not dry when she returned she would copy a couple of the sunset scenes. At least she would have something productive to show for her day.

To her surprise Marcus was in the shop. 'Where's John?' she asked. 'Day off?'

'Hardly. Nicola's having a bit of time to herself. I offered to look after the shop so Bryony and John could take the girls down to the playground.'

'I'll wander down that way. I can call in on Saffron. I've undercoated some pieces of wood, but I need to find the exact measurements she needs for the lids.' Ronnie frowned. 'How long does gloss paint take to dry? The undercoat seems to be taking ages.'

'You'll need to leave it for at least twenty four hours if you want to paint over it,' Marcus advised her. 'If you try to put more paint on before the base is dry you'll just end up with a sticky mess.'

Ronnie pulled a face. 'I'm not sure this is a good idea. At least I know what I'm doing with water colours. Can you save a lettuce for me, please? I'll collect it on my way back, along with some tea and coffee.'

Ronnie walked down to Saffron's shop. As usual there were tourists milling around, handling the goods that were on display and replacing them haphazardly. Ronnie was pleased that her pictures were in protective polythene and displayed up on the walls, whilst the stock was kept behind the counter. There was no way the visitors could handle and soil them. Waiting until Saffron had finished serving; she passed her time looking at the boxes which had a photograph of Spinalonga on the lid. Her heart sank. There was no way she was going to be able to reproduce such a detailed, miniature picture in gloss paint on a piece of wood.

Saffron stepped over to her side as the woman left the counter. 'You look worried, Ronnie. Have you got a problem?'

Ronnie nodded. 'I thought I'd try to make a start on the box lids. I've been looking at these. There's no way I can produce anything half as good. I can scale down to a certain extent and keep everything in proportion, but to get this much detail would be impossible. I'm experimenting with the gloss paint Vasi brought for me, but I'm not at all sure that it's suitable. Oil paints would probably be better.'

'Can you get some from Aghios Nikolaos?'

'I can, but they're very expensive and I've never tried working with them before. Even if I was successful the lids would cost you double the amount you're selling the boxes for at the moment. I don't think it's feasible.'

Saffron eyes roved over the customers in the shop. She often found there was something missing at the end of the day and she knew she had not sold it. Occasionally items had turned up where they had slipped behind something else or ended up amongst other goods, but she was sure some tourists were not averse to pocketing whatever they fancied if they thought she was not looking.

She frowned. 'Hold on a minute. I want those children out of here. They are just playing around and making a mess.'

Ronnie watched whilst Saffron insisted the group of young teenagers replaced the items they held in their hands onto the display stand and left the shop. 'Out,' she said sternly. 'If you want to buy you come in one at a time. Understand?'

They obviously did understand as truculently all the youngsters except one left the shop. 'Buy?' the girl asked and held up a pair of earrings.

Saffron smiled at her. 'Of course. Present?'

The girl nodded. 'For Mamma.'

Saffron proceeded to place the earrings into a small box and gift wrapped it neatly, waiting patiently whilst the girl counted out her money on the counter. Saffron took another look around the shop and returned to where Ronnie was standing.

'It's a ploy they use. They come in as a group and I can't watch all of them. They move things around and then one will slip something into their pocket. If I confront them they pretend not to understand. Anyway, what were we saying; are you sure you need oil paints? I visited a man in England and he had some incredibly delicate paintings that had been mounted on box lids. I couldn't afford to buy his work to sell here, but I know Uncle Yannis invested in some bits and pieces that he offered at a special price.'

'Would he mind if I went and looked at them?'

'I'm sure he wouldn't. Why don't you go up to the taverna and ask John to 'phone him and tell him what you want?'

Ronnie shook her head. 'Marcus is up there. John is down at the playground with his girls and Bryony. I'll wander in and have a look. If I can't make myself understood then I'll ask John to speak to him and go back another day.'

Ronnie walked into Uncle Yannis's shop. There were a few tourists of an older age group looking around, speaking quietly and behaving decorously. She had a feeling that Uncle Yannis would not have permitted a group of youngsters to enter his premises. He smiled at her from his position behind the counter where he sat with Ourania and Marisa. His business could not be so brisk as to need three people to serve the customers and she guessed it was more a way of passing the day for the two elderly ladies.

Ronnie wondered how she would explain her errand and looked around to see if she could see any of the items she thought Saffron meant. There were no boxes with painted lids on show and Ronnie approached him tentatively.

'Boxes?' she asked.

Yannis shook his head. 'Next shop.'

'No, English boxes. Saffron said you had English boxes.'

Yannis frowned, as if interpreting each word. 'Ah, English,' he said at last, pushed Marisa's magazine to one side and pointed to a selection of items in a display case.

Saffron peered at them. There were pendants painted with butterflies or ladybirds, some of the insects alighting on flowers and others showing just the flower or a small posy along with paper weights that had an abstract design. 'Boxes?' she asked again.

This time Yannis spoke to his wife and she lifted her magazine. In the glass case were some small silver boxes with a painting inset in the lid.

'See?' asked Saffron and Yannis nodded, unlocked the back of the case, spread a piece of velvet on the counter top and placed three small boxes on it for Saffron's inspection. She picked each one up in turn, examining the delicate work. One showed children playing; another where a family was having a picnic and the third was a man in a dress suit offering a bouquet to a lady who was wearing a crinoline. Each one was so perfect that she thought it must be a transfer she was looking at.

Carefully she opened the lid and read the tiny label. She could just make out the words "Hand Painted by Jack Morrison." She turned it upside down and read the price tag. Yannis was asking seventy five Euros for the piece. Even allowing for his profit margin it must have cost him at least fifty Euros. It was no wonder Saffron said she could not afford to stock them.

Ronnie handed it back to Yannis and shook her head. 'Expensive.'

Yannis smiled. 'Very good. Hand paint.'

'Beautiful,' agreed Ronnie, 'But expensive.' She looked at the pendants and paper weights again and Yannis hurried to take a selection out of the case for her. Again they were exquisite, but no item was priced at less than forty Euros.

'Thank you for showing me.' Ronnie hoped he recognised her as the artist who sat down on the quay and not disappointed that she was not a prospective customer. She would have to ask John to explain why she had visited the shop.

Ronnie returned to Saffron's shop and waited whilst she finished wrapping two of the small plates that had a photograph of Spinalonga transferred onto them.

'I've been down to Yannis's shop. The boxes he has are beautiful. I couldn't possibly produce anything as perfect as those. Why don't you have a transfer put on like you do for the plates?'

'It would have to be painted, then copied and laminated to the box. I did investigate the possibility, but it's a different technique from placing a transfer onto a plate. It would be expensive and also mass production, whereas an original hand painting is special.'

Ronnie shook her head. 'I'm willing to experiment with the gloss paint, but I'm not prepared to go and buy a quantity of oil paints and find I can't work in that medium. Why don't you send the man in England a photograph of Spinalonga and ask him if he would make the lids?'

Saffron smiled. 'You saw the prices Uncle Yannis was charging? They are imperfect items in Mr Morrison's eyes and he offered them to me at a reduced price. I still couldn't afford to stock them.'

'Well,' Ronnie sighed, 'I'm willing to try, but I'm not very hopeful of being successful. I'll work on the wood in between reproducing the other paintings for you. Even so it will be a slow process. Marcus told me I should allow gloss paint twenty four hours to dry before I try to paint over it.'

Ronnie left Saffron's shop and walked to the end of the village. As she passed the Kyriakos's taverna he waved to her.

'Come. Sit in the shade and have a frappe.'

Ronnie hesitated, she enjoyed looking at the view from the taverna, but she had intended to have a short walk whilst she thought about the decorated enamels she had seen in Uncle Yannis's shop and then visit the children's playground. Jack Morrison's work was incredible and she would like to find out more about his techniques. His amazing results could be due to the paint he used, along with his artistic gift. If that was the case, with practice, she should be able to reproduce something that was acceptable. It could be worth her while to approach the artist and ask for information. She would look his name up on the internet when she returned to her apartment and see what she could find out.

'You look very serious, Miss Ronnie. Problem?' Kyriakos raised his eyebrow at her.

'No, not really. I was talking to Miss Saffron about painting pictures of Spinalonga on wooden boxes. I have tried using gloss paint, but I can't get the detail. I had a look at the enamels Uncle Yannis sells and I was wondering if I could contact the artist.'

'You can paint on the wood?'

Ronnie shrugged. 'The painting is not the problem. It's trying to make it small enough to fit on a box lid is impossible.'

Kyriakos looked back at the entrance to the taverna. 'You would paint a picture of Spinalonga on wood for me?'

'Why would you want a picture of Spinalonga? You can see the island from here.'

'I have an idea. Whilst we talk I think of it. Above the entrance I have a picture of Spinalonga. It is painted by you, signed by you, and when my customers admire it and ask who is the artist I can tell them you have painted it. I also tell them they can buy copies from Miss Saffron's shop. Is a good idea. Yes?'

Ronnie smiled at his enthusiasm. 'I'll think about it.'

'No, come.' He walked across to the doorway and Ronnie followed him. 'Look,' he spread his arms across the opening. 'It has to be a little wider than the door but not too high. Little bit of sky and little bit of sea, most is of Spinalonga. I will pay you, but you make just for me. Not for any of the other tavernas.'

'Would Mr Giovanni agree that you could put up a picture?'

Kyriakos shrugged. 'Why not? When I go to pay my rent I will speak to him.'

'Well if he has no objection I suppose I could try. When you've spoken to him you'll have to tell me exactly the size you want and it will take some time. I may not have it ready until the end of the season.'

'That is no problem.'

'I can't tell you how much it will cost.' Ronnie frowned. 'I can ask Mr Vasi to buy the piece of wood when you have given me the measurements.'

'Wait.' Kyriakos hurried inside and returned with a metal rule. He handed it to Ronnie and proceeded to stretch it across the doorway. Taking his order pad he wrote down the measurement. He reduced the width by a third and wrote down the height he wanted. 'There,' he said triumphantly. 'There are the measurements.'

September 2010

Ronnie drove up to Neapoli and wandered through the old streets gazing at the architecture, some of it dilapidated and in sore need of repair, but still reflecting the ancient grandeur of the town. Until 1904 Neapoli had been the capital of the Prefecture of Lassithi and as such had boasted a University and also an orphanage for boys. Ronnie wondered where the unfortunate girls who happened to be orphaned had been housed. The orphanage had closed many years ago and was now a small museum for a collection of archaeological artefacts from the surrounding area. It was hard to believe that the small town had once been so important.

She visited the Cathedral and then sat at a cafe across the square and sampled the local drink – soumada- but did not find the sweet almond flavour to her taste at all. It was quite an effort to empty her glass and she took a mouthful of water from her bottle to clear her palate. She would walk a short distance away and order a coffee; that should finally take away the taste.

Whilst she ate some lunch Ronnie studied the map. It would be practical to spend the remainder of the afternoon in the town and drive back to Plaka via Kastelli. She had visited the Lassithi plain the previous week and discovered a fascinating Folk Museum, with genuinely old furniture and dummies wearing the authentic costume of the bygone age. Now she just had Ierapetra left on her list of possible attractions for when her mother and great uncle arrived. She did not want them to be bored, but nor did she want to exhaust them by trying to cram too much into their fortnight.

There were plenty of short drives to local villages or areas where they would have a spectacular view and on some days that could be enough for them.

Before they arrived she needed to have a stock of paintings ready for Saffron and John had arranged for him and Nicola to visit Mili during the week offering to take her with them. She had accepted with alacrity, but also with a slight feeling of guilt. After visiting Lassithi and photographing the old mills that were silhouetted against the sky she had shown the subsequent paintings she had made to Saffron who had immediately requested more, and she was trying to complete the wooden panel that Kyriakos had requested for above the taverna doorway.

John drew up outside the apartments and Ronnie waved from the balcony, picked up her bag and walked out to the car.

'Hi, Nicola. Hi, John. You didn't tell me we were to have company.' She tickled Skele's ears as he pushed his head through the open window at her.

'You don't mind having him in the back do you? He'll settle down once we start to move again.'

'Of course I don't mind. Provided he gives me my fair share of the seat. Move over Skele. I need to be able to sit down.' Ronnie gave the dog a push and he swayed his body, but left his feet firmly planted on the seat. 'John, ask him to move, please.'

John turned round and grinned. He pointed to the far side of the seat and commanded Skele to sit. The dog obeyed immediately.

'That's all you need to do,' he explained to Ronnie. Skele looked at her as she climbed into the car and she was sure he was smiling, amused by her inability to communicate with him.

'Good dog,' she said and he moved towards her. 'No, you are not sitting on me. You'll make me far too hot.'

'Skele.' John spoke firmly and the dog moved his paws from Ronnie's knees. 'Ignore him, Ronnie. He's teasing you. I'll open the window on his side so he can stick his head out. Let me know if you're in a draught.'

As soon as the car began to gather speed Skele stuck his head out of the window, his ears being blown back. Every so often he would withdraw his head and shake it vigorously before leaning out again. John drove steadily along the main Highway until they reached Heraklion. Once the town was behind them he turned onto a secondary road that was signed for Arolithos.

'I thought we'd use the old road. It's quicker and much prettier than driving on the Highway. We'll join it again at Stavromenos. The turn off for Mili is only about ten minutes along the road from there. On the way back we could have a quick swim at Platanias. You did bring your gear, didn't you, Ronnie?'

'Did you tell me to?'

John nodded. 'I'm sure I did. You always carry your swimming gear wherever you go in the summer.'

'Don't worry, I've brought it. More importantly – has Skele got his?'

'Left the house wearing it,' confirmed Nicola. 'There are a couple of old towels in the trunk and John will give him a rub down before he's allowed back in the car and make him sit on one. Giovanni won't want his car smelling damp and doggy.'

'Why didn't you bring yours?'

'Saved taking out the girls' car seats, but I didn't tell Dad that Skele was coming with us. I said I needed the back seat as we were taking you up to Mili.'

'John's always been devious,' remarked Nicola to Ronnie.

'Only by omission,' answered John indignantly. 'I never tell a lie. Had he asked me if I was taking Skele I would have told him the truth.'

'You told a whopper to the girls this morning. They saw us getting the car ready and wanted to come as well.' Nicola turned in her seat towards Ronnie. 'John told them we were taking the car into the garage and would soon be back.'

'I knew once Mum and Bryony distracted them they would

forget all about us. They're quite used to being passed around.'

'You make them sound like parcels,' laughed Ronnie.

'Maybe we could stick some stamps on them and send them away?' suggested John, and Nicola looked at him reproachfully. He shook his head. 'I'm only joking. I wouldn't want to be without those two now. I enjoy watching them interact with each other.'

'Yes, you miss out in some ways if you are an only child.'

'Your Mum didn't think about having another one?' asked Nicola.

'I think she was probably so traumatised when my father went to prison that she didn't look at another man for years. By the time she married my step father I was twelve. If she had given me a sibling the age gap would have been too great for us to ever play together.'

'I'm glad I didn't have any siblings,' announced John. 'I freely admit that I was spoilt rotten by my grandparents and aunts and uncles. I don't think I would have wanted to share their attention with another child.'

'You're still spoilt,' Nicola reminded her husband. 'Your clothes are washed and ironed and your meals prepared. You don't have to do any shopping or cleaning.'

'What about the time I spend up at the taverna cooking? Doing odd jobs for Dad, running errands for Mum and helping with the girls?' replied John indignantly. 'At least you're at home all day doing as you please.'

Nicola winked at Ronnie. 'Fine. We'll do a swap one day next week. You can stay at home and look after the girls. When I come back from the taverna I'll expect our room to be clean and tidy, the ironing done and the girls to have had their tea. I'll ask Bryony to come up to help me so you won't be able to call on her and have to manage on your own. You can tell me later how much time you had to yourself to do as you pleased.'

'I'm sure Grandma Marisa would stay home from the shop to help me,' grinned John.

'That's just the kind of trick you would pull. Men!' Nicola gave a mock sigh. 'I should have looked for an American millionaire.' Nicola squeezed John's knee.

'You wouldn't have had two lovely little girls then. He'd have been more interested in going off to make money than in you. You wouldn't be driving along in a beautiful country about to take a romantic walk with your beloved husband in a magnificent gorge and meet an extremely interesting old man.'

'I might find the interesting old man more interesting than the husband you think I'm so enamoured of,' Nicola warned him.

John chuckled. 'Wait until you've met him. He must be about ninety, has hardly any teeth and a hook in place of a hand.'

'You never know what attracts a girl. Isn't that so, Ronnie?'

'Can I reserve judgement until I've met him? I don't want to fight you for him, Nicola.' Ronnie realised the interchange between John and Nicola was no more than a friendly teasing.

'If it comes to that Skele and I will go for a walk and leave you to it.'

At the sound of his name Skele drew his head back into the car and looked at John. 'Not long now, Skele, then you can have a run.'

Skele seemed to digest the information, then pushed his head back out through the open window.

John turned off onto the side road and drew in to a space that had obviously been created for vehicles to park safely. He passed Skele's lead to Ronnie and she attached it firmly to his collar.

'He's very good and obedient, but I don't like to take a chance and let him loose. A car could come around the corner quickly.'

'Maybe we should keep him on a lead until we've seen Tassos. He might not like dogs,' suggested Nicola.

''I thought we'd take him for a run first, then he can be tethered outside and he won't make a fuss.'

'Are you planning to walk the whole gorge?' asked Ronnie. 'It's quite a distance to the top and back.'

'I'd like to, but not today. If you want I can always drive up later and meet you at the village.'

Ronnie shook her head. 'I've done it once. I'm more interested in meeting this old man. I imagine he only speaks Greek so you'll have to tell me what you talked about later.'

'I'll try to keep you briefed and then John can fill in the details later. If you get too bored you can always say you have to go to take Skele for a walk and I'll explain why you're leaving.'

Ronnie smiled at Nicola gratefully. She was not sure how long she would be able to sit there listening to them conversing in Greek and not understanding a word.

John tied Skele to a convenient tree just before the steps to the taverna. They had walked for nearly an hour, allowing the dog to run free and root around in the undergrowth. He now settled down with his head between his paws and looked at John trustingly.

'Be a good, quiet dog. We'll not forget you and could well bring you back a treat.' John filled the plastic bowl he had carried with him with water and placed it on the ground along with a handful of dog biscuits before giving Skele a pat on his head.

Tassos was sitting at the far side of the taverna, overlooking the gorge just as he had been when John had visited him before. 'I do hope he remembers me,' muttered John as he approached.

A woman came out from the cooking area and intercepted the group. John spoke to her rapidly in Greek. 'I came to see your father earlier this summer and he told me about his life as a pedlar. I'd like to talk to him some more and introduce him to my wife. Even if it isn't convenient to speak to him we would still like some lunch, please.'

Anastasia looked at her father dubiously. 'You were with him a long time when you came before. He was very tired afterwards and I think you may have reminded him of incidents he would prefer to forget. Have a seat and I'll ask him if he feels up to speaking to you again.'

'Of course. We'll understand if he refuses.' John looked over to where Tassos was sitting. The man raised his hook in greeting, but John did not know if that meant he recognised him or if it was his customary welcome to visitors.

'His daughter is going to speak to him.' John interpreted for Ronnie.

'Suppose he does refuse to speak to you?' asked Nicola.

John shrugged. 'I have to accept that, but I'll be disappointed. I want to ask him about his life when he was on Spinalonga. I know old Uncle Yannis's version, but I'd like to know Tassos's opinion.'

Anastasia returned to them. 'He will talk to you. He remembered you said you would bring your wife to meet him.' She looked from Nicola to Ronnie.

'This is my wife, Nicola,' John indicated her with his hand. 'Our friend is Ronnie. She was the lady who, quite by chance, found your father for me. We've left our dog tied to a tree down there. Is that alright?'

Anastasia nodded. 'We're not supposed to have dogs in the taverna. What can I bring you to drink?'

'Three small beers, please, and what can you offer us to eat?'

'Keftedes, calamari, chicken, beefburger, omelette, all with chips and salad.'

Nicola and Ronnie chose chicken and John opted for keftedes. 'You wouldn't have any sausages, I suppose?'

'You would rather have sausage?'

John shook his head. 'Not for me, but to give to our dog. It will be a reward for him for being good.'

'I'll see what I can do.'

John led the way over to the table next to Tassos and held out his hand. 'I'm pleased to meet you again. I'd like to introduce my wife, Nicola and our friend, Ronnie.'

Tassos held out his left hand and both girls touched it with a semblance of a handshake. 'I remember you. You're the man with all the questions.'

'And you're the man with all the answers,' replied John.

Tassos chuckled. 'So what did you want to talk to me about this time?' he asked.

'Well,' John leaned forward, 'Old Uncle Yannis was happy on Spinalonga. When the island was finally closed he was desolate. He never envisaged that they would have to leave their homes. All he had petitioned the government for was the new medical treatment.'

Tassos shrugged. 'It was different for them. They accepted they were incurables. I wasn't ill. I had no place over there amongst sick people. They repaired their houses, started up their businesses and made a life for themselves. I couldn't do that.'

'But you said you worked over there as a cobbler,' protested John.

'I patched and made good for those who were able to wear a boot and move around, but I realised I would soon run out of customers. What would I do then? Sit and do nothing all day long like so many of them?'

'Couldn't you have grown vegetables or kept chickens?' suggested John.

'I only knew how to mend boots, besides I had no garden.'

'So what did you do to pass the time?'

Tassos shrugged. 'We talked together and I kept trying to think of a way I could return to the mainland.'

'Whereabouts did you live?'

'On the hill above the square with many of the others.'

'Did you share your house?'

Tassos shook his head. 'I was not prepared to have sick people living in my house. I could have become infected. I was prepared to meet with them and talk in the open air. That way the germs would be carried away. I didn't want any of them in my house, touching my belongings or using my plate or cup.'

John smiled to himself at the man's ignorance of the transference of the disease.

'From the first day I arrived all I thought about was leaving the accursed place.'

'What about your neighbours? Did they think you were being unsociable or did they understand?'

'I had a good relationship with them. Most people were friendly enough, but I didn't fit in. I kept to myself. I wasn't prepared to take one of the women and pretend I was living a normal married life in an ordinary village. I don't think I would have done so even if I had been sick. It ended in tragedy for so many of them.'

'When their partner died, you mean?'

Tassos nodded. 'Then and when they took their children away.'

'What?' Neither John nor Nicola could believe what they had just heard. 'Who took them away?'

'The government. They said that healthy children should not be on the island. They were allowed to stay with their parents until they were about two years old, then they were taken.'

Nicola felt tears coming into her eyes. She could not imagine how she would feel if anyone took their daughters away. 'Where did they go?' she asked.

'Sometimes a relative was willing to take them in; if not they were sent to an orphanage.'

'Did the parents ever see them again?'

Tassos shrugged. 'I've no idea. All I remember is the heartbreak when they were taken from their mother's arms. Fo and Aristo lived next door to me and I could hear their sobbing each night through the walls after their daughter was taken.'

'Couldn't the doctor have done anything to prevent the children from leaving?'

Tassos's lip curled in disgust. 'He was the one that made the arrangements. Excused himself by saying that it was the law. He could have turned a blind eye to the babies who were born and the authorities would never have known about them.'

'What about Father Minos? Couldn't he do anything to help?'

Tassos shook his head. 'He had to be careful. The doctor didn't like the fact that the Priest would give a blessing to those who wished to live together as man and wife. That was another thing that was against the law, getting married. Father Minos had wanted to intercede on the parents' behalf but he was begged not to. The people were frightened that if he did the government would insist he left the island.'

'Old Uncle Yannis never mentioned any of this in his notebooks,' protested John.

'Why should he? He had no children. He was only interested in rebuilding and improving our quality of life over there. Don't misunderstand, I'm grateful for that or I would probably have been sheltering in the tunnel the way others used to before he arrived. I wouldn't have had a little house to call my own. Everyone on the island owed Yannis a debt of gratitude, along with Spiro. Without him there would have been no hospital where the truly ill could spend their last days being cared for.'

John shook his head sadly. 'He considered Doctor Stavros was a saviour. I find it hard to believe that he could be so hard hearted about the children.'

'He was a good doctor; he did his best for us. You could see how exhausted he was when he left after his weekly visit. He didn't have the energy or time to start a tussle with the government on our behalf, and he probably thought that to move the children away to a healthy environment was better for them.'

Anastasia appeared bringing their meals, along with two cooked sausages on a separate plate for Skele and John smiled his appreciation. 'Two sausages. Now that really will be a treat for him.'

'Enjoy your food,' she said and returned to the kitchen area.

'I'm not sure I can,' said Nicola in English. 'Not after hearing about the children.' A tear rolled down her face. 'Imagine what it would be like to have Jo and Lisa taken away.'

Ronnie looked at Nicola in alarm. 'You don't mean someone is trying to take the girls away from you?'

John shook his head and placed his arm around Nicola. 'It was a long time ago, Nick. You mustn't be upset by it. No one would consider doing such a thing these days. I'll explain later, Ron, but there isn't anything to worry about.'

Tassos looked at Nicola in concern. 'I didn't mean to upset your wife. You asked me and I told you what had happened.'

John released Nicola and pulled out his wallet, withdrawing a photograph of Joanna and Elisabetta. He held it out for Tassos to look at.

'These are our daughters. My wife is imagining how she would feel if they were taken away from us in six months time.'

'You would at least have a photograph. Those parents had nothing but memories to sustain them. Stassa,' Tassos called. 'I'll have a brandy.'

'You haven't had your lunch yet,' protested Anastasia.

'I'll have that afterwards. Mushroom omelette.'

'I haven't any mushrooms. You'll have to have ham or cheese.'

Muttering beneath his breath at the inevitable change to his menu, Tassos looked at John. 'Do you want a brandy? You look a bit shaken.'

John shook his head. 'No thanks, I'm driving and I've already had a beer. It was just rather a shock when you told us about the children. I had no idea. In fact, I'd never even thought about children being born over there as Old Uncle Yannis hadn't mentioned them.'

'Children are born as and when.' Tassos lowered his voice. 'I told you about Stassa and her circumstances. Sometimes I say too much. I trust you never to tell her, even after I'm gone.'

'I wouldn't dream of doing so,' John assured him. 'You're her father.'

Tassos nodded. 'I have been since the day she was born. She knows no different, nor her brothers.'

'I promise, on the heads of my daughters, that I will never tell her,' John answered solemnly.

Tassos leaned back and closed his eyes, then opened them again. 'Who else have you told?'

'Only my wife,' John assured him. 'She will be bound by the same oath as I am.'

Anastasia brought over an omelette, accompanied by a small glass of brandy. 'You've let your food go cold,' she admonished them. 'Shall I reheat it for you?'

'I'm afraid we were so engrossed in talking that we forgot to eat. It's fine as it is. We must make a move when we've eaten. We've quite a long drive back.'

Anastasia nodded. She would not be sorry to see them go. Her father would be tired after their visit and as he had asked for a brandy he was evidently unsettled by their conversation.

John fed Skele pieces of sausage and then untied him and picked up his water bowl. 'You were very good. You can have your freedom back until we reach the road.'

Skele loped along beside them, stopping to sniff at the grass, following a scent for a few yards before catching them up again.

'So what did you talk about?' asked Ronnie. 'What were you saying about your children?'

'Tassos said that any children who were born on Spinalonga were taken away from their parents after about two years and sent to relatives or an orphanage.'

'Why?'

'The government or health authorities thought they would become leprous if they stayed there. They were just so ignorant about the disease! Old Uncle Yannis had never mentioned them and I suppose I was pretty stupid not to have thought about children being born to the couples. I just assumed their sickness made them infertile.'

'What about Anna?'

'She wasn't born there. She was taken over just before the island was controlled by the Germans and lived with Uncle Yannis and his wife. It wasn't until after Phaedra had died that Father Minos finally told him that she was his natural daughter. I should have thought about other children when I read that.'

'Tell me how it happened.'

'According to Old Uncle Yannis the girl who ran his lodgings in Heraklion was a prostitute. She had a child and she told Father Minos that Yannis was the father. When the war broke out she and Anna went down to Aghios Nikolaos. She had married and her husband thought they would be safe there. She abandoned Anna and the child was caught stealing. She had a birthmark that another doctor diagnosed as leprosy and she was sent off to the island.' John tried to précis the information he had read in his great uncle's notebooks. 'It was whilst Uncle Yannis was in Heraklion that he was diagnosed, so he must have already had the disease when Anna was conceived.'

Ronnie looked at John dubiously. 'Can anyone be certain she was your Uncle Yannis's daughter? You say the woman had a husband. Couldn't she have been his child?'

John shook his head. 'I only know what I've read in the notebooks. She didn't get married until she knew she was pregnant.'

'But if she was a prostitute anyone could have fathered the child,' protested Ronnie.

'Very true, but she assured Father Minos that Yannis was the father. Old Uncle Yannis's sister was a very capable artist. You will have seen some of her work displayed in Uncle Yannis's shop. He values them highly and would never sell them. Anna's work was exactly like hers in style. I told you the prints that Uncle Yannis has on sale were Anna's drawings.'

'I didn't realise. I thought they were all done by the same person.' Ronnie gave a rueful laugh. 'As an artist I should have noticed any differences, but then I've never actually compared them.'

'I expect everyone makes the same mistake. When you put

them side by side you can see that Anna's are less mature, the pencil lines not as bold and confident as great grandmother's were. I'll ask Uncle Yannis to get out Anna's drawings and then we'll make a date or you to come down one evening and you can look at them.'

'Can't I look at them in his shop?'

'There are a good many that he has never reproduced. Flora was quite horrified when Uncle Yannis suggested the pictures that showed her should be copied and sold. She was adamant that he was not to do so. He hasn't copied any of Old Uncle Yannis or his wife. They were no longer around to ask for permission, so he selected those that he thought would offend no one.' John clicked his fingers and Skele came to his side to allow his lead to be clipped to his collar. 'It was a shame Anna wasn't on Spinalonga at the same time as Tassos. If I had seen a picture of him he might have been easier to trace.'

'I don't see how,' remarked Nicola.

'Someone may have recognised him as the pedlar.'

'Pretty unlikely as he stopped being a pedlar after he lost his arm.'

John shrugged and opened the car door. He was loath to admit that Nicola was right.

Ronnie had enjoyed having her mother and great uncle staying. They had marvelled at the beauty of the area and could understand Ronnie's desire to come back and paint the scene time and again. Saffron had arranged for them to visit her and Vasi at their house, closing her shop early so she was able to prepare a meal, and the other evenings they had patronised the local tavernas in Plaka and Elounda.

Ronnie had driven them to the various outlying towns and villages that she had explored and on three occasions had taken them up to Heraklion so they could visit Knossos, the museum and wander around the waterfront and town. Her mother had been more impressed by the waterfront at Rethymnon, where the tavernas crowded together and vied for custom. She had taken them to Mili and walked down to the taverna, explaining how John had finally traced the old man who raised his hook in greeting as they arrived.

It was with some trepidation that she had taken them to Spinalonga, accompanied by John. She had no desire to experience a hand on her shoulder or someone sighing again. However hard she tried to convince herself that she had imagined the incidents she knew she would never have the courage to spend time on the island alone.

Ronnie had not mentioned her unnerving experiences to either of them, but she watched them both closely as they walked around, listening enthralled as John related the history of the island. Her mother and Uncle Alex did not appear to have any unexplained ghostly feelings, although she saw her uncle shiver on a couple of occasions, despite the warmth of the day.

Charlene settled herself comfortably in the back seat of the car. She was enjoying her visit to Crete and was glad she had made the effort to make the long journey. It was good to see Ronnie so happy and relaxed and having met Saffron and her relatives she would have no qualms about her daughter returning the following year.

'I thought I'd drive you up to Kritsa today. We'll stop at the little church with the frescos on the way. When you've had enough wandering around we'll have some lunch and drive back through Kastelli and I can show you the house covered in flowers that I've told you about.'

'How did people get around without a car?' observed Charlene.

'They walked,' replied Ronnie cheerfully. 'They knew the short cuts over the hills.'

'Or had a donkey,' added Uncle Alex. 'Trouble is, Charlene, I would have been riding the beast whilst you walked.'

'No wonder some of the older women look so tired and worn out.'

'That's partly the sun and also where the country women have worked out in the fields since they were children. The town people work terribly hard during the tourist season. You've seen for yourself how the tavernas and gift shops are open all hours. There's no nine 'til five or shift work. They tend to rely on relatives to help them out so they can have a bit of time to themselves.'

'I'm certainly glad we went to America.' Uncle Alex shook his head. 'I worked hard, but at least I had regular time off and a holiday each year.'

'The men seem to have more time to themselves than the women,' observed Ronnie. 'When they've done their housework, shopping, washing, prepared meals and dealt with their children they take out their needlework and spend the evening sewing or knitting. The men tend to go off to a drinking place and spend the evening playing cards or watching football on the television. Amongst the older generation it's still a man's world.'

By the time Charlene and Alex had viewed the church of Panagia Kera, wandered around the narrow whitewashed streets of Kritsa and examined the hand crafted goods for sale, Ronnie could see that both of them were tired. She was pleased she had arranged an outing fairly close and they would not have a long journey back to the apartments. It would take no longer to drive through Kastelli than to retrace their journey along the main coast road and she did want her mother to see the house with the flowers.

Ronnie drew off the road into the space by the water cistern. As she climbed out she waved to a man across the road.

'He was the one who came and changed my wheel when I had a puncture. I'm not sure what he does in that building behind him. I'd love to ask, but I think he speaks as much English as I do Greek. There's the War Memorial.' Ronnie indicated to the monument inscribed with the names of the villagers who had lost their lives during the invasion of Crete by the Germans.

'I've become really interested in the memorials. It is so sad.

They have so many names that are the same that whole families must have been wiped out. Each one has a symbol of some kind on the top. Sometimes it is easy to interpret, you know, doves meaning peace, crossed guns denoting a battle, but others are more difficult to understand and probably have a significance just for that village.'

'Was there a battle up here?' asked Charlene.

'From all I've read and heard there were battles or skirmishes just about everywhere. The Cretan resistance organised ambushes and carried out guerrilla warfare. If an allied soldier was found in your village you'd be accused of hiding him and half a dozen people would be shot as a punishment. There may not have been a battle just here, but the memorial is a record of the local people who lost their lives fighting either the Germans or the Italians. The Cretans were amazingly courageous and defiant. They were determined not to be cowed by the occupation.'

'We are a proud and courageous people,' smiled Alexandros.

'I thought you told me you were an American.' Ronnie looked at her great uncle with a sly smile.

'I am an American when I am in America. Now I am in Crete I feel like a Greek.' He shook his head sadly. 'I wish I could understand the language. One or two words are familiar, but nothing more.'

'You'll have to go to lessons so that the next time you come you'll be able to converse like a native.'

'You're planning to return then, Ronnie?'

'I think so. I have some plans for the winter, then I'll return to New Orleans for a few months and come back out here at the end of March.'

'What plans are they?' asked her mother. 'I thought you were going to return home at the end of October?'

'That was my original idea. I'm waiting for an answer from a man in England. I asked him if he would be willing to give me a course of lessons. He agreed but I'm waiting for him to send through some dates that are convenient for him either at the end of October or beginning of November. It could mean I'm there for a week or a month so it would be foolish to return to New Orleans and then come back to Europe.'

'What about Thanksgiving?'

'I promise I'll be home by then.' Ronnie smiled at her mother.

'Who is this man? What do you know about him? I don't like to think of you going off to a foreign country to see some unknown man. You do hear of the most awful things happening to girls travelling on their own.'

'Saffron and Vasi have met him. They've been to his house and met his wife. Don't worry, Mom. He might well refuse to share his techniques with me. Nothing is settled yet. Now, if we walk around the corner here you'll see the house where someone obviously loves gardening. Have you ever seen such a riot of colour in such a small area? It's breath taking.'

Ronnie stood and waited whilst her mother and Alexandros gazed at the tiny patio, crammed full with pots containing flowering plants. On every sill there were planted window boxes, their greenery and blossoms trailing down the front of the house. Even the steps leading to the front door had plant pots sitting on them, leaving just enough space for a foot to be placed.

'Do you think the owner would mind if I took a photo?'

Ronnie shook her head. 'I've taken one each time I've visited and no one has ever come out and shouted at me. I imagine the owner is very proud of their hard work and is only too pleased to share it with tourists.'

Charlene took a photograph and then took a step backwards. The next thing she knew she was sitting on the ground.

'Mom, are you hurt? What happened?'

Charlene shook her head and pointed to the hole in the road. 'I didn't realise that was there. It threw me off balance. I don't think I've done any damage.'

Alexandros and Ronnie bent down and assisted Charlene

to her feet. She winced as she put her weight on her right foot. 'I've twisted my ankle.' She tried again. 'I'm sorry, but it's really painful. I don't think I can walk any further.'

'I'll drive the car up. We'll call in at the medical centre at Elounda and have it checked out.'

'I'm sure there's no need for that. It's just a twist. It will be fine by tomorrow.'

Between them they helped Charlene to the end of the road and Alexandros waited with her for Ronnie to bring the car. It was parked only a few yards away, but Charlene was wincing whenever she put any weight on her foot.

The doctor at the medical centre confirmed that Charlene had only a slight sprain. He bandaged it tightly and recommended that she rested for a couple of days. If it was no less painful by then she should go to the hospital for an X-ray.

'It's all very well him telling me to go to the hospital for an X-ray in a couple of days, but we're due to fly home on Wednesday. I can't miss the flight just because my ankle still hurts.'

'Would you like me to take you into the hospital now?'

Charlene shook her head. 'No, it's more comfortable now he's strapped it up for me. Let's wait and see how it is tomorrow. Thank goodness it happened right at the end of our holiday or it would have spoilt everything. As it is we've been to so many places, thanks to you, Ronnie.'

'I've enjoyed taking you out. It was a good excuse for me to make visits a second time.' Ronnie did not mention that she was disappointed not to have been able to show them more of Kastelli and the abandoned house that she found so attractive. 'Did you ever find those old photographs you said you had, Uncle Alex?'

'I know where they are now, but I've not gone through them. I'll have a look at them when I get home. If I find anything interesting I'll put it to one side to show you.'

'I'd like to see them anyway. I probably won't know any of the people in them or recognise the places, even if I've visited.

Everywhere has changed so much over here according to the locals. Even Plaka was only a ruined village until Giovanni and Marianne started the self catering business.'

October 2010

Ronnie carried the wooden panel for Kyriakos carefully along to the taverna. She had no idea how Kyriakos planned to fix it, but with John's help she had nailed a narrow baton on the front and back. It gave the piece of ply wood added strength and she hoped it would stop it from buckling in the sun.

Kyriakos was delighted. 'Miss Ronnie, you are so clever. I will be the envy of all the other tavernas. You keep your promise and do not make for them however much they offer you?'

'I won't make one for any other taverna, Kyriakos. How are you going to fix it?'

Kyriakos smiled. 'I have arranged for a piece of wood to be fixed there,' he pointed, 'and another just above the door frame. Now, I will pay you your bill and when you return next season you will see how good it looks.'

Ronnie packed the two warm jumpers and the winter coat that her mother had brought over at her request. She would no doubt need those whilst she was in England. Her summer wear she packed into a separate case as she planned to leave it, along with her easel. Giovanni had agreed that she could leave it there during the winter months, but if she did not return to collect it at the beginning of the season he would throw her belongings away.

'I'll be back,' Ronnie assured him. 'I'd like to rent the same apartment again. I given it a thorough clean and thrown out all my rubbish.'

Giovanni smiled. The girl had been no trouble at all, never lost her key or complained that something was not working. Even when the apartments had been fully occupied and visitors had been tramping past her door at all hours of the day and night she had not asked to be moved to quieter rooms. He would check out the apartment after she left, but he did not expect to find any problems.

'I will make sure it is ready for you. You have my telephone and e-mail address? Just let me know when you are arriving and I will make sure all is in readiness for you.'

'I've said goodbye to everyone so all I need to do now is wait for the bus. I've very little luggage and plenty of time before my flight. If I hang around too long I might change my mind and decide to stay here for the winter.'

Giovanni shook his head. 'I do not think you would enjoy living in the apartment during the winter. There is no heating and there are days when it is very cold and wet. The apartments are for summer holidays only.'

'I'll believe you,' Ronnie smiled easily. 'Here is my key; and thank you for everything.'

Saffron locked the door of her shop and pocketed her keys with a feeling of relief. She would not do any work this evening. She would be able to devote her time to Vasi. She had the winter months to check her stock and place orders ready for the next season. She sighed. Did she really want to work so hard next year? She had thought the shop would give her something to occupy her days. She had not realised how time consuming it would be. This evening she would cook a meal for Vasi, they would share a bottle of wine and make plans, hopefully for a vacation in England so she could see Marjorie again.

Vasi took Saffron's hand and led her out onto the patio. 'We need to talk,' he announced. 'There is a big problem.'

Saffron looked at him anxiously. 'Is it your father?'

Vasi shook his head. 'No. It is us. Throughout the season I

have hardly seen you. Every day you have been down at your shop. When you returned in the evening after our meal you would sit and work on the computer ordering stock or making up your accounts. We no longer had a life together.'

Saffron paled. Was Vasi going to tell her he did not want her living with him anymore? 'I thought you approved of me having the shop to keep me occupied whilst you were working.'

'I do, but you devoted too much time to it. You have neglected our relationship and worn yourself out. Next season you need someone to help you so you can have some free time. Why don't you ask Ronnie to run the shop a couple of days a week?'

Saffron sighed. 'Ronnie only wants to paint. Sometimes she sits out by the quay all day and another time she goes somewhere else or only stays for an hour or so. I don't think she would be reliable.'

'If you paid her a wage for working in the shop she would have to be reliable.'

'I suppose so.'

'You do not like the idea?'

'I don't think she would agree. As an artist she considers herself a free spirit. She always has a stock of pictures for me when I need them, but she likes to move to new locations and produce something different. I don't think she would like to be cooped up in a shop for hours.'

'Then you must close the shop one day a week,' said Vasi firmly. 'You cannot work these hours every day throughout next season.'

'The locals work like that.'

'For them it is necessary. They have to make enough to enable them to live throughout the winter. This season has been hard for them. Many places have had to close and the staff have had to find other work. You do not have to rely on your shop for an income.'

'Are you suggesting I should employ an out of work chambermaid or waitress?' asked Saffron.

Vasi shook his head. 'No, of course not. You need someone you know and trust. You do not want to arrive the next day and find half of your stock has disappeared.'

'What about your friend, Yiorgo's wife?'

'Barbara would not be suitable. She speaks only Greek, besides she has her family to look after and she would have to travel in from Aghios Nikolaos. She refused to move to Elounda when I offered this house to Yiorgo. Barbara is a village girl. She is a good wife and mother, an excellent cook and handy with her needle, but she does not have enough education to be able to run a shop. I could have offered Yiorgo work at one of the hotels, but it would only have been as a handy man and cleaner. He would not have been able to work as a waiter or receptionist. He is an exceptionally good boat man and that is where his heart lies – at sea. I was more than happy to give him that opportunity.'

Saffron sighed. 'I will think about employing someone, Vasi. I admit I didn't realise how difficult it was to run a shop efficiently. When I started it I was expecting it to be more of a hobby than a business. Uncle Yannis always seems to have plenty of time.'

'Uncle Yannis deliberately runs his shop at a loss now. He has plenty of money to live on and he does not have to pay tax if he has not made a profit.'

'But he bought the enamel pendants and I've seen the prices he's charging for them.'

Vasi smiled at her. 'Saffie, do not be so naive. Uncle Yannis does not mind whether he sells them or not. Each year they sit there they will be counted as useless stock and can be deducted from his assets.'

'So why did he refuse to let me stock certain items and buy them himself?'

'He cannot tell the tax man that he has sold nothing all season. He would not be believed. He needed some cheaper items to draw customers in. That way he can claim that the business is running at an overall loss. Eventually he will have to close down as his age catches up with him. He will then offer you his stock, which he will claim is at cost price. If you buy it he will declare that he had to clear everything by selling it at a loss.'

'And the tax man will believe him?'

Vasi shook his head. 'No, but Uncle Yannis will make quite sure the man cannot prove otherwise. His writing is shaky, maybe he wrote down the figure correctly, but then misread it when he added up the amounts. His memory is not so good. He is sure he has the paperwork filed somewhere. The tax man will have to return when he has found it.'

Saffron's eyes opened wide. 'Is that really what happens?'

'Of course. When you have balanced your books for the year I will help you to complete a tax form. If ever your returns are questioned you explain that the form was in Greek and you did your best.'

'Surely they would want to know why I hadn't asked you for help?' Saffron looked at Vasi dubiously.

Vasi shook his head and sighed heavily. 'You are so independent. You wanted to prove to me what a capable business woman you are, but, of course, you made mistakes through ignorance and inexperience.'

'It's dishonest,' protested Saffron.

Vasi looked at her earnestly. 'Saffie, why should you work hard all season and then give most of your earnings to the government? What will they do with it? They will grant their employees a rise in their wages.'

'But surely it's used for the police and fire brigade, along with maintenance of roads and buildings, the schools, refuse collection?'

'We have already paid those expenses in with our water and electricity bill. Believe me, Saffie, the extra money they prise out from us is used only for their benefit.'

'I don't want to end up in jail.'

Vasi smiled and took her hand. 'I promise you will not.

Everyone makes false claims on their tax forms. If they are detected they apologise for the error, say it was accidental, and pay whatever amount they owe. It would take the authorities forever to prosecute each offender and if they sent them to jail there would be no room for the criminals. Besides, this year you should not be eligible for tax. You had to invest in your stock.' He placed his finger on her lips. 'Why are we talking about taxes and accounts when we at last have an evening when we can enjoy being together? I am sure you are tired and would like to go to bed early.'

Ronnie sat with Jack in the small room at the back of his house that he called his studio. She felt nervous as he placed a small sheet of copper on the table and placed an oval wooden template near the edge.

'We'll start with something easy. If you want to learn how to paint enamels you have to learn the basic technique of cutting the shape you want to work with. Make a wooden template and draw round it using a thick pencil.' He worked as he spoke. 'Then cut the shape out as close to your line as possible. Make sure you don't go inside or it will end up unsymmetrical. You can always file off a nib. Now your turn.'

Ronnie held the wooden template firmly in place and drew around as he instructed. Jack picked up a small pair of shears, designed for cutting metal, and cut around the oval he had drawn. He held up the perfect oval of copper and scrutinized it carefully before handing the shears to Ronnie and waited for her to do the same.

'Not bad for a first attempt,' he smiled. 'Put the template back on top and if any part looks irregular use the glass paper to smooth it down. Go gently, just a stroke at a time. You don't want to take off too much.'

Ronnie followed his instructions and waited until Jack had held it up and declared himself satisfied. 'You'll soon get the knack of doing that,' he assured her. 'Now it needs to be cleaned.'

He placed three small bowls on the table and donned a pair of thin rubber gloves. 'You can get all this from a chemist,' he explained. 'Once you have explained what you need the acid for there should be no problem obtaining a small supply. Always make sure you are wearing gloves. You don't want to get the acid on your fingers and it is essential that the copper is spotlessly clean.'

Ronnie watched as he immersed the two copper ovals into the acid bath and after a short while transferred them to the one that had an alkaline solution. He removed his gloves and donned a fresh pair before removing the copper and placing it into a bowl of distilled water and washing it thoroughly.

'Now do you know which is the reverse side of the copper?' asked Jack and Ronnie shook her head.

'Both sides look the same to me.'

'Quite right. Whichever side we do not apply the enamel to first we call the reverse. Make sure it's a nice even layer. You don't want to have lumps or bumps or it won't fire evenly.'

Jack inspected Ronnie's work and opened the door to his small kiln. He removed a shelf that had been specially adapted by him to hold the enamels during firing without damaging the edges and very carefully balanced the two pieces of copper inside.

'This will only take two or three minutes,' he announced. 'Don't put your bare hand inside when you take them out. It's incredibly hot. You'll need an asbestos glove.' He waited until the timer on the kiln rang and switched it off. Gently he opened the door and lifted out the shelf.

'We'll leave those to cool off and then we have to repeat the process again to enamel the other side of the copper. Once you get into a routine you can get on with something else whilst you wait. I usually cut my blanks in one go. As soon as one goes into the kiln I start to clean the next. That way I can keep the production going.'

'How many do you make in one day?'

Jack shrugged. 'Probably about thirty. Once they have been enamelled and fired on both sides they can be carefully stored and used as I want. I've learnt by experience that it is more practical to make up a batch of enamels and do the painting at a later date. That way you only have one thing at a time to concentrate on. If the timer goes off when you're in the middle of a delicate piece of brushwork you're likely to spoil it, and if you leave the enamel in the kiln until it's convenient for you to remove it all sorts of unexpected results occur. I'll show you some later.' Jack touched the underside of the copper with his finger. 'Nearly ready.'

Ronnie waited patiently until Jack had repeated the procedure with the baths of acid, alkali and water, removing the black copper oxide that had formed during the firing on the reverse of the shaped copper.

'Do you always use white enamel as a base?' asked Ronnie.

Jack shrugged. 'It depends upon your final design. You can use any colour you want.'

'Suppose I used pale blue and then decided I'd rather have white? Could I enamel it again?'

'If you changed your mind before firing you could clean it and start again. If you've only fired one side you can do the other side whatever colour you want. Once both sides are fired it's more practical to put it aside and use it another day. Start afresh. Once these have fired we'll take a break and have a coffee.'

Ronnie sat in the kitchen with Jack and his wife, Susan, and sipped her coffee. Whilst she drank Jack quizzed her about her own art work and she told him how she had decided to go to Crete and work as an artist for the season.

'I sell my paintings to the woman who has the gift shop there. I understand she visited you last year.'

Jack nodded. 'She wanted to purchase enamels to sell there, but decided they were too expensive.'

'Saffron sells items that are within the price range of the

ordinary tourist. Not the mass produced tourist rubbish, she leaves that to the other shops in the area. Her Uncle Yannis has a very expensive gift shop. I understand he bought some of your enamels.'

'And you plan to supply him when you have mastered the technique?'

Ronnie shook her head. 'Do you remember she discussed small boxes with a photograph of Spinalonga on the lid?'

Jack nodded. 'I gave her the name and address of the supplier of the boxes and where she could purchase trimmings.'

'They've been very popular. John fixed a photograph of Spinalonga on the lid and then Saffron asked if I could paint a picture of Spinalonga. I tried, using different mediums, but I was not at all happy with the results. She showed me your catalogue and I thought I might be more successful if I painted on enamel and that was attached to the lid.'

'Very ambitious of you,' smiled Jack. 'Painting on enamel is completely different from painting a picture. You have to become used to working through a magnifying glass.'

'So you don't think I'll be able to do it?'

Jack shrugged. 'We'll see. You can try your hand at the painting and see how you get on.'

'Suppose I ruin them?'

'You won't be able to do that. Have you finished? Come on, then, back to work.'

'Now the first thing to do, of course, is to decide on your design. Have you a photograph of this island with you?'

'I didn't bring it with me today.'

Jack nodded. 'No problem. You can bring it along tomorrow. Have a look through my photographs and choose something you like.'

'Do you always work from a photo?' asked Ronnie.

'It depends. A photo can give you guide lines on perspective.

If I am making a decorative design I usually draw it out first on a sheet of paper and decide on the colours. You need to have everything ready before you start to paint.'

Ronnie looked through Jack's photographs and selected one of a windmill. In the foreground was a pond and in the field at the side was a horse.

'That doesn't look too difficult,' she commented, 'but I don't do animals. Can I leave it out?'

'Of course. Now, decide what shape enamel would be suitable. You have the height of the windmill to take into account, remember.'

Ronnie picked up the oval enamel that had been cooling beside the kiln. 'Suppose I turned this so that its height was greater than the width.'

Jack nodded. 'Fine. What colours do you need?'

'Well, blue for the sky and the pond, brown for the windmill, green for the grass.' Ronnie looked at him in surprise. It was obvious to her the colours she would need. 'Maybe some black to outline the windmill.'

Jack opened a cupboard. On every shelf there was a small pestle and mortar, along with glass jars of coloured powdered enamel. He removed the basic colours Ronnie had requested and set them, along with a pestle and mortar, on the table at the side. Beside them he placed some small clean palettes and tubes of pigment.

'You'll only need minute amounts of the enamel. If you want to change the shade add a pin head amount of pigment just before you're ready to use it.'

'Where should I start?' asked Ronnie.

'The same as if you were painting on paper. The background.'

'So I'll start with the sky. Can I add some white to the blue? The colour there is far too harsh.'

'Place a little on your palette and add the pigment.'

Jack handed her a paintbrush and Ronnie looked at it in

amazement. 'This only has three hairs.'

'Quite sufficient for painting a large area like the sky or grass. You'll use one that has only one hair for the more intricate detail. Are you ready? If so I'll add the lavender oil. As soon as I've done that start to work as quickly as you can. Only paint the area that will be the sky. There's no point in painting the whole background, besides it costs too much.'

Jack used an eyedropper to add some lavender oil to the ground enamel on Ronnie's palette and she dipped the end of her brush in and looked at the oval enamel that was set beneath a magnifying glass. Frowning in concentration she began to paint an even layer of blue over the top two thirds.

'Now the grass,' instructed Jack and Ronnie repeated the process with the enamel and the pigment.

'Won't the colours run?' asked Ronnie anxiously.

'The lavender oil dries almost immediately. You can paint up to it and over it. Just be very gentle.'

It took Ronnie almost an hour to complete her picture of the windmill and when she had finished she eyed it critically. 'It doesn't look very good.'

Jack nodded. 'I agree. I suggest you try again.' He picked up a damp tissue and wiped it across the paint, removing it completely.

Ronnie had mixed feelings as she looked at the blank, white enamel. She felt aggrieved that her painstaking work had been so easily obliterated, but relieved that she had not ruined the enamel base. Cautiously she commenced painting the sky again whilst Jack took the other oval enamel and began to replicate her work. His brush strokes were much swifter and more confident than hers and he laid aside his completed work long before she had finished the windmill and started painting the pond.

He waited patiently until she finally laid her brush down and compared them. 'Better,' he acknowledged. 'I'll fire mine and then you can add the finishing touches to yours after lunch.'

They joined Susan in the kitchen where she produced a steak and kidney pudding and vegetables. She placed a heaped plate before Ronnie and then looked a little disconcerted.

'You're not vegetarian?' she asked.

Ronnie shook her head. 'Not at all. I enjoy meat and fish. This smells delicious. It's very good of you to say I could have lunch here.'

'Half the day would be gone if you walked back to the hotel and had lunch there,' observed Jack.

'I could always bring a sandwich with me.'

'You need something warm inside you. You're not in Crete now.'

Ronnie smiled, feeling guilty. She had accepted their offer of a mid-day meal and planned to have a snack later rather than another meal. It would also help her budget. She had not realised how expensive it would be to stay in a hotel for two weeks, despite being in the country and not in London. She had also paid to have a taxi from the airport to the village and been horrified at the cost.

Ronnie spent the afternoon making two more attempts at reproducing the picture of the windmill to her satisfaction. It was far more difficult than she had realised by looking at Jack's work and her respect and admiration for him increased. In the time that it had taken her to paint two enamels he had painted six, two of them had only been small bunches of flowers, destined to be set in silver and worn as pendants, but the others were of country scenes and he planned to mount them on boxes.

She shook her head in despair. 'I don't think I will ever be able to paint these decently.'

Jack smiled at her sympathetically. 'It isn't everyone who can paint on enamels professionally. It takes a good deal of practise in the first place. If you were able to master the techniques in two weeks you would be a genius. I can only show you the method and after that it would be up to you.'

Ronnie sighed. If she had not paid the two week's tuition fee and her hotel bill in advance she would have seen if she could change her flight date and return home immediately. As if sensing her despondency Jack patted her hand.

'You've done very well for your first day. Bring in that photo you want to try to reproduce tomorrow and we'll see how you manage that. Next week you can paint the windmill again and compare it with your earlier one. I guarantee you'll be more satisfied with the result then. Come on, time for a cup of tea and then Geoff will walk you back to the hotel.'

'Geoff?'

'My son. He'll be in from work any minute.'

'It's very kind, but I don't need anyone to take me home. I know my way.'

'I'm sure you do, but it's dark out now and you have a very dangerous road to cross and a nasty corner to negotiate. Susan and I would be much happier to know Geoff had seen you safely back.'

Ronnie stretched her stiff shoulders. Secretly she was relieved not to be walking home alone. One side of the road did not have a pavement, only a steep bank, and where she needed to cross over, although there was a small roundabout, the traffic had appeared never ending that morning. Whilst Jack was talking he was tidying his studio, ensuring that the enamels he had fired were cooling safely, the electricity to his miniature kiln was switched off and the plug pulled out of the socket.

'Can't be too careful when dealing with electricity. You never know when a wire has begun to wear and will short out and start a fire.'

Ronnie nodded. She did not know if Jack had ever visited Greece and seen the state of some of the electric wiring over there. She heard the front door close and Jack straightened up with a smile.

'There's Geoff now. We've finished up just in time.'

Geoff sat at the kitchen table with them and drank a second cup of tea gratefully.

'Hard day?' asked his mother sympathetically.

Geoff pulled a face. 'Just the usual, really. Deliveries were late. Fran had missed the sell by date on some yoghurt, and, of course, Mrs Fielding found them. I swear that woman looks at every sell by date each time she comes in. She didn't even want to buy yoghurt. Said she had "just noticed" the date. All she wanted was a pack of biscuits and she brought those back later to say the top two were broken and demanded that we changed them for a fresh pack. She made me open four packs of rich tea, and when I found an undamaged pack she then said she'd changed her mind and thought she'd prefer to have digestive.'

Ronnie curbed her desire to laugh. 'What happened to the packets you had to open?' she asked.

Geoff pointed to the plate on the table. 'You're eating them. I put the money in the till and brought them home. Good job I'm able to buy goods at a discount price from the shop or I'd be penniless.'

'Good job you're not at Fortnum and Mason,' said Jack. 'Mind you, we'd be living off the fat of the land, not making do with a pack of broken biscuits.'

Geoff walked down the hill to the main road, Ronnie at his side. 'I understand you are an artist. How did you get on with my father today?'

'His work is amazing. I had no idea you had to make up the enamel bases yourself. I thought you just bought a batch already made.'

'Dad worked out that technique for himself. Did he show you the procedure?'

Ronnie nodded. 'Compared with the painting that's the easy part.'

'What kind of painting do you usually do?'

'Landscape watercolours. They're on a somewhat larger scale. I've never tried painting whilst looking through a magnifying glass before. I didn't find it easy.'

Geoff took Ronnie's elbow. 'This is the safest place to cross the road. At least you can see the traffic coming. There's no pavement on the other side, so keep behind me and walk as close to the verge as you can.'

Ronnie followed Geoff's instructions and was relieved when they rounded the corner without incident and she was able to walk on a pavement again.

'Thanks for coming with me,' she said. 'I'm used to walking in the dark without a pavement, but not with so much traffic around. I'd hate to live in that house on the corner.'

Geoff nodded. 'I agree. They lose their front wall frequently. On one occasion a car actually went through their front window.'

'How awful. Was anyone hurt?'

'No, fortunately the occupants were upstairs in bed at the time and the driver only suffered minor injuries. Had they been in their garden or the lounge watching the television at the time it could have been far more serious.'

'Very frightening and to do that amount of damage he must have been travelling very fast.'

'I heard he was a visitor to the area. Obviously he wasn't familiar with the road. What are your plans for this evening?'

Ronnie frowned. 'I thought I'd make some notes about the work I've done today; then e-mail my mother before I go to bed.'

'Fancy a quick drink?'

Ronnie hesitated. It was only just after six and the notes and e-mail would certainly not fill her evening. 'Why not?' she smiled.

Geoff opened the door of the pub and steered her towards an empty table. 'We'll grab that one before the regulars start to arrive and monopolise them all. What would you like?'

'A dry white wine would be nice if they sell it by the glass.'

Whilst Ronnie removed her coat Geoff went up to the bar,

returning with a glass of wine and a pint of beer. 'Cheers,' he said before taking a long draft.

'So,' said Ronnie, 'I gathered from your earlier conversation that you work in a shop. What do you do, apart from dealing with your difficult lady customer?'

Geoff smiled. 'I'm a manager of a convenience store. We sell a variety of goods including food. Do you want to know a secret?' He leaned across the table towards Ronnie and winked. 'My customer, Mrs Fielding, is fictitious. I make up little stories about her. Makes Mum and Dad think I enjoy working there.'

'And you don't?'

Geoff shook his head. 'I started work in the store during my school holidays and they asked me to stay on. It seemed like a good idea at the time, but it's a total dead end and pretty boring.'

'So why don't you leave?'

'What would I do? I've not been to Uni.'

'Are you artistic like your father?'

'No, I take after Mum. Could never keep in the lines even as a child. At least I have a job. I know of a good many chaps who are on benefits. Sims would leave as well if he could find something else.'

'Who is Sims?'

'The other manager. I work eight 'til four and he does four to eleven.'

'At least you have decent hours. What do you do with yourself during the evenings?'

Geoff smiled somewhat self-consciously. 'I watch the stars.'

Ronnie looked at him uncomprehendingly.

'I'm interested in astronomy. I have a high powered telescope and I watch the movement of the stars and record them. I'm hoping I might get a job at the Observatory at Greenwich one day. It's one good thing about living out in the country. It's dark, not like in the towns, so most of the time I get some good sightings.'

'I can't tell one cluster of stars from another,' admitted Ronnie.

'If you like we'll go outside when we've finished our drinks and I'll point out some of the easier ones to distinguish.'

Ronnie shook her head. 'I honestly don't think I'd be any the wiser; and it's cold out there now.'

'Cold? It isn't cold yet.'

'It is to me. I've come here from Crete. I was wearing summer clothes last week.'

'That accounts for your sun tan. How long were you there?'

'Five months.'

'Five months! That's some holiday.'

Ronnie laughed. 'It wasn't a holiday, well, not all of it. I was producing landscapes for a local gift shop. I went out for a holiday in April and met the family who are related to my ex-partner. Saffron suggested I could make a living by supplying her with original watercolours and I decided to give it a go.'

'That was brave.'

Ronnie shrugged. 'I knew that if it didn't work out I could always return to the States and find some work. I'll probably do temping for five months to make some money when I go back home and then I'll return to Elounda for the summer season.'

'It sounds a wonderful life,' observed Geoff enviously.

'I'm not complaining. It can be a bit lonely sometimes.'

'Why is that?'

'I don't speak Greek and the family I know are pretty busy. They have apartments, a shop and taverna and all the family work non-stop during the season. At least I could please myself what hours or days I worked and when my mother and uncle came out I took a couple of weeks off.'

'So if you're a landscape artist why have you come here for my father to show you how to make enamels?'

'It's a long story.' Ronnie finished her glass of wine. 'Would you like another?'

Geoff shook his head. 'Thanks, but I ought to get back. Mum will have dinner waiting. How about if we arrange to have a drink tomorrow when I walk you home and you can tell me more about your decision to paint enamels.'

Ronnie found trying to copy the photograph of Spinalonga onto enamel even more difficult and demanding than reproducing the windmill. Jack had insisted she made her own enamel base from a piece of copper and whilst she did so he selected the paints he would be using later.

'Why do I need to make another base? There are plenty on the shelf.'

Jack looked at her sorrowfully. 'If you don't know how to make them what will you do when you run out?'

'Couldn't you supply me with them ready made?'

'I could, but I would have to charge you for the materials and my time along with the cost of the postage. If they were lost or delayed in the post, or you wanted a particular shape, what would you do? Far better to know how to make the bases yourself. It will probably take time before you manage to fire them to perfection, but you'll just have to keep trying.'

Ronnie frowned. 'That would mean I needed a special kiln like yours.'

Jack looked at her in amusement. 'Of course. Did you think you would be able to paint the enamels and send them back to me for firing? The paint would be rubbed off or smudged. You need to have all your own materials to hand.'

Ronnie bit her lip. 'I'm not sure I could afford the range of equipment that you have.'

'I suggest you see how you get on with the painting before you make any decisions about purchasing. I'll not try to talk you into buying a kiln and enamels if I don't think you have the ability. I have very high standards. I wouldn't want you to produce mediocre work and say you were taught the techniques by me.'

Ronnie's face flamed as she placed the enamel into the kiln. She had too much respect for him to say that her standards were just as high as his.

Having coated both sides of the copper with enamel paint and fired them she had propped the photograph in front of her and tried to replicate the picture she was looking at.

'Why haven't you painted the sky or the sea?' asked Jack. 'That will be far more difficult to fill in than paint over.'

'I want to concentrate just on Spinalonga at the moment. You've told me how expensive the paints and lavender water are and I don't want to waste more than I need to. Once I'm satisfied that I can reproduce it decently I'll paint the background and see how I get on.'

Jack nodded. He thought it unlikely she would be satisfied with her work for some considerable time. The amount of detail she was trying to add was too complicated. He would have to talk to her whilst they ate their lunch and try to persuade her to be less ambitious.

Ronnie listened to Jack and tried to follow his advice as she painted during the afternoon. Without the detail of the fortress wall and the buildings the island lost its character. She tried to add some darker lines to define the houses and then it looked clumsy and amateurish. At the end of the afternoon she felt thoroughly dissatisfied with her day and was pleased to help Jack clear away when they heard Geoff arriving.

He raised his eyebrows to her in a silent question as she entered the room and she shook her head. 'Not good. How did your day go?'

Geoff winked at her. 'Not too bad. One chap complained that we didn't stock printer cartridges. I tried to explain that there were so many different kinds that it would be impossible for us to stock them all. He said if we called ourselves a convenience store we should stock everything that people needed.'

'That's somewhat unrealistic. We have a number of convenience stores in Elounda, but they are really for your basic food and medical supplies. I have to go into Aghios Nikolaos if I want to buy art paper or paints.'

'I recommended he tried the stationers, although I knew they didn't stock them either.'

'Why did you tell him to go there then?' asked Jack.

'Get him out of my hair. Telling me he needed a new black cartridge urgently did not make one appear on the shelf.'

'Did Mrs Fielding come in?' Susan leaned forward eagerly.

Geoff shook his head. 'Not today unless it was whilst I was having lunch; probably too busy eating her digestive biscuits.'

Ronnie smiled to herself. No doubt the story about the man wanting a replacement cartridge was as fictitious as Mrs Fielding.

'I've told Mum we're going to have a drink together tonight and she said she'd put my supper in the oven.'

'I don't want to cause her any inconvenience,' frowned Ronnie.

'She doesn't mind. She's only too pleased to think I have a girl friend.'

Ronnie eyed him dubiously. 'I could hardly be called your girl friend. We only met yesterday and we are *only* having a drink together.'

'It's alright.' Geoff grinned at her. 'I won't start making unwanted advances to you. I like you, but as you say, we only met yesterday. Bit soon to start planning a long-term relationship. I'm interested to hear why you have come over to England to learn how to paint enamels and you said it was a long story so I exaggerated a bit to Mum. Made her think you were going to drag me up to your room screaming and shouting.'

'I hope you didn't,' exclaimed Ronnie in horror. 'What will she think of me?'

'Don't worry. It's my sense of humour. I like to get a rise out of people. I told Mum we were going to have a drink and you were going to tell me all about Crete and which constellations you can see from there.'

'Which what?'

'Constellations, stars.'

Ronnie shook her head. 'I'm sorry, Geoff, but to me stars are bright little lights up in the sky. They look very pretty.'

Geoff sighed dramatically. 'Well, I supposed it was too much to hope that a girl as beautiful as you would also be interested in astronomy.'

'Geoff, you are trying to flirt with me. Either we have a sensible conversation or I shall go straight up to my room and not even have a drink with you this evening.'

'You're just trying to get out of it because it's your turn to buy.' Geoff spoke in an injured tone.

'I am not,' replied Ronnie indignantly and then realised that once again Geoff was joking. She shook her head. 'I never know when you are being serious.'

'I am quite serious when I say I would like to know what made you come over to England to learn about enamel painting.' Geoff opened the door of the pub for her.

'Do you want a pint?' asked Ronnie.

Geoff shook his head. 'You get the table and I'll get the drinks.'

'That's not fair. You got them last night.'

'I'm not a fair person. You grab that table whilst it's free.' Ronnie hesitated and Geoff took a step towards her. 'Do as you're told, or you'll look awfully silly when I pick you up and sit you on the table.'

Ronnie suppressed a smile. She had an idea he would be quite capable of carrying out his threat.

'So,' he settled himself across from her. 'Tell me why you came over here to my father.'

'It really goes back to last year when Saffron and Vasi came over. Saffron saw your father's enamels in one of the shops and thought they'd be ideal for the gift shop she was planning to open. He explained how they were made and she realised they were well outside her budget. Anyway, when I visited Plaka and she saw my landscapes she offered me a free lance job. I paint, she buys, and then sells them to the tourists for a profit.'

Geoff frowned. 'I hope you're making a reasonable percentage for yourself. Maybe I should come out as your business manager.'

'I thought you said you were being serious. John, her nephew, is a photographer and he has taken photographs of Spinalonga that he attaches to the lids of boxes. Saffron wondered if I would be able to reproduce the island on enamel and mount it on a box. I'd tried painting directly onto wood and it just wasn't successful, so I agreed to come over and see if your father could teach me the techniques.'

'And has he?'

Ronnie nodded. 'I know the technique, but I don't think I'll be able to paint them for Saffron.'

'Why's that?'

'I'm finding the actual painting difficult. It's very different from painting with watercolours. It has to be done through a magnifying glass and you have to work quickly as the paint dries so fast. Even if I could do it I don't think I could afford the equipment. I'd have to ask your father to send me the blank enamels.'

'That wouldn't be a problem.'

'I'm sure it wouldn't, but the enamels and the lavender water are very expensive and I would still need a special kiln like your father has to fire them. Even if I decided to invest in the equipment I would have to charge Saffron so much for each painting that it wouldn't be a viable business proposition for her. It's a shame because boxes with a picture of Spinalonga on the lid are a bit of a novelty at the moment for the souvenir hunters.'

'What's so special about it?'

'You really want to know?' Ronnie delved into her bag and brought out the photograph she had taken to Jack's to copy. 'It was a leper colony.'

'Don't tell me they built those walls,' Geoff shook his head sceptically as he looked at the photo.

'No, the walls and bastions are from the Venetian era. The Turks took over the island and built their homes there and after they had left the houses were just left to decay. The lepers were sent there and made their homes in the less ruinous buildings. Eventually one man managed to persuade the inhabitants that they were quite capable of repairing their houses and the island became a very pleasant place to live. It's been abandoned again now for fifty years and a good deal of money is being spent on safety and renovation. The tourists love it. They go over in their droves and although they take photos they often like to take a souvenir home to remind them of the island.'

'Have you been there?'

'Of course. It's just across the bay from where I live. The family I know had a relative who lived on the island for years. John, the photographer, knows all about the history of Spinalonga.'

'Why was it abandoned?'

'After the War tests were done on the people who were still alive and they were sent over to the hospital in Athens. No one lived on the island any longer.'

'There you are; ideal location for you to have a studio.'

Ronnie suppressed a shudder, remembering her uncanny experiences whilst she had been over there. 'I don't think so. Too many people around most of the time. Now, would you like another drink? This time it is definitely my turn.'

'Are you twisting my arm and trying to get me drunk?'

'No, I'm offering you a second pint of beer.'

'Then I'll accept, thank you. Are you having another?'

Ronnie nodded.

'That's good. I'd like you in a mellow mood as I have something I want to ask you.'

Ronnie felt her heart sink. She enjoyed the easy relationship she and Geoff had developed and did not want it to be spoilt by him proposing they became more than friends. She waited her turn at the bar and returned to their table with their drinks.

'What is it you want to ask me?'

Geoff looked at her over the top of his tankard. 'Cheers,' he said. 'What are your plans for this weekend?'

'Plans?'

'Yes, you know. You will get up in the morning, have breakfast and then ...?'

'I hadn't thought about it.'

'Would you like to go up to London? We could go to the Tate or the National or any other art gallery that you fancy, unless you'd rather go to the Planetarium.'

'What's that?'

Geoff grinned wickedly. 'The Royal Observatory at Greenwich. It's where you can see the configuration of the stars and their relationship to the planets. It's quite fascinating.'

Ronnie eyed him sceptically. 'It might be quite fascinating to you, but I doubt I would mean very much to me! I'd love to visit one of the London art galleries, but wouldn't you find it boring looking at pictures?'

'I can always take a book to read. How about if I pick you up in the car at nine and we'll drive to the nearest railway station and take a train from there to Victoria?'

Ronnie enjoyed her day. It was a relief not to be looking through a magnifying glass trying to improve her brush strokes . Geoff was good company and patient with the time she took as she wandered from gallery to gallery admiring the paintings on display. He had insisted they took some time out for lunch and then accompanied her as she returned to the rooms she still wanted to visit. Finally he turned to her with a rueful smile.

'I've had it,' he admitted. 'My feet ache and I have a crick in my neck. I'm going down to the cafeteria for a cup of tea and I'll wait for you there until you've seen enough. They don't close for another hour so you can continue to go around if you want. Don't worry about me. I can always have a second cup.'

Ronnie took him at his word, assured him she would be able to find the cafeteria and hurried into the next room. She could not believe how many paintings there were hanging on the walls and she was sure that if she spent a week there she would still not see everything that was on display.

'So?' asked Geoff as they took their seats on the train. 'Did you enjoy your day?'

'It was wonderful. I saw pictures I'd only ever seen reproduced before in art books. Thank you, Geoff.'

'No need to thank me. I'm pleased you had a good day and it gave me something different to do.'

'What do you usually do with yourself on a Sunday?'

'Bit of a lay in, bit of gardening if the weather's decent, any odd jobs that Mum needs, watch a football match on the T.V. and generally mooch around until it gets dark enough for me to look at the stars.'

'That doesn't sound very exciting. Don't you meet up with friends?'

'Most of my mates are married. Occasionally we meet for a quick pint, but their wives expect them to spend Sunday at home.'

'What about the ones who are not married?'

'Same scenario. They have a regular girl friend and spend Sunday with them.'

'So why aren't you married or going out with someone?'

'I've had a couple of serious relationships but they didn't lead to anything permanent. No doubt I'll meet the right girl one day. Maybe you'll be the right one.'

Ronnie shook her head. 'I'm not looking for a relationship with anyone, besides, I'm only here for another week.'

'Couldn't you extend your stay or come back again later?'

'I can't afford to do either. I managed to live in Crete on my earnings, but for staying in England and paying for tuition I had to dip into my savings. I can't keep on doing that.'

Geoff sighed and shrugged. 'Oh, well, that looks like another prospective wife has turned me down. What would you like to do next weekend?'

Ronnie considered; she did not want to give Geoff the impression that she was interested in becoming his girl friend, but she was only in England for eight more days. There would be no harm in going out for the day with him next week.

'I'd quite like to go to London again and visit the British Museum.'

'Phew.' Geoff wiped his hand across his brow. 'That's a relief. I thought you were going to choose another art gallery. I've had my fill of gazing at pictures. Today will probably last me for the rest of my life.'

'Were you really that bored?' asked Ronnie anxiously.

'No,' Geoff smiled at her. 'I found it quite interesting, but I wouldn't want to repeat the experience next week. The Brit is a good choice. There's a tremendous amount to see there, the artefacts have been collected from all over the world.'

'You've been there, then?'

'On a number of occasions. I'm not quite such an ignoramus as you may think. I find the enormous Egyptian statues awe-inspiring.'

'I'd like to go to Egypt,' sighed Ronnie.

'So would I,' agreed Geoff. 'Shall we go together?'

Ronnie giggled. 'Geoff, will you stop propositioning me?'

'You can't blame a chap for trying,' he smiled back.

Ronnie was looking forward to her trip to the British Museum with Geoff. She was disappointed and disheartened by her painting on enamel. She could finally produce something acceptable, but she knew the amount she would have to charge Saffron would make her work prohibitive. Jack had complimented her on her patience and tenacity, and suggested she stayed in England longer so he could help her to improve her technique and eventually employ her as one of his artists.

She had declined the offer. 'I promised my mother I would be with her for Thanksgiving and my flight is booked. I can't afford to stay at the hotel indefinitely and there's no point in me looking for accommodation here when I plan to return to Crete at the end of March. If everything goes sour on me over there I might well remind you of your offer and come back to England.'

'Geoff will miss you.'

'I've appreciated his company and him taking me up to London.'

'He ought to get out and about more. Stuck in that shop all day and then he spends his evenings looking at the sky. How does he ever expect to find a girl to share that kind of life with him?' Jack shook his head dolefully.

'I'm sure there are some girls who are ardent stargazers. He has tried to educate me, but I still can't distinguish one group from another.'

'I'm not surprised,' Jack agreed. 'Still, at least I never had to go and sit on a river bank whilst he fished or attend football matches and watch him play. Enjoy yourself tomorrow and don't forget to come on Monday to say goodbye to us before you leave.'

Ronnie sank back on the seat of the train. 'I'm exhausted,' she announced.

Geoff smiled at her. 'The British is just too much to take in. You could do with a week up there to be able to absorb and appreciate the different cultures from around the world.'

'What about the Elgin Marbles?' asked Ronnie mischievously.

'Beautiful sculpture.'

'No, I mean what do you think about them being in England rather than where they belong in Athens.'

'I don't give it a second thought. That's a problem for the politicians to sort out. I have just enjoyed looking at the ones we have.'

'Suppose they were plaster casts and the originals were back in Athens?'

Geoff shrugged. 'I doubt if I'd know the difference and I'm sure there would be few others who would know they were fake. Just because they've been copied doesn't mean they've lost their beauty.'

'Difficult,' remarked Ronnie. 'If they made copies they ought to tell the public they are not the originals and then the visitors could feel cheated. If you don't tell them and someone finds out it becomes a scandal.'

'After all the controversy about returning them to Athens I doubt if they'd get away with not telling the public they were copies. Athens would shout it from the housetops that the originals had been returned. How do you feel about them?'

'Well,' Ronnie considered. 'Part of me feels they should go back. They belong to Greece. The other part of me says thank goodness they were brought over here and looked after. Do the Greeks deserve to have them back? For years they didn't appreciate their ancient monuments. Once the novelty of having had them returned had worn off would they continue to look after them properly?'

'No doubt the Greeks would say they'd look after them better than we had and the Brits would not believe them. We'd be forever sending someone over there to report back on their condition.'

'Actually the museum in Heraklion is fabulous. All Cretan finds, of course, but they are well looked after and labelled. The museum down in Aghios is rather old fashioned and they have started building a new one.'

'When will it be finished?'

'Goodness knows. The Greeks take their time to do things and much of the public building work stops during the summer as the workers go back to their seasonal jobs.'

'Have you been to the Acropolis?'

Ronnie shook her head. 'That's in Athens.'

'What about Knossos?'

'I've been there and it's pretty amazing due to the reconstruction that was done years ago. You really feel that parts of it looked like that when people lived there.'

'Did they live there? I've read a book that puts forward another theory. It was an enormous mausoleum, a real city for the dead.'

'How come?' asked Ronnie doubtfully.

'I can't remember all his reasons now, but they were all very logical and plausible. I've got a copy at home. Would you like to borrow it?'

'I'll not have time to read it before I fly home.'

'That's no problem. You can take it with you. I can always get hold of another copy. I'll look it out for you tonight and you can collect it when you come to say goodbye to Mum and Dad tomorrow. I'll walk back to the hotel with you as usual and then I wondered if you'd have dinner there with me? If so I need to tell Mum not to make anything for me tomorrow.'

'I'd like that,' said Ronnie and meant it. She would miss Geoff and his humour.

'It's been a pleasure having you here,' said Susan. 'I know I didn't see much of you as you were working with Jack, but you were no trouble at all.'

'I enjoyed meeting you. You made me feel like part of your family and you are a superb cook. Every meal I shared with you was absolutely delicious.'

'Cooking is a hobby for me. I enjoy making new dishes. They're not always a success and then I tweak them a bit with my own ideas and that usually improves them.'

'I should have come to you for cookery lessons rather than wasting Jack's time.'

'You didn't waste his time. He continued with his own work whilst he tutored you. He said you were a good pupil and he's only sorry you're not going to stay here and eventually become one of his artists.' Susan took a cake from a tin and placed it on the table. 'I made this today. It's from a recipe I haven't tried before. When Geoff arrives we'll have a slice and you can give me your opinion.'

Geoff walked with Ronnie back to the hotel and escorted her into the dining room. He ordered a bottle of wine and whilst they studied the menu Geoff lifted his glass.

'I've had one of my serious moods come over me,' said Geoff and Ronnie looked at him warily. 'I know you're flying back to the States tomorrow and then plan to return to Crete, but could we keep in touch? E-mail pen pals.'

'I don't see why not. You can tell me about Mrs Fielding.'

'Do you know what she did today?'

'Go on, tell me.'

'She went through every apple in the tray and picked out any one that had the slightest speck. She then brought them over to me and said they were not fit for sale at the price displayed and could she have them cheaper as they were imperfect goods.'

'What did you say?'

'I told her that if they were not perfect then they were not fit for sale at any price. I gathered them up and after she'd gone I put them back in the display.'

'Was there anything wrong with them?'

Geoff shook his head. 'Nothing. They were just the usual marks you get on the skin of an apple. She went and picked the others over again and finally bought two. I put my finger on the scale and she had to pay ten pence extra. I rang up the correct amount and put her ten pence into the charity box.'

Ronnie laughed. 'What did your Mum think of that one?'

'I haven't told her yet. I thought I'd try it out on you first.'

Ronnie shook her head. 'And I fell for it. Suppose your Mum ever wants to meet Mrs Fielding? What will you do then?'

Geoff shrugged. 'She could be away on holiday or moved to Scotland to be near her relatives. I'm sure I'll think up some excuse.'

'Have you ever tried writing, Geoff? You have such a fertile imagination.'

'It's one thing thinking up little incidents to amuse Mum, but no one else would be interested. Here's the book I promised you about Knossos.' Geoff pulled the slim volume from the pocket of his jacket.

'Are you sure you don't want it back? I could post it to you,' offered Ronnie.

Geoff shook his head. 'No, hold on to it and I may come to collect it.'

'To the States?'

'No, but I may decide to have a holiday in Crete.'

'Really?'

'Why not? I've visited France, Italy and Switzerland. Time to go a little further afield. If I do come would you be able to take a couple of days off to show me around?'

'I'm sure I could manage that. My time is very much my own over there. Let me know when you've made up your mind and know your dates. I could book you in at the self catering apartments where I stay.'

Geoff took his diary from his pocket. 'I'm on holiday from twenty first of June until the fourteenth of July. How would that fit in with your plans?'

Ronnie looked at him in surprise. 'You'd already decide you were going to holiday in Crete, hadn't you?'

'My decision depended upon your reaction. Had you said you would be far too busy to spend any time with me I would have taken it as a snub and gone elsewhere. Even so, I would still have given you this.'

Geoff delved into his pocket again and brought out a small package. Ronnie gave a giggle.

'You're like a magician. How many more items do you have hidden in your pockets?'

'Nothing else. At least I won't be lopsided when I walk home as I was walking here.'

'I didn't notice.'

'Maybe I have a natural lean.' He handed the package to her. 'Open it.'

Tentatively Ronnie unwrapped the small box. She hoped desperately that it would not contain a ring. She liked Geoff and was prepared to spend some time with him if he came to Crete, but there was no way she was going to commit herself to a relationship. She lifted the lid and gave a little gasp.

'That is beautiful.' She looked at the small pear shaped enamel, hanging from a slender silver chain with a painting of a forget-me-not.

'You really like it?' asked Geoff eagerly.

'I love it. Your father made it, of course.'

'May I put it on for you?' Geoff rose and walked behind Ronnie, taking the pendant from her and fastening it around her neck. 'I wanted you to have a souvenir of your time in England and a forget-me-not seemed very appropriate.'

'Oh, Geoff, you are such a nice kind man. Thank you very much. I shall treasure this.'

Geoff returned to his seat and raised his glass. 'To our next meeting on Crete.'

November 2010

'How did your painting course work out? Did you find it useful?'

Ronnie shook her head. 'It was very interesting, but it isn't practical for me. Jack showed me how to make and cut enamels and then he explained how I needed to grind up the enamel to make the paint. You apply it with lavender water. You have to work looking through a magnifying glass and often your paintbrush has only one hair.'

'Really?' Alexandros raised his eyebrows.

'When you're satisfied with the results you fire the enamel in a special little kiln and that sets the paint.'

'Suppose you're not satisfied?' asked Alexandros

Ronnie grinned. 'Then you wipe it off and start again. I've brought some of my better examples to show you. Tell me what you think.'

Alexandros examined the small enamels. 'They're amazing. Did you really paint these?'

Ronnie nodded. 'Compared with the work that Jack produces these are rubbish. Look at this one.' Ronnie held up the forget-me-not pendant that she was wearing. 'Jack made this and you can just see how perfect it is.'

'It's very pretty. How much did he charge you for that?'

Ronnie blushed. 'He didn't. It was a gift from his son.'

Alexandros raised his eyebrows and Ronnie's blush deepened. 'Tell me more about your young man.'

'There's nothing really to tell. He's very nice. He insisted on walking me back to my hotel each evening as it was dark. We used to have a quick drink together and chat. He took me up to London to the Tate Gallery and the British Museum and we enjoyed our day. There was nothing more to it than that.'

'Really? That was all? What a shame.'

'Uncle! I really do not need a man around to complicate my life.'

Ronnie did not tell her great uncle that she had received a long e-mail from Geoff. He had told her all about Guy Fawkes, the history of the plot to blow up Parliament in 1605. The discovery of the plot and the saving of King James I was an event that was still celebrated all over England with bonfires, guys and fireworks. One of the most famous celebrations took place in a town close to where he lived and he had mailed copies of the photos he had taken of the event. They showed people in fancy dress and carrying flaming torches who were taking part in processions leading to open fields where large bonfires were lit and effigies burnt.

She had replied, telling Geoff the history of the American Thanksgiving celebrations that had begun in 1621. In that year the Pilgrims who had sailed from England to America held a thanksgiving service for their survival and the fruition of their crops. The tradition had continued down the centuries, being declared a public holiday; although it was now used as an excuse to provide a table groaning with food so you could feast until you could eat no more rather than a religious service of thanks for your well being.

Uncle Alex smiled at her vehemence. What it was to be young and independent. He had declared he had no need for a woman in his life until he had met Millie, then he had changed his mind.

'So tell me more about this painting you've been studying.'

'Well, it's far more complicated than I thought. My idea of painting an enamel of Spinalonga and fixing it to the lid of a box is impossible. Jack said he would send me the blank enamels, but I would still need a special little kiln, the paints and lavender water;

they're expensive to start off with. I would also need somewhere like a studio where I could store everything and work. The whole project is too expensive to be feasible. I'd have to charge Saffron a small fortune for each one and I can't see the tourists being willing to pay that amount for a souvenir. Uncle Yannis bought some of Jack's reject stock and he's having a problem trying to sell that.'

Ronnie wrapped the enamels and placed them back into her bag. 'Did you find anything interesting amongst the photos?' Her eyes strayed to the table where there were various small piles of snapshots and a box.

'Yes, I did. I thought I'd talk to you before I showed you any photos. It will probably come as a bit of a shock to you. It did to me. I had no idea.'

Ronnie frowned. 'What are you talking about, Uncle Alex?'

'You're grandmother was adopted. She wasn't my sister.'

'Adopted? How come? Surely you must have known? Did Grandma know?' The questions came tumbling from Ronnie's lips.

'Amongst the photos I found a sealed envelope. I expected to find more photographs inside. Instead there were old papers written in Greek. I had no idea what they said so I went along to the Embassy and asked them to translate them for me. There were the official documents giving my parents' permission to enter the States with their children. There was also a letter and according to the translation by the man at the Embassy Vivi was given to my parents.'

'What! You can't just give children away.'

'I'll show you.' Alexandros took to sheets of paper from the table. One was old and yellowed and the other looked fresh. He handed the new sheet to Ronnie and she read the words in disbelief.

*The girl known as Paraskevi is given into the custody of
Yiorgo and Maria Roussakis to be nurtured by them in mind,
body and spirit until she is of a mature age.*

'Is that legal?' asked Ronnie.

Alexandros shrugged. 'I presume so. On the original paper there are three signatures at the bottom and I imagine they were those of her parents and an official.'

'May I see?'

Alexandros handed her the original letter and Ronnie screwed up her eyes. 'These signatures are hardly legible. Do you recognise any of them?'

'They mean nothing to me.'

'So she wasn't called after a relative after all. Why was she adopted?'

Alexandros shrugged 'Maybe my mother could not have any more children. Maybe her mother had died.'

'So my grandmother was adopted by your parents when she was a tiny baby?'

Alexandros shook his head. 'No, we collected her when she was about two, I think. My Mamma told me I was going to have a sister. I was quite ignorant about reproduction at that time. I thought everyone went to collect their children. Mamma became quite cross with me, I remember. I asked if we could choose because I would rather have a brother. She told me not to be silly and said that I must be kind to Vivi and look after her.'

'Goodness,' Ronnie smiled. 'You were an innocent. Did you find her original birth certificate?'

Alexandros shook his head. 'I expect that is in Crete somewhere.'

'And Grandma never knew that she was adopted?' Ronnie shook her head wonderingly. 'Why didn't they tell her?'

'They may have kept quiet about it thinking the American authorities might send Vivi back to Crete.'

'Could they have done that?'

'I've no idea. The adoption may not have been legal, just an agreement between the parents. They wouldn't have wanted it investigated by immigration if that was the case.'

Ronnie wrinkled her brow. 'So the couple I understood to be my great great grandparents were no relation to me. In fact you're not my great uncle. You're no relation to me either.'

'Does it make a difference?'

'It makes me feel odd. One minute I had relatives and now I haven't. It doesn't change the way I feel about you, Uncle Alex. You can love someone who isn't a blood relative.' She assured him. 'Did you never ask your mother why they had collected Vivi? You obviously realised how children were conceived when you were older.'

'I did ask her once. She told me I was being ridiculous and imagining things; Vivi had always been with us.' Alexandros's eyes twinkled at her from behind his glasses. 'I think Vivi was probably born out of wedlock. Later her mother wanted to marry a man she had met and he refused to accept the child. That could be why my parents never told her. They didn't want her to feel she had been rejected.'

'So, in fact, we could have a number of relatives that we know nothing about?'

Alexandros shrugged. 'We could, but I shan't lose any sleep over them.'

Ronnie sighed. 'I would like to know who grandmother's real parents were and why she was adopted.'

'What difference does it make?'

'None at all, really, I'm just feeling curious. Where did they go to collect her?'

Alexandros shook his head. 'I don't know, but it can't have been very far from where we lived. They drove there and back in one afternoon.'

'You say they *drove* there? In a car, do you mean?'

Alexandros smiled and shook his head 'No they had a couple of donkeys and a small cart. My grandfather and father used to ride off on a donkey every day.'

'To go to work? What did they do?'

'I imagine so, but I have no idea of their occupations.'

'Did everyone in the village have a donkey and cart?'

'I expect so, but I really don't remember, Ronnie. Do you still want to look at the photos? There's one of the cart with my grandfather holding the donkey.'

'Of course,' answered Ronnie at once. 'Did you recognise any of the people in them?'

'Only my parents. The elderly couple I assume were my grandparents. One or two of them have names written on the back, but the others are a total mystery to me.'

Ronnie examined each photograph carefully. 'These ones of the couple you think were your grandparents are fascinating. Have you seen how much gold jewellery your grandmother is wearing? It must have weighed her down. Your grandfather has the baggy trousers with a dagger in the waistband. There's another of him with ammunition over his shoulder and a rifle in his hands. Did he go shooting or was he going off to a war?'

'He'd probably dressed up for the photograph. Look, in this one he just has a white shirt under his waistcoat, no sign of any weapons.'

'Would he have worn those clothes for work?'

'I imagine so. It wasn't until later that the Western style of dress became popular.'

Ronnie placed the photographs of Alexandros's grandparents to one side and looked at those of his parents. In a number of photographs his mother was shown in the company of another girl. They were both dressed simply in blouses and skirts, their hair tucked up beneath a scarf.

'Who was the girl with her?' asked Ronnie.

'I don't know. Possibly a friend.'

'Did she have a sister? They do look quite alike.'

Alexandros shook his head. 'I never heard mention of one.'

'So as far as you are aware you had no aunts or uncles on either side of the family?'

'That's right. I'm the last of the Roussakis men. This branch of the family ends with me.'

'It's unusual. Most of the families I know seem to have hundreds of relatives.'

'They tend to claim distant cousins as relatives, whereas we don't usually go further than a second cousin. My grandparents may have had siblings, but if they did I never remember hearing them talk about them and I can't recall ever having any visitors to the house.'

'No visitors?' queried Ronnie in surprise.

'There was a man who came once. I only remember because it was an unusual event. My parents seemed rather upset after he left and my grandmother was crying. I was sent out to the yard to play. Maybe he brought news of a death in the family.'

Ronnie sighed. 'It's so frustrating. I want to know so much more about the family.'

'I'm sorry. I'm not a lot of help,' apologised her great uncle.

'I'm not blaming you. You were a little boy and couldn't be expected to remember. I don't remember the details of when my father was sent to prison. I know a policeman came to the house and my mother crying when my father was taken away by him. I know I kept asking when he was going to come home and then I cried when Mom told me he wouldn't be home for a long time, but nothing more. Where's that photo of your grandfather with the donkey and cart?'

Alexandros handed it to her and Ronnie giggled. 'That is amazing. You hardly ever see anyone actually riding a donkey these days.' It was hard to make out the features of the man standing at the head of the donkey, behind him was a stone wall and arched door and just to one side part of a window could be seen with an ornamental grill.

'I only remember riding in it once. I was so excited. I seem to think my grandfather drove us to the coast to catch a ferry to mainland Greece.' Alexandros wrinkled his brow. 'I expect all our belongings were in the back along with my mother and us children.'

'Were you seasick on the journey?'

'Not that I can remember.'

'How many weeks did it take for you to reach America?'

'Goodness knows. We spent most of the time in a cabin with my mother. I expect she was frightened we would fall overboard if we roamed around on our own. I think that one was taken when we were on the boat.'

Ronnie looked at the two children, their unsmiling mother holding them firmly by the hand. Ronnie felt sorry for her. To leave your home and go half way across the world to an unknown country must have been a daunting experience. Added to that was her responsibility for the well being and safety of her children. No wonder she was not smiling.

Ronnie began to sort through the photographs of Alexandros and Vivi as children, sometimes alone, together or with one or other of their parents. She began to put them into some sort of sequence.

'These ones of you are obviously taken when you were quite a little boy, probably about two or three, judging by your height. You were so like your father even then.'

Alexandros sighed. 'It became even more noticeable as I grew older, particularly after Pappa shaved off his moustache.'

Ronnie examined the photographs of her grandmother as a child. 'She reminds me of someone.'

Alexandros chuckled. 'I'm not surprised. You're the image of her.'

'Me?' Ronnie looked at him in surprise.

'Forget her old fashioned clothes. Look at her face, the shape of her nose and chin, then look at yourself.'

Ronnie rose and walked over to the mirror and studied her reflection carefully. 'I suppose I am like her,' she smiled. 'At least I'll know how I'll look when I get old.'

Ronnie spread the remainder of the photographs out on the table in front of her. 'I do wish they had put a name on the back of all of them so we would know who they were. I'm sure this girl is the same one who was in that photo with your grandmother.' Ronnie held it up to the light and turned it first one way and then the other. 'There is something written on the back, but it's so faded and indistinct that I can't make it out.'

She sighed deeply. 'If only you could remember where you lived on Crete I'd take copies of these photos back with me, go to the village and ask some of the old people there if they could tell me who the people were. I know they wouldn't be alive now, but someone would be bound to remember them. Were there any more papers in the envelope?'

Alexandros shook his head. 'Nothing.'

'What about death certificates for your parents?'

'I have those, but they only give their last address in America. That's not a lot of help.'

'What about your birth certificate? Does that say where you were born?'

'I only have my nationalisation papers from when I officially became an American citizen. Goodness knows what became of my birth certificate, if I ever had one.'

'You must have had one.'

'Not necessarily. I understand that officialdom was very slack in Crete before the war.'

'Would you let me make a photocopy of the paper about my grandmother being given into your parents' care? I'd like to take it back to Crete with me and find out if it is a legal adoption certificate. If so I should be able to trace where she was living earlier and who her parents were.'

'You can, but I doubt you'll be able to find out anything. It's too long ago.'

Ronnie wagged her finger at him. 'Don't be too sure. I'm going to ask John for some help. He knows the right people to ask for information. Remember how I told you he had found that old man who seemed to have done a disappearing act.'

Ronnie was deep in thought when she left her great uncle. Had her grandmother really been adopted; and if so, why? She had begged Alexandros to search through his loft and see if he could find anything more to shed light on the situation. She wished she could return to Crete sooner and ask John where she should start looking for family records. As it was she had to visit the employment agencies again and see if she could find some temporary work for the winter months.

April 2011

Ronnie pushed her bag into the overhead locker and took the aisle seat. She was suffering from a mixture of emotions. She was sad to have left her mother and uncle in America, but looking forward to returning to Plaka. Geoff had asked her to spend a week in England when she had to break her journey to make the European connection at Heathrow and she had considered the idea before mailing him to say she could not afford either the money or the time.

He had replied that she would be welcome to stay at his parents' house, but again she had declined the offer. Grudgingly she had agreed to change the time of her flight to Crete so he could journey up to Heathrow and spend a couple of hours with her. He had seemed so delighted to see her again that she now felt guilty that she had refused to spend longer in his company. She consoled herself with the thought that when he visited Plaka in June she would hire a car and devote her time to taking him to places of interest.

She fastened her seat belt and hoped it would not be too long before the 'plane took off. She was anxious to arrive in Crete before darkness so that once again she would have the pleasure of seeing the expanse of the bay spread before her with Spinalonga sitting as a guardian at the far end. She had mailed both Giovanni and Saffron of her impending arrival, but they had neither of them offered to collect her from the airport and she hoped she would be able to find a seat on the small bus that delivered the tourists to their hotels.

As the engines started up and the familiar force of the take off pushed her back in her seat she closed her eyes, took a deep breath and tried to relax. She hated take off and landing. She opened her eyes again when the air hostess asked everyone to attend to the instructions that must be followed in the event of an emergency. She felt slightly irritated. She knew where the exits were situated, how to use an oxygen mask and to remove her shoes before using a chute to evacuate. The procedure was just a way of taking the passengers' minds off the uncertain moments whilst the 'plane left the ground and became airborne.

As the hostess began to advertise the duty free goods that were available on board Ronnie opened her book. If she was able to read a few pages she would probably drop off to sleep for an hour and the journey would seem quicker. The girl sitting next to her was rummaging in the net pocket attached to the seat and finally turned to Ronnie.

'Would you mind if I borrowed your flight information brochure? Mine seems to be missing.'

'Not at all.' Ronnie handed it to her. 'You can keep it. I don't find them particularly interesting.'

'I'm only looking to see if they have the perfume my mother wears at a bargain price. I try to buy it on the flight out, then when she visits me I have her birthday present ready and waiting.'

'That's a clever idea,' remarked Ronnie. 'If they haven't got it on board you might be able to buy it from the duty free shop on your way back.'

'It will be too late then. My mother will be out in July.'

'Are you working in Crete?'

The girl nodded. 'I'm employed by a travel firm to check health and safety. I go around to all the hotels they have on their books and make sure the electrical fittings are in order, tiles on the floor are not chipped, the swimming pool is kept clean, check their safety certificates are up to date. That sort of thing.'

'It sounds interesting, but I would have thought it should have been done before the season started.'

'Most of them are closed and you can't get access. If you do go early and find defects they promise they are just about to rectify the problems and then you have to go back again anyway to make sure they've done as they said.'

'This keeps you busy all season?'

Caro grinned. 'I make sure it does. I have to do follow ups and it gives me a summer in the sun. The only downside is that I have to go back to England with my reports each month. What about you?'

'I'm an artist. I work on commission for one of the gift shops.'

'Now that really is interesting. Whereabouts?'

'Plaka.'

'I know, that's down by that island, isn't it? Thank goodness I haven't been asked to go over there and do a health and safety check. I'd probably have to recommend it was closed down.'

'Have you ever been there?' Suddenly Ronnie felt defensive on behalf of Spinalonga.

'No, I've only seen photographs.'

'Reserve your judgement until you've visited. I understand that a tremendous amount of work has been done over there to make the buildings safe. If a tourist has an accident over there it is likely to be their own fault.'

'I gather you have been over?'

'On a number of occasions. I did some painting over there.'

'Really? I've got some hotels to visit in Elounda – that's not far away is it? Maybe we could meet up when I'm down that way and we could go over together?'

Ronnie nodded. It would be good for her to have someone new that she could meet up with occasionally, and she was sure that if she went to Spinalonga whilst tourists were swarming all over the island she would not have any strange feelings. 'I'm Ronnie.'

'Caroline, but I'm always known as Caro. So where do you live whilst you're over there painting? Have you got your own villa?'

'I wish! No, I rent a self catering apartment.'

'I hope the accommodation I've been allocated is decent. I'm going to be based in Aghios Nikolaos as most of the hotels I have to check out are there. At least I have a car provided for when I have to go out of town. I always feel sorry for the visitors who don't realise that although they have the beach at their doorstep it's difficult to get anywhere else unless you hire a car.'

Ronnie nodded her agreement. 'I found it quite frustrating at first. Whenever I wanted to go into Aghios Nikolaos I was waiting around for buses unless I could arrange a lift with friends.'

'You don't have a car?'

'I don't really need one. When my family visited last year I hired a car so I could take them out.'

'How are you getting down to Plaka today? Are friends meeting you?'

'I'm not expecting anyone. I mailed them my time of arrival and I've heard nothing back so I'll try to get a seat on the tourist bus that goes to the different hotels. If that isn't possible I'll have to catch the ordinary bus to Aghios Nikolaos and then I'll take a taxi to Plaka.'

'I can drive you down to Aghios Nikolaos if you don't mind waiting around whilst I collect the car.'

'Would you? That would be a tremendous help.'

'You can show me the way. I was based up in Chania last year so I don't know this end of the island at all.'

'It isn't difficult and it's well signed, not like when you drive off into the country.'

Caro rolled her eyes. 'Tell me about it. You can drive around in circles. You check the map, follow the signs and still can't find the village because the sign with its name on has been knocked down. Are you having a drink? I see they're bringing the trolley.'

Talking to Caro, hearing about the various horrors she had found in hotels the previous season made the flight pass quickly for Ronnie. She had not read any of her book and nor had she dozed to pass the time. She described her art work and the time she had spent in England the previous year trying to master the art of painting enamels.

'Jack was terribly patient with me, but I realised that I didn't really have the talent and it would be terribly expensive to set up my own studio.'

'Did you paint the pendant you're wearing? I've been admiring it.'

Ronnie held it up towards Caro. 'No, Jack painted this and it was a gift.'

'That was kind of him.'

Ronnie blushed. 'Actually it was his son who gave it to me.'

Caro raised her eyebrows. 'Romance?'

Ronnie shook her head. 'Not really. I only knew him for a couple of weeks. He's very nice and we've kept in touch. He wanted me to break my journey on my way back to Crete and stay in England for a week with his family, but I decided it wasn't a good idea. He's coming to Crete for a holiday at the end of June and we'll see how that pans out.'

'I hope it works out for you both.'

'What about you?'

'No. I'm happy to play the field, but I'm not ready for any permanent attachments. If Mr Right should come along so be it, but I'm not looking. I just want to enjoy myself. Oops, was that the undercarriage going down? We must be nearly there.'

Ronnie waited patiently whilst Caro completed the formalities for her car hire. She had looked to see if anyone had come to meet her, but there was not a familiar face to be seen amongst those who were greeting the arrivals.

'Well, that's sorted,' announced Caro. 'Now all I have to do is find the car, then the exit from the airport and then the correct road for Aghios Nikolaos. Nothing to it!'

Ronnie drew up outside Giovanni's house and asked her taxi to wait. She only had to collect the key for her apartment and she assured him she would be no more than a few minutes. Bryony answered her knock and looked at Ronnie in surprise.

'Hi, there. You're a day early. We weren't expecting you until tomorrow. Come in.'

Ronnie frowned. She had mailed Giovanni to say the day she would be arriving. 'I only need the key to my apartment. I have a taxi waiting.'

'Send him away. One of us will take you up in the car.'

Ronnie hesitated and Bryony gave her a little push. 'Go on, or you'll be paying him a fortune for nothing.'

Giovanni handed Ronnie the key to her apartment. 'I mailed you this afternoon to say I would meet you tomorrow at the airport. What made you come a day early?'

'I haven't. I said I would be arriving on Wednesday.'

'Today is Tuesday.' Giovanni smiled at her. 'You must have worked out the time difference incorrectly. It's no problem. Your apartment is ready.'

'Provided I have a bed for the night somewhere. I'm shattered.'

'I'll get you some bits and pieces for the morning,' promised Bryony. 'You'll need some milk and bread. The shop won't be open until later in the week, but let us know if there's anything you need.'

Ronnie smiled at her gratefully. Now she had finally arrived all she wanted to do was go to bed and sleep for as long as possible. She had sent her mother a text message from the airport to say she had arrived safely and she would check her other mails tomorrow.

Ronnie pottered around her apartment, unpacking the clothes she had left there and her painting materials. She felt completely disorientated, but knew this was due to the time differences she had experienced over the last two days. The day was overcast and she wished the sun would shine so that Plaka was as she remembered from the previous year.

It was mid-day when she heard a knock at the door and opened it to find John standing there.

'I thought I'd let you know that I'm at the shop. There's nothing fresh yet. I've come up to put the freezer on and just give it a general clean up. Tins and packet goods are available.'

'That was thoughtful of you, John. Have I got time to check what I have in my cupboards and make a list?'

John nodded. 'I'll be there for at least an hour. Come over when you're ready.'

Rapidly Ronnie checked her cupboard. She certainly needed a fresh bag of rice. Her container had 'things' hopping around in the bottom and she emptied it hurriedly into the rubbish. The pot of jam had crystallized and there was a film of mould on the top. It joined the rice in the rubbish. Pasta, sugar, coffee, tea and jam she would be able to purchase from John, and if she could then have a lift as far as his home she would only have a short walk to Elounda where she could buy some fresh fruit and vegetables. She made a separate list, adding eggs, bacon and salad items.

John was mopping the shop floor when she arrived and she stood in the doorway. 'I don't want much. I've brought a bag and if you could pass it out to me I won't need to walk over your clean floor. I'll go into Elounda and pick up some fresh bits later.'

John held out his hand for her list. 'It won't take long to dry. I'll get this for you and if you're happy to wait until I've finished up here I'll drive you in to Elounda. The buses aren't very regular at the moment.'

'I'd be grateful. Waiting at a bus stop and never knowing if the bus will turn up is so frustrating. I don't mind having a taxi back if I have a heavy bag. Do you think it's going to rain?'

'No, this cloud will clear in another couple of hours. Are you in a rush or do you want to have a coffee? I'd like to hear what you've been up to.'

'Actually I want to talk to you and ask your help.'

John raised his eyebrows. 'More early morning visits to Spinalonga?'

Ronnie shook her head. 'I have a mystery I'd like you to solve if you can.'

'Hold on, I'll make the coffee then you can tell me.' John walked carefully back across the damp floor, returning a short while later with two cups of steaming coffee and placed them on the wall beside Ronnie. 'No tables and chairs out yet, so we'll have to make do with sitting on the wall.'

'No problem.' Ronnie was pleased she had decided to wear her jeans rather than shorts.

'So tell me about this mystery you want me to solve.'

'Well, you're good at finding out about people and where they came from. You found that old man, Tassos.'

'Well, you actually found him,' admitted John.

'That was just a fortunate coincidence. You did all the background investigation. Would you be able to look into my ancestry?' asked Ronnie.

'Do you have a skeleton in the cupboard?'

'I'm not sure. When I went home Uncle Alex had looked out the old family photos and he'd also found some papers amongst them. They were written in Greek and he took them to the Embassy to have them translated. One was permission for the family to enter America and I've photocopied the other one so I could show it to you. According to the translator my grandmother was virtually given away.'

John raised his eyebrows. 'You don't just give children away.'

'That was my reaction. I thought maybe the translator had misread the Greek and it was actually a legal adoption agreement. There are three signatures on it, but no government stamp or seal or anything.'

'Didn't your great uncle know that she wasn't his true sister?'

'No one knew. Her parents had never told her or anyone else as far as I can gather. Uncle Alex thinks it may have been just an agreement between families and if the immigration authorities had found out they would have sent my grandmother back to Crete.'

John nodded. 'That would explain why they kept the information to themselves. I'll have a look at it for you, but it's doubtful that I'll be able to find out anything. She could have come from anywhere on Crete, even if she was the daughter of a relative.'

'Uncle Alex said his parents drove somewhere one afternoon and collected her. It must have been near where they lived to be able to do the round trip in just a few hours.'

'She may have been brought from somewhere else on the island. Did they walk or have a donkey?'

'Uncle Alex says his grandfather had two donkeys and a cart.'

'Two donkeys and a cart? They must have been quite a wealthy family. What work did his grandfather do?'

'Uncle Alex doesn't remember. He said his grandfather and father went off on a donkey each day. When they emigrated they ended up in Dallas and his father worked in a flooring factory.'

'What year did they leave Crete?'

Ronnie shook her head. 'Uncle Alex was a little boy. He thinks he was about six.'

John held up his hand. 'Hang on a minute.' He walked into the shop and returned with an order pad. 'Give me your uncle's full name and that of his parents and I'll have a look. I can't promise anything, mind you.'

'Would you, John? I'd be terribly grateful. I'd like to know who I really am.'

'You might not like what I find out.'

Ronnie shrugged. 'I'll take that chance. It would be better than not knowing anything at all.'

'How old is your Uncle Alex now?'

Ronnie wrinkled her brow. 'Seventy seven, coming up seventy eight.'

'So if his memory is correct that he was five or six when Vivi was 'collected' she would be about seventy two or three now.'

'According to her death certificate that Mom has she died aged sixty two ten years ago.'

'So someone, probably your mother or uncle, knew her date of birth.'

Ronnie shook her head. 'After Uncle Alex told me Vivi had been adopted I asked Mom if she had a birth certificate for her mother. She said she had never seen one or found one amongst her papers, but Vivi had always said her birthday was nineteenth of August and she was born in nineteen thirty seven.'

'I wonder if she was right or if she was just told that date,' mused John. 'Birthdays and age have never been that important to the Cretans until recently. Your Name Day is still your main celebration.'

'You'd have to know how old you were to get married and also when you were old enough to draw your pension,' protested Ronnie.

John grinned. 'If your parents agreed you were of an age to get married then the ceremony took place. You could retire from work whenever you pleased. If you had sufficient work years credited to your name you were entitled to a pension. Of course, if you had plenty of money you didn't need to worry about having the credits.'

'Suppose you're a fisherman or farmer? How do you prove you've worked enough years?'

'The authorities accept your identity card as proof of your age, although they know the information is not always accurate.'

'That doesn't mean that you've worked for the required number of years, though.'

'Most manual labourers have worked a good deal longer. They probably started when they were about thirteen and most of them continue until they're well into their seventies and no longer physically able.'

'So does your Uncle Yannis get a pension?'

John nodded. 'And Aunt Ourania and Grandmother Marisa.'

'But they still work in the shop.'

'Of course. What would they do with themselves if they were sitting at the house all day? They no longer depend upon it for a living, but it's a very good tax loss.'

Ronnie frowned. 'What do you mean? Tax loss?'

John grinned at her. 'They have to declare their pension, of course, and they own the shop premises. Uncle Yannis claims to have had a loan to help him equip the shop and is still repaying that. The stock they have has depreciated, custom has dropped off, there are breakages and damages to be taken into account along with the increase in utility bills.' John shook his head and sighed dramatically. 'He is shouldering a big loss.'

Ronnie looked at him wide eyed. 'Surely the tax officials would want details of the loan he is paying off. Where did he get it from? The bank?'

'From my father, of course. He would have borrowed the money one day, arranged the same sum to be borrowed from the bank and repaid my father. My father would then have asked Uncle Yannis for a loan and the same would have happened in reverse. Money would have been moved from one bank account to another so many times that it would be almost impossible to track it down and prove there isn't money outstanding from one person to another.'

'And no one investigates?'

'Not if you have a good accountant. He will make sure the trail is so difficult to follow that no one wants to spend the time or effort. It could cost more in an employee's wages than the amount that was recovered.'

'Is your father running at a loss?'

'Of course,' answered John immediately. 'He has empty properties that are not giving him a rental income, wages to pay to everyone, the upkeep of the house and self catering apartments, stock for the taverna that has gone out of date and has to be thrown away. It is difficult to make ends meet.'

'But the apartments were full all last summer,' protested Ronnie.

'Were they?' John raised his eyebrow quizzically. 'You paid my father in cash each month therefore your apartment must have been empty all season.'

'John! Do you mean that?'

'Holidays that are booked through the companies are paid for directly into the bank. There is no need for cash payments to be entered into the accounts. There may only be half a dozen all season, but it helps when you have to balance your income against the expenditure to ensure that your accounts show you are running at a loss.'

'It sounds more complicated than running true accounts. What happens if you are found out?'

'You hold up your hands and admit you have made an error. You apologise. It was an oversight. It will not happen again. You are usually given a small fine and told to be more careful in future.'

'Has that ever happened to your father or Uncle Yannis?'

John smiled. 'A while ago when Bryony and Marcus came over. According to his accounts my father was paying Bryony for far more work than she would be able to do in a week. He claimed she was working up in the taverna all day, as a chambermaid in the morning and also as an assistant in the shop during the afternoons. It was queried, but my father explained that the taverna and shop were one and the same. It had just been a small oversight on his part to claim she was there all day. Whilst she was working as a chambermaid Marcus was in the shop, so the money was correct, it was just the name that was wrong. He omitted to mention that he was paying Marcus to act as a maintenance man.'

'John, it is totally dishonest.'

'Of course,' John shrugged. 'We know it is; our accountant knows it is; the tax collector knows we do not tell the truth and the government is powerless to claim the money we owe. Why do you think Greece is in such a financial mess?'

Ronnie shook her head in despair. 'If that is the way affairs are run in Greece now what must they have been like seventy or more years ago? Maybe that paper that says my grandmother was given into the care of Yiorgo and Maria Roussakis would be recognised as a legal adoption paper at the time.'

'It's possible. Let me have a copy of that paper and write down all the details you can think of regarding your uncle and I'll see what I can do. I'll look up your grandmother first. If the date you have given me is correct then her birth should be registered. If I find her I can look up the adoption records. If I can't find anything under births or adoption we'll have to look elsewhere. Do you know where on Crete the family were living at that time?'

'Uncle Alex says they lived somewhere called Castle something.'

'I'll have a look at the map and see if I can get a clue. Nowhere springs to mind, but I only really know this area. I can also have a look at the Census for Yiorgo and Maria Roussakis and see if their names appear. They would have had to produce their identity cards to be allowed to emigrate. I could try looking at the shipping lists and see if I can find their names amongst the passengers. That could be a starting point. It might even say whereabouts on Crete they had lived and give your great grandfather's occupation.'

'What are you doing, John?' asked Nicola, looking over his shoulder at the computer screen.

'Trying to find out some information about Ron's grandmother. She reckons her grandmother was given away to her uncle's parents.'

'*Given* away? That's not possible.'

John shrugged. 'Who knows? The child may have been in an orphanage and the paper that Ron has just relates to when she was collected and the actual adoption papers have been lost over the years. I've been trying to find out if there was a girl born on nineteenth August nineteen thirty seven and called Paraskevi '

'And was there?'

John grinned. 'Fifty four.'

Nicola laughed. 'Oh, well, better than a hundred and fifty four. What do you do now?'

'I start with the death certificates for people with that name. If I can find them for females with that birth date I'll be able to cross them off. That should reduce the number a little.'

'What about those that remain?'

'I look for marriage certificates.'

'But Ronnie's grandmother was married in America.'

'Exactly. I can cross off every Paraskevi born on nineteenth August nineteen thirty seven who has either died or married. With a bit of luck I should be left with just one that I can't tie up and that should be Ron's grandmother and her parents' names should be recorded along with her birth.'

'And if that doesn't work?'

'I'll have a look at the population Census, but I haven't got a lot of hope there. If Ron's grandmother was born in nineteen thirty seven and the family left for America in nineteen thirty nine or forty she wouldn't be recorded, any more than her uncle would be. I can check the shipping lines and see if I can get an exact date when the family left for America, but to be honest, I don't hold out much hope of finding out anything.'

Bryony was enjoying herself. For the first time in weeks she felt she was actually being useful. Marianne had left the organisation of the Easter festivities for her to arrange. She had made copious lists of the different foods they would need, visiting the butcher in Elounda and ordering chicken, pork, beef and a whole lamb to be barbecued.

Vasilis and Cathy had been invited, along with Vasi and Saffron and she continually checked the number of guests and the amount of food to ensure there would be sufficient.

'Would you mind if I asked Ronnie to come along?' asked

Saffron. 'I know she isn't family, but she fits in well and I would feel a bit guilty about leaving her on her own at this time.'

'John has already asked her,' smiled Bryony. 'Did you know she has asked him if he can look into her family background? Apparently her grandmother was adopted and she would like to know more details.'

'I had no idea. Has John had any luck?'

'Not that I know of, but he may be waiting to tell her his findings at Easter.'

'I feel a bit guilty about John,' admitted Saffron.

'Why? It was all due to you that he is so well and happy again.'

Saffron shook her head. 'Not me, credit must be given to the neurosurgeon. No, last season I arranged with John that he would shrink some photos of Spinalonga for me and I would attach them to some of the wooden boxes. I've found a supplier who will laminate them straight on to the wood and he's not expensive if I buy a quantity at a time. I must admit fixing them to the lids was terribly time consuming. It will be a job I shall be pleased to relinquish. I need to be able to spend less time at the shop and be at home for Vasi this year.'

Bryony raised her eyebrows as Saffron continued. 'His father has taken over the management of the Central again so Vasi doesn't have to make the journey to and from Heraklion every day. We hardly saw each other last year as I was at the shop every day and then working on accounts or ordering during the evenings. If it's like that again this season I can see that it could cause problems between us. I really need an assistant, but where do I find someone I can trust?'

'Are you seriously looking for someone to help you in the shop?' asked Bryony and Saffron nodded.

'They need to be able to speak decent English and be accurate and honest. I suggested his friend Yiorgo's wife to Vasi, but he said she wouldn't be suitable. Ronnie likes to go off and paint as she wishes and certainly would not want to be tied to regular days or hours. I can't think of anyone else.'

'You could think of me.' Bryony blushed as she made the suggestion.

'You? But you're busy working here.'

Bryony shook her head. 'I'm not really busy. I used to spend most of my time keeping Grandma company, along with helping Marianne with some of the meals and a bit of cleaning. John has taken over the shop and taverna; we all clean our own rooms, so it's just the lounge and kitchen that needs attention and Nicola often does that whilst the girls are having an afternoon nap.'

'I thought you were helping Nicola, so she could have a bit of time to herself.'

'Some days I'll play with them for an hour or so, or take them out with Nicola, but it isn't regular and Nicola is coping well with them now they're that little bit older.'

'Would you really consider helping me up at the shop?' Saffron could not think why she had not thought to ask Bryony before. 'We could work out some convenient times for you and I'd pay you, of course.'

'What would I have to do?' asked Bryony. 'I'm not good with my hands like you are.'

'You'd only have to serve the customers, put out more stock as necessary and keep an eye open for any shoplifters. I can assure you that you would be busy all day.'

'When would you want me to start?' asked Bryony eagerly.

'Come up during the morning next week and I'll show you where everything is. I'll spend the first couple of weeks up there with you until you feel confident to cope on your own for some of the time. If you don't enjoy being there you're free to say and I'll have to try to find someone else to help me.'

'I'm sure I'll like it.' Bryony was secretly elated. She could have asked Giovanni to employ her as a chambermaid to occupy herself, but she had no desire to spend every morning cleaning the self catering apartments. 'I'd better go and see if Marcus has finished digging the barbecue pit,' she said, longing to go and tell her husband that she was going to be working for Saffron.

May 2011

Ronnie found Caro good company on the occasions when they were able to meet. She always had a fund of amusing stories about the various hazards she had encountered at the hotels during her visits and the excuses the owner had tried to make to cover his shortcomings.

Ronnie had warned Saffron that Caro was making health and safety checks at the various hotels her company used and Saffron passed the information on to Vasi.

Vasi frowned. 'Do you know when she is coming?'

Saffron shook her head. 'She just arrives apparently. At the moment she is concentrating on the hotels in Aghios Nikolaos, then she will let Ronnie know when she is visiting Elounda. She wants Ronnie to take her over to Spinalonga.'

Vasi nodded. 'Aghios Nikolaos is no problem. Her company do not include me in their brochure. Elounda is different and also Hersonissos. The managers have not reported any problems to me, but I will do my own check to ensure they have not missed anything.' He placed his arm around Saffron. 'It is so good to come home to you each evening and know you will be spending time with me, rather than poring over accounts or sitting at the computer ordering more stock.'

Saffron kissed his cheek. 'You were very patient with me last year, but you were quite right. The situation I had worked myself into was impossible. Bryony is more than happy to come to the shop three days each week. It has taken so much pressure off me.'

Three weeks later John closed his computer with a sigh. 'I can't find any trace of Ron's grandmother. I've cross checked all the girls named Paraskevi who were born in August nineteen thirty seven and I haven't a single one left unaccounted for.'

'If Ronnie says that is the date her grandmother claims to have been born, it could well be incorrect. She could have been called Paraskevi after a relative, not because she was born on a Friday. In that case she could have been born any day of the week. You could be looking in the wrong month or even the wrong year.'

'Nicola!' groaned John. 'Do you mean I've got to do it all again?'

'That's up to you. You can honestly tell Ronnie that you've looked and not found any trace of her grandmother.'

John shook his head. 'I can't. I've only looked for that one Friday. I'll have to look at the other Fridays in the month and if that doesn't turn up anything then I'll have to go through the whole year. If only her grandmother's birth certificate could be found it would make everything much easier. Ron's asked her uncle to go through absolutely everything to see if he can find out any more information, but she hasn't heard anything positive from him yet. He says he's found a few more photos, but no documents.'

'It's a shame you didn't have this project to keep you occupied during the winter.'

John shrugged. 'I wish she'd mailed me in November when her uncle first told her. I could have made a start then, but she says she's in no rush. Her mother and uncle are visiting again in September and she has said it would be nice to tell them then what I have found out. At the rate my investigation is going the answer will be nothing,' ended John gloomily.

'Something is bound to turn up. You're only going back seventy years.'

'Her uncle doesn't even remember the name of the village where he lived!'

'Why don't you look at the Census for nineteen thirty one?'

suggested Nicola. 'His parents should be on that.'

'It won't tell me anything about Ron's grandmother, though. She's the one I need to find.'

'If you can find his parents on the Census you'll know what work his father did and which village they lived in. Once you've found them on that you can look at the Census for nineteen forty one and see if they are still there. If his father was a farmer or fisherman he could be difficult to track down, but once you know the village there must be some record of him or some old person who remembers them going off to America. It wasn't something people did every day of the week. Grandma lived to be a hundred and up to a couple of years ago her memory was good. It was only recently that she became confused over the sequence of events.'

John sighed. 'I'll decide tomorrow whether to look for other girls named Paraskevi or start on the Census. I want to spend some time with the girls before they have their tea and bath.'

'No chasing, please, John.'

John shook his head. 'I thought I'd take them down to the beach and they could dabble around in the rock pools.'

'You won't let them go in the sea, will you? It isn't warm enough for swimming yet.'

'Promise,' John assured her. 'It needs two of us to do that safely anyway. If they can find a few crabs and shrimps in the pools they'll be more interested in those than going swimming. Don't worry, Nick. I'll look after them properly.'

'I know you will, but they can move so fast now. Maybe if I came with you and sat at the top of the beach? Then if they took off in different directions we could catch one each.'

'I'll put their wrist restraints on and attach them to me. They won't be able to stray far.'

'They won't like that.'

'Then they won't be going to the beach,' said John firmly. 'They have to learn the rules. Remember when you first came to stay? I wasn't even allowed to paddle unless Mum or Dad was down there with me and I could swim quite well by then. You have an hour to yourself and don't worry about them.'

John enjoyed being down in the sheltered cove with his daughters. As Nicola had predicted, they had objected to having a rein attached to their wrists, but once down on the beach they became engrossed in looking in the shallow pools. John lifted each one up onto the rocks and moved a stone from the bottom of the pool. A small crab scuttled away and Lisa squealed whilst Jo crowed with delight.

'You don't have to be frightened, Lisa. It's only a crab.' John dipped his hand in the pool and brought the crab out. 'Look, it's very tiny.'

Lisa looked at the tiny crustacean and shuddered. 'No,' she said and shook her head.

'Alright, we'll put him back in. Shall we look for a shrimp?'

John moved them from pool to pool and both girls watched with fascination as a tiny fish darted away from the side as their shadow fell across it. He encouraged them to put their fingers into the water and Jo began to splash.

'No, that's not a pool to play in. That's where the little fish lives. I'll find you a pool to play in later.' He pulled a sea snail off the rock and placed it on the bottom of the pool, hoping it would crawl back to the side, but it lay there motionless. He had more luck with a sea anemone, passing his fingers close to the waving tentacles so that it withdrew them, spreading them out again as soon as he took his hand away.

'He's looking for his tea,' explained John.

'Cake,' suggested Jo and John shook his head.

'He eats teeny weeny little fish called plankton unless he can catch a shrimp as it goes past. Come on, we'll find a pool big enough for you two to have a paddle, then we'll go back home and you can have your tea.'

Jo promptly sat down in the pool and kicked her legs, splashing her father and sister. Lisa joined her, but was far more restrained, letting the water run through her fingers and then rubbing her wet hands across her hair. Jo laughed, and not to be outdone she stood up, bent over and put her head down into the pool. She emerged gasping and spluttering as John raised her up.

'You're not big enough yet to understand you have to hold your breath,' he admonished her. 'No, Lisa. You are not to do it.' He held her firmly. 'Let's go and say goodbye to the little fish and then I'll take you back to your Mamma. You can tell her you've seen a fish, a crab and an anemone.'

'Moni,' said Lisa.

'Anemone,' corrected John. 'Anemone, try and say it again.'

Lisa shook her head. 'Fish.'

'Yes we saw a fish. What else did we see?'

'Cwab.'

'That's right, Jo, we saw a crab.' John picked up a girl in each arm and began to climb back up the steps to the house. Once on the patio he closed and locked the gate behind him before removing the restraints from their wrists and allowing them to run into the house.

'John!' Nicola admonished him. 'I thought you promised you wouldn't let them go in the sea.'

'I didn't. They managed to get in this state whilst playing in a rock pool.'

Nicola eyed him doubtfully.

'Honestly. Lisa ran her wet hands over her hair and Jo put her head under the water. Tell Mamma what you saw in the pool, Jo.'

'Cwab.'

'And what else?'

'Moni,' added Lisa. 'Fish.'

'What's a "moni"?' asked Nicola.

'Anemone,' John translated. 'Come on, girls. Let's get you cleaned up and some dry clothes. Then you can go and have your tea.'

'Cake?' suggested Joanna hopefully.

John turned his attention to the Population Census of Crete dated 1931. The documents were divided to cover the different Prefectures of the country and John started from Chania in the north planning to work his way methodically through Rethymnon, Heraklion and Lassithi. In many cases the writing was difficult to decipher due to the poor handwriting and careless storage before the details had been placed on microfilm.

Roussakis, with various spelling variations, appeared to be a fairly common name. He listed each one he came across along with the family members, their ages, occupations and the village where they lived. As his lists grew longer he began to despair of ever finding Ronnie's great grandparents and wished he had looked for all the girls who had been born in 1938 and called Paraskevi. He did not know which would have been more time consuming.

It took John more than six weeks, scrutinizing the lists each evening after the girls had been put to bed, finally deciding that he had found every Roussakis who was recorded as living on Crete in 1931. Spread across the island he had found three hundred and thirty four men named Yiorgo Roussakis, and twenty two of them had married a woman called Maria; all but two had extended families.

If they lived in a reasonable sized town they had a street and house number recorded, but those who lived in the villages had no such details. In many cases the name of the village to which the information related was unreadable where the page had been creased and the information not transferred when it was copied.

Now all he had to do was to repeat the process for the 1941 Census and decide who was missing and why. He also hoped that the names of the villages would be readable.

Painstakingly he checked and cross checked the entries, deleting each one from his hand written lists if they still appeared on the 1941 Census. Whilst doing so an awful thought occurred to him. Yiorgo could be the name Ronnie's great grandfather was known by, but it may not have been his given name. John looked back at his original lists. He might well have to go back and check the other Roussakis families again. He groaned at the thought. He just hoped that before he was faced with that possibility he found one of the men named Yiorgo Roussakis, married to a woman named Maria, who fitted the age group and was not on the 1941 Census.

'John.'

'Mmm.' John did not look up from the list he was checking.

'If you do find a couple who appear to be Ronnie's great grandparents what are you going to do then?'

John placed his cursor on the line he had reached, sat back and stretched. 'I'm hoping I'll be able to find the name of the village where they lived. I can then look and see if there are any adoption records for the area.'

Nicola frowned. 'I thought they were confidential.'

'Names and details would be, but there should be a record of how many children were adopted each year.'

'And then?'

'Then it will be up to Ron. She could try approaching the capital of the Prefecture and ask for a search to be made for the date her grandmother was adopted and any details that are available about her natural parents.'

'Would they give them to her?'

'I'm not sure. It's long enough ago that it happened. Her grandmother's natural parents are obviously no longer alive.'

'There could be other relatives.'

'I don't think Ron's looking for an extended family. She just wants to know her immediate genealogy.'

'I have a friend coming over to Crete for a visit in a few weeks.' Ronnie smiled at Caro. 'We'll have to meet up for a drink whilst he's here.'

Caro raised her eyebrows. 'The man in your life?'

'Not really. He's the son of the artist in England where I went for a couple of weeks.'

'What does he do?'

'He's joint manager of a convenience store.'

'Really?' Caro looked at Ronnie in surprise. 'I would have thought you'd have been going out with someone in the art world.'

Ronnie shook her head. 'I'm not actually going out with him. He used to walk me back to my hotel each evening and we would have a drink together. He took me up to London a couple of times and we had dinner together on my last evening.'

'Must be serious on his part to come over here to see you. How serious are you?'

'We're just friends,' replied Ronnie vaguely. 'We've kept in touch by e-mail and he asked if I'd show him around a bit if he came over for a holiday.'

'So where's he staying? With you?'

'In the same self catering apartments, but not with me.'

'I bet he wanted to stay in your apartment with you.'

'He didn't suggest it and I didn't offer. I told you, we're only friends'

'So what's he like?'

'Quite amusing.' Ronnie recalled the stories about the fictitious Mrs Fielding.

'Tall, short? Dark, fair?'

Ronnie considered. 'Medium height I suppose and his hair is medium brown.'

'Hmm. A 'medium' man. He doesn't sound that exciting.'

'Maybe that's why we're only friends.'

'I'll give you my opinion when I've met him. When's he arriving?'

'On the twenty first and staying until the fourteenth July. I hope he likes swimming as I'm not sure I know enough different places to take him to each day.'

'There's Knossos and the Heraklion museum.'

'That goes without saying, but that only takes up two days.'

'I'll see if I can think up anywhere for you.' Caro looked at her watch. 'I must go. I have to be at a hotel at two fifteen and it's nearly two now. I'll be in touch when Mr Medium is here.' Caro picked up her bag and with a wave of her hand sauntered down the waterfront towards the hotel where she would probably spend the remainder of the afternoon.

June 2011

Ronnie waited at her apartment for Geoff to arrive from the airport. She had not offered to go up to meet him, arranging for him to travel down by the mini-bus and arrive with some other guests later that afternoon.

She had taken the opportunity during the morning to clean her apartment and ensure that there were supplies of tea, coffee and milk in the apartment that Geoff was to occupy. She was not sure if she really wanted him to be around for three weeks and hoped he would be willing to go off on his own some of the time and leave her to paint. Maybe she should have suggested that he only spent two of his three week holiday in Crete, but it was far too late now to change arrangements.

As he alighted and waited for his case to be off loaded Ronnie walked forwards. 'Hi, Geoff. Good to see you again. How was your journey?'

'Ronnie! I'm so pleased you're actually here. I thought I might be left to find my own way to my apartment.'

'I told you I would be here waiting for you. I have your key, so grab your case and follow me. It isn't far.'

Geoff followed Ronnie dutifully as she led the way to the apartment block and pushed open the door. 'Here you are; number three. There's no one above you so you should be quiet enough. I'm across the hallway at number four. You can always give me a knock if you have a problem.'

'What kind of problem is included?' asked Geoff with a lift of his eyebrows.

'Running out of milk first thing in the morning,' answered Ronnie severely.

'Lost key at midnight?'

'I'll make sure Giovanni leaves a spare with me.' Ronnie opened the door and ushered Geoff inside. 'You should have everything you need for tonight. I've put some milk in your fridge and there's tea and coffee in the cupboard. We can go over to the taverna for breakfast tomorrow. It's also the local shop so you can buy anything else you think you might need.'

'It's a long time until breakfast,' complained Geoff.

'I'm not suggesting that you wait until then for your next meal,' smiled Ronnie. 'I'm going to leave you to unpack and when you're ready give me a knock. I'll show you around Plaka and we'll have a meal here this evening.'

'You could stay and talk to me. I won't be long unpacking.'

'We have three weeks in which to talk. If we start talking now we could have run out of conversation by next week.'

Geoff watched as Ronnie backed out of the doorway and closed the door after her.

He pulled back the cover on the bed and looked at the crisp, clean sheets. He bounced up and down and found the mattress comfortably sprung. Next he looked into the small bathroom and was relieved to see it was spotlessly clean.

He had entered into conversation with a couple during the flight and they had raised their eyebrows in horror when he said he was staying in self catering. They told him about sheets that were not sent to the laundry for weeks on end, just ironed to make them look fresh, of bathrooms that smelt of drains where the plumbing was so antiquated, and warned him not to leave a morsel of food around as the cockroaches would be in immediately. They had confided that they never stayed in less than a five star hotel and they had taken a chance on one in Elounda that only had four stars.

They were not at all sure if it would come up to their standards.

Geoff smiled to himself as he placed his T-shirts and underwear into a drawer and took his toiletries into the bathroom. The room was larger than his bedroom at home and he had to share the bathroom with his parents. He opened the door to the patio and took a deep breath of the Cretan air. He tried to differentiate between the assortment of scents that assailed his nostrils and decided he could smell herbs, flowers, the sea and best of all, from somewhere was coming the smell of a barbecue with a tantalising aroma that made him realise he was very hungry.

He washed his hands and face, changed his slacks and donned a clean shirt. He wondered if there was anywhere he would be able to take his laundry or would he be expected to wash his clothes by hand. He would have to ask Ronnie. He ran his hand across his chin and decided he only needed to run his razor quickly over his face, followed by a quick splash of aftershave and then his toilet would be complete.

Ensuring he had his key safely in his pocket, along with his wallet and passport, he crossed the hallway and knocked on Ronnie's door.

'Am I respectable enough to escort a young lady out for dinner?' he asked as she opened it.

Ronnie eyed him up and down. 'Just about. There's one thing missing.'

Geoff looked at her in surprise. 'What's that?'

'A jacket or pullover for later. It's still beautiful at the moment, but when it gets dark it can get quite cold.' Ronnie picked up a large woollen wrap and placed it over her arm.

'If you were a lady you would offer me your wrap if you saw I was cold.'

'If you decide not to bring a jacket with you and feel cold that's your problem, not mine,' answered Ronnie with a smile.

'Two seconds.' Geoff unlocked his door and emerged back into the hallway moments later with a jacket slung over his shoulder.

'Am I properly dressed now?'

'For this evening, yes. I hope you have shorts, tees and sandals with you for during the day.'

Geoff smacked his forehead. 'Did you tell me to bring them?' He looked at Ronnie in mock alarm.

'I most certainly did.'

Geoff smiled at her. 'Then I have them with me; along with swimming trunks and a beach towel.'

'Sun glasses and sun screen?'

'I doubt if I'll need sun screen at this time of year. You said it wouldn't be too hot.'

Ronnie shrugged. 'Suit yourself, but don't expect me to commiserate with you if you get burnt.' She made a mental note to purchase some from John the following morning and keep it with her in her bag.

Ronnie introduced Geoff to Saffron as they passed her shop and waved to Uncle Yannis. She explained to Geoff the relationship and when he looked puzzled she laughed.

'Don't even try to work it out,' she said. 'Greek relationships are difficult enough, everyone is claimed as a cousin, however far removed, but their family is even more complicated because half of them were born in America.'

Geoff shrugged. 'Oh, well, I suppose there is something to be said for having two sets of grandparents and one uncle and aunt. Don't you agree?'

Ronnie was about to explain about the adoption of her grandmother and changed her mind. 'I only have one uncle,' she said. 'I recommend we eat here tonight.' She led the way to a table outside Kyriakos's taverna. 'Have you ever had octopus?'

Geoff shook his head. 'Is that what I can smell cooking?'

'We'll ask for a small portion for you to try. It isn't everyone's taste. What about calamari?'

'I'm pretty sure I've had that before.'

'Well, I suggest you leave the ordering to me. I'll ask for a selection of dishes and you can try all of them. If you don't like them just say so. It's no problem.'

In halting and basic Greek Ronnie ordered small helpings of tsatziki, taromasalata, olives and bread, to be followed by octopus, calamari, keftedes, dolmades and chicken kebabs, whilst Kyriakos smiled and scribbled items on his order pad. That way she felt sure Geoff would find something palatable and a salad and bread would be brought to them automatically.

'You speak Greek,' remarked Geoff admiringly and Ronnie shook her head.

'I'm trying to learn, but it's difficult. I can ask a simple question, but I don't always understand the answer and have to ask for them to repeat it in English. I've ordered a carafe of the local wine, but you can have beer if you prefer.'

'When in Rome, do as the Romans.'

Ronnie shook her head sadly. 'Your geography is a bit astray. You happen to be in Greece.'

Geoff shrugged. 'Alright, when in Greece, do as the Greeks.'

'That's better. Now, what would you like to do tomorrow? I'm happy to hire a car and take you around, but I don't want to do that and then find you plan to spend the day on the beach.'

'Where should I visit whilst I'm here?'

'Well, I've earmarked a day to visit Knossos, another for Heraklion to include the museum, Spinalonga obviously, and there are other archaeological sites we could drive to if you're interested. There's a lovely little folk museum up on the Lassithi Plain and the views up there are wonderful with all the old windmills, although very few of them actually work now.' Ronnie began to work her way steadily through the small dish of olives.

'How about if we had a day on the beach tomorrow and then did some visiting later in the week? I'd hate the weather to change and not have a swim whilst I'm here.'

Ronnie smiled. 'It's very unlikely the weather will change now. It may be windy on occasions, sometimes a bit cloudy, but

I certainly wouldn't expect it to rain.'

'I could have left my umbrella and galoshes behind. It would have saved me from being overweight."

'Have you really brought them with you?'

Geoff grinned and shook his head. 'No, you told me you had wall to wall sunshine and I believed you. I did bring my mackintosh, though.'

'Truly?'

'It could be pouring when I arrive back at Gatwick.'

Ronnie returned to the ideas she had formulated to occupy some of Geoff's time. 'We could travel into Elounda by bus and spend the morning wandering around, walk over the Causeway and have lunch at an excellent taverna. Do you like walking?' she asked.

Geoff looked at her solemnly. 'I never complained about walking you back to the hotel, did I?'

'That was ten minutes down the road. I'm talking about walking for two or three hours.'

'Up hill and over dale?'

'Up hill certainly. There are some unspoilt little villages just up from Elounda. You can drive up there, but the streets are narrow and parking can be difficult. It's easier to walk. If you are into proper walking I could take you to Kritsa Gorge.'

'Let's see how I get on climbing up to the villages. Is all this food for us?' Geoff eyed the array of dishes being placed on the table in disbelief.

'This is called a meze. It's just a small selection of the main dishes that are available. If there is anything you particularly like you can have a larger helping as your main course the next time you visit. Just take a little of everything, add some salad and a piece of bread. There's no rush. In Greece you take your time over your evening meal. Sometimes it lasts for hours. As friends pass by they see you and come in, another round of drinks are ordered and some more meze and before you know it the evening has flown by.'

'A bit like spending the evening in the pub.'

'I suppose so,' agreed Ronnie somewhat doubtfully.

'Bit frustrating if you only wanted a quick bite to eat before going on to the theatre or cinema.'

'That's something you certainly won't be doing down here,' smiled Ronnie. 'There is no cinema or theatre.'

'So what do the people do with themselves?'

'In the summer most of them are working. If they have some time off they spend it with friends in a bar or playing cards. The older generation tend to sit out on their balconies, their daughters take the grandchildren to visit them and they chat over a glass of wine whilst the children play.'

'Wow, it sounds too exciting for words.'

'It's just a different way of life over here. The evenings are warm, so what could be more pleasant than sitting outside, sharing a bottle of wine and chatting to your friends?'

'Surely they have the television?'

'Of course, but they don't spend the evening with their eyes glued to the screen unless there are football or basketball matches. They watch more during the winter, of course.'

Geoff considered Ronnie's words. 'I suppose that's true of most of us, really. Mum often watches a soap whilst Dad is immersed in a book.' Geoff topped up Ronnie's glass. 'What do you do with yourself in the evenings?'

Ronnie shrugged. 'It depends. Sometimes I add a few finishing touches to some paintings or clean my apartment. I may sit out on the balcony and read for a while.'

'You don't meet up with friends?'

'Occasionally. Most of the people I know are from Yannis's house; the man we waved to as we passed the shop. I'll visit them if I'm invited, but I wouldn't just arrive.'

Geoff raised his eyebrows. 'You wouldn't be welcome?'

'I'd be made more than welcome, but I would feel embarrassed. They have their own routine for relaxing when their working day

171

has finished. I meet up with Caro sometimes when she is in this area.'

'Caro?'

'We'll arrange to meet up with her and have a drink one evening. She's a health and safety inspector for one of the travel companies. She checks that everything is in order at the hotels the company uses. I think you'll like her. She tends to have a number of amusing stories to tell.'

'Yes? Do you want to hear the latest saga of Mrs Fielding?'

'Go on,' sighed Ronnie. 'No doubt you're dying to tell me what you've thought up this time.'

Geoff grinned. 'Well, she came into the shop and began to pick over the strawberries. When she decided she had a perfect punnet she removed all the stalks. She brought an empty punnet over and asked for it to be weighed along with the stalks. She then demanded an extra strawberry to make up the weight of the punnet and stalks to agree with the weight stated on the price label. She said she couldn't eat the stalks or the punnet so she didn't want to pay for them.'

'I don't believe you.'

'I don't expect you to, but I'm sure Mum will appreciate it. I'll have to think up one or two incidents that happen over here and embellish them.'

'You're hopeless.'

'And helpless. I need to visit the gents and I don't know the word or how to ask for directions.'

'Go towards the back of the taverna. Someone there will guess what you want and point you in the right direction and there will be a picture of a man on a door. It's not difficult.'

With his jacket still slung over his shoulder, Geoff walked beside Ronnie away from the taverna and towards the apartments.

Geoff halted and looked up at the dark sky. 'If it's always as clear as this I'll have to spend some nights down on the beach looking at the stars. They're so clear and the constellations are at a slightly different angle. I'm sure I'd be able to observe some stars here that aren't visible in England.'

'If you sleep on the beach people will think you're a vagrant and you'll be reported to the police in Aghios Nikolaos. I shall disown you.'

'You wouldn't leave me languishing in gaol, would you?'

Ronnie nodded. 'It would be far too embarrassing to admit that you were a friend of mine.'

'I wouldn't actually sleep on the beach. I would only be laying there looking at the stars.'

'Tell that to Mr Christos when he arrests you. What time do you want to meet tomorrow for breakfast?'

'What time do you suggest?'

Ronnie considered. 'I would say eight. You have to remember that we are two hours ahead of English time, so your body may be telling you it's six. It only takes a day to catch up so it's worth while ignoring the difference tomorrow morning. John is usually at the taverna by eight so we can go over whenever we're ready. I can buy some bits and pieces for a picnic lunch at the same time.'

'Bits and pieces like we had tonight?'

'Don't get excited. My menu will not be as comprehensive. I'll get cheese, ham and tomatoes and make up some rolls. Did you enjoy the food you had tonight?'

'Very much. I'm not sure I'd want a large plate of that pink stuff, though.'

'You mean the taromasalata. That isn't meant to be eaten as a main dish. We can go somewhere else tomorrow evening and you can try some different bits and pieces.'

'Shall we go for a drink?' asked Geoff and Ronnie shook her head.

'You can if you want. There are plenty of places open, but it's almost eleven and definitely my bed time.'

'Is that an invitation?'

'No, it's a polite way of saying goodnight to you.'

'Oh, well, you can't blame a chap for trying.'

Geoff grinned at her and Ronnie felt nonplussed. He seemed to find her attractive and would make suggestive remarks, but when she rebuffed him he accepted her answer with a good grace.

Ronnie had found spending a complete day on the beach boring and was relieved when Geoff said he would like to visit Knossos or Heraklion the following day. She arranged to hire a car for two days with a proviso that she might wish to extend the hire for longer. She knew it would be no more expensive to hire for two days each week rather than the complete week and that meant that if Geoff became bored with sight-seeing and preferred to lie on the beach the car would not be sitting idle.

She was pleased with Geoff's reaction to Knossos, his admiration and interest in all he saw made him a pleasure to be with. He was anxious to visit the museum the following day to see the finds that were on display and Ronnie was quite happy to spend the day wandering through the various rooms and discussing the artefacts with him. He bought a guide book and during their drive back to Elounda he spent most of the time looking through it.

'We'll have to go back,' he suddenly announced firmly.

Ronnie slowed and signalled that she was pulling in at the side of the road. 'What have you left behind?' she asked.

'Nothing, but I don't remember seeing that pot.'

'Geoff! You saw so many different pots how can you possibly know if you saw that particular one? It's too late now anyway. The museum closes at six.'

'Oh, well, we can always go back tomorrow.'

Ronnie compressed her lips. 'We'll see. It would be better to leave it a while and have another look around just before you go home.'

'I could always drive up alone tomorrow if you didn't want to come.'

Ronnie shook her head. 'I've only hired the car for these two days. It's booked out to another couple for the remainder of the week,' she lied glibly. She trusted Geoff's driving in England, but was not sure if he was capable of driving safely in Crete. 'I thought you could have a culture rest and spend the day on the beach. I need to take a bit of time out to catch up on my work for Saffron, otherwise I'll have to be working every day next week and there'll be no time for us to go anywhere.'

'When are you taking me over to that island?'

'Sunday would be best. It's a bit quieter than the other days and if we go early we should have about an hour before the crowds start to arrive. I've asked John if he'll take us over in his boat and then give you a guided tour. He knows more about Spinalonga than anyone else. If you get bored with the beach let me know and we can walk around Elounda and up to the local villages. I can hire a car again next week and we can drive up to Lassithi and have a look at the villages away from the coast.'

'I'm in your hands. Where are we eating this evening?'

'I thought we'd drive into Elounda. There are masses of tavernas there and I can return the car at the same time. It will be easy enough to get a taxi back to the apartment. Just decide whether you'd like to eat in the town or on the waterfront.'

'What do you recommend?' asked Geoff after he had studied the menu.

'It will all be good and they serve quite large portions. I suggest you choose just a main meal. Whilst it's cooking they are bound to bring a dip of some sort and olives for us to nibble on. You can always have a sweet afterwards if you need topping up.'

'If I had a pork fillet what would come with it?'

'Chips and salad.'

'Steak?'

'Chips and salad. Don't expect vegetables like you have at home.'

'So all I really have to decide is which meat I would prefer?'

Ronnie nodded. 'I'm going for chicken fillet in a mushroom sauce.'

'I'll try the pork fillet.' Geoff lounged back in his chair. 'I'm thinking of coming out here to live.'

'Are you?' Ronnie looked at him in surprise.

'Why not? You have wonderful weather, staggering scenery and fabulous food. What more could I ask for?'

'A job could help.'

'Darn, I hadn't thought of that.'

Ronnie was watching the tourists strolling along the waterfront comparing the menus at the different tavernas. 'Oh, there's my friend Caro.' She waved her hand and Caro walked over to them Geoff rose and having been introduced asked Caro if she would care to join them.

Caro shook her head. 'Thanks, but I'm on my way to a date. I've decided we are eating over by the Causeway and he's buying me lobster.'

Ronnie raised her eyebrows and Caro smiled.

'He owes me. I gave him forty eight hours to get his electrical certificates done or I would slap a closure order on him. They were still not ready when I went back and he said if I was agreeable to meet him for dinner this evening he would have them ready for me.'

'Could you really have him closed down?'

Caro nodded. 'It would only take one phone call and he knows it. Will you two be around tomorrow evening? We could meet up for a drink then.'

Ronnie nodded. 'We'll see you in the bar just down from the church; the one with the green seats.'

'It's a date. I'll be there at seven. 'Bye.'

Ronnie and Geoff were waiting at the bar, their drinks before them when Caro arrived. 'Hi there. Sorry I couldn't stay last night, but Mr Groper was waiting.'

'Mr Groper?'

'He has one of those unpronounceable surnames, but he's like an octopus. Whichever way you move he's touching you, and I'm not talking just about your arm. I kept moving as far away as possible and still he tried to get his hand up my skirt at every opportunity. As he poured my wine he made sure his hand brushed across my boobs. Finally whilst we were finishing our dessert he started stroking my buttocks. I'd had enough by then.'

'What did you do? Throw your wine in his face?'

'No, I promised Mr Groper I would soon be back and went to the ladies. On the way I asked the waiter to take a bottle of their most expensive champagne to the table and to have a glass poured and waiting for me. I then sneaked out of the taverna and drove back to Elounda. I don't know how long Mr Groper waited for me to return, but he certainly had a hefty bill to pay.' Caro sat back with a satisfied smile.

Geoff roared with laughter. 'Serves him right. That was no way to treat a lady.'

'Did you get the certificates?' asked Ronnie.

Caro shook her head. 'Of course not. He was trying to bribe me to buy more time. I phoned my company this morning and delivered the closure notice an hour later. The guests have been moved and he will have to foot their bill at their new hotel. I informed the Greek authorities that his electrical certificates were not up to date and they'll be paying him a visit now. It's going to cost him a good deal more than the meal I stung him for to get the hotel re-opened.'

'I must remember this story to tell my mother. It's better than my Mrs Fielding anecdotes.'

'What are they?' asked Caro and Ronnie sat there, bored as Geoff recounted the stories she had heard before about the mythical lady, whilst Caro squealed with laughter..

'I can top that,' said Caro eventually when he finished. 'Last year when I was working in Chania various guests checked in to a hotel. Two separate couples went to separate tavernas for a meal.

Afterwards both the ladies decided they would have an early night whilst the men decided to have another drink before turning in. A couple of hours later when the first man returned to the hotel he realised he didn't have his key. Not wanting to wake his wife he went to reception and asked if he could obtain a spare. He was asked his room number and he knew it began with a three, but nothing more. The night clerk asked for his name and he gave it as Potter. The clerk checked the reservations and handed him the key to room three two one.

'He went up, opened the door and without putting on the light, began to undress quietly so as not to disturb his wife. He could not find his pyjamas that he was sure he had placed under his pillow and decided the maid must have moved them and it wouldn't hurt him to sleep in the buff. Man number two left the bar where he had been drinking and returned to the hotel. He had his key and let himself into his room, went straight into the bathroom and undressed. Walked over to the bed stark naked and threw back the sheet only to find there was already a naked man in his bed.

'Well, you can imagine the hullabaloo that followed. He was shouting at the intruder, the wife was screaming, the police were called, total mayhem. When everyone had calmed down, and both men had dressed themselves, it turned out that both men were called Potter. By sheer chance they had been given rooms on the same floor. Mr Potter Two was the rightful occupant of room three two one and Mr Potter One should have been given the key to room three one two.'

Geoff had been giggling like a schoolboy whilst Caro told the story. 'What happened next?' he asked eagerly.

'Rather shame-faced Mr Potter One was escorted to his own room and deposited there for the night. The next day the two couples met up and Mr Potter One apologised and bought them dinner. I understand they spent most of their holiday fortnight together and became firm friends.' Caro poured herself another glass of wine.

Ronnie sat silently. She was not at all sure she believed the story Caro had told any more than Geoff's tales about Mrs Fielding.

'So tell me exactly what your work entails.' Geoff leaned forwards.

'Well,' Caro took a mouthful of her wine and began to explain her duties. Ronnie listened politely. She had heard this before.

'It sounds really interesting,' said Geoff as she finally finished.

'You could join me one day and see just how boring it can be.'

'I'd like that. It would certainly be something different to say I had done whilst on holiday.'

'How about tomorrow?' asked Caro. 'Had you two anything special planned?'

Ronnie shook her head. 'We'd thought about hiring the car again and going up to Lassithi, but that can be done another day.'

'How would tomorrow suit you, then Geoff? I've a couple more hotels to do in Elounda. I'm giving Mr Iliopolakis a surprise at eight thirty.'

Ronnie nearly said she knew Vasi and then thought better of it. It could be a better idea to telephone Saffron and ask her to tell Vasi that a check on the hotel was to be carried out the following morning.

'That's fine. Where shall I meet you?'

'I'll drive up to the apartments and collect you. Be ready at eight fifteen. Do you want to come down, Ronnie?'

Ronnie shook her head. 'I'll be happy to spend the time painting.'

'That's settled then. Where were you two going to eat? I found a decent restaurant just across from here that doesn't charge the earth. Shall we go there?'

Ronnie was not sure she wanted to spend the rest of the evening in Caro's company, but there was no way she could refuse. 'Give me a few minutes. I need the ladies.'

Leaving Geoff and Caro at the table Ronnie made her way

inside the taverna. Once into the toilet she pulled out her mobile and pressed in Saffron's number.

'I've only got a couple of minutes,' she said. 'I'm with Caro, the health and safety representative. She's planning to be at Vasi's hotel in Elounda at eight thirty tomorrow. It's a surprise visit and I'm sure there is no problem, but I thought he might like advance warning. She closed a hotel down today because they were unable to give her electrical certificates for this year, so it could be as well if Vasi had those to hand.'

Saffron sucked in her breath. 'Thank you, Ronnie. I'm sure everything is in order, but I'll let him know.'

Vasi frowned when Saffron told him he was having a visit from the health and safety inspector the following morning. He knew his electrical certificates were out of date and no health and safety representative would accept excuses. He pressed Giovanni's phone numbers into his mobile and Saffron heard him having a conversation in Greek.

'Giovanni, I have a problem. I know I am to have a visit tomorrow morning from health and safety and my electrical certificates are out of date. Do you know anyone who would be able to provide me with some current ones immediately and do a check later?'

Giovanni smiled to himself. He had never known Vasi be caught out before. 'I'll speak to John. I believe he knows someone. I'll get back to you.'

John grinned. 'I'm sure Dimitris would be delighted to earn some extra money. I'll run him up to Vasi's house. Give Vasi a call back and ask him to have his old certificates to hand; oh, and tell him to have five hundred Euros in his pocket.'

Giovanni raised his eyebrows. He knew that what John was planning was completely illegal. 'Just don't get caught out,' he warned.

John shrugged. 'I'm only giving a friend a lift.'

Dimitris hesitated when John explained the position Vasi was in. 'All you need to do is copy out his old certificates and date them for a week or so ago.'

'I don't want to lose my licence. I gained my qualifications whilst I was doing my National Service. If they found out I had done anything underhand I could have it rescinded.'

'Vasi is honest. I'm sure if you can help him with his current problem he'll ask you to do an electrical check next week to ensure everything is in order and from then on he'll be a regular customer. It will be worth your while, Dimitris.'

Dimitris sighed. 'I just hope you're right.'

Vasi had his old certificates ready for Dimitris when they arrived.

'I'll go and chat with Saff,' announced John. 'I don't understand electrics, so I'll be no help to you.'

Dimitris looked at the fifteen pages of electrical certificates and frowned. 'John explained what you needed, but I can't just copy these. If someone decided to check they would never believe that there were no faults found anywhere. Did you have to renew any plugs or sockets last season or make any additions to the wiring?'

Vasi nodded. 'I had to replace two showers where the element had gone, and light bulbs, of course.'

'They're appliances. I'm talking about basic wiring.'

Vasi shook his head. 'As far as I'm aware there are no problems.'

Dimitris sighed. 'In that case I'd better make up a few.' He spread the sheets out before him and studied them carefully. 'Right, we'll say there were two cracked sockets in the kitchen and one not working in room two three four; a loose light switch in room three zero seven and another in room one five two. Two exterior lights were not working due to a loose connection. That should be reasonable. If any faults are picked up you'll have to say they have happened since the check and you'll get them rectified immediately.'

'Of course,' agreed Vasi. 'I'd be grateful if you would come in next week and do a genuine electrical check for me. I know I should have organised it before the season started, but you can have access to the guests' rooms whilst the maids are doing the cleaning.'

'What date do you want me to put on the certificates?' asked Dimitris.

'March or early April would be best.' Vasi placed two hundred Euros on the table beside Dimitris.

Dimitris looked at the money, wondering if he should pocket it. Vasi added a further one hundred Euros and pushed the notes towards him. 'I appreciate that you were prepared to come out during the evening.'

'I'll have to date them for April. I didn't leave the army until then. It will take me a while so I suggest you join Mr John and Miss Saffron. I'll give you a shout when I've finished.' Dimitris pocketed the money without further qualms.

Feeling himself dismissed Vasi joined John and Saffie on the patio. Saffron poured him a glass of wine and smiled.

'I won't ask why Dimitris is here or what he is doing. When Ronnie 'phoned I assured her there would be no problems.'

Vasi smiled at her. 'Nothing major, just a bit of paperwork that needs to be updated. I'll make sure I'm at the hotel early and warn the staff to be on their best behaviour.'

Throughout the evening Geoff and Caro carried out an animated conversation, virtually ignoring Ronnie's presence and she felt thoroughly miserable. Geoff seemed to be genuinely interested in all aspects of Caro's work for the travel company and Caro was only too delighted to explain legalities, interspersed with amusing anecdotes that had happened on various other Greek islands.

It was past midnight when Caro finally decided she would drive them back to the apartments before returning to Aghios Nikolaos. Ronnie was relieved they would not have to hire a taxi. Geoff had paid his share of the meals they had eaten out at the tavernas, but not offered to share the cost of the car hire or contribute towards the petrol; even the entrance fees to Knossos and the museum had been paid by her. So far he was having a cheap holiday.

Caro left them with a wave of her hand and a reminder to Geoff that she would be waiting for him at eight fifteen.

'She's such a nice girl,' he remarked to Ronnie. 'It's really good of her to say I can go to a hotel with her tomorrow.'

'I'm pleased you liked her. It will certainly be something different to do whilst you're here.'

Geoff returned to the apartment having spent the day with Caro. He could not stop talking about the way he had spent his day.

'The owner of the hotel was there when we arrived. He seemed a nice man and spoke excellent English. Caro said I was a trainee and asked if he minded me accompanying her whilst she did her checks. She asked for his electrical and fire certificates and he produced them immediately. She pointed out various things on them to me, like the date and any defects that had been recorded, as if I was really training to do the job. She made a note of the problems that had been recorded; then she asked to check the rooms and the kitchen where it said there was a fault. They had been rectified as the owner said.'

Ronnie nodded. She did not know if someone had worked during the night to ensure that everything was in order, but she was pleased she had not mentioned that she knew Vasi Iliopolakis.

'Caro asked me to check the cleanliness of the Gents toilets whilst she checked out the Ladies. We did that three times throughout the day. I had to check that they were clean, flushed properly, had enough toilet paper, the basins were clean and the hand driers were working. She said the toilets are often clean enough first thing, but by mid-day they've run out of paper or have become soiled and no one has checked on them. These all appeared fine. All she could find was a tap that had developed a drip between her first and second visit.'

Ronnie tried to suppress a yawn. 'I'm not boring you, am I?' asked Geoff anxiously.

Ronnie shook her head. 'Not at all,' she lied. 'I was later to bed last night than usual and now my lack of sleep is catching up with me.'

'You could have had a siesta.'

'I wasn't feeling tired then. So what else did you do?'

'Well, we checked the kitchen to make sure the ovens were clean, extractor fans working, no 'nasties' lurking in dark corners and fresh food was actually fresh. Caro even looked in the dishwasher to make sure there wasn't any greasy scum. I'm sure I wouldn't have thought of doing that. She asked to do a random check on the rooms, along with the ones that said they had needed to have attention from the electrician. The maids had finished the cleaning and they had certainly done a good job. The showers were clean and there were fresh towels. That was another thing Caro did that I wouldn't have thought about – she checked the hem of the shower curtains to see if they were dirty.'

Ronnie made a mental note to check her shower curtain. She had not taken it down to wash since her arrival.

'The bedding was clean, the bedroom floors had been mopped; even the balconies had been swept. The only fault we could find was a fire door on the second floor. It was somewhat stiff to open. A little old lady would have had a struggle and could have panicked if she were really trying to escape from a fire. We went along to a sandwich bar and had some lunch and then Caro said we would go back to the hotel whilst she completed her check sheets and wrote up any instructions she wanted to give to the owner. We sat in the lounge by reception and as soon as Caro saw some of the guests arriving she approached them and asked if she could talk to them about the hotel. They mostly gave it a glowing report. One woman complained that the coffee at breakfast could be hotter and a man said he would like more bacon to be available. When Caro mentioned this to the chef he said the temperature of the coffee would depend upon how long the water had been sitting in the machine. Once it drops below a certain temperature it automatically begins to heat up again. You can be unlucky if you take your coffee just before the element kicks in again. As regards the bacon, he said the dishes were refilled as soon as they were seen to be running low, but you could be unlucky and take your helping just before the dish was replenished. Caro suggested we went there to eat one evening so we could see what the food was like for ourselves.'

Ronnie nodded. 'Talking of food has made me feel hungry. Do you want to walk into Elounda or stay in Plaka tonight?'

'I'm easy. We're making an early start tomorrow to go over to Spinalonga, aren't we? In that case it could be wise to stay local and have a reasonably early night.'

Geoff was interested in Spinalonga. He listened carefully to John and asked intelligent questions, with none of his usual facetious remarks and took a quantity of photographs. Ronnie made sure she kept close to the two men, not wanting to experience any more inexplicable sighs or feel that someone was watching her. As the first of the visitors began to disembark from the large boats that brought them from Aghios Nikolaos John turned to Geoff.

'Have you seen enough? Now the big boats have arrived it will be too crowded to see anything properly. We can always come over again next Sunday if you wanted.'

Geoff agreed and John led the way back down to the old port entrance where he had moored his boat. 'Go back and stand by the gateway, Ronnie. I want one last photo.'

'Would you like me to take one of both of you?' offered John.

Geoff shook his head. 'No, Mum and Dad don't need to look at me in a photo. I'm there in the flesh.'

Dutifully Ronnie took up a stance at the gateway. Just as Geoff was about to take the photograph she gave a gasp and turned around.

'John,' she made a strangled sound and began to walk backwards away from the entrance.

'You moved just at the wrong moment, Ronnie. Go back and let me try again,' Geoff called to her.

'No.' Ronnie shook her head vehemently. 'I want to go now.'

John reached her side and took her arm. 'Problem?' he asked and raised his eyebrows.

Ronnie nodded. 'She was there. I'm sure she was sobbing.'

John nodded. He would not try telling Ronnie that any sound she had heard was either the wind or the waves as he knew she would refuse to accept the explanation.

'That's not a good place for a photo.' John shook his head at Geoff. 'The light isn't right. You'd never see Ron. She'd be in the shadow of the doorway.' John jumped into his boat and helped Ronnie aboard. She gave him a shaky, but grateful smile. 'You're welcome to look through the photos I have of Spinalonga, Geoff. If there's anything there you think you'd like just let me know.'

'Thanks.' Geoff was perplexed. There was no reason why he should not have taken a photograph of Ronnie standing in the archway. The light had been perfect. Her reaction had been very strange. He would have understood if she had refused previously to have any photographs of herself taken, but she had stood leaning on the Morosini Fountain in Heraklion whilst he photographed her without protest, along with many other locations.

They accompanied John back to the taverna where he insisted on cooking them a late breakfast and Geoff began to regale John about his visit to the hotel with Caro. John winked at Ronnie, but made no mention of his visit to Vasi with Dimitris.

'Thank goodness we don't have to worry about her dropping in on us,' declared John. 'We take our bookings from a different company. Provided we send them copies of our electrical and fire safety certificates they don't bother us further.'

'You mean no one comes and inspects the apartments for damage or cleanliness?'

John shook his head. 'The maids clean the apartments every day and if they notice any damage they report it to us. If there is mouldy food in the fridge or the cooking facilities are dirty they are cleaned when the visitors leave. Most people are pretty good, but why should you expect the cooker to be cleaned every day if you are a dirty cook? Wipe it over yourself, the same as you would if you were at home. You certainly won't find our apartments dirty when you arrive. Our reputation depends upon everything being in order and visitors recommending us.'

'I could ask Caro if she would do a check for you if you wanted,' suggested Geoff and John looked at him in amazement.

'Why would I want her to check out our apartments? She doesn't work for our holiday company.'

'She could pick up any small thing that you hadn't noticed. The only notes she had to give to the owner of the hotel in Elounda were about a dripping tap and a stiff fire door. Apart from those two things he received a glowing report from her.'

'I'm pleased to hear it,' remarked John drily.

'We'll go back in a couple of days and see if he's fixed them,' announced Geoff. 'They need to be attended to. If the drip gets worse it could end up flooding the toilet and the fire door needs to be opened easily. No one would want to hear of a disaster due to a stiff door.'

John and Ronnie exchanged glances. By the way Geoff was talking you would think he was the health and safety inspector.

'So what are you to planning for the remainder of the day?' asked John.

'I thought it might be a good day to walk up to Mavrikiano, have a snack lunch there, then walk through to Pano Elounda and we can see the filming they are doing. From there we can drop down to Kato Elounda and into Elounda proper. Depending on the time and how energetic Geoff feels we could then walk over the Causeway. I could show him the mosaic and we could either stay there for a meal or walk back to Elounda.'

'Sounds as if I should have brought my hiking boots.'

'I think you'll manage in your sandals. The alternative is to spend the remainder of the day on the beach or wander around Elounda. You decide and let me know.'

Geoff shrugged. 'I'm happy to take part in the walking tour. By the way, I forgot to say that Caro insisted on inspecting the drains. She made the handyman take up the covers so she could ensure there were no blockages and they didn't smell.'

'No doubt she had her drain rods tucked under her arm to unblock them if necessary,' remarked John, sotto voice and Ronnie giggled. 'Any more to eat, either of you? It's such a long walk to Mavrikiano.' He winked at Ronnie. 'I could make you some sandwiches to keep you going.'

Geoff frowned. From the way Ronnie had talked the village was hardly any distance away.

'I think we'll manage,' Ronnie assured John with a smile. 'If Geoff faints from lack of nourishment I'll call you.'

'I'll send Skele up to find you with a packet of sandwiches strapped to his back,' promised John and began to clear the dirty dishes from the table.

'Who's Skele?' asked Geoff.

'John's dog. He's lovely. Where is he this morning, John?'

'I'll collect him from Dimitris when I've been to Church. No doubt you'll see him around at some time, Geoff.'

'What breed is he? We had a beautiful poodle that was a prize winner at Crufts. He came top of his class.'

'Breed? Goodness knows. What Skele lacks in looks he makes up for in intelligence. He's a dog in a million.'

Ronnie looked at her watch. 'If we want to be in Mavrikiano for lunch we ought to think about moving or everyone will be having their siesta.' She did not want to become involved in a long discussion about the merits of different dogs.

Geoff found the walk to Mavrikiano well within his capabilities.

'By the way John spoke I thought it was going to miles up into the hills, but it's only a short way up from the town. Is this where the townsfolk used to live?'

'A good many of them still live up here, particularly the older generation. For years the houses would stand empty after the elderly owners had died, then the European visitors began wanting houses where they could stay during the summer and the younger people saw a way to make money. They cleared out the rubbish, put in a modern kitchen and bathroom and gave everywhere a coat of paint. Now a good many of them are holiday lets. They're ideal for families with children who would find a hotel too expensive and apartments like Giovanni's too small.'

'Are they inspected by health and safety?' asked Geoff.

'For goodness sake, you've become obsessed with health and safety. I have no idea.'

'They should be. Caro made me realise just how important it is for every property to be checked out.'

'I doubt that you'd be very popular with the locals if you started asking for electrical certificates or to check their drains. Now, hopefully we are early enough to be able to sit out on the balcony and look at the view whilst we eat. They do a fabulous crab salad. Everything is freshly made and good, but that salad is out of this world.'

The service was slow as the taverna began to fill up with more customers, many of them from the film set that had been built in Pano Elounda. A very old man sat in a corner and everyone greeted him deferentially as they entered.

'Who is he?' asked Geoff.

'Manolis Foundoulakis, I believe. He's advising the film makers.'

'What's the film about?'

'Spinalonga. He claims to be the only survivor from the time when the leprosy sufferers were sent over there to live.'

Geoff shifted uncomfortably in his chair. 'Is it healthy having him around in a taverna? I mean, suppose he's infectious.'

'Of course he isn't infectious. John told you that when the tests were finally carried out after the war most of the sufferers were found to be burnt out. No doubt he was and that's why he came back to his home village. Had he still suffered from the disease he would have been taken to the hospital in Athens.'

Geoff looked pointedly at his watch. 'How long will it take us to walk to this other village? I'd be interested to see the film set they've built.'

'About a quarter of an hour. It's only just along from here.'

'Then shall we make a move? I've eaten far too much and if we sit here much longer I shall fall asleep.'

Ronnie nodded and signalled that she would like the bill. She had an idea that Geoff would have been quite happy to stay longer had she not told him Manolis once lived on Spinalonga.

Ronnie and Geoff waited patiently whilst a scene was shot a number of times until the director declared he was satisfied. As the cast took a break they were allowed to walk through the village street where an arch had been constructed and the houses had fibre glass exteriors attached to make them resemble the houses on Spinalonga. Three elderly ladies sat on a bench, obviously enjoying being the centre of attention, as the director explained how he would like them to behave in the next sequence.

'I suppose they don't want a handsome young Englishman as a leading man?' queried Geoff. 'I've also fancied becoming an actor.'

'I don't think so,' smiled Ronnie. 'They have their own main actors and they're using the local people as extras. I've heard that just about everyone had a small part during the winter filming.'

'What about John? Is he in the film?'

Ronnie shook her head. 'He and Nicola agreed their twin girls could be used for short periods of time provided Nicola is with them. It's useful to have twins. If one is off colour the other one can be filmed and it means neither of them need to be in the limelight for very long. They are so alike to look at that no one will ever know that two different children were used.'

'I should obviously have come over during the winter.'

'If you had been asked to take part I think you would have been playing a German. You don't look a bit Greek.'

Geoff grinned. 'I could still have claimed to be a film star. Oh, they're filming again. Can we stay and watch for a while or will we be in the way?'

'We'll soon be told to move if we're disturbing them.' Ronnie leant against the wall whilst Geoff watched every action avidly, finally agreeing to walk on to Kato Elounda when the scene had been satisfactorily concluded.

As they reached Elounda Geoff decided he would like to stop for a drink at the bar where they had met Caro the previous evening. He looked at his watch.

'I'm sorry if I've spoilt your plans by spending so long watching the filming. Do you think we could leave the Causeway walk until another day?'

'No problem,' replied Ronnie. 'We can always have a wander around Elounda for the remainder of the afternoon.'

'At the moment I'd be quite happy to sit for a bit longer and have another beer.'

Ronnie sat there patiently, making her frappe last, whilst Geoff sipped his second beer slowly and continually looked around.

'You'd never know it was a Sunday,' he remarked. 'All the shops and tavernas are open for business.'

'They probably didn't open until about ten. That gives the owners time to go to Church. After that Sunday is just another trading day during the season. It becomes very different during the winter months. I understand that most places are closed and even the little supermarkets are only open for a few hours each day.'

'Catching up on the sleep they've lost during the season, no doubt.'

Ronnie shook her head. 'According to Saffie after a couple of weeks of idleness they begin to think about refurbishment for the next season, and there's the olive picking, of course. Everyone becomes involved in that.'

Geoff nodded absently and cast a surreptitious glance at his watch.

'Do you want to look around the gift shops?' asked Ronnie.

'Not particularly. I'll pick up some bits from the duty free on my way back to keep Mum and Dad happy. Oh, there's Caro.' A broad smile crept across his face.

Caro approached from across the road. 'I thought it was you two I could see sitting here. What have you been up to today?'

Geoff launched into a long description of their visit to Mavrikiano and Pano Elounda to watch the filming. As Ronnie listened to him and saw the glances he kept giving Caro she had an idea that they had arranged to meet and that was why Geoff had spent so long over his beer and declined the walk over the Causeway.

'What have you been doing today?' asked Ronnie of Caro when Geoff finally stopped talking.

Caro shrugged. 'This and that. Cleaned my apartment, bit of shopping, popped in to one of the hotels I had visited last week and checked that the kitchen had been given a really thorough clean as they had promised.'

'I understand from Geoff that the hotel you visited together was all in order.'

Caro nodded. 'I had the impression that Mr Iliopolakis was expecting us.'

'He'd probably heard from the other hoteliers that you were in the area.' Ronnie hoped she did not have a guilty look on her face. 'Where are you visiting next week?'

'Well, I thought I'd descend on the hotels on the road to Istro. Provided I don't find anything too terrible I should be able to cover a couple each day and return to Aghios in the late afternoon. The following week I'll have to make the journey down to Ierapetra. I'll need to stay down there as I have six hotels to check and they're quite large ones. There's little point in keep driving up and down each day. Now, where shall we eat tonight? I have the car so we could drive over to the taverna on the Causeway.'

Ronnie felt unreasonably aggrieved as Geoff agreed readily to Caro's suggestion. She had spent a considerable amount of time working out an itinerary that she thought would keep Geoff both interested and occupied whilst he was staying in Plaka, now Caro appeared to be taking over the arrangements she had planned so carefully.

Once again Caro and Geoff monopolized the conversation. Mentally she drifted back to the experience she had on Spinalonga that morning. She was convinced that she had heard a woman sobbing, but if that was so, why hadn't either John or Geoff heard the sound also?

'Hey, Ronnie, I asked you a question.' Caro tapped her arm and brought her back from her daydream.

'Sorry, I was thinking about something.'

'You didn't look as if you were on our planet,' observed Caro. 'I asked if you would like to come down to Istro tomorrow with us. Geoff's keen to see somewhere else. I'll just do one check tomorrow and then we could visit Gournia later in the afternoon.'

Ronnie shook her head. 'Thanks, but I really should catch up on some painting. You and Geoff go down and enjoy yourselves.' Ronnie had been looking forward to taking Geoff to Gournia, but she certainly did not want to spend most of the day sitting around whilst Caro visited the hotels looking for problems.

July 2011

Ronnie collected her easel and paints and walked down towards the Plaka waterfront. As she reached Saffron's shop she hesitated and then entered.

'Good morning, Saffie. I'm having a painting day. Do you have any particular requests?'

Saffron shook her head. 'Just the usual selection, please. Your friend not with you today?'

Ronnie shook her head. 'He's going down to Istro with Caro. She has to check a hotel down there and then they plan to go on to Gournia.'

Saffron raised his eyebrows. 'You didn't want to go with them?'

'I didn't fancy talking hotel safety all day. They seem to have one track minds. All either of them seem able to talk about are drains and plugs and whether the showers and bedrooms are clean. I don't know if she has spoken to Vasi, but I get the impression that his hotel was certainly passed.'

Saffron nodded. 'She gave him his certificate on the spot and said she would drop in some time later just to check that the faults she had found had been rectified. Thanks for 'phoning. It meant Vasi had all his paperwork to hand, which always gives a good impression.'

'Caro said she had an idea that Vasi knew he was going to be inspected and I told her the other hoteliers had probably told him.'

'Vasi appreciated your call. No one likes a visit from health and safety without prior warning.'

'Geoff offered her services for a check on Giovanni's apartments.'

'What did Giovanni say to that?' asked Saffron.

'It was John she suggested it to and he said his father didn't let the apartments through her company so there was no need for her to trouble herself.'

'She was probably just being nosey or hoping to get another customer to add to her books.'

Ronnie picked up her easel. 'Well, I'm going to enjoy myself today without having either of them around. I'll bring you some paintings later,' she promised.

Ronnie showered and changed from her shorts and T-shirt into a blouse and skirt. She imagined that Geoff would be back in Plaka, no doubt accompanied by Caro, by about seven and then she would suggest they ate locally. She liked to patronise the tavernas in the area, particularly Kyriakos, and it would also mean that if she became too bored with their conversation she could excuse herself and return to her apartment.

At ten she was still waiting for them and becoming concerned. Had they had an accident? She pressed in Caro's number on her mobile and when it was finally answered she could hear laughter and music in the background.

'Hi, Caro. I was just wondering what time you and Geoff were planning to return to Plaka for a meal this evening.'

'Oh! Oh, I'm sorry, Ronnie. I should have called you. I didn't realise you would be waiting for us. We're actually in Aghios and having a meal now.'

'That's no problem.' Ronnie spoke through gritted teeth. 'Have an enjoyable evening.' She closed her mobile feeling cross. Caro could easily have 'phoned her earlier to say they were not returning until late.

Ronnie walked the short distance to the taverna on the waterfront at Plaka. Kyriakos greeted her with a smile and looked at his watch.

'You are just in time, Miss Ronnie. I have no customers so I was about to close early.'

'I can go elsewhere if it is not convenient.'

Kyriakos waved her towards a seat. 'For you of course it is convenient. You are alone this evening? Your friend is not with you?'

Ronnie shook her head. 'He's spending the evening with some other friends.'

'So, what would you like to drink?'

Ronnie considered having whisky or vodka and then thought better of it. 'I'll just have a glass of white wine, please.'

'And to eat?'

'Whatever is still available. Please don't cook anything especially for me.'

'I will speak to the chef.' With a flash of his white teeth Kyriakos went inside and she could hear him conversing with the chef. He returned moments later with a bottle of white wine and two glasses.

'You will not mind if I join you?'

Ronnie shook her head. 'Not at all.'

'I have asked the chef to make you up a large meze. He said he would cook if you wanted something different.'

'That sounds fine. I'm always happy with a meze.'

Kyriakos poured a glass of wine for each of them and they wished each other good health. 'So, what have you been doing today?'

'I was painting. I needed to catch up with the orders for Saffron. I had taken some time off so I could go to Knossos and the Heraklion museum with Geoff. He is on holiday, but I am not.'

'And he is enjoying his stay on Crete?'

'I believe so. He has enjoyed the places we have visited and is very happy with Greek food.'

'So he should be.' Kyriakos blew a kiss with his fingers. 'Greek food – it is the best; and Cretan food is the best of the best.'

Ronnie smiled and Kyriakos frowned. 'Yes? My English is not right?'

'Your English is very good, but in this case it would be better to say "the very best".'

'My food at my taverna is the very best. Yes?'

Ronnie nodded. 'I'm sure other tavernas would claim theirs was better, but I prefer to eat at your taverna when I am in Plaka.'

'That is good. Ah, here comes our meal.'

The chef emerged from the interior with a large tray loaded with an assortment of small dishes that he proceeded to place on the table before them.

'I'll never eat all this!' exclaimed Ronnie.

'I will help you,' Kyriakos smiled. 'If it is not eaten tonight it will have to be thrown away. Not everything is able to go into the fridge.'

The chef drew a second table over to them and began to place further dishes on it. Kyriakos smiled at her. 'Usually you have a fish meze or a meat meze. Tonight you have both. Please,' he waved his hand, 'Enjoy.'

Kyriakos waited until she had helped herself to a variety of foods and then began to fill his own plate. Between them they made amazing inroads into the taromasolata, tsatziki, humus, olives, keftedes, dolmades, smoked pork, sausage, chicken, octopus, calamari, whitebait, salad, hard-boiled egg and cheese. Finally Ronnie sat back.

'That was marvellous. I couldn't eat another thing.'

'Sometimes it is good to come to eat just when I am about to close. Now, I have a special treat.'

Ronnie looked at him in horror. 'I can't eat any more, honestly.'

Kyriakos smiled. 'This, I know, you will be able to manage. One moment.'

He collected up a number of the empty dishes and hurried

back into the taverna. He returned a few moments later with some crystallized orange and lemon slices.

'This is very special,' he announced solemnly. 'My mother makes this to her own recipe. She does not tell her neighbours how it is made, but they agree that hers is the best. I serve it only to my very special customers.' He held the plate out to Ronnie and she speared a slice of lemon on her fork.

'Oh,' the sweetness of the sugar and the sourness of the lemons mingled together on her taste buds giving a delightful sensation. 'That is incredible.'

Kyriakos held the plate out to her again and this time she took an orange segment. The taste was very different from the lemon and just as delicious, being unexpectedly full of juice.

'May I?' Ronnie eyed the plate again and Kyriakos pushed it towards her.

'It is all for you.'

'No, one more piece of each, then I must stop eating,' said Ronnie firmly. 'Just put my name on the remaining pieces for when I come the next time.'

'Now you would like coffee?'

Ronnie shook her head. 'I won't sleep if I have coffee this late. Do you realise it's after one in the morning? I am sorry, Kyriakos, you were hoping to have an early night.'

Kyriakos shrugged. 'If I had returned home I would probably have fallen asleep in front of the television. I have had far more pleasure sitting here chatting with you, sharing a meal and watching your enjoyment. I will fetch some raki; then you will sleep soundly.'

'I've already had far too much wine.'

'Raki is for the digestion. I will escort you home, although you will not be drunk.'

'I am only just down the road,' protested Ronnie.

'No matter, I will walk with you and see you safely into your apartment.'

Ronnie slept soundly and was finally awoken by a knocking on her apartment door. Hastily she forced her arms into her wrap and opened it a crack. Geoff stood there, concern written all over his face.

'Thank goodness you're alright.'

'Why shouldn't I be?'

'I knocked your door when I arrived back last night and there was no answer. I thought you were having an early night. Then when I knocked earlier his morning you still didn't answer and I began to get a bit worried in case you were ill or anything.'

'I had rather a late night. What is the time? Nine? Goodness, I've really overslept. Give me half an hour to make myself respectable and then we can decide what you would like to do today.'

Geoff frowned. 'I thought you said we were having a car today and driving to some of the outlying villages. I could have gone down to Istro again with Caro.'

Ronnie took a deep breath. 'Geoff, we mentioned having a car, there was no definite arrangement made. Had you returned earlier yesterday we could have discussed what you wanted to do today.'

Geoff shrugged. 'Blame me, of course. I'll be down on the beach if you want to join me.'

Ronnie was not sure if she did want to join Geoff for a day on the beach. He was obviously annoyed that he was not going to spend the day in Istro with Caro. She showered leisurely, donning her bikini beneath her T-shirt and shorts, picked up her towel and a book and finally made her way down to the beach.

Geoff had been in for a swim by the time Ronnie joined him as the drops of seawater still glistened on his back.

'Was it warm in the sea?' asked Ronnie.

'I enjoyed it,' he answered without turning his head to look at her. 'I got too hot to wait for you to arrive.'

'Fancy another dip now I'm here?'

'No. I'm having a sleep.'

Ronnie placed her towel on the sun bed to make a pillow, removed her shorts and T-shirt, picked up her book and settled herself comfortably. If Geoff was annoyed with her he would just have to get over it so they could have a sensible conversation about activities during the remainder of his stay.

Geoff began to snore irritatingly and Ronnie closed her book. She would go for a wander through the village, Saffron or Bryony would be at the gift shop and John might be at the taverna. She could buy some bread, cheese and olives for a snack lunch and have a chat at the same time. She dressed herself in her shorts and T-shirt again and left her book and towel on the sun bed to indicate to Geoff that she would be returning, slipped her feet into her sandals and walked up to the road.

Bryony was busy, a coach party of tourists had arrived and were fingering the variety of goods on display, picking them up, showing them to a friend and placing them back haphazardly. Whilst she wrapped and accepted the money for the items purchased Bryony was also trying to watch for any pilfering that was taking place. Ronnie entered and walked up to the counter.

'Morning, Bryony. I'll hang around for a while until your customers have thinned out.'

Bryony gave a relieved smile. 'If you could just keep an eye out.'

Ronnie nodded. 'I'll do that whilst you serve.'

It was half an hour before the coach party began to make their way back to where they coach was waiting for them and Bryony let out a sigh of relief.

'I'm sure they don't come in en masse so they can take things, but I do find it a worry trying to watch them and serve at the same time.'

'Saffie said it was usually the children who try to slip off without paying.'

Bryony nodded. 'I know, and I don't think I've lost anything yet. It can be difficult to tell when they put things down anywhere they fancy. I thought someone had taken a framed picture the other day and then I found it. They'd left it outside in the sun. What are you up to today? Not painting?'

'Geoff fancied a day on the beach so I decided to join him. He's snoring his head off so I don't think he'll miss my company.'

'Saffie said he was going around with the girl who did the health and safety checks at his hotel and behaving as if he were her assistant.'

Ronnie shrugged. 'I suppose it's something different for him to do. Personally I don't see the attraction. Is John up at the taverna? I thought I'd buy some bread and cheese for our lunch. I can nip back to the apartment and make up a sandwich.'

'I'm sure John would do that for you.'

'I know, but he charges customers extra for ready-made rolls or sandwiches. I know he'd do them for me for nothing and then I'd feel guilty. Actually, feeling guilty reminds me, I haven't paid Kyriakos for the meal I ate there last night.'

'What did you have?'

'I was terribly late and he was just about to close. The chef made up a fabulous meze of the food that was left over from the day and we shared it.'

'You and Geoff?'

'No,' for some reason Ronnie blushed. 'Kyriakos shared it with me. Geoff was in Elounda with Caro.'

'Well, I'm sure Kyriakos will know you have not run away. I'm going to make myself a coffee now everything has quietened down. Will you join me?'

Ronnie shook her head. 'No, thanks. I'll go up to see if John is there and then go to see Kyriakos as I go back to the beach.'

'Well, if you want a break from Geoff's snoring I'll be here this afternoon.'

Ronnie walked up to the main road and along to the taverna.

'Late breakfast or early lunch?' asked John as she entered.

'Neither.' Ronnie shook her head. 'I just want a few bits to make up some rolls for lunch on the beach.'

'What do you fancy? I'll do them for you.'

'There's no need, really. I can go back to the apartment and make them up.'

'I won't charge you any extra.'

'I know,' Ronnie sighed. 'That's why I don't like you to make them for me.'

'Don't be silly,' grinned John. 'You're not a tourist, you're a local. Besides, I wanted to ask you about your experience on Spinalonga on Sunday morning.' John sliced open the rolls as he spoke.

Ronnie frowned. 'You just think I'm imagining things.'

John nodded. 'I do think it's all in your imagination, but I'm intrigued. Why should you imagine you hear and feel people over there? Have you ever had any psychic experiences?'

'Not that I can recall. It only seems to happen when I'm on Spinalonga and far enough away from other people that they can't hear anything.'

'What exactly did you think you heard when you stood by the entrance gate?'

'A woman was sobbing.' Ronnie looked at John with distressed eyes. 'She sounded quite desperately unhappy. It was the kind of sobbing you hear from a relative when a loved one has died unexpectedly. Totally heartbreaking.' Tears came to Ronnie's eyes as she recalled the moment. 'I'm probably just being stupid, but when it happened it seemed so real.'

'I think you're just over sensitive. Have you been up to Pano and watched any of the filming? They are really playing on peoples' emotions. When the film comes out there won't be a dry eye amongst the viewers.'

'I watched a bit with Geoff on Sunday, but I've not seen any of the other scenes. That can't possibly be affecting me. I'm probably just being stupid and imagining things.'

'I thought I might go up to Mavrikiano and speak to old

Manolis. He might remember something unusually sad happening.'

Ronnie shrugged. 'I'm sure a number of very sad events happened over there, but I can't see how they can possibly affect me. Oh, John, you've made those rolls look delicious. I was going to make do with cheese and a few olives.'

John wrapped the rolls and placed a scoop of olives into a separate bag. 'Enjoy your lunch. I hope your Geoff can keep awake long enough to eat one.'

'He's not "my" Geoff. He's just a friend.'

'Actually I'm pleased to hear that. I can't say I took to him particularly. You're worth a better man than him, Ron.'

When Ronnie returned to the beach Geoff was sitting up and talking on his mobile 'phone. He finished the conversation quickly and turned to her.

'I thought you'd gone off to do some painting or something,' he remarked belligerently.

'I went to get us some lunch. It's only some rolls, but we can have a proper meal this evening.'

'Caro said she should be back from Istro about seven and would meet us up here at eight.'

Ronnie raised her eyebrows.

'We could go to that place we went to on my first evening,' continued Geoff.

'I went there last night, but I'm quite happy to go again tonight. If he happens to be busy there are a number of others and they all serve excellent food. Have you tried the baked fish? It's particularly delicious.'

'Caro doesn't eat fish.'

'There are plenty of other dishes on the menu for her. Just because she doesn't eat fish it doesn't mean you can't try it.'

Geoff shrugged non-committally and Ronnie sighed. 'Are you happy to stay on the beach this afternoon or would you rather do something else?' she asked as she handed him a roll.

'I'll stay down here, but if you want to go off and paint or something you don't have to stay with me. I am capable of looking after myself. I won't swim out too far and I'll put some sunscreen on when I come out of the water.'

'I could do with completing a few jobs. I'll do those and if I have time I'll come back for a late swim. If I don't make it I'll see you at eight and when Caro arrives we can decide where to eat.'

Ronnie walked away from the beach feeling disgruntled. She had been looking forward to Geoff's visit and totally changed her routine to accommodate him. She was thankful that she had not made any firm arrangement to hire a car again this week. She could only think of visiting Kritsa, Napoli and Kastelli and driving around the Lassithi Plain. Those excursions would only occupy three days and she wished now that he was returning to England at the end of his second week.

Remembering that she had still not paid Kyriakos for her meal the previous evening she detoured to walk past his taverna and he greeted her with a welcoming smile.

'What would you like, Miss Ronnie? Frappe, juice, wine? Some lunch, maybe?'

Ronnie shook he head. 'I came to pay for the meal I had last night. The wine must have gone to my head as I completely forgot about paying the bill.'

Kyriakos shook his head. 'There is nothing to pay. You ate the scraps that would have gone into the rubbish bin.'

'I'm sure none of the food I ate would have been thrown away. It was all delicious, and there was the bottle of wine also.'

'I asked to share your drink and I ate some of your meal. No, there is nothing to pay. You were my guest.'

Ronnie frowned. 'That doesn't feel right.'

'The next time you come I will give you a bill. If you bring your friend and he is paying it can be a big bill.' He winked at her conspiratorially. It annoyed her that Caro would hand Geoff ten Euros and he would accept it; then divide the bill for their meal between himself and Ronnie. She did not see why she should be subsidising Caro.

'We may come this evening.'

'That is good. I will look forward to seeing you. Now you are here you will have a drink?'

'Only if you let me pay for it.'

Kyriakos gave her a soulful glance 'A friend should be able to buy a friend a drink.'

Ronnie shook her head. 'Not when it is his business. You will never make any money if you always treat your friends, Kyriakos.'

Kyriakos shrugged. 'All I ask is enough to pay my bills and the rent to Mr Giovanni each month. Money – pouf – you cannot eat it and it cannot keep you healthy. There are more important things in life than money.' Kyriakos motioned Ronnie to sit down and sat opposite her, indicating to the waiter that he should bring them some drinks.

'My grandmother told the story her mother had told her about the greedy tax man. She was a little girl at the time, but she remembered the worried faces of her parents when they knew the tax man was coming. He would want to know how many kilos of olives they had harvested and how much they had been paid for the oil. He would then sit at their kitchen table and work out how much tax they owed. Always it was more than they had calculated. They knew he had added on an amount for himself.'

'Was that how he earned his wages?'

Kyriakos shook his head. 'He had a regular salary, but this was his way to make a fortune. When the farmers said they could not pay the extra charge he agreed to hold it as a debt until the following year. The problem for the farmers was that it happened year after year until they were deeply in debt. He would then offer to take the crop from an olive tree or the rent from a property they owned in place of drachmas. He assured them the arrangement would be to their advantage as the government was insisting they paid their debt in full immediately. He was offering them a solution to their problem. Within twenty years many of them had given away half of their olive crops and many of the village houses. Gradually he became a very wealthy man.'

'What a crook! How they must have hated him.'

Kyriakos nodded. 'They certainly did. They hated him and they feared him. He married the daughter of a land owner who had once owned most of the village. My grandmother said when the man had no houses left to give the tax man took his daughter as payment. He still continued to collect the rents and overcharge the farmers. If he walked down the main street he would hear the villagers hissing behind his back, sometimes one would spit at him, but he did not seem to care. Whenever he attended Church the priest reminded the congregation that the sins of the fathers were visited on the children and he would look directly at the tax man.'

'And he took no notice?'

Kyriakos shook his head. 'He did not appear to care about the hostility of the villagers and took no heed of the priest. When it became necessary for his daughter to marry a local man he invited the whole of the village to the wedding feast.'

'I hope they refused to go.'

Kyriakos chuckled. 'They went, apparently, sniggering no doubt at her predicament, ate their fill and took as much as they could carry home with them saying it was their due.' Kyriakos became sombre again. 'Sadly for the family the priest's words became true. The daughter miscarried. The hastily arranged wedding to preserve her good name had been in vain.'

'That can happen to anyone,' protested Ronnie.

Kyriakos continued as if she had not spoken. 'Village people do not forget that a girl has been free with her favours. Virginity is valued. A year or so later she gave birth to a boy. The old man was delighted. He arranged a large Baptismal party for the child and once again the villagers took advantage of the food and drink on offer. The priest attended and wished health and good fortune for the infant, but once again reminded the gathering that the sins of the fathers were visited on the children. It was not long afterwards that the younger daughter stopped walking down the village street and then she disappeared.'

'Why?'

'My grandmother did not know, but the girl was not seen again. A rumour went around that she had run away as her father would not let her marry the young man of her choice.' Kyriakos shrugged. 'Another child appeared a few years later and it was shortly after that the family left the area, leaving just the old couple behind.'

'Where did they go?'

'I've no idea. Again there was a rumour that the older daughter had discovered where her father hid his money and stolen it. Within a few months of them leaving the old man seemed to lose his mind. He would spend his days writing figures on a piece of paper and when the Germans invaded he insisted they owed him taxes. At first they laughed at him, but when he threatened them with his gun they shot him.'

'What happened to his wife?'

'As far as I know she continued to live in the village and was looked after in her final years.'

'So the crooked tax man had one daughter who ran away to be with her lover, the other robbed him and moved away with his grandchildren, and he was shot by the Germans. I suppose you could say the curse was fulfilled, but I think it was his poor wife who suffered most.' Ronnie had been so enthralled by the story that she had not touched her drink.

'You do not like pomegranate juice?'

'Oh, yes, I do.' Ronnie picked up the glass and took an appreciative mouthful. 'I was just so intrigued by your story.'

'On the life of my grandmother it is true as she told it to me.' Kyriakos crossed himself.

'I am not doubting you,' smiled Ronnie. 'I wish I could speak Greek so I could ask your grandmother for more details.'

Kyriakos shook his head. 'That is not possible. She died three years ago.'

'So what happened to all the olive trees the man owned?'

'Gradually the villagers took back what rightfully belonged to them. They tended the trees and harvested the crop. No one ever arrived to place a legitimate claim to them or their houses and eventually they considered they belonged to them again.'

'No one has ever come back?'

Kyriakos shook his head. 'Not as far as I know. I am sure if a relative had appeared the news would have been passed from village to village very rapidly and reached Elounda within a day.'

'Where did the tax collector live?' asked Ronnie.

'He had the big house in Kastelli. It is not that far away.'

'Oh, I know the one. It's completely derelict. Such a shame as it must have been magnificent.'

'Once, maybe, but now it is inhabited only by ghosts.'

'Do you believe that?'

Kyriakos shrugged. 'I have no reason to go to Kastelli. It is only what I hear.' He spread his hands. 'You see why I am not a greedy man? When eventually I marry and have children I would not wish my sins to be passed on to them.'

'You really believe that would happen?'

Kyriakos shrugged. 'Who knows? I would not like to take the risk.'

Ronnie finished drinking her juice. She was not sure she believed the story Kyriakos had just told her. It could well have been something his grandmother had made up to make him behave himself when he was an unruly youngster or to explain why the house was derelict.

When Ronnie returned to the beach for a swim there was no sign of Geoff. He might have gone to a taverna for a drink or even decided he had had enough sun for one day and returned to the apartment. She stripped down to her bikini and dived into the sea, swimming out strongly for a few yards to avoid the other bathers before turning onto her back and floating lazily in the current.

Something touched her leg and she inadvertently let out a small scream and began to kick wildly. Once she was a few feet away she saw the cause of her alarm as a young man lifted his goggles and removed his snorkel from his mouth.

'So sorry,' he called. 'I didn't mean to frighten you. I just didn't see you.'

Ronnie managed to smile. 'No problem,' she called back. The pleasure from her swim was now diminished and she stroked her way leisurely back to the shore. She sat on the beach and watched as parents played with their children in the water and one or two foolhardy swimmers thought they could reach Spinalonga. The island was further away than it looked and the currents were unpredictable. She thought about the story that Kyriakos had told her and wondered if John would be able to corroborate it if she paid him a visit at the taverna.

She slipped her shorts and T-shirt over her damp bikini and picked up her bag. As she reached the top of the beach a young man hurried up to her.

'I really do apologise. I hope I haven't spoiled your afternoon on the beach.'

Ronnie frowned, then realised it was the young man who had been snorkelling. She shook her head. 'Not at all. I had only planned to come down for a short while.'

'You're the artist lady, aren't you?'

Ronnie nodded. 'I paint water colours.'

'The ones on sale up at the gift shop? I bought a couple of those.' He blushed. 'I suppose you wouldn't sign them for me.'

Ronnie smiled in amusement. 'They are signed, but I'll sign them again if you wish.'

'I meant personalised signing; one for my Mum and another for my aunt.'

'No problem. Are you staying locally?'

'In the self catering apartments.'

'Then you know the taverna and general store? I'm just about to go up there and have a chat with the owner. I'll probably be there for at least half an hour, maybe more.'

A broad grin spread across the man's face. 'I'll meet you there in about ten minutes.'

Ronnie continued up to where she could see John was busy serving customers and waved to him. 'Do you need a hand?' she asked.

'The dish washer could do with being unloaded and some of the dirty crockery put in ready for the next wash.'

Ronnie dumped her bag and began to remove the cups, saucers, glasses and plates from the dish washer, whilst keeping an eye open for the young man with his pictures. When she saw him approach and look around for her she wiped her hands and walked outside to greet him.

'I'm sorry. I didn't realise you were working here. I didn't mean to interrupt you.'

'I'm not actually working. I could see John was busy and he asked if I would unload the dish washer. Had I not arrived he would have managed perfectly well without me. Come and sit down. Would you like a drink?'

'No, I'm fine, really. The owner won't mind us sitting here if we don't buy anything to eat or drink, will he? I don't want to be a nuisance.'

'Not at all. I want to talk to him and that won't be possible until this little rush of customers is over. Are you enjoying your stay?' Ronnie sat down beneath an umbrella and indicated that he should do the same.

'It's beautiful here. I know I ought to go off and visit some of the other parts of the island, but I just can't seem to drag myself away. I haven't even been as far as Elounda yet.'

'How long are you here for?'

'Only a week.'

'You really should do a bit of exploring rather than spend all your time on the beach.'

'You must know the area pretty well. Where do you suggest I go?'

'Well, you could visit the villages just above Elounda and return later in the day for a swim, or a swim in the morning and then a walk over the Causeway and have a meal at the taverna there. You've been to Spinalonga, I expect.'

The young man shook his head. 'Not yet. I keep saying I will go tomorrow.'

'You would only need a morning or afternoon over there, still plenty of time for snorkelling.'

'I haven't found anything very exciting under the water around here,' he admitted. 'I was hoping to see some octopus hiding in the rocks.'

'Why don't you take your snorkelling gear to Spinalonga with you? When you've had enough of walking around you could swim around the rocks. I've heard octopus can be found out there.'

'Would I be allowed?' he asked eagerly.

Ronnie shrugged. 'You just do it. Someone will shout at you if it is forbidden and you just pretend not to understand. Just be careful of the currents and make sure you don't get your foot caught between the rocks. Now where are these pictures you want me to sign? Wait whilst I get a cloth to make sure there isn't anything sticky on the table.' Ronnie returned inside and reappeared with a clean cloth, wiping the table carefully. 'What would you like me to put?'

'Well, one just to Mum with love from Owen and then your signature underneath and the other the same but to Aunty Jean.'

Ronnie pointed to the "Ve-Va" on the front of the picture. 'Do you want me to sign that or my full name?'

'Your full name, please.'

Ronnie took a pen from her bag and signed each water colour as he had requested. 'There you are Owen. I hope they like them.'

'I'm sure they will. Thank you so much, Veronica.'

'Veronica! Goodness, no one ever calls me that. I'm Ronnie.'

Owen replaced the pictures inside their protective envelope and rose, holding out his hand. 'Thank you. I'm so pleased I've met you.'

'I'll probably see you around,' Ronnie smiled. 'Enjoy the rest of your holiday.'

'I'm sure I will and I'll take your advice. I will turn my back on the beach and walk up to one of the villages.'

'If you go to Pano Elounda you'll see a film being made. They've made the village resemble the main road on the island.'

'Really? I'll definitely go there and then when I go to the island I can see how authentic it is. I might even see some famous film stars.'

'I doubt that, somehow, but I'm sure you'll find it interesting.'

As Owen walked away John raised his eyebrows at her? She shook her head and waited until he had satisfied the last of his customers.

'I'm sorry, I haven't finished unloading the dish washer.'

'No problem. Who's your friend?'

'A young man who frightened the life out of me by touching my leg whilst he was snorkelling. He was waiting for me at the top of the beach and asked me to personalise a couple of pictures he's taking home as gifts.'

'Fame at last.'

'Hardly. I would need more than that to make me famous. Actually, John, I was on my way up to ask you about something Kyriakos told me.'

'What tall stories has Ackers been telling you?'

'Ackers?'

'That's the name his friends know him by. What did he tell you? Did he claim to be a multi millionaire or a poverty stricken peasant?'

'Neither,' smiled Ronnie. 'We were talking generally and he said he was not interested in making his fortune as money did not always lead to happiness. To illustrate his point he told me a story that he claimed his grandmother had told him about a wicked tax collector.'

'Which one? They are all corrupt.'

'The one that had the big house in Kastelli. When he went to collect the taxes that were due from the olive farmers he always asked for more than they owed. He offered to make up the difference to the government himself by accepting the crop of an olive tree each year or the rents from the villagers as payment. Over the years he became very wealthy, but one of his daughters ran away, the other married and robbed her father before moving away with her husband. The old man became senile and when the Germans invaded he presented them with a tax bill. Obviously they refused to pay him and he threatened them with his gun. Needless to say they shot him.'

John nodded. 'I know the house you mean and the villagers say it belonged to a tax collector. It's been derelict as long as I can remember. I don't know how true Ackers's story is about the family. I could ask Uncle Yannis to see if he remembers anything about him, but he was only a boy during the war.'

'It's not important,' smiled Ronnie. 'When I was in Kastelli I noticed the house and thought how magnificent it must have been. I'm not sure I believed all Kyriakos told me about the family's misfortunes. He probably exaggerated or the truth has become distorted over the years. He said his great grandmother told his grandmother and she told him.'

John shrugged. 'Who knows? Village stories have some truth in them, but they become embellished over the years. The house probably did belong to the tax collector and I expect he was amongst a number of men who were shot by the Germans. As for being cursed by the priest and his family leaving him, that has probably been added over the years to make the story more dramatic.'

'Do you think his name will be on the War Memorial up there?'

'It could be. Do you know his name?'

Ronnie shook her head and laughed. 'Even if I did know his name I wouldn't be able to read the Greek lettering. I still struggle with a menu written in Greek.'

John shook his head in mock despair. 'One day, when there is time, we will teach you Greek.'

'I know I ought to make the effort, but you all speak English so well that it seems unnecessary. I'm off to have a shower, then I'll see if I can track down Geoff. We're meeting Caro at eight.' Ronnie rose and picked up her beach bag.

'Enjoy your evening.'

Ronnie pulled a face. 'I enjoy their company individually, but when they are together I don't seem to exist.'

Ronnie emerged from her apartment shortly before eight. Geoff was sitting on the wall outside and appeared to have forgotten his previous bad temper.

'You look very nice,' he complimented her.

'Thank you. I thought about your suggestion to take Caro to Kyriakos's taverna and I'm quite happy to go there. It saves spending time discussing where else to go.'

'You're sure? I just thought the food there was good and Caro would enjoy it.'

'It's no problem. What did you do with yourself for the rest of the day?'

'I wandered around Plaka for a while and then decided to return to the apartment and have a shower. I spent some time on my lap top, catching up with my parents and various bits and bobs. What did you do?'

'Finished my jobs and had a late swim. Went up to the taverna and had a chat with John. Nothing exciting. What do you want to do tomorrow? We could hire a car if you want to drive out to the villages.'

Geoff looked slightly embarrassed. 'Can we decide after I've spoken to Caro? She may be visiting somewhere interesting.'

'Just let me know tonight so I can organise car hire first thing in the morning if necessary. If I leave it too late the tourists could have booked them all and we don't want to have to go to Aghios Nikolaos. By the time we get there half the day will be gone.'

Kyriakos was not surprised to see Ronnie arrive with Geoff and Caro. He greeted her effusively and brought out a selection of bread rolls, olives, tsatziki and taromasalata for them to eat with their drinks whilst they discussed the menu.

'I'm having the prawn saganaki,' decided Ronnie finally.

Caro shook her head. 'I don't eat fish, particularly prawns. Fish are either cannibals or scavengers. At least animals are given suitable feed.'

'Not always,' Geoff reminded her. 'Remember the outbreak of mad cow disease that caused such a panic? The cows had been fed their own species that had been processed into animal feed.'

Caro shuddered. 'I seriously considered becoming a vegetarian. I've decided chicken kebabs and salad for tonight. What are you having, Geoff?'

'I'm going to follow Ronnie and have the prawn saganaki. I can eat chicken in England.'

Caro shrugged. 'Be it on your own head. I was going to suggest that we drove down to Pahia Ammos tomorrow. I only have one hotel there to check out so we could have a drive through the villages and find a secluded bay for a swim. You won't want to do that if you're feeling ill.' This time Caro did not extend the invitation to Ronnie.

'I'm sure I'll be fine. If I have any ill effects I'll call you to save you the drive up here.'

Ronnie felt disappointed. She was obviously not going to be expected to hire a car and drive around the local villages. She had planned to return to Kastelli and copy the names from the War Memorial to ask Kyriakos if the name of the tax collector had been included amongst those who had lost their lives.

'I'll make my own arrangements for eating tomorrow evening,' she assured them both. 'That way you will be under no pressure to hurry back.' She would be able to economise by cooking herself an omelette; continually eating out was having a disastrous effect on her savings.

As usual Geoff appeared enthralled by Caro's description of the various faults that she had found at the hotels and the dire threats she had made to the managers. By the time the waiter appeared with the saganaki Ronnie was thoroughly bored and wished she could join Kyriakos who was standing on the thoroughfare, encouraging passersby to come in to sample his food. Her time spent with him the previous evening had been far more entertaining and interesting.

He seemed to sense her eyes on him and looked over and winked at her. Ronnie hastily lowered her eyes to her plate and pretended not to have noticed. A couple studied the menu and he was soon ushering them to a table, where the waiter bustled over carrying some olives and nuts. Ronnie was amused to see the tourists had not been given the same selection of appetisers as they had been offered. Kyriakos was back on the thoroughfare, plying his trade, advertising his taverna as serving the best food in Plaka and Ronnie was amused by the crestfallen expression on his face if they refused his entreaties.

As he passed her chair she heard him murmur 'How is a poor taverna owner going to pay his rent if the tourists do not patronise him?'

Whilst he escorted a family to a seat at the far side Ronnie saw Owen standing hesitantly peering at the menu.

'Would you mind if I invited Owen to join us?' she asked. 'I believe he's on holiday on his own over here.'

Both Geoff and Caro were so engrossed in discussing the merits of air conditioning in the rooms as opposed to electric fans that they did not appear to hear her. She slipped from her chair and walked to where Owen was standing.

'Would you care to join us?' she asked. 'I'm afraid we're half way through our meal, but you'll be welcome.'

Owen blushed with pleasure. 'I hope you didn't think I was hanging around outside hoping to be invited. I thought I should wait until the man came back to show me to a table.'

'It is a Greek custom to join your friends when you see them in a taverna. There is no formality. Another table is brought over and more chairs and sometimes a couple becomes twenty or more people enjoying themselves. Come and meet Caro and Geoff.'

Owen followed Ronnie to the table and without asking Kyriakos produced another chair. The dishes of appetizers were replenished and a menu thrust into Owen's hand.

Geoff and Caro looked at him in surprise and Ronnie explained how she had met Owen. 'As he's holidaying on his own I thought he might appreciate joining us for a meal.'

Owen placed the menu on the table unopened. 'I'm afraid the names of the dishes mean very little to me. Could I have whatever it is you're eating?' he asked Ronnie. 'It smells absolutely delicious.'

'Prawn saganaki. Try some.' She pushed her plate towards him and he dipped a small piece of bread into the sauce.

'That's for me. I've seen people eating interesting looking things, but I didn't like to show my ignorance and ask what they were. I had steak and chips last night and chicken and chips the night before. I'd really like to sample the local dishes.'

'Most of the taverna owners speak very good English. If you ask them they will tell you what the main ingredients are. They won't make you feel ignorant or stupid, unless you ask them the same question the following night,' added Ronnie.

'I must remember that,' smiled Owen. 'I have a bad habit of asking the same question over and over again.'

'Really? Do you have an exceptionally bad memory?'

Owen shook his head. 'I'm in the police force. You keep asking a suspect the same question hoping the suspect will slip up and give a different answer. If they do you ask them to explain the discrepancy and they tie themselves in knots trying to extricate themselves.'

Ronnie laughed. 'That sounds amusing, but in reality it must be quite different. Do you have to deal with hardened criminals?'

'Not often; I mainly work on the computer records. I came from a small town in Wales and we didn't seem to have organised gang crimes. It was quite an eye opener when I reached the city.'

Whilst Owen had been talking Geoff and Caro had stopped their conversation and were listening avidly.

'Do tell me more,' urged Geoff. 'I've always thought I would like to be a policeman.'

Ronnie was surprised. She had never heard Geoff express any desire for police work before and she decided he was just being polite and trying to keep Owen in the conversation.

Owen shrugged. 'It isn't very exciting. I entered when I had finished Uni and that meant I was able to avoid traffic duties and pounding the beat. Occasionally I get to interview suspects, but I spend most of my time typing up the reports and checking paperwork.'

'Are you licensed to carry a gun?'

'Goodness no. I've held one, but I had no inclination to fire it.'

'All the police over here carry guns,' Caro informed him.

'Actually I've not seen a policeman since I left the airport.'

Ronnie smiled. 'The nearest police station is in Aghios Nikolaos. The one they had in Elounda was closed down. Lack of crime.'

'That's good to hear. A shame there aren't more places in the world like this.'

'If there were you'd be out of a job,' observed Geoff. 'So how would I apply to join the force?'

'Just walk in to your nearest station and ask them where you should apply if you want to stay living locally. Different areas have different head offices. No good applying to Birmingham if you want to live in Norwich.'

'They would tell me, just like that?'

'Of course. It would then be up to you to contact them and ask for an application form. They can send it on line for you to complete and return. You would be notified if they thought you unsuitable or called to the head office for an interview. What work are you doing at the moment?'

'I'm the manager of a convenience store.'

'Responsible for the takings and the accounts?'

Geoff nodded.

'Well, that's a point in your favour. It says you are honest. How about you, Caro? What work do you do?' Ronnie noticed that Owen's eyes lingered on her as he asked the question.

'Health and Safety. I inspect the hotels and report back to a travel firm.'

'Now that does sound an interesting job. How long are you here for?'

'All season.'

'I understand everything closes down over here in November so what do you do in the winter months?'

Caro shrugged. 'This and that. Sometimes I'm asked to check on a hotel in England if the firm are planning to hire rooms there over Christmas.'

'So what happens if you give them a bad report?'

'Unless it's a structural defect that could seriously endanger peoples' lives the hotel is given an opportunity to put things right. Most things like cleaning up their kitchen, repairing broken tiles, removing obstructions from in front of the fire doors, can be dealt with pretty quickly.'

'And if it's structural?'

'I refer that immediately to my office and they send a structural engineer to assess the problem. The hotel is closed until he gives it a safety certificate.'

'Is that why you closed the hotel in Aghios Nikolaos?' asked Ronnie, remembering how proud Geoff had been of her decision.

Caro shook her head. 'No. That was a combination of faults that meant it was sub-standard. We moved our visitors out, but we cannot stop others staying there. That decision would have to be made by the Greek hotel inspectors.'

Once again the whole conversation seemed to be revolving around Caro and her work. Ronnie sat there listening and wondered if Owen was truly interested or just being polite. As they finished their main course Kyriakos appeared at their table.

'How was your meal?'

'Delicious, thank you. Can we see the sweets menu, please,' asked Owen.

'I will bring for you.'

Ronnie smiled to herself. She knew Kyriakos had no dessert menu, but would bring a selection of fresh fruit to the table accompanied by a small carafe of raki.

Caro wiped her wet grapes carefully on her napkin before popping them in her mouth. She saw Ronnie looking at her and shook her head.

'You can't be too careful. I know they've been washed, but what water did they use? It's fine for drinking in the town, but this is a village. They could be using water from a stream and somewhere else someone has done their washing in it.'

'I haven't seen a single stream in this area,' remarked Ronnie. 'I'm not saying there aren't any during the winter when it rains, but they've certainly all dried up now.'

Caro shrugged. 'Would you mind if I left you? I've had quite a busy day and I still have to drive back to Aghios. I'll be here for you at eight, Geoff, unless you tell me you have been struck down with food poisoning during the night.' She handed Geoff ten Euros and pushed back her chair.

'I'll walk with you to your car.' Geoff rose also and pulled another fifteen Euros from his wallet. 'Can we leave you to pay the bill, Ronnie?'

Ronnie nodded. She could hardly refuse to let them leave until she had seen the amount they owed and shared the total, although she was certain she was going to be out of pocket as usual. She hoped Owen was not expecting her to treat him.

'Just a moment, can I have a photograph?' Owen picked up his camera.

'Why would you want a photo of me?' asked Caro scowling.

'A souvenir of a very enjoyable evening when strangers took pity on a lonely traveller.'

'Come on, Caro. A photo won't take a second.' Geoff placed his hand on her arm and stood behind the chairs with her. Owen quickly took a photo. He glanced at it and shook his head. 'Can I have another? I seem to have cut off Geoff's head.'

Smiling Geoff obliged by bending his knees so he was nearer to Caro in height, but this time Ronnie noticed Caro looked down so her face was almost hidden in shadow. Ronnie was about to suggest to Owen that he tried a third time when he declared himself satisfied and Geoff and Caro took their leave.

Ronnie signalled to Kyriakos that they were ready and as soon as he reached their table Owen spoke up.

'I'd like to pay my share separately, please.'

'No problem. And Miss Ronnie, all three on one bill?'

Ronnie nodded. 'They've left me their money.'

She looked across the thoroughfare to where Caro and Geoff stood by the sea wall. Geoff was pointing up at the stars and as he did so he slipped his arm around Caro's waist and drew her to him. She looked up at him he bent his head and kissed her.

Ronnie felt a pang of jealousy that was swiftly followed by relief. Geoff had never attempted to kiss her for all his innuendo and suggestive remarks. When he had first arrived in Crete she had expected him to try to move their relationship forward and then she would have seriously considered his attention. Now she was not sure if she even liked him.

Owen read the total on Ronnie's bill and frowned. 'They have not left you enough. Shall I go across and tell them?'

Ronnie shook her head. 'I'm sure they'll sort it out with me tomorrow.'

'Are you planning to return to your apartment or would you like another drink?' asked Owen.

Ronnie considered. 'Just one would be very nice. It's alright for you holidaymakers, you can sleep in. I have to be disciplined and get up for work.'

'I'd like to hear more about your art. What made you come over here to work?'

Ronnie laughed. 'I came on holiday with my partner, the partnership went sour, but I decided to return.'

'You just took a chance that your pictures would sell?'

Ronnie shook her head. 'It's a bit complicated. I had a verbal contract with the gift shop.'

'That was very trusting of you. How did that come about?'

'It's quite a long story. Are you sure you want to hear the details?'

'I am truly interested. Besides, I see the taverna owner has brought us a bottle rather than a glass. We cannot drink all that in five minutes. Is Geoff from your previous relationship that went wrong?'

'Certainly not. I am not interested in Geoff as a prospective partner. If things work out for him and Caro they have my blessing.'

Ronnie found talking to Owen easy, and the bottle of wine rapidly emptied. Ronnie giggled. 'I've had far too much to drink. I thought policemen were supposed to protect young ladies, not lead them astray.'

'I'm not your usual sort of policeman. Now, I will ask the taverna keeper to add the wine to my bill and then I will escort you to your apartment.'

'To prove you are a conscientious policeman?'

'To prove I am a gentleman. You will have to lead the way and then tell me how to return to my apartment.'

'I don't think you'll find it difficult. There are only the two blocks of self catering apartments here. I have some rooms on the ground floor of one, so you shouldn't get lost finding your way home. I'll pay Kyriakos and then I really must leave.'

Whilst Ronnie paid Kyriakos, Owen took a surreptitious look at the photographs he had taken. It could just be a coincidence of likeness, in which case his colleagues would laugh at him and say he had had too much sun. On the other hand he could, purely by chance, have found a person who was of interest to them.

Geoff knocked on Ronnie's door when he returned from Pahia Ammos, looking very self satisfied.

'Enjoyable day?' asked Ronnie and Geoff blushed.

'Yes, very,' he mumbled. 'Actually, I wanted to talk to you about something?'

Ronnie raised her eyebrows. 'Go ahead.'

'Would you think me very awful if I moved out of the apartments and went down to Ierapetra with Caro next week?'

'You've already paid for your accommodation here, you can't ask for a refund just because you want to go off somewhere else.'

'I realise that. It's no problem. I wouldn't want to take all my gear with me anyway so it's convenient to be able to leave it here. It's just that, well, I asked if you'd spend your time with me and I truly thought we'd spend the weeks together getting to know each other better.'

Ronnie took pity on him. 'Geoff, we're friends, nothing more. If you want to spend your time with Caro that's fine with me.'

Geoff sighed with relief. 'I just didn't want to offend you or anything.'

'You won't offend me. All I will say, Geoff is that you should beware of holiday romances. They often fizzle out once the holiday is over.'

Geoff shook his head. 'That won't happen with Caro and me. We're soul mates, meant for each other.'

'Then I can only wish you both well. Forget about me and enjoy your time together.'

'Ronnie, you really are one of the nicest, most understanding girls I've ever met. I'll obviously see you again before I have to return to England, but even then I'd like to keep in touch. Friend to friend.'

'Of course.' Ronnie stepped forward and kissed Geoff lightly on the cheek. 'I hope everything works out for you both and I shall look forward to receiving a wedding invitation in the near future.'

'End of the season probably, when Caro returns to England.' Geoff pulled his key from his pocket. 'I must shower and change. Caro said she would give me an hour to freshen up, then we would go somewhere special to eat.'

Ronnie closed her door. 'Well, well, well,' she said quietly to herself. 'Who would have thought those two would have found each other so attractive.' She pulled off her T-shirt and fanned herself with it. She would prepare a salad, then have a shower to cool down before cooking her omelette. It would be pleasant to sit out on her balcony for her meal that evening and it was almost a relief to know she would not have to make conversation to anyone.

Owen looked in the tavernas at Plaka for Ronnie, but saw no sign of her. He knew where she lived having walked her home the previous evening, but he was not going to call on her formally. He very much wanted to talk to her again, but wanted their meeting to appear casual and unplanned. No doubt he would see her whilst she was out painting the following day and he would make the most of any opportunity that arose.

As he strolled down to the beach he could see her inside the gift shop talking to the owner and decided it would be inappropriate and obvious if he interrupted. He would go for his swim and hope that when he returned he would see her painting. It would be an ideal time to stop and admire her work and chat about his plans for the day. In return he hoped she would tell him if she was meeting her friends.

To his annoyance there was still no sign of Ronnie when he left the beach. The sun had been stronger than he realised and even his dark skin was turning red and he debated the wisdom of spending the remainder of the day on the beach. He decided he would have a cold shower, wear the lightest shirt he had brought, smother himself with sun screen, take plenty of water and investigate the nearest village. Provided he kept to the main road until he came to the side road that led to Mavrikiano he should be able to hail a passing taxi if he found the heat too much to bear.

To his surprise the walk was not as arduous as he had anticipated. He took advantage of any shade there was and climbed the hill slowly. Once in the village it was cool in the narrow streets and he wandered leisurely, stopping first just for a drink and then deciding to eat at the small taverna. He sat out on the balcony and looked down at the town of Elounda and the village of Plaka. Both were far larger than he had realised. Elounda reached back into the foothills and Plaka was trying hard to imitate her neighbour, the houses gradually creeping up the hillside.

The selection of meals he was offered for his lunch took his breath away. He had expected to be offered half a dozen dishes accompanied by chips and salad, but he found it difficult to choose from the variety the taverna keeper reeled off.

'Could I have some dips and a beetroot salad?' he asked. 'I think that will probably be sufficient.'

'Of course. There will be plenty more available if you still feel hungry. You would like another large beer?'

'I certainly would. It was pretty hot walking up here.'

Theo grinned at him. 'It is warm. If you came in August then it would be hot.'

Owen ate his lunch leisurely, trying to decide whether to walk on to Pano Elounda or retrace his steps to Plaka and have another swim. Finally the urge to be in the cool water took precedence and having paid his bill, replenished his water bottle and rubbed a further layer of cream onto his bare arms and neck he took his leave. The other villages could be tackled another day, and he really should be sensible and walk up to them during the morning before the sun was at its height. The coolness he had appreciated on first arriving in Mavrikiano now felt chill and rather than hugging the shade he strode openly in the sunshine. He noticed that the elderly people who were sitting in the shade of their doorways had a cardigan or pullover on and wished he had thought to bring one with him. As he reached the level ground of the main road leading to Plaka the heat hit him again. He looked back at the tiny village, now almost hidden from view. No one would believe the temperature could change so dramatically within such a short distance.

Arriving back at the apartments, feeling as hot as he had done earlier in the day, he stripped off rapidly, donned his swimming trunks beneath his shorts, picked up his snorkelling gear and decided he definitely needed a swim. He would then have a short siesta before deciding where to have a meal that evening.

Ronnie looked in her fridge. She had some cheese, along with an egg, some limp lettuce and a soft tomato. It was an unappetizing selection and having had an omelette the previous night she was disinclined to have the same meal again. She should have thought earlier and bought some supplies from John. She had neglected stocking up on food whilst Geoff had been staying as they had gone to a taverna every night to eat. Now she must get back into routine again and cater for herself.

'Your friends not with you this evening?'

Ronnie looked round in surprise. She had not heard Owen approach her table.

'No, they've gone down to Ierapetra.'

'May I join you?'

'Of course. Have you been on the beach all day? You look a little over-cooked.'

Owen laughed. 'I probably am. I walked up to Mavrikiano and had a delicious late lunch there. Have you tried their beetroot salad?' He kissed his fingers. 'I've never tasted better.'

'Probably because the roots were pulled from the ground this morning and freshly cooked. It wasn't very sensible to walk up there at mid-day. Why didn't you go earlier?'

'I went for a swim and then it was a snap decision. I could either waste my day lying on the beach or I could do something a bit different and more interesting.'

'I'm pleased to hear you visited the village. It has so much old world charm. I took Geoff up there, but he seemed more interested in watching the filming in Pano. I had planned to take him to some other villages, but when Caro suggested he went to the hotels she was checking out he jumped at the chance to see somewhere different.'

'I don't know that I'd want to spend my day poking around peoples' kitchens. How long did you say you known them?'

'I met Geoff when I was in England last fall, autumn to you,' Ronnie smiled. 'He seemed a very pleasant young man and asked if I would take him under my wing if he came over here on holiday. I'd planned various excursions that I thought would interest him and he seemed happy enough to spend the time with me until he met Caro.'

'I had the impression they were a long standing item.'

Ronnie shook her head and laughed. 'It's a whirlwind romance. Geoff told me last night they are planning to get married at the end of the season.'

'How long have you known Caro?'

'Only a few months. We met in the 'plane coming over and began talking. Until Geoff arrived we'd meet up about once or twice a month and have a drink together, but once she had met him she became a permanent fixture.'

'You don't mind that she has taken your companion?'

'No, we were only friends, nothing more. He's not my type. He makes up the most outrageous stories. They sound very plausible at the time, but he admits they are completely fictitious. At first it's amusing, then it becomes boring. He's also a star gazer.'

'Is Caro also a star gazer?'

'I have no idea. I know she makes up tall stories the same as Geoff. Some evenings they spent their time each trying to be more outrageous than the other.'

'So they will have some months apart. That will be a test for their relationship.'

'Oh, I'm sure they'll manage to meet up when Caro returns to England each month to give her report to her travel firm.'

'She has to do that?'

Ronnie nodded. 'She says it's the only down-side of the job. She says it's such a pain having to fly back to England just for a few days each month.'

'I would have thought in these days of technology she could have used the e-mail service. It would certainly be a good deal cheaper and less time consuming.'

'We don't always receive a signal down here. It's due to the mountains. Sometimes you can't use the internet for days. It can be very frustrating and I can understand why a travel firm are reluctant to rely on the information reaching them by the time they need it.'

'You didn't want to go down to Ira – Ira – whatever it is with them?'

'Ierapetra.' Ronnie shook her head. 'I really need to settle down to work. I've taken a number of days off recently whilst Geoff has been here. I have to make sure I leave Saffron with a stock of pictures in September. My mother and uncle are coming over and I certainly don't want to have to spend my days painting whilst they're here.'

'Have they visited you before?'

'Last year. I took them to all the usual tourist attractions and then we just drove around the villages. They have said they'll be quite happy to drive around again. I'll just have to change the route so they think they're going somewhere new. I thought I might take them up to Mili again. They can't manage the gorge walk, but they thought the area around the taverna was beautiful.'

'How far away is that?' asked Owen.

'Up by Rethymnon. It's at least a three hour drive. Bit far to walk.'

Owen grinned. 'I've managed Mavrikiano today and I'm planning to walk into Elounda tomorrow morning and then up to those other two villages.'

'Don't forget you want to go to Spinalonga.'

'I have three more days and the boats seem to go out all the time.'

'Take my advice, go to Spinalonga tomorrow. Sometimes a very high wind develops and can last for a couple of days or more. The boatmen are reluctant to go out then, sometimes even forbidden by the port authorities. The villages are unlikely to be blown away.'

Kyriakos brought some fruit to their table and a small carafe of raki. 'It is good to see you again this evening, Miss Ronnie. You have shown your friend the painting you did for me.' Kyriakos pointed to his doorway.

Owen stood up and moved forward for a closer look. 'That really is something,' he remarked. 'It is the first thing you notice when you walk past the taverna, but I didn't realise you had painted it, Ronnie. I thought you only did water colours.'

Ronnie smiled at him. 'It was a bit of an experiment. Fortunately Kyriakos was pleased with the end result.'

'Miss Ronnie is very talented. You have seen her pictures in Miss Saffron's shop?'

'I have bought a couple,' Owen assured him. 'That was how we came to know each other.'

'You will come here again tomorrow, Miss Ronnie?'

Ronnie shook her head. 'This is my last treat for a while. I now have to economise and cook my own meals again.'

Kyriakos's face fell. 'I hope you will still visit me, for a drink and a chat.'

'Of course. I always enjoy talking to you. I'd like to hear more about your grandmother. I have a number of questions I want to ask you about her. I will come in some time during the day when you are quiet. The evening is not suitable.'

Kyriakos beamed at her. 'You are always welcome, Miss Ronnie. How am I to make up the bill?'

'Two separate, please,' Ronnie answered quickly. She did not want Owen to think she was expecting him to pay for her.

'Will you allow me to pay your share?' asked Owen and Ronnie shook her head.

'Thank you for the offer, but I prefer to be independent. If you pay for me I shall feel obliged to meet you tomorrow and treat you. It can end up being difficult. You may wish to eat somewhere else tomorrow but would feel you had to come here and spend the evening with me.'

'That would not be a hardship,' Owen smiled. 'I enjoy your company.' Owen poured a small glass of raki for each of them and held his out. 'To successful painting. May you become world famous.'

Ronnie pulled a face. 'That's not very likely. Here's hoping you enjoy the remainder of your holiday.'

August 2011

Ronnie was surprised by the e-mail she received from Geoff. He started conventionally by thanking her and saying how much he had appreciated all she had done for him whilst he was visiting Crete. He then continued by asking if she had seen or heard anything from Caro. She had told him her mother would be visiting her for the last two weeks in July and she would return to England with her so she could present her monthly report to her company at the beginning of August.

He had arranged to meet her and her mother at the airport and drive them to her mother's house. It would be an ideal opportunity for him to meet her. He had also arranged to take Caro to visit his parents that weekend. He had taken the day off from work, but on arriving at the airport he had received a brief text saying "Plans changed. See you."

He had tried to call her, only to be told that her mobile was switched off. Despite wandering the arrivals department for over two hours there had been no sign of her or her mother and her 'phone was still switched off. Since then he had tried to contact her every day without success. He could only think that her mother had been taken seriously ill or her mobile was either lost or stolen.

Ronnie frowned. Even if Caro's original mobile was no longer in her possession she would immediately have purchased a new one. Ronnie pressed in the numbers she had for Caro's 'phone and was asked to leave a message. Ronnie debated whether to ask Caro to 'phone Geoff and decided against mentioning him. She called the number again and asked Caro if they could meet up for a drink.

She answered Geoff's mail as best she could, assuring him that it was most likely that something had happened to Caro's mobile and consequently she may have lost his number. She added that she had asked Caro to meet her and she would then ask her about the problem and give her both Geoff's mobile number and his e-mail address.

Geoff replied, thanking her for her trouble, and also saying that he had met an interesting man on the flight home. He worked at the airport in security, checking the screens as the luggage was scanned. Geoff was full of enthusiasm for the job and was thinking of applying.

Ronnie smiled as she read it. When she had first met him he said he was hoping to work at the Observatory at Greenwich. A couple of weeks ago he had been full of enthusiasm for working in health and safety, then he had asked Owen how he could join the police force, now it seemed he wanted to be involved in security work at the airport. She had an idea that Geoff would remain a convenience store manager for the rest of his life, dreaming of bigger and better things, but never taking the first step towards moving on.

Caro returned Ronnie's call the following day and arranged to meet up that evening for a drink. 'I won't be able to stay very long, but I have something rather nice that I'd like to show you.'

Ronnie smiled to herself. No doubt Caro was wearing an engagement ring. She would let Caro tell her about her marriage plans with Geoff and not spoil her pleasure by saying Geoff had already told her.

Caro strolled casually across the square in Elounda to where Ronnie was waiting. She slid into the seat opposite and scrutinised the list of sundaes that were on offer. Ronnie glanced at her hands. She was definitely not wearing a ring.

'I thought I'd treat myself. Then I really must stick to my diet. I found I had put on three pounds when I weighed myself last week.'

'It doesn't notice,' Ronnie assured her.

'You may not be able to see it, but I know it's there. I'll go for strawberry. I know there will be lashings of cream and a chocolate sauce. Really decadent. What about you? Are you going to join me in wickedness?'

Ronnie shook her head. 'I'd rather have a selection of sorbets. I'll go for a mango and a lime. That should be refreshing.'

'You didn't *walk* here from Plaka did you?'

'Yes, it doesn't take very long.'

'You really should get a car.'

'I don't need one. I can walk or use the bus. I know plenty of people who will give me a ride if they are coming this way.'

'My car has just been upgraded,' announced Caro smugly. 'That's what I wanted to show you. It's that nice looking little blue number over there.' She waved her hand. 'I told my firm the one I was using was just about to die on me and would cost an arm and a leg to repair. They agreed that I could get a new one.'

'Was that when you were over there at the beginning of the month?'

Caro nodded and her earrings sparkled in the sun. 'I actually had some decent weather whilst I was there. That makes a change.'

'Did you meet up with Geoff?' Ronnie tried to make the question appear innocent, although she knew the answer.

Caro looked at her scornfully. 'Why would I want to do that?' she asked.

'I thought, from the way Geoff spoke, that you had an arrangement to meet when you returned to England with your mother.'

Caro shrugged and laughed. 'He wanted me to visit his parents. I can't think of a more boring way to spend an afternoon.'

'Actually his father is very interesting to talk to and his mother is charming.'

'No, it would give the wrong impression. He would think I was seriously interested in him.'

'I thought you were going to show me an engagement ring and tell me you two were going to be married.'

Caro raised her eyebrows. 'Whatever gave you that idea? Geoff was an amusing diversion. He was so gullible. I have no intention of marrying a convenience shop manager.' She fingered her earrings as she spoke. 'My sights are set somewhat higher than a shopkeeper.'

'Geoff is a very nice man,' protested Ronnie.

'Yes, nice is the word. Mr Medium. Last week I met the most delicious man you could imagine. He has a yacht moored in Aghios Nikolaos and he's *loaded,* I mean *seriously* loaded.' Caro pushed her hair back to show her earrings to their full advantage. 'Those are just for starters. I aim to have the matching necklace by the end of the week. He's ripe for the plucking. I found him lonely and miserable because his latest girl friend had chucked him for someone even more loaded. I played the sympathetic, shoulder to cry on, card until he was hooked. Now he's found me he seems to be getting over his previous love affair pretty quickly,'

Ronnie stood up and in doing so deliberately pushed the sundae dish into Caro's lap. 'I hope you enjoy your sundae along with your new and loaded companion. You disgust me, Caro. I thought you truly cared for Geoff and I know he was absolutely head over heels in love with you. I feel hurt on his behalf that you were just using him as a distraction. I won't be calling you again and don't bother to call me.'

'You've ruined my skirt.' Caro sounded furious. 'Sour grapes just because your boyfriend preferred me.'

Ronnie walked away, shaking with anger. She had been instrumental in introducing Geoff to Caro and now she had to break the news to him that the girl she had considered a friend had been using him to pass the time and amuse herself. She wondered how much money Geoff had spent on her whilst they were in Ierapetra and hoped it had not amounted to anything more than expensive meals.

Feeling thoroughly miserable she plodded slowly along the road, not turning to look when she heard a car draw up beside her. If it was Caro trying to make amends she was not interested.

'Miss Ronnie, you would like a ride?'

Ronnie hesitated. She suddenly felt very weary. 'Thank you, Kyriakos.'

He leaned across and opened the door, waiting whilst she adjusted the seat belt. 'You are not happy, Miss Ronnie? I was in the grocer's shop and I saw you get up and leave your friend. She shouted after you, but you did not look back. You have had a disagreement?'

'I'm disgusted with her.'

Kyriakos raised his eyebrows. 'We will go to the taverna. We will have a drink together, maybe I will be able to find some of the crystallized fruit that my mother makes and you enjoy. You will tell me your problems and then you will feel better.'

He smiled at Ronnie and she gave a wavering smile in return. She suddenly felt rather close to tears.

Ronnie helped Kyriakos carry in the bags of groceries and took the carafe of wine and glasses he handed to her back to a table outside. When he joined her there were four pieces of crystallized fruit sitting on a saucer and he placed them in front of her.

'My mother always says that if you are upset you should eat a little of something that is very good and it will help you to recover.'

'I like your mother,' Ronnie managed to smile as she popped a piece of lemon into her mouth and allowed the taste, both sweet and sour to explode to the joy of her taste buds.

Kyriakos poured a glass of wine for each of them. 'You wish to tell me the problem?'

Ronnie hesitated. She had no idea if Kyriakos could be trusted to be confidential, but then she decided she did not care if word went around about Caro's behaviour. If the gossip reached her new found companion he could decide for himself if he wished to continue to see her. Geoff was not there to be hurt or embarrassed.

'Well,' she began, 'you remember when we came to your taverna Caro appeared to be besotted by Geoff.'

Kyriakos nodded. 'They appeared very much in love.'

Ronnie shook her head. 'Geoff was, but she was playing a game.' She related to Kyriakos that Caro had led Geoff to believe that she was serious, but as soon as he returned to England she had immediately discarded him for someone who appeared to have plenty of money.

Kyriakos patted her hand. 'She is not a nice lady. If she comes to my taverna again I will refuse to serve her. I will tell her every table is booked. She took your friend from you and has thrown him away like a piece of rubbish. She will be repaid for her bad treatment. Remember the greedy tax man.'

'Geoff and I were only friends. I am not concerned with Caro. I just feel so sorry for Geoff. He is going to be badly hurt.'

'You have to tell him?'

'What else can I do? I was responsible for introducing them, but I had no idea that Caro was so devious.'

Kyriakos pushed the saucer of fruit a little closer to her and Ronnie selected a piece of orange.

'You must not blame yourself. If you did not know her nature how could you warn him? Many of the girls who work over here come not only for the sun, but also to find a man who is willing to pay all their expenses. They do not go with the local men, but choose a holiday maker who is unattached. They are not nice girls. They are not like you, Miss Ronnie. You work honestly for your living.'

Ronnie sat at her lap top and began to compose a letter to Geoff. The time she had spent with Kyriakos had calmed her down and she began to think of ways to break the news of Caro's duplicity to Geoff as gently as possible. After a number of attempts, she read her final mail through.

"Hi, Geoff, I managed to contact Caro today and we met for an ice cream in Elounda. We talked about you, of course, and I think Caro feels she acted hastily whilst you were here. I can only suggest that you do not keep trying to contact her, but give her some time and space.

You may also have been influenced by the surroundings whilst you were here. Now you are back in England and working I am sure that Crete seems like a dream and maybe you were both rather carried away in a romantic situation. I am always your friend. Ronnie. P.S My regards to your parents."

Ronnie pressed "send" and sat back with a sigh of relief. She hoped Geoff would read between the lines and accept that their grand passion had been no more than a holiday romance. She certainly did not want to tell him in any detail about their conversation or that Caro had found a new man to dance attendance on her.

She must now concentrate on building up a stock of paintings that she could leave with Saffron whilst her mother and uncle visited and she must also ask John if he had managed to find out anything about her grandmother.

Ronnie was in the midst of checking her stock of paper, paints and brushes when there was a tentative knock on her door. She stiffened. If it was Caro she had no desire to speak to her. She opened the door a crack and Kyriakos stood there, a shy smile on his face and holding the saucer with the two remaining pieces of crystallized fruit.

'You did not eat them, Miss Ronnie. I hope you do not mind, but I brought them over for you.'

'Oh, Kyriakos, that was such a kind thought. Why didn't you put them back with the others?'

Kyriakos shook his head. 'Once they have been taken out it is not good to put them back in. They should be eaten.' He pushed the saucer into her hands. 'Have them before you go to bed. They will make you feel good and help you to sleep well.'

He walked away as Ronnie stammered her thanks. For the second time that day she felt like crying. Kyriakos had been so kind and understanding.

John laid an array of papers out before him on the table and smiled at Ronnie.

'I'm not sure that the information I've managed to find is very much help to you. I've tracked down a number of families with the surname Roussakis, but I've not found anything conclusive. I tried the passenger lists, hoping there would be a couple and their children listed as going to America, but there were a number of sailings each week, often with two hundred or more Greeks on board. There's no certainty they went from Piraeus, they may have gone from Egypt.

'I decided I could be wasting my time and turned to the population Census for 1931. I have no idea how accurate the information is. I understand that someone visited each village and recorded the details of the inhabitants. I made a note of every Yiorgo Roussakis that I came across. Some of them would have been too young to be your relatives and others too old, so I took them off. You don't know the year your great grandparents married, I suppose?'

Ronnie shook his head.

John sighed. 'Well, I narrowed the possibilities down to six families in 1931. They were in the right age group. I checked against the 1941 Census and there is a different location for one family. In 1931 they were living in Kato Paleokastro. They were farmers and had two daughters and a son. It's quite likely that the daughters had married by 1941 so they would be listed under their husband's name. I think the parents had gone to live with one of them as a couple named Yiorgo and Maria Roussakis are recorded as living in Galouvas with a Yiorgo and Anna Demopolakis.

Their son could be in the army and over on the mainland of Greece which would account for him not being listed. I haven't discounted them altogether, but I think they are unlikely to be the family you're looking for.'

'Where's Galouvas?' asked Ronnie.

'It's a village in the Chania Prefecture. That leaves just one other possibility. There's a Yiorgo Roussakis living in a village somewhere in the Lassithi Prefecture. Of course the entry is in a section where the name of the village is unreadable. The people are listed under their family names, not the villages, so those that come before and after are no help in providing a clue. There's no wife mentioned, although it says he's aged eighteen. There's also a Despina and Panayiotis Roussakis listed who would be the correct age to be his parents.' John held out his hands in despair.

'So is there no way we can find out where they lived?' asked Ronnie.

John shook his head. 'The occupation shown for that Yiorgo Roussakis is a trainee clerk. He could have worked in Aghios Nikolaos, Neapoli, Ierapetra or even Kritsa. Kritsa was an important town still at that time. I've tried comparing the information from the 1931 Census with that of 1941. Yiorgo Roussakis is no longer registered. He may well have met an untimely death, of course, or just not been around when the information was being collected. A man would have been sent out to an area to record the inhabitants and their occupations, but people could easily have been missed off or duplicated. The information was then transcribed by someone else for the Prefecture and yet again to encompass the whole of Crete. Any amount of errors could have occurred whilst information was being re-entered. Spelling your name, even today, can be a bit haphazard. Roussakis could be spelt with a double "s" when you signed your name, but on your original identity card it could be spelt with one.'

Ronnie gave a little laugh. 'Like the story you told me about Mr Christos.'

'Exactly,' agreed John. 'I can try going through both the Census records again to see if I have missed something. If we knew the name of the village we could see if there are any records of birth and death for the intervening years. They should be recorded somewhere, but I'm afraid people were a bit careless about registering the birth of a child; likewise with a death. If you lived way out in the country you waited until your next visit to the town, then you could find the office was closed and by the time you finally got around to making the entry you had forgotten the exact date. At least when it became law after the war for everyone to carry an identity card it made people more conscientious. Before then you could probably go your whole life without officially existing. I'll carry on looking if you want, but I think you could end up disappointed.'

Ronnie shook his head. 'You've spent more than enough time searching for them. I'll tell Uncle Alex that you haven't had any success. Maybe I could have another look through the old papers and photos when I return home and if I can find anything I think might be relevant I'll let you know.'

Week One
September 2011

Ronnie tidied her apartment and delivered her collection of art work to Saffron.

'My relatives are arriving today.' She explained as she handed her the three large folders. 'There should be plenty there to keep you going, probably until the end of the season, but if there is anything special you want just let me know.'

'Thank you,' Saffron felt the weight as she took the folders from Ronnie's hands. 'Goodness, you have been working hard. You'll have to bring your mother and uncle up to have a meal with us whilst they're here.'

'They'd love that. They really enjoyed meeting you both last year; along with the rest of your family.'

'Better to meet us in small numbers rather than *en masse*. What time do they arrive?'

'Their flight should land at two, so I'm going into Elounda now to pick up the hire car and drive up to meet them. I hadn't the heart to tell them to take the shuttle.'

'I should hope not. After all they haven't seen you for months.'

'They'll probably soon be fed up with having me around all the time.' Ronnie raised her hand and made her way up to the taverna.

'Are you really going in to Elounda this morning, Kyriakos? I can easily walk in or take a taxi.'

'I have said that I am driving in, so I will do so.'

Ronnie frowned. She was not sure that was the answer to her

question. Kyriakos spoke excellent English and he did not usually make mistakes. She had a sneaking suspicion that he had only said he was going into the town because he knew Ronnie needed to be there to collect the hire car.

As Ronnie walked across to the arrivals terminal she came face to face with Owen.

'Well,' she smiled, 'this is a surprise. I wasn't expecting to see you back in Crete so soon. Are you going down to Elounda? If so I can give you a lift when I've met my mother and uncle.'

Owen shook his head. 'That's very kind of you to offer, but I have people meeting me and I'm going to Aghios Nikolaos. Things are a bit complicated at the moment but I'd like to have a chat with you whilst I'm here. Could we meet for a drink?'

Ronnie frowned. 'Is this a way of asking for my mobile number?'

'It would certainly help and could save me a wasted journey. I know where to find you in Plaka but you could have gone out anywhere for the day.'

Ronnie opened her mobile 'phone and read the numbers to him which he entered into his own mobile.

'I have to go.' Owen raised his hand to two men who were approaching. 'I promise I will be in touch.'

'Have a good holiday,' said Ronnie automatically and continued towards the terminal.

Ronnie was surprised when Owen called her two days later and asked if he could meet her. 'There's something I would like to talk over with you and it isn't really suitable to discuss it over the 'phone.'

'I'm a bit occupied at the moment,' frowned Ronnie. 'My relatives are visiting and I've been taking them out each day.'

'It really is quite important and I shouldn't take up more than half an hour of your time.'

Ronnie hesitated. 'Well, I suppose I could dump them on the beach for the morning.'

'Provided they won't mind. I could be with you in an hour. Can we meet at the taverna that belongs to your friend? The one you did the painting for. I know my way there.'

Ronnie giggled. 'At least he doesn't change the name each season like some of them seem to do. I'll be waiting there for you.'

Ronnie sat in the shade of a large umbrella with a glass of mango juice. Kyriakos hovered around her, trying to tempt her to eat something, but she refused.

'I'll only be here about half an hour. Then I'll have to collect the beach babes and feed them.'

'Beach babes?' Kyriakos looked puzzled.

'My mother and uncle. I've agreed to meet that policeman who was on holiday over here. He says he needs to speak to me and if I'm going to be accused of a crime I would rather my mother didn't know,' smiled Ronnie.

'He is not going to arrest you?' Kyriakos looked at her in alarm.

'I'm not expecting to be arrested. He just said he wanted to talk to me about something important. I don't think I've done anything worse than park illegally in Elounda whilst I've been living here. Oh, at least he's on time. That's a point in his favour.'

Owen drew his car onto the piece of waste ground at the side of the taverna and greeted Kyriakos with a smile. 'Could I have a small beer, please?'

Kyriakos nodded. Why should a policeman need to see Miss Ronnie?

Owen shook Ronnie by the hand and sat down opposite, waiting until Kyriakos had placed a cold beer on the table in front of him.

'Another mango juice, Miss Ronnie?' and Ronnie shook her head.

'I'm fine, thank you. What did you want to speak to me about, Owen, that could not be said over the 'phone?'

'I appreciate you giving up your time whilst your relatives are visiting. I'm only here for a couple more days and I wanted to speak to you about your friend Caro.'

Ronnie snorted. 'I no longer consider her to be a friend. We fell out over her treatment of Geoff. I actually threw her sundae into her lap.'

'What happened?'

'I walked away.'

Owen smiled. 'No, I meant between Caro and Geoff.'

'She said he had been nothing more than an amusing diversion for her.' Ronnie spoke indignantly. 'She was boasting to me that she had already found a rich yacht owner. He had bought her some expensive earrings and she was planning to have the matching necklace by the end of the week.'

'You had no idea that her feelings for your friend were not genuine?'

Ronnie shook he head. 'Had I known then the kind of person she was I would never have considered her as a friend.'

'Then the news I have for you will come as no great surprise. Miss Caroline Law was arrested this morning.'

'Arrested! What for? I mean, she didn't steal the earrings, did she?'

Owen shook his head. 'I have to apologise. I was not strictly honest with you when I was here earlier in the year.'

Ronnie raised her eyebrows and Owen continued. 'I am in the police force, but in the fraud section. I was genuinely over here on holiday and it was by pure coincidence that I thought I recognised someone we wanted to investigate further. I sent her photograph back to London and when I returned to work I was told it was a match. We did some discreet checking and then I was sent back out here with the necessary paperwork for the local police to arrest her and to arrange her extradition back to England.'

'What?' Ronnie could not believe her ears. 'Caro has been arrested?'

'Unfortunately she has been a very foolish and greedy young lady.'

'You mean she doesn't work for a travel firm?'

'Oh, yes, she does exactly as she claims and is very efficient and held in high regard by her company. She has been working for them for the last ten years. She earns a good salary, but thought of a way to make a good deal more. Her mother was genuinely disabled, a spinal injury, and when Miss Law was offered the opportunity to work abroad she insisted she had to return to England each month to visit her mother and check on her welfare. The firm agreed. Unfortunately after her mother died Miss Law decided to take advantage of the situation. She continued claiming her mother's disability and unemployment benefit whilst she was employed full time and enjoying her European travels.'

'But how? Surely it was obvious that she was not disabled.'

'She used her mother's X-rays if she needed to prove her imaginary injury and would arrive at the offices on crutches. An employee was taking a smoking break outside and happened to see her throw the crutches into the boot of a car, walk around to the driver's side completely unaided and drive off. It sent alarm bells ringing and her name was added to a list of claimants to be investigated.'

'You didn't know she was working over here?'

'We had no idea. Once we became suspicious we called at her address, only to find that she no longer lived there and when we called at her new apartment we still received no answer. When she visited the offices she had numerous excuses; just moved, a hospital appointment that day, been visiting friends, out shopping, all the usual evasive tactics. We don't have the resources or finance to put anyone under continual surveillance so our visits were haphazard and her excuses plausible.'

'Surely you could have written to her and made an appointment.'

'We tried that and she claimed she had never received any

such letter. If we sent it recorded delivery she refused to accept it. Said it had come to the wrong address and she knew no one of that name.'

'Didn't you try telephoning?'

'We tried, but the number she had given us was discontinued. She claimed she could not afford the telephone bill.'

'But her travel firm? Why didn't you contact them? Surely they would know her mother had died.'

'We had no idea where she was working and as far as they knew she was returning to England each month, ostensibly to visit her mother, but in reality it was to go to the benefits office and sign on.'

'Didn't anyone check her signatures against her mother's?'

'Her mother's name was Celia and she always signed herself just C Law. She had rather large, childish writing. Very simple to copy.'

Ronnie let out a breath. 'So what will Caro be charged with?'

'Claiming benefits to which she was not entitled. She will probably be given a term of imprisonment due to the length of time she has been claiming and the thousands she has received. Her employment with the travel firm will be terminated and they may well ask for reimbursement for all the air fares they have paid on her behalf.'

Ronnie shook her head. 'Are all criminals stupid? Why risk losing a good job and going to all that trouble just for some extra money?'

'Well, some are more foolish than others. Some manage to get away with their crimes for a number of years, but we usually catch up with them in the end.'

'It's Geoff I feel sorry for. I've already had to mail him and say that Caro felt she had made rather a hasty decision and needed some time and space to consider getting married. I know I was evading the truth, but I wanted to let him down as gently as possible. Now I will have to mail him and tell him she was nothing but a cheap crook and he is better off without her.'

'I'm sorry to be the bearer of such unpleasant news.'

Ronnie shook her head. 'I have no sympathy for Caro. She deserves any punishment she gets. It just shows; Kyriakos was right when he said she would be repaid for her treatment of Geoff.'

'Kyriakos?'

'The taverna owner. He gave me a ride home after the sundae incident. I was so cross and upset that I confided in him.'

'Then no doubt he'll be pleased to know that his prophecy came true.'

'Is it alright for me to tell him? I won't be breaching a confidence or anything?'

'No, you can tell him.' Owen rose and held out his hand. 'I appreciate your time. I felt I should let you know as I believed her to be your friend. I hope when we meet again it will be under more pleasant circumstances. I plan to visit Crete again next summer and I can't think of a more beautiful place than here.'

'What did your friend want?' asked Charlene when Ronnie arrived on the beach.

'It's a bit of a long story. I'll tell you later. What would you like to do this afternoon? There isn't really time to go very far. I thought maybe we could have some lunch and then drive up to that village where you hurt your ankle last year. Provided you don't go falling down pot holes again you should enjoy walking around the village and there is a magnificent house up there that I'd like to show you.'

When Ronnie arrived in Kastelli there were already two cars parked in the space between the War Memorial and the water cistern. She hesitated, the only other space was directly in front of a gateway to the house and she could see the occupants were in their garden. No doubt she would be shouted at and waved away if she tried to leave her car there. She drove slowly on up the road where a lane led off and she swung into it.

'I should be out of the way if I park up on the verge. You two get out. I don't want either of you falling into a ditch.' She edged the car forwards and as far onto the grass as she could.

'I think we could probably walk through that side road. It would save having to walk along the main road. Just be careful how you go, Mom. It's a bit uneven and make sure you look behind you before you step back to take a photo.'

Charlene smiled. 'I was very lucky last year. It would have been awful if I had broken my ankle. Hobbling around for those last couple of days over here was bad enough.'

'It helped us to get through the queues at the airports, though,' added Alexandros.

Ronnie led the way down the narrow, unevenly paved street. Along one side ran a whitewashed wall, straggling greenery trailing down at intervals sometimes covering the blue painted wooden doors. On the opposite side of the road the houses were tiny, many of them in disrepair with their doors padlocked and blue painted shutters closed across the windows.

'Are they made to paint their houses all the same?' asked Charlene and Ronnie shook her head.

'There are no street lights so it's practical to have the houses white and blue is a traditional colour to ward off evil spirits.'

Ronnie could see a woman had lifted her curtain and was peering at them through her grimy windowpane. A surprised look passed across her face and she crossed herself before letting the curtain drop back into place.

'I'd love to see inside one of these traditional houses,' remarked Charlene.

Ronnie tried the door of an obviously derelict house, hoping she would be able to open it a chink and see inside, but it was firmly locked. She tried the next and the door gave easily, but was held in place by the chain. 'Shall I?' she said, and began to wriggle the nail that held the chain in place back and forth until it came away in her hands.

Gingerly she pushed the door open and looked into the dark interior. 'Oh!' She took a step backwards.

'What's wrong?' asked Charlene.

'I think someone might still be living in there. There's furniture and things around.'

'Come away then.'

'Let me see.' Alexandros took Ronnie's place at the door. 'No one lives here now.' He looked around the main room where there was a jumble of furniture, table, chairs, a bed, with the coverings mouldy and decaying, and religious pictures still adorned the walls.

'But why has it been left furnished?' asked Charlene. 'It looks as if she has just gone out for her shopping.'

Ronnie pulled the door closed. 'The houses are not turned out and put up for sale here when someone dies. No one wants them so they leave them as they were when they were last occupied. Maybe in the future a family member will decide to renovate the house and sell it, but until that time it will just sit there. It's only in the last twenty years or so that foreigners have started to invest in property over here and some of the derelict properties have been sold or renovated.'

The woman who had looked at them through her window hobbled along the road towards them and Ronnie turned with her back to the door so she would not see that it was slightly ajar.

The woman stopped and studied Alexandros, muttered something unintelligible before crossing herself and walking on.

'What did she say?' asked Ronnie.

Alexandros shook his head. 'I don't know, but it didn't sound very welcoming.'

'I think we ought to fasten that door and go.' Charlene glanced after the woman nervously. 'She may have seen you go in and thought we were stealing something valuable.'

'I can assure you there was nothing of any value in there. Where's this house with flowers, Ronnie? Are you sure we're walking down the right road?'

'It's at the end of the road just past the big house.' Ronnie continued further up the road. 'This house must have been fabulous when it was in good repair. It's such a shame that it's been left to become a ruin. Imagine how it must have looked originally.'

Alexandros placed his hand on the wall to steady himself. His face had drained of colour and Ronnie looked at him anxiously.

'Uncle Alex, are you alright? You look awful.'

Slowly Alexandros turned towards his great niece. 'I know this house. This was where I lived when I was a little boy.'

'You lived *here*?'

'I'm sure I did. Last time we came I thought the water cistern looked familiar. I remember being told not to play near one in case I fell in. The War Memorial wasn't there, of course, and they have cisterns in many of the villages, so I thought that was why I recognised it. Now I've seen this house I *know* I lived here.'

Ronnie looked at her great uncle in awe. Questions were tumbling around in her brain. She recalled the photograph her uncle had shown her of his grandfather standing beside the donkey. Part of a large house had been in the background, three stone steps leading up to the arched front door and to one side had been a window with a decorative grill. How stupid she had been not to realise the house they were now looking at was the same as the one in the photograph. Even the name of the village should have given her a clue, Uncle Alex had said he lived in a village called Castle and they were standing in Kastelli.

'So who did your parents sell it to when they left Crete? Who has let it decay through neglect?'

Alexandros shook his head. 'I've no idea. There might be some papers hidden away relating to the sale.'

Ronnie peered through the broken window. 'There's still furniture inside. Everything has been left, just like the little house we looked into.'

Alexandros looked through the next window and sucked in his breath. He suddenly felt most disorientated as he looked at a scene that was familiar from his childhood memories.

'Maybe my parents planned to return and then Crete was invaded and they decided there would be nothing to return here for and forgot about it,' he said shakily. 'After all they had a home in Dallas.'

'But this house must have been worth a fortune. How could they just forget about it? Let's find the taverna. There's bound to be someone there who can speak English and we can ask them about the house.'

Ronnie led the way back down to the main road. A group of men had gathered beneath a tree opposite and the old lady was talking to them animatedly and pointing towards Alexandros. They were regarding him curiously.

As Alexandros approached them they looked away and ignored him. The woman gave an audible hiss, crossed herself again and walked away.

'Maybe they don't welcome strangers in this village,' said Charlene nervously. 'Can we go back to the car?'

'Uncle Alex,' called Ronnie. 'Mom wants to leave.'

Alexandros followed them down the main road towards the lane where Ronnie had parked the car. He felt confused and unsettled, wishing he could ask the reason why the group of men had been so unfriendly and the woman was clearly disturbed by his presence.

The cars were no longer parked beside the water cistern and a man working in the garden of the house called over to a woman who was sitting at the table, an array of brightly coloured wools before her.

'Is this enough, Margaret?'

'I'd like a bit more.' She bent her head back down over her sewing.

Ronnie stopped. The couple were evidently English. 'Can you help me?' she called.

'Are you lost? This is Kastelli. Continue down the road through the village and you'll reach Elounda. Turn and go back the other way for Neapoli.' The man called back to her and returned to cutting lavender sprigs.

Ronnie shook her head. 'No, we're not lost. We just wanted to ask some questions about the village and we don't speak Greek.'

'Come into the garden. Make sure you close the gate behind you. I don't want the dogs to get out.' The woman spoke to them without looking up from her sewing.

'What are you making?' asked Ronnie as she looked at the assortment of knitted pieces spread out on the table.

'Lavender dolls.'

'May I see?'

The woman indicated a knitted doll to Ronnie. 'Smell it,' she instructed and Ronnie held it up to her nose.

'That's beautiful. How do you make them?'

'Just make a little sachet to contain the lavender and place it inside the body. When I've stuffed the rest I join the limbs and head to the body.' Margaret finished off the sachet she had been stitching, snipped the cotton and placed it in a box by her side.

'Do you sell them?' asked Ronnie.

'To the medical centres; they sell them on for funds.'

'What about the gift shops in Elounda?' Ronnie had never seen any of the dolls for sale.

'I wouldn't be able to make enough to keep them supplied. They'd probably want dozens at a time.'

'Suppose you made them for just one shop?' Ronnie was thinking of Saffron's gift shop. 'May I buy one?'

'Certainly. Three Euros.'

'They're worth far more than that,' Ronnie assured her as she took the coins from her purse.

'I don't do it to make my living. It's just one of my hobbies. Anyway, what did you want to ask about the village?'

'Well, it's really about the large derelict house. Do you know who owns it?'

Margaret shook her head. 'The big house, Alan. They want to know who owns it.'

'Why? Are you hoping to buy it?'

'Is it for sale?' asked Ronnie eagerly.

Alan shook his head, wiped his hands down his trousers and approached the table with another bunch of lavender. 'Not that I've heard.'

Ronnie looked disappointed. 'So do you know the owners?'

'No, it's been derelict every since we moved here, six, seven years ago.'

'Do you know why it's been left to decay?'

Margaret shrugged and pushed some stuffing into a small knitted arm. 'Some say when the Germans came they shot the people who lived there.'

'That can't be right,' protested Alan. 'I've been told the owners moved away before the war and have never returned.'

'There are all sorts of rumours in the village. Goodness knows if any of them are true. Everyone tells a different story about the girls who lived there. I've heard that one ran away with her sister's husband,' added Margaret.

Ronnie felt herself go cold. What was it Kyriakos had said? The younger daughter had run away as her father had refused to let her marry the man she loved. If the man in question was her brother-in-law and he reciprocated her feelings the situation could have been intolerable for both sisters. Maybe that was why the older daughter and her family had moved away. Now her great uncle was saying he had lived there as a child. She placed her hand on Alexandros's arm and shook her head at him. For some inexplicable reason she did not want him claiming that he had once lived there.

'So it's just going to sit there until it crumbles into the ground,' said Ronnie sadly.

'Or until someone comes forward and proves they own it.'

'How would they prove that?'

Alan shrugged. 'No idea. People out here didn't make written Wills leaving their goods to relatives. It was just accepted that your children inherited whatever you possessed.'

'Would you like a cup of tea?' Margaret placed the doll she was working on to one side. 'I'm just about to make some.'

Ronnie shook her head quickly before her mother or Alexandros could accept. 'No, thank you. We've taken up enough of your time. We're meeting friends in Elounda and need to get back in time to take a shower. Thank you for the doll. I'll make sure we shut the gate behind us.' She indicated with her head towards the road. 'Come along, Mom. We're really running late now.'

'What was the rush to get away, Ronnie?' asked Charlene as she climbed into the car. 'A cup of tea would have been very welcome. They seemed nice people. I would have liked to have chatted some more with them.'

'We may be able to come up and visit them again at some time,' Ronnie replied vaguely. 'I just felt we'd intruded and the offer of tea was almost an excuse to get rid of us. From the way they spoke it sounded as though they don't really know anything at all anyway, just the village rumours.'

As Ronnie drove down the road leading back to Elounda she saw one of the men who had been standing beneath the tree detach himself from the group and stroll over towards the house, obviously to ask the occupants the reason for the strangers' visit. The others looked after the departing car and the old lady shook her fist. Ronnie saw their actions from her wing mirror and shivered. Why were the villagers suddenly so hostile towards them?

'Are you absolutely certain you lived in that village when you were a little boy, Uncle?' asked Ronnie.

Alexandros nodded and took a sip of the brandy he had ordered. 'I don't remember that nice house where we visited the English couple, but I'm sure there was a building there, probably a farm.

254

As we walked along the village street it seemed familiar, but most of the villages we have visited have side roads that look like that. It was when I saw the big house that I became certain. As I looked through the window I recognised the furniture. There was the dresser on the far wall where the best china was kept, and I could just see the small table at the side of the room where I remember seeing my grandfather sitting and writing.'

Ronnie rested her chin on her hands. 'Uncle Alex, I've heard some bad stories about the people who lived there. I don't know how true they are. Would you prefer that I stopped searching for your parents?'

'If you do that you have no chance of finding out about your grandmother.'

Charlene looked between her daughter and her uncle. 'You both seem to forget that Vivi was my mother. I didn't know she was adopted and I'd like to find out the truth. Whatever stories abound in the village are probably wildly exaggerated, and even if they are Gospel truth what harm can old gossip do to us now?'

'You're right, Charlene. If John is willing to continue searching you and your mother have a right to know exactly how Vivi came into the family.'

Ronnie smiled in relief and gratitude to her mother. Now she knew where her great uncle had lived she was more intrigued than ever by the story of her grandmother's adoption and would very much like to know if the story Kyriakos had told her about the tax collector's family had any truth to it.

'Do you want to stay here?' she asked. 'I really feel I should return to the apartment and call Geoff. I was going to mail him with the news about Caro, but somehow that seems too uncaring and impersonal. I can drive back down and collect you later.'

Charlene looked at her watch. 'Why don't we sit here and have another drink? I enjoy watching the activity on the waterfront. When we've had enough we can start to walk back to the apartments. You can always meet us half way.'

'Is that alright with you, Uncle Alex? I don't want to find you collapsed in a heap at the roadside.'

'You take your time. It could be a difficult call. We'll stay here and have a taxi back when we're ready to leave. It's further back to the apartments than Charlene realises.'

Ronnie smiled at him gratefully. She was certainly not looking forward to telephoning Geoff.

'Hi, Geoff, it's Ronnie here.'

'Ronnie, good to hear from you. How are things in Crete?'

'Fine, but I need to talk to you. Are you at home? You're not driving or anything, are you?'

'No, I've been home over an hour. We've had a cup of tea and I've told Mum today's story about Mrs Fielding.'

'Then forget about her and listen to me. It's about Caro.'

'Caro? She's alright isn't she? She hasn't had an accident or anything? I still haven't heard from her and after I received your e-mail I thought maybe I should give her a bit of space, after all, she has her work to concentrate on.'

Ronnie took a deep breath. 'Please, Geoff, just listen to me for a few minutes. I went up to the airport to meet my mother and uncle and I bumped into Owen. Remember him? The policeman who had a meal with us one evening?'

'Yes.' Geoff sounded apprehensive.

'He arranged to come and see me this morning.'

'I thought he was keen on you. He must be serious to have returned so quickly.'

'No, Geoff, listen. This has nothing to do with me. Owen is in the police force as part of the fraud squad. They investigate people who've been cheating on their benefit claims. Caro's mother was in receipt of a disability allowance and after she died Caro continued to claim it.'

'Goodness, no wonder Caro hasn't contacted me. The poor girl. Her mother must have died very suddenly. I do wish she'd contacted me. I could have helped her with the paperwork. It often happens that by the time the paperwork has gone through the allowance has been paid for a couple of extra weeks and you just have to send it back.'

'Caro was claiming it deliberately. Her mother died some years ago.'

'No, that can't be right. She said her mother was visiting her in Crete and they were flying back together when she came over to England to report to her company.'

Ronnie took a deep breath. 'Caro did not have to come over to England to report to her company. She came over to sign on at the benefit office. She was pretending to be disabled.'

There was silence on the other end of the telephone.

'Geoff? Are you still there?'

'Yes,'

'Do you understand what I'm saying? Caro's mother died some years ago and Caro has been defrauding the benefit office. She's received thousands of pounds from them.'

'How?'

'According to Owen she had an arrangement with the travel firm to come over once a month to visit her mother. She did not tell them when her mother died. She used crutches whenever she had to sign on and had her mother's X-rays to back up her claim. By chance she was seen putting the crutches into the back of a car and driving off.'

'There must be some mistake.'

'There's no mistake, Geoff. Owen took a couple of photos, remember. He thought Caro's face was familiar to him. He sent them back to London and his colleagues checked them out. He had come back over here with an arrest warrant for her and she is going to be taken back to England.'

'So why did he come to see you?' Geoff sounded belligerent.

'He thought we were friends. I think he also wanted to find out if I knew anything about her scheme.'

'But you are friends.'

'We had a disagreement, but that's not important. Geoff. I am truly sorry that I've had to tell you this. I wish I'd never introduced you.'

'I don't believe it.' Geoff's voice rose and he sounded slightly hysterical. 'You're making this up because you thought I was interested in you and I found Caro more attractive. You're just being spiteful.'

'Geoff, I swear I'm not. I wouldn't do that to you. You're a decent man, but I never thought of you as more than a friend.'

'What am I going to do?' Geoff sounded near to tears.

'There's nothing you can do, Geoff. Caro was not the person she led you to believe she was.'

'Why did she do it?'

'The fraud? Well, I suppose she just saw an opportunity and was greedy.'

'No, I mean to me.'

'Maybe she was a little carried away and things moved a bit faster than she had anticipated.' Ronnie did not want to add to Geoff's misery by saying that Caro had merely used him for a couple of weeks and immediately found a new companion once he had left.

'What am I going to say to my parents and my friends?'

'Why don't you tell them that you've had second thoughts; that it was a holiday romance that cooled once you had left Crete.'

Ronnie heard Geoff sigh deeply and guessed he was trying hard to control himself. 'Will Caro be in the newspapers or on the news?'

'I have no idea. I hope not for your sake.'

'Will this policeman want to come and interview me?'

'I really don't know. I haven't made any arrangement to see Owen again. If I do see him I'll telephone you.' Ronnie felt confident that there would be no accidental meeting between her and Owen and hoped he would not seek her out. 'I didn't want you to hear the news any other way, but I'm so sorry, Geoff.'

Geoff hesitated. 'Yes, well, I suppose I should say thanks for 'phoning.'

The telephone went dead and Ronnie looked at it in surprise, then realised that Geoff had curtailed the call.

Week Two
September 2011

John listened to Ronnie's news with growing interest and excitement.

'I can't believe how stupid I was not to recognise the house from the photograph and associate the name Kastelli with Castle.'

'Never mind. Now I know where to start looking. If your uncle is sure he lived in Kastelli his father must have been the unmarried Yiorgo Roussakis who was living there with his parents. If he married a local girl, and it sounds as if he married the girl from the big house, the records should be held either at the church in Kastelli or archived in the Lassithi records office. If I can track those down they will tell us who Yiorgo Roussakis married and the date. It should also give us the names of the girl's parents. I can then look them up on the Census'

'How will that help?'

'Background information. There may have been other family members living there. I can also look in the records for your uncle's baptismal records and also see if there is anyone in the village with the name Paraskevi who could have been adopted by his parents. If I find that she was baptised in Kastelli the names of her parents should be recorded.'

Ronnie frowned. 'Assuming that Uncle Alex's father is the man who lived in Kastelli and he did marry the girl who lived in the big house that would make him the grandson of the greedy tax collector.'

John grinned. 'Does that worry you?'

Ronnie shook her head. 'As such, no. I only have Kyriakos's story to go on. It could be completely untrue, but it was rather unnerving when we were there. The villagers were really hostile, no one would speak to us; a woman spat after us and crossed herself. Why would they behave like that?'

John shook his head. 'Maybe they mistook you for some tourists who had been a nuisance in the village on another occasion.'

'The English couple who live there were friendly enough, but they didn't know anything about the house or the previous occupants. The woman said the Germans had shot the people living there, but the man said the younger daughter had run away because she loved her sister's husband.'

John raised his eyebrows. 'That's interesting and if it's true it would certainly have been the scandal of the village and the story would have been passed down the generations. Mind you, any tax collector was hated by all the villagers. All sorts of untrue and malicious rumours could have been circulated about him and his family.'

John grinned at Ronnie. 'We still hate the tax man. He no longer rides around to collect the money, but we're all convinced that the government demands more than their entitlement. Now I know where I'm looking I'll check the 1931 Census again and see who else was living in Kastelli at that time. The peoples' occupations were recorded so it should say if a tax collector was living there. I can't see him being happy in an ordinary village house if he had become a wealthy man, so it's more than likely he occupied the big house.'

'Would he have built the house or bought it from someone else?'

'That would depend upon how old it is. He may have accepted it as a debt from some unfortunate tax payer. I'll see if I can find out who was living there in the 1921 Census. After that I'll try tracking down the marriage and Baptismal records. I'd like to be able to find them on the internet, but I think it doubtful anyone would have thought village records were important. I'll just have to hope they are in Aghios Nikolaos or Neapoli and haven't been archived in Heraklion or Athens. Leave it with me, Ron, but I can't guarantee that I'll have come up with any results whilst your family are here.'

John studied the Census for 1921. The writing was cramped and difficult to decipher in many places, but at least the name of the village of Kastelli had not been obliterated. Yiorgo Roussakis was listed there as a boy aged eight. His father was a farmer and his mother was listed as the same. From there John moved up and down the list, looking at the occupations given. Most of the people appeared to have been farmers which was no great surprise to him. The Priest was Father Constantinus and his place of residence was listed as the Church. No doubt he had a small house to one side of the religious building.

Within a few lines was the name Alesandros Danniakis, his age given as fifty one and his occupation was that of a tax collector. Below Sofia Danniakis aged twenty four was listed as his wife and the names of two girls, Maria aged eight and Fotini aged six followed.

John frowned. Was Sofia really his wife or could she have been his daughter? If their ages were correct she was twenty seven years younger than her husband. He squinted at the age recorded for Alesandros, but there was no mistake, it clearly said fifty one, not thirty one.

He drew a sheet of paper towards him and made a rough family tree. He would check the Census of 1911 and see if Alesandros had been married previously. Sofia could be the daughter of a first marriage and her father having married a second time could have been widowed with two young girls to care for. It would have been natural for the older girl to become a mother to them and as such the listing of her as Alesandros's wife was a mistake.

John closed the screen and opened up another that covered

the Census for 1911. He immediately searched for Kastelli and the list of villagers. Yiorgo Roussakis was not listed and nor was there mention of Alesandros Danniakis. John scrolled up and down looking for any further clues, but there was nothing else to help him.

With a sigh he closed the page and entered the name Alesandros Danniakis and the year as nineteen eleven. He hoped he would not find there were hundreds of men with the same name listed as living in all areas of Crete at that date. Painstakingly he examined each entry as he brought up the details, finally having a list of three who would have been the correct age for the man he was searching for. To his delight the occupation for one was given as a tax collector, but there was no mention of a wife and the man had lived in Aghios Nikolaos.

'It has to be him,' muttered John to himself, 'But how did he end up in Kastelli?'

John closed his eyes, they were sore from looking at the screen of the computer for so long, but he was loath to finish searching. He drew the sheet of paper towards him again and began to add some notes. He would have to find the records of marriages that had taken place in Aghios Nikolaos between the years of nineteen eleven and nineteen twenty one. If Alesandros was recorded as marrying a woman called Sofia at least that question would be answered.

John checked the records again; there was definitely no Alesandros Danniakis listed as living in Kastelli in nineteen eleven, so he must have moved to Kastelli either when he married or shortly afterwards. He tapped his teeth with his pen. In the village community it was the custom for the woman to have a house provided by her father as her dowry. That could mean that the woman came from Kastelli and if they had been married in that village his search should be quicker and easier.

Feeling encouraged John searched for the records of all the marriages that had taken place in the village after nineteen eleven and two hours later he was rewarded. Alesandros Danniakis was recorded as having married Sofia, daughter of Maria and Theodopolous Angelakis, when she was aged fifteen in nineteen sixteen.

'John, are you ever coming to bed?' asked Nicola.

'I'm actually getting somewhere. I'm sure I've found Ron's great grandparents.'

Nicola yawned. 'If you have then they'll still be there tomorrow. Give it up for tonight, it's nearly midnight.'

'I'm not sure I'll be able to sleep.'

'Yes you will. I'll make sure of that.'

John grinned at her. 'I thought you were tired?'

'Not that tired.'

'In that case I will leave it until tomorrow.' John closed his computer. 'By the looks of things Ron's great grandmother was married when she was fifteen – and our parents thought we were too young!'

'They always married young in those days. Fifteen to twenty one are supposed to be the best years for child bearing.'

'Talking of child bearing,' John traced Nicola's breast with his finger. 'The girls are coming up for two.'

'And still hard work. Give it another six months and I might consider your proposal.'

'By then you'll be coming up for twenty three, past your prime.'

Nicola giggled as John took her in his arms. 'You might be past yours.'

'Never,' John assured her. 'You'll still be trying to fend me off when I'm an old man of ninety.'

The following evening John turned his attention back to the marriage records for Kastelli. He narrowed his search to begin in nineteen thirty two as he knew Yiorgo Roussakis was listed as unmarried in nineteen thirty one. He trawled through the lists, which were not unduly long, until he saw that Yiorgo had indeed married the tax collector's daughter in nineteen thirty two. He completed the family tree down to that date and scrolled through the remainder of the records until nineteen forty one, but there was no record of Fotini having married.

He placed her name and a question mark beside it, along with a number of possibilities. At the top of the list was "died". He looked at the deaths recorded for the village during nineteen thirty one and nineteen forty one expecting to find her name recorded there but he could find no reference to her and he shook his head in puzzlement. Maybe Fotini had run away from her home with a young man. When he had finally tracked down Ronnie's grandmother he might look for her again. He could find out which young men had left Kastelli and see if they were listed as living elsewhere with a woman named Fotini.

John turned back to the records of Baptisms and easily found that Ronnie's great uncle had been baptised in nineteen thirty four. He moved the cursor down year by year looking for Paraskevi but her name was not recorded. He could only conclude that she had been adopted from an orphanage.

Annoyed that he could still find no trace of Ronnie's grandmother he began to pull up the pages that covered the orphanage records. There was no girl called Paraskevi who matched her age group in the records for the Lassithi Plateau. He tried looking at the other orphanage records for Crete and found twenty three girls with the name, but when he subsequently checked with the nineteen forty one Census all the girls were still living at the orphanage.

Totally frustrated by his lack of success John called Ronnie and said he had come to a dead end.

'Come and tell my mother and Uncle what you have found. I know Uncle Alex is interested to know more about his grandparents. I think you've done wonders to find out anything at all.'

'It wasn't that difficult,' said John modestly. 'It was just a question of looking down some old lists.' He did not add that it had taken him hours to check and recheck the data.

'There you are, Mr Roussakis,' John laid the papers before Ronnie's great uncle. 'I have the names of your parents and the date they were married. Both of them had been born in Kastelli. Your father must have been a very intelligent young man to have become a government clerk. His parents were farmers and it's doubtful if either of them could even write their name.'

'Where would he have received his schooling?' asked Ronnie.

'Probably the village priest. My old Uncle Yannis received his first tuition from Father Theodorakis here in Plaka. Thanks to the priesthood after a while most of the village men and some of the women could read and write.'

Alexandros studied the family tree that John had handed to him. 'I remember my grandfather as an old man, but I never realised how much younger than him my grandmother was. She seemed old to me at the time. How did he manage to persuade a young girl of fifteen to marry him? I'm surprised her parents allowed it.'

'Maybe there was something about her that did not attract the young men. She may have had a squint or been deaf and her parents knew she had little chance of making a better match.'

Alexandros shook his head. 'I don't remember her having a squint and she did beautiful embroidery. I'm equally sure she wasn't deaf. In her photographs she looks quite an attractive woman.'

John shrugged. Villagers, particularly in those days, had been riddled with superstition. If she had a mole on her face or wart on her arm they would say the devil had touched her.

'Your father and mother had your Baptism recorded, but I can't find out anything at all about Paraskevi. Your mother's sister disappears and her death is not recorded, so it does sound as though the story that she ran away could be true.'

'Oh,' interrupted Ronnie. 'Remember the photos you showed me of the two girls, Uncle? You said one was your mother, but you didn't know who the other one was. That was probably Fotini.'

'So I had an aunt I never knew about. I wonder what became of her.'

'I could try looking at the names of the village boys and see if one of them is no longer on the Census. If I put his name in and looked through I might find one with a wife called Fotini.'

'She's not really important. I'm more interested to know where Vivi came from.'

'I can't find any record of her at all. I've looked in the Baptismal records and covered a number of years in case you were mistaken about her age, and I've also tried the orphanages to see if she had been placed in one after she was born. There's nothing. It's as though she never existed.'

'She must be somewhere,' insisted Ronnie. 'Is there anywhere else you could look, John?'

'I can only think that she was baptised somewhere else and the records were lost when the Germans were here. They did a tremendous amount of damage and after they left some of the records had to be reconstructed from memory.'

'That's probably the answer,' agreed Alexandros. 'You should be quite grateful, Ronnie. I am the grandson of the evil tax collector, but you are no relation to him.'

Ronnie sat there with a frown on her face. Finally she turned to her uncle. 'Do you realise what that could mean, Uncle Alex?'

'That I am a wicked man?'

Ronnie shook he head impatiently. 'Your parents had no other children. There is no sign of Fotini, but even if she did marry and have children you would still be the oldest grandchild. You must be the owner of the house in Kastelli.'

'Me? Don't be silly, Ronnie.'

'Remember what the English couple said. The people did not make Wills. It was understood that their children would inherit.

267

After your grandparents died the house should have gone to your parents and subsequently to you.'

'Actually Ron's right,' agreed John. 'If there are no other living relatives that house is yours.'

'And what would I do with a wreck like that? It would cost a fortune to rebuild and I don't want to come over to Crete to live at my age.'

'So it will just disintegrate.' Ronnie shook her head sadly.

'Unless you want it?'

'Me?' Ronnie looked at her uncle in surprise.

'If I am legally the owner then I am at liberty to pass it on to you as a gift.'

Ronnie smiled at him and squeezed his arm. 'I really appreciate the thought, Uncle Alex, but we don't actually know if you are the owner. I could never afford to put it back into good repair anyway.'

Charlene took John's pen from his fingers and turned the sheet of paper with the family tree over. She frowned in concentration as she jotted down figures and added them up. Eventually she looked up.

'I can,' she said.

'What!'

Alexandros and Ronnie looked at her in amazement. Ronnie shook her head. 'You have no idea how much it would cost, Mom.'

'I'm not hard pressed. I invested wisely, thanks to you, Alex, and I have a large amount sitting in the bank doing nothing useful. I always planned to give it to you for a house of your own when you decided to get married, Ronnie. Why shouldn't you have it now and repair the family home?'

Ronnie felt tears coming into her eyes. 'Oh, Mom,' her breath caught in her throat. 'I can't let you do that. Suppose, just suppose I did repair the house and then I decided to leave Crete. What would happen then?'

'You'd sell it, of course,' answered Charlene practically.

'It isn't actually my family home.'

Charlene shrugged. 'It's as good as. If Alex can prove he owns it and signs it over to you I'm prepared to finance the restoration. What do you say?'

Ronnie looked between her mother and her uncle. Alexandros nodded.

'But if I did restore it what would I do with it? It's far too large for just one person.'

'You could do whatever you wanted. Sell it, rent it, turn it into a small hotel, get married and have ten children. The choice would be yours.'

'I don't think I'll go for the ten children option.' Ronnie laughed shakily. 'I can't thank either of you enough.'

John smiled at her. 'Well, I may not have been able to find your grandmother, but it looks as though I have found you a house. Don't start work on it just yet. It would probably be best if Mr Roussakis spoke to my father. He would know the best person to consult. There are probably all sorts of formalities that will need to be gone through to prove the house does belong to you.'

Week One
October 2011

The apparent disappearance of Fotini niggled away at John. He returned to the Census lists and studied them carefully. He had not missed her through his eyes being tired. She was definitely not on there. He looked through the names of the young men who had lived in Kastelli at the time and all but three had remained living there, taking a local girl for their wife. Two men who had moved away had married, but their wives were not called Fotini. The third disappeared and John began to search in the hope that he would be able to discover he was the mysterious lover of Fotini. To his disappointment, when he finally consulted the register of deaths, he found the man had died due to an accident whilst working on the reconstruction of the harbour arm at Heraklion.

A horrible suspicion came into John's mind. Had the girl been murdered and her body never discovered? If that was so there could only be three suspects; the mysterious lover, her father in a fit of violent rage or Yiorgo Roussakis if he was having an affair with her.

John turned the suspects over in his mind. If Yiorgo had found his sister-in-law was carrying his child he might well have murdered her to prevent the truth coming out. It was unlikely that the lover would have committed the crime. When a young man found that he had made his girlfriend pregnant he usually went to her father, cap in hand, apologetic and humble, and asked to be allowed to marry her as soon as possible. Either possibility, once known by her father could have caused him to act irrationally to save the family name. John did not want to speculate down that route.

'What do you think, Nick?'

'That you have a nasty, suspicious mind.'

'No. Seriously, Nick, I can't think of any other explanation.'

'I think you should leave it. If her father did kill her and dispose of her body he can't be brought to justice now. The only people the discovery would hurt would be Ronnie and her family. Why do that to them?'

'If Mr Roussakis does own the house and gives it to Ronnie let's hope she doesn't find a body under the floor or walled up in a room.'

'John, I know you've done a tremendous amount of work finding Uncle Alex's grandparents, but a thought has occurred to me. Suppose Uncle Alex was told the house was his and then a descendent of Fotini came forwards and claimed it?'

'I don't see how they could, besides, unless Fotini had a child before her older sister your uncle would still be the oldest descendant.'

'Their mother was married at fifteen. She may have been married even younger.'

'There's no mention of her in the Marriage records.'

'I know, but you've said yourself that very often births and death were not recorded accurately. It could have been the same with marriage. There's even a chance that she did run away with a young man and they never married.'

'She should still show up on the Census,' frowned John.

'Not if she deliberately avoided giving her details. She may have been frightened that her father would find her and drag her back home,' reasoned Ronnie.

'Then I can't see any way that we can ever find out about her, any more than we can find anything about your grandmother.'

'Do you think there's anyone old enough in Kastelli who would remember the family?'

John shrugged. 'It's doubtful. Your uncle is in his seventies. You'd need to find someone at least ten years older than him.'

'What about the old lady I told you about who spat after Uncle Alex and crossed herself. Why would she do that?'

John smiled at her. 'What you're really trying to say is "will I go to Kastelli and find out".

'Would you?' asked Ronnie eagerly. 'If no one remembers anything I promise I'll give up searching then.'

Ronnie felt incredibly nervous as she drove up to Kastelli with John. He parked beside the water cistern and before crossing the road he and Ronnie looked at the names engraved on the War Memorial.

John shook his head. 'His name is not there.'

Ronnie followed John across the road to where the men were gathered beneath the trees. They smiled to each other; no doubt he was another tourist requesting directions.

John greeted them and made some small talk before finally asking if there was anyone living in the village who would remember the family who had lived in the big house.

The men exchanged glances. The English couple said their visitors had asked if the house was for sale. What was the sudden interest in the big house? They scratched their heads, pretending to consider, one suggesting a name only for the person to be discounted by another. John realised they were waiting for him to make it worth their while to impart any information to him. He pulled some Euro notes from his pocket.

'It is very important to the young lady accompanying me to find out the history of the family who lived there before the war.' He held a ten Euros note out.

'Old Kassie might know something,' suggested one as he took the note from John's hand.

'Where would we find her?'

The man looked down at the Euros note he held and pursed his lips. John offered another ten Euros note which was seized hastily.

'She'll be in her house, no doubt.'

'Where's that?'

The man looked down at the notes again and John shook his head. 'If you are unable to tell me I'll ask your village priest.'

The man gave him a sour glance. 'I'll take you there, but she might not talk to you.'

John took that to mean that he would have to pay the old lady for any information she was willing to impart. He beckoned Ronnie forward.

'He says he will take us to the house where an old lady lives. There's no guarantee that she will remember anything.'

Ronnie had seen how much cash John had handed over to the men. 'Have you got enough money? This is becoming expensive.'

John grinned at her. 'Knowledge always comes at a price and no doubt there'll be more to pay yet.'

The man was already striding off down the road and John and Ronnie hurried to catch him up. They passed the house that had been a riot of colourful flowers earlier in the year and turned into the side road where the big house stood on the corner. Ronnie could not resist giving it a quick glance as she walked by. Was it really going to belong to her?

Stopping before one of the tiny houses the man rapped on the door and opened it. 'Kassie, are you there? There are some visitors to the village who want to ask you about the old days.'

The curtain was lifted and the old woman peered out at them.

'John, she's the old lady who spat at Uncle Alex's and then crossed herself,' Ronnie said nervously.

John raised his eyebrows. 'Then she might well know something. May we come in?' he called.

He and Ronnie walked down a step into the tiny living room, John having to bend his head to avoid bumping it on the lintel. Old Kassie sat on an upright chair next to a small table by the window where there was a television set. On the far side of the room there was an old rusty cooker with a bowl on the shelf beneath a tap and some chipped crockery. A truckle bed took up the remaining space by the wall by the door and in the dim light it was just possible to make out the religious icons and photographs that covered the walls.

Ronnie blinked in disbelief. Did this old lady really live in this one room? She edged her way carefully into the small amount of space that remained. Kassie looked at them warily and the man who had accompanied them stood in the doorway protectively.

John held out his hand to Kassie and took her gnarled fingers in his. 'I'm very pleased to meet you. The young lady accompanying me is called Veronica. She does not speak Greek.'

Kassie looked at Ronnie and held out her hand. Dutifully Ronnie touched it with her own, hoping she would not be expected to eat or drink anything the old lady decided to offer them.

'What do you want to know? What happened during the war? How we were forced to live off snails and grass? How the soldiers raped the women, some girls as young as seven or eight and old women like me? They didn't care.'

John shook his head and placed a ten Euros note on the table. 'We'd like to know anything you can remember about the people who lived in the big house.'

The old lady eyed it. 'My memory's not so good these days.'

Hastily John added another note.

'What do you want to know about them?' Kassie spat onto the floor and crossed herself. She looked at the notes on the table. 'My grandmother said the old couple were nice enough. She used to scrub their floors and clean the windows. Wealthy family, owned most of the houses in the village until the tax man started calling. Each year he demanded more and more and they began to give him the village houses as payment. He collected the rent, but if the occupant said their roof leaked he told them to get it repaired. If their shutters were rotten he said they should get new ones. In the old days if such a thing had happened the old man would have arranged for repairs.

'Eventually the old couple had nothing left. The family were destitute. All they had was the house and the wife's gold jewellery. My grandmother said he gave them the choice; give me your house or I take your daughter.'

John did a rapid calculation. This must have been Sofia, the daughter of Maria and Theodopolous Angelakis. 'Why didn't she give up her jewellery?'

'It was family jewellery. Their daughter would have inherited it eventually as she had done. He knew that. They gave him the house and moved into one of the village houses. The following year he returned. He said they still owed money and this time he claimed their daughter as payment.' Kassie sucked her gums. 'According to my grandmother she was quite a prize. Prettiest girl in the village and from a good family, whereas he was an old man.'

'They let him marry her?' John was horrified.

Kassie spread her hands. 'They had no choice. Had they refused he would have taken her by force. Better to have her legally married to him than ruined forever and possibly bearing his child. They probably hoped he was too old to give her any children and he would die soon leaving her a respectable and wealthy widow, able to make a decent marriage.'

John held up his hand. 'Just a minute, please. I have to tell my friend this in English.' John recounted rapidly the story Kassie had told him.

Ronnie nodded. 'That accounts for all the jewellery my great grandmother was wearing in the photograph. It was family heirlooms. I wonder what became of it?'

John placed another note on the table. 'What happened?' he asked, knowing full well that the tax man had not died until much later.

'The girl, despite having been forced into marriage with the man, was not prepared to abandon her parents. She was pregnant within the year and insisted her parents came back to live in the house so her mother could care for her. She had a healthy daughter, but claimed she was too weak after giving birth to look after the child so her parents stayed on. I don't think the tax man cared. He had what he wanted; a young wife, a child, a big house and her parents were no more than his servants.' Kassie spat on the floor again and crossed herself.

Ronnie felt nauseated by the old lady's action and hoped she would not repeat the process too frequently.

'Within another year the girl was pregnant again and another girl was born. No doubt he had wanted a son, but for some reason there were no more children. The girl accepted her situation. She never complained about her husband or accused him of mistreating her. He allowed her parents to continue to live in the house and he doted on his daughters, despite their waywardness, even insisted the village priest gave them schooling along with the boys.'

'What happened to the girl's parents?'

'Her father had an accident when he was out in the fields cutting grass for the tax collector's donkey. The scythe hit his leg and cut into an artery. His wife found him lying in a puddle of his own blood when he did not return home. My grandmother said she seemed confused after that; would go up to the field looking for him, forget she was cooking and let the food burn. One day she tipped a pan of boiling water over her feet. She neglected the injury and ended up with blood poisoning and died a few weeks later.'

John nodded. He had heard stories like this before; injuries neglected that became infected and in the days before antibiotics were available the sufferers inevitably died.

'So the girl was left to run the house and look after the children on her own?'

Kassie shook her head. 'Mr Danniakis employed my mother to go and do the rough work. She liked the girl, even became friends, but the children did as they pleased even when their father was home. Their mother indulged them. As they became older they were allowed to walk down the village street or out to where the boys were working in the fields without their mother with them. Maria, the older one, took a liking to one of the boys. He was working as a clerk down in Aghios Nikolaos and would walk back to the village each weekend. She would be waiting for him and ended up pregnant.' Kassie spread her hands. 'It was only to be expected. My mother knew what was going on. She had heard Maria talking to her sister, confiding in her, telling her what Yiorgo had in his trousers.'

John smiled to himself. He wondered if the girl had decided Yiorgo was a better catch than one of the farm boys or whether Yiorgo had set out deliberately to make the girl pregnant knowing her father would insist he married her?.

Kassie took a breath. She was obviously now relishing in the salacious details. 'Her father arranged a hasty marriage, and everyone knew why. She lost the child so she could have waited and had a proper wedding. Yiorgo went to live in the big house with them. Thought himself way above us villagers, then, just because he'd married the daughter of the tax collector and worked in Aghios Nikolaos. My mother remembered him when he was a little boy playing in the dirt outside his mother's house.'

'What work did he do in Aghios?'

'Something to do with a shipping firm. Just a clerk in an office no doubt, but by the way he carried on you would have thought he owned the ships. Made sure each Sunday that he was seen pressing a gift of money into the hands of the priest whilst all we could give him were a few eggs or some bread. Good thing when they did up and leave. We didn't want the likes of them here.'

'Just because they had more money than the villagers?'

She shook her head. 'I'll get to that.' Kassie looked pointedly at the money lying on the table and John added another five Euros.

'That we could put up with. There's always someone with more than you have. It was the younger girl, Fotini, who was the problem. She was following in her sister's footsteps, always out and looking for the boys.'

'So she became pregnant as well?' John sat forward eagerly.

Was this when he was going to find out that Yiorgo had been having an affair with his sister-in-law?

'Maria was expecting again and this time she had a boy. Everyone was delighted. He was fit and healthy, despite Maria having had a hard time. I remember him. A beautiful little boy, despite being the image of his father. It was after his Baptism that the villagers became aware that something was not quite right. It was the middle of summer and Fotini was not going out to walk down the village street wearing a flimsy blouse and lifting her skirt too high, saying she was cooling her legs. If you walked past the house you could see her gazing out of the window, but as far as my mother knew she never left her room.'

John frowned. 'Why not? Was she ill?'

Kassie nodded. 'The old man bought a cart and we thought we would see him driving through the village with his family in the back, but he just left it to one side of the house. My mother said there was a strange atmosphere in the house and incense was being burnt in every room. She was forbidden to enter Fotini's room, a slop bucket was placed outside each morning and when she had emptied it she had to knock on Fotini's door to let her know she had returned it.'

'Why were they keeping her a prisoner?' asked John. Could this have been to keep her apart from, Yiorgo and was this the reason she had run away?

'They did not want her near them. She was incurable.'

'What! You mean she had leprosy?'

Kassie shrugged and crossed herself, but this time she did not spit on the floor. 'Who knows? Rumours began to go around the village. My father did not want my mother to go to the big house and work there. He was frightened she would bring infection back to us if the girl was sick. My mother went up to the house to tell them she was not going to work there any more and found Maria and her mother crying. Fotini had run away and her room needed to be cleaned. They would pay her well if she would stay and do it immediately. Whilst she was cleaning the room she had the window open and saw Mr Danniakis return driving the cart. The two women rushed outside to him and he took both women into his arms. "It was confirmed. They have taken her away," she heard him say.'

John felt a rising excitement. It had not occurred to him that Fotini could have been taken to Spinalonga. That would explain why she was no longer listed on the Census. As far as the government of the time were concerned the incurables on Spinalonga did not exist.

'My mother told my father what she had heard and very soon the whole village knew her father had taken her away in the cart. My father forbade my mother to go back up there to work for them, although they said their daughter had gone to the hospital for an operation and not survived. No one believed them.'

'Do you know what happened to her after that?'

Kassie shook her head. 'I was about ten. Why would I be concerned about her?'

'Is that why Yiorgo and Maria decided to go to America?'

Kassie looked at the money again and John added another five Euros. He sensed that Ronnie was anxious to know what the old lady had told him, but he did not like to interrupt her flow.

'That was later, after the girl came. The cart was scrubbed out as well, but never used. One day they harnessed the donkey and Yiorgo and Maria drove off. When they returned they had a little girl with them. For weeks they kept her hidden inside with them; then one morning the donkey was harnessed to the cart again. Maria and the children sat in the cart surrounded by boxes and parcels and the men sat on the front seat. Later the old man returned alone and the villagers were told they had gone to America to start a new life.'

'So the tax collector and his wife were left alone in the big house?'

Kassie nodded. 'He was an old man by then. He no longer

went out on his donkey to collect taxes. After a while he sold the donkeys. Sofia began to grow her own vegetables and keep chicken. From being the wealthiest family in the village they became no better than the rest of us. The tax collector was rarely seen except at church and he was avoided. Often he would go up to someone and tell them their taxes had not been paid or their rent was due. Sofia would take his arm and persuade him to return home and check his papers again.'

John frowned. 'If he owned the cottages in the village surely he had plenty to live on with the rents coming in?'

Kassie shrugged. 'Later Sofia told me they had used all their money and borrowed more so they could send Maria and Yiorgo to America. The rents were being used to pay off their debt.'

'So what happened to them eventually?'

'The war came and by then he was so confused that he demanded taxes from the Germans. They laughed at him and said he was a senile old man. He walked into the village with his gun and began to shoot at them. They immediately shot him.'

'Is his name on the War Memorial?' asked John.

Kassie shook her head. 'He did not die in battle or defending his home and family. He died through his love of money.'

'And his widow?'

'She was left on her own. I looked after her when she could no longer help herself. She talked to me.'

'Did she tell you anything about the girl who was sick?'

'She never mentioned her.'

'Did she ever hear from her daughter in America?'

Kassie shrugged. 'I've no idea.'

'So after Sofia died the house was just left empty?'

'No one claimed it.'

'What about the village houses?'

A crafty look came over Kassie's face. 'They belong to us now. No one has asked for rent for over fifty years. They are ours.'

John was not prepared to debate the legalities of ownership, but he would be interested to know if their claim for ownership was legal.

John added another five Euro note to the pile that had grown steadily. 'There's just one more thing: My friend visited the village a few weeks ago with her uncle and mother. You spat at them and the villagers were hostile. Why?'

'I recognised him. It was Yiorgo returning to claim back our houses.'

John shook his head. 'No it was not Yiorgo. It was his son. You said he was the image of his father as a little boy. As he grew up he still looked like him. I assure you he had no intention of claiming back your houses. Until a short while ago he did not even know he had been born and lived here.'

'So why did he come?'

John waved his hand towards Ronnie. 'She is trying to trace her grandmother who was the girl taken into the family. I've been trying to help her, but I can't find her. When the lady's uncle said he had lived here as a little boy I thought someone in the village might remember something and be able to help.'

Kassie smiled a toothless smile. 'I've told all I know.'

'And I am very grateful to you.' John rose and indicated to Ronnie that they were leaving. He took another twenty Euros note from his pocket and picked up the others from the table. Kassie's eyes widened in alarm and flashed with anger. Was he only going to give her twenty Euros? He pressed all the notes into her hand and she clutched them to her flat chest.

Ronnie touched the old lady's hand and said "thank you" in Greek. She could hardly wait to get outside into some fresher air and also to hear the information that had been imparted to John.

'How much do I owe you, John, and were her memories worth it?'

'They certainly were. I was so stupid. The one place I didn't look for Fotini and it was so obvious! We'll drive back to Plaka and then I'll tell you everything she said.'

'I'm not sure I can wait that long. Can't you tell me now?'

John grinned at her. 'I don't think it would be a good idea to stop and tell you in Kastelli. I'm not at all sure how much English the villagers understand. Wait until I tell Nick. I know just what she'll call me – a big palookas. She always does when she finds out I've done something stupid.'

Ronnie looked at him in puzzlement. 'But what have you done that was stupid?' she asked.

'It's not what I have done, but what I didn't do.'

Ronnie sat with John and Nicola on the patio at Uncle Yannis's house overlooking the bay and with a view of Spinalonga. Nicola had asked Marianne to look after the girls so John could tell her at the same time as he passed the information on to Ronnie.

Ronnie listened carefully as John told her how the tax collector had demanded the teenage girl as his wife.

'What a horrible man he was,' she remarked.

'I'm not sure he was that bad,' argued John. 'Old Kassie said his wife never complained about his treatment and she stayed with him. I presume she could have gone to America with her daughter. I think he was exceedingly greedy but he may have genuinely fallen in love with the girl.'

'All right,' conceded Ronnie. 'Benefit of the doubt. Uncle Alex's grandmother was a bit of a loose woman. You have to concede that.'

'Probably no more than some of the other village girls, but she was caught out. What about her sister? Did she become pregnant?' asked Nicola.

'They kept her a prisoner in her room for as long as they could.'

Nicola's eyes widened in horror. 'No wonder the girl ran away.'

John smiled triumphantly. 'She didn't run away. According to Kassie her father took her away in the cart. Haven't you guessed or are you both as dense as I was?'

The two women looked at him; then Nicola's hand went to her mouth. 'You mean she was leprous?'

'That's what Kassie led me to believe, but she had no proof, only the words her mother was supposed to overhear. Assuming she was right, the whole family would have been worried that they would be infected. No doubt Maria was terribly concerned about her son. If the villagers realised the dilemma the family would have been ostracised or even driven away from the area.'

'So they went to America,' stated Ronnie.

John shook his head. 'Not immediately. It was a few years later when they adopted Vivi that they left Crete.'

'So we're really no further forward in finding out who my grandmother was,' said Ronnie, thoroughly disappointed.

'I have an idea, but before I tell you I'd like to check out a few facts. At the moment we don't know for certain that Fotini was leprous and sent to Spinalonga. I'm going to ask Doctor Papanakis if I can have another look at the old records for the island.' John spread his hands. 'If Fotini doesn't turn up there, then I really do not know where else to look.'

Week Two
October 2011

John drove into Aghios Nikolaos and waited until Doctor Papanakis had seen his patients before he entered the room. At first the doctor did not seem to recall him at all. John explained that he had been there over two years ago when he was searching for details of Tassos and recognition dawned on the doctor's face.

'I was hoping you still had those old records and you would give me permission to go through them again.'

'Who are you looking for this time?' asked Doctor Papanakis.

'Bit of a long story, but an American friend of ours has Cretan ancestry. I've managed to trace her family back to the village of Kastelli, but there's a member of the family missing. She appears on the 1931Census, but not on that of 1941. There's no record of her death. She's just disappeared.'

'What makes you think she was on Spinalonga?'

'According to an old lady in the village a girl was ill and it was rumoured she had been an incurable. If she was sent to Spinalonga there should be a record of her transfer to Athens after the war or her death at an earlier date. I hadn't realised that the people on Spinalonga were not included in the Census.'

Doctor Stavros smiled at John's ignorance. 'They were included at the time, but the records have never been made available to the public. Some people, even now, are somewhat sensitive about their ancestry.'

'Where are the records kept?'

'Athens,' replied Doctor Papanakis and John's face fell.

'I can't possibly go over there. May I look through the old records you have, please?'

Doctor Papanakis sighed. 'Well, you've looked at them once so I see no reason why I shouldn't let you look at them again.'

'You didn't throw away any of those that I had sorted and put to one side, did you?' asked John anxiously.

'I've not bothered with them. I have enough to keep me busy with my current patients without looking at sixty year old records of dead people. I've deposited some more recent records down there and I trust you not to be nosey and look at those.'

'The only one that would be of any interest to me would be my great grandmother's and I know exactly how she died. She was just over a hundred and she wasn't ill, just worn out. I promise I'll not look at any except those relating to Spinalonga. I'd be happy to bring them up here and you could keep an eye on me.'

'I don't think that will be necessary. When did you want to make a start?'

'A soon as possible. Our friend is going back to America at the end of the month and I know she'd love to be able to tell her great uncle that she has found his missing relative.'

Doctor Papanakis nodded. 'Come along after lunch tomorrow. I should be working in my office, trying to catch up with my paperwork.'

John could hardly wait to return to the doctor's office. Throughout the morning he looked at his watch. He should have asked the doctor what time he went to lunch. If he went early he could be back by twelve thirty, but if he did not go until later he would be forced to wait outside until the doctor returned.

Just after one John knocked on the doctor's door and hoped it would be answered. To his relief the doctor stood there, looking disgruntled at having been disturbed.

'I'm sorry, I'd forgotten you were coming or I'd have left the door unlocked for you.'

'I'm sorry I had to disturb you,' apologised John. 'If I can complete my search today I won't need to be a nuisance to you again.'

John was optimistic in hoping he would complete his search for Fotini in one afternoon. He had forgotten just how many people had lived and died on Spinalonga over the years. There was no chronological record, Doctor Stavros had added their names to his ledger as he examined them and simply ruled a line with a date beneath when the person died. He would have to examine every page for a woman named Fotini Danniakis.

Four hours later he was no closer to ending his search and he heard the doctor's tread on the stair. 'I've leaving now and I will need to lock up. Have you found the person you're searching for?'

John shook his head. 'I think I'm almost half way through. May I come back tomorrow and continue?'

Doctor Papanakis shook his head. 'It is my day off tomorrow. The surgery will be closed. You will have to return another day.'

John bit back his disappointment. 'Very well. May I come the day after? If I could start searching in the morning I would probably be finished by the end of the afternoon.'

The doctor considered. There was no reason why John should not spend the day in the cellar. 'You will have to leave whilst I am at lunch. I cannot allow you to be on the premises alone.'

'Of course. That will be no problem.' John placed a marker in the ledger. There were two further volumes that he had not yet opened.

Ronnie waited impatiently for John to tell her the result of his search. She had mailed her great uncle and asked him not to contact the American Embassy in Athens. Giovanni had recommended he spoke to Adam Kowalski as the man was fully conversant with Greek law and also spoke the language fluently.

"I really don't think you should do anything until John has managed to find out what happened to your grandmother's sister.

It's possible that that she had children and their descendants could have a claim on the house. I certainly wouldn't want you to get into a long and expensive legal battle on my account. As soon as John has any news for me I will let you know and then we can discuss it further when I come home for Thanksgiving."

Ronnie did not mention their visit to Kastelli and the information Kassie had imparted. There was no certainty that the girl had been leprous, she really could have had an illness confirmed, been admitted to a hospital and died. John could easily have missed the information and she did not feel she could ask him to check a second time.

John opened the ledger and began to turn the pages. An hour later he was successful. There was her name "Fotini Danniakis" and the date recorded by Doctor Stavros was nineteen thirty four. Now all he had to do was see if she had survived the war and been sent to the hospital in Athens or succumbed to starvation or her illness.

He read the doctor's abbreviations and copied them carefully. If he was unsure of their meaning he could always ask Saffron about the medical shorthand as he had done previously. It appeared that over time the infection had spread from her right arm, across her shoulder and over the back of her neck. Feeling elated John was about to close the ledger, then remembered he had not seen a date of death or transfer recorded. He turned the page and sucked in his breath.

Pregnant. The word jumped out at him. The girl was pregnant. How he wished the doctor had been more conscientious about dating his entries. Hurriedly John read on down the page. The doctor appeared to have examined her, however cursorily, on a regular basis and the pregnancy seemed to have taken a normal course. Finally it was recorded "F. 19.08.37".

John sat back, convinced he had discovered Ronnie's grandmother, but how had she become to be adopted by her aunt and uncle? He continued to read down the page, but there was nothing of any significance before he reached the line drawn across the page and the date of Fotini's death in 1943. He began a quick search through the other ledgers to see if he could find any reference to a girl called Paraskevi. He found three, but they were all mature women and could not be the child he was looking for.

He stacked the ledgers neatly back onto the shelf and returned upstairs to the doctor.

'Thank you very much, Doctor. I found the lady I was searching for. Would you have a few moments to spare so I could ask you a question?'

'I'm not conversant with the treatment for leprosy. Thankfully there are very few cases nowadays and if I should come across one I immediately send them to the hospital for the diagnosis to be confirmed. I believe they are given Chemotherapy to halt the progress of the disease, but more than that I can't tell you.'

John shook his head. 'It isn't actually a medical question. The woman I found is recorded as having given birth to a daughter. What would have happened to her? There's no mention of her at all.'

Doctor Papanakis frowned. 'How would I know? She may have died in infancy, but assuming she survived and was healthy she would have been sent to the orphanage.'

John smote his forehead with his hand. 'What a fool I am! Tassos told me that the children stayed with their parents for the first two years of their lives; then they were sent to an orphanage if relatives were not willing to accept them. Do you have any records here of children who have been adopted?'

Doctor Papanakis shook his head. 'I don't have those. They are kept under lock and key at the Town Hall. They are legal documents and highly confidential.'

'I don't want to look through them all. I just want to know if the girl who was born on the island was adopted by her relatives or whether she went to an orphanage.' John pulled the piece of photocopied paper from his wallet and handed it to the doctor.

Doctor Papanakis read the words and shook his head. 'Hardly

a legal adoption certificate. As I understand the law any children who are sent to an orphanage are not adopted by them, just taken into their care. Did you look in the ledger that related to the children? It's possible there is some reference to her there.'

'I didn't know there was one! I only looked through the ledgers where Doctor Stavros had made a list of the inhabitants that he treated.'

Doctor Papanakis looked at his watch. 'If you want to go back down to the cellar I can give you another hour and a half.'

He had hardly finished speaking before John was on the stairs leading back down to the cellar. He scanned the shelves where the old records were kept, pushing the books to one side until he came across a slim, dog-eared book that had been half hidden by the bulkier volumes. Rapidly he began to read the names, running his finger down them. Most of the boys appeared to have been admitted to the orphanage in Neapoli, whereas the girls had been sent to live with nuns in various areas of Crete.

He noted, sadly, that no children had been sent away from Spinalonga after the occupation of Crete and sincerely hoped that due to the deprivations the people had suffered that no children had been born during this time. It was unlikely they would have survived the starvation their parents had experienced.

John had almost given up hope of finding Paraskevi's name when he found a few pages at the back of the book. Many of them were blank, but some names had been entered with a number beside them. Three quarters of the way down the page John saw Paraskevi Danniakis with the number forty seven written beside it. At the back of the ledger was a thick, sealed envelope.

John looked up the stairs and at his watch. There was no sign of the doctor and he should have another quarter of an hour before the doctor said he had to leave. Taking his penknife, John slit the flap of the envelope open carefully, hoping it would be assumed that the gum had given way over the years. Inside were a collection of handwritten documents, each with a number and bearing the signature of Doctor Stavros and usually another two people.

Quickly he flicked through them until he found number forty seven. He spread it out in front of him and took the photocopy from his wallet again. The wording was exactly the same, but this time the signatures were readable. The names of Fotini Danniakis and Aristo Lenandakis appeared in shaky writing, with Doctor Stavros's name scrawled beneath and the date, twelfth September nineteen thirty nine. How he wished he had brought his camera with him. Hastily he copied the names, date and the number of the document into his notebook before replacing all the papers back into the envelope and making an attempt to reseal the flap.

Details of Ronnie's ancestry were gradually coming together.

'I've found her!' John declared as he walked out onto the patio.

'Who was lost? Joanna or Elisabetta?' Marianne asked anxiously.

'Neither,' smiled John. 'I've found Ron's grandmother. Where's Nick?'

'She said she was taking the girls up to the park. She called Ronnie and she was going to help her keep an eye on them.'

'That's even better, then. I'll go up there and I can tell them both at the same time.'

Ronnie looked at John in delight as he described how he had searched the old records for Spinalonga and found her great great grandmother listed as an occupant.

'I hope she wasn't too badly affected,' said Ronnie with a frown.

'I only know that the records said it was her right arm, across her shoulder and over her neck. The doctor hadn't recorded the severity. It may have been just one or two unsightly patches.' John tried to be reassuring. 'I can also tell you who your great great grandfather was,' he announced triumphantly.

'Who?' asked Ronnie avidly.

'Patience,' John admonished her. 'Fotini is recorded as being pregnant and having Vivi on nineteenth August nineteen thirty seven, so Vivi was correct when she claimed that was her birthday. She isn't mentioned again, but I managed to have a look at the children's records. Most of the children went off to orphanages when they were about two. I think the boys were probably sent in batches as the date is the same for a number of them. The girls seem to have been sent to live with nuns, more or less singly. Once I found your grandmother I didn't look at any of the other records.'

'How awful to have to send your child away.' Nicola looked over at the twin girls playing happily in the sand pit.

John remembered Tassos saying he could hear the couple who lived in the house next to his sobbing after their child had gone. He wondered if that was Fotini and Aristo and wished he could remember the names the old man had given to his neighbours. He would not mention the memory to Ronnie.

'So what did it say?'

John pulled the photocopied paper from his wallet. 'Exactly the same as this. No doubt one was for Yiorgo and Maria Roussakis and the other was kept in the doctor's records. On the one the doctor kept the signatures are quite legible, Fotini Danniakis and Aristo Lenandakis, with the doctor's signature underneath and the date that she left the island; twelfth September nineteen thirty nine.'

Ronnie wrinkled her brow. 'That date would agree with Uncle Alex being about four years older than her and them arriving in America in nineteen thirty nine.' She gave a wry smile. 'So my great great grandmother was not married.'

John shrugged. 'Lepers were not allowed to marry. From all I read in old Uncle Yannis's memoirs many of them lived together for years and Father Minos was willing to give them a blessing. He considered he and Phaedra were married. As Aristo Lenandakis also signed the paper so he must have accepted that he was Vivi's father.'

Ronnie looked at John dubiously. 'I suppose you wouldn't be

able to find out anything about him, would you?'

John burst out laughing. 'I knew you were going to ask me that question. I'll have a look during the winter months, but he could have come from anywhere in Greece. The chances of finding him are very slim.'

'I know, but I'd appreciate you giving it a shot when you have the time.' Ronnie smiled happily. 'I really do appreciate all the trouble you've taken, John. I hadn't mentioned our visit to Kastelli to my mother or uncle. I had intended to tell them when I returned home for Thanksgiving, but I can't wait that long. Now I can mail them and tell them all about the family and explain why the villagers appeared so unwelcoming.'

'Do you plan to do that now or will you come to have a celebratory drink with us this evening? I think we have to welcome you into the family properly now we know your links to Spinalonga.' John raised his eyebrows at her and Ronnie felt her stomach lurch. Was that why she had experienced such unsettling events when she was on the island?

'I'd love to.' She hugged first Nicola and then John. 'I can't think of a nicer family to belong to.'

John helped Nicola to bath the girls, and, as usual met with her disapproval a he tickled their necks and they squirmed and wriggled.

'John, we need them to be asleep by the time Ronnie comes. I'm sure she'll want you to tell her all the details again about her great great grandmother.'

'I'm pleased I never mentioned to Ron that I thought Yiorgo might have been having an affair with Fotini or that he or her father could have murdered her.'

'I told you that you had a nasty mind.'

'No, I haven't,' protested John. 'I was just considering every possibility. When you think about it, what would be more natural than her giving her child into the care of her sister and brother-in-law? Two people she felt she could trust.'

'That doesn't explain why they went off to America so soon afterwards.'

'Well,' considered John. 'Kassie's mother, like all the village women, no doubt loved to gossip. She may even have made a habit of eavesdropping at doors and open windows. I'm sure she knew all sorts of details about the family that they would rather have kept private.'

'I wonder what other secrets they had.'

'Who knows, but if old Kassie was right about her mother overhearing the conversation and it was repeated amongst the villagers they would have had their own idea where Vivi had come from. Sooner or later she would have heard rumours and the family would have had no way of disproving them. The poor girl could have been ostracised and her life made miserable. I think they did the right thing.'

To Ronnie's surprise when she opened her computer to mail her mother and uncle she had an incoming message from Geoff. He heart sank. She really did not want to get into a discussion with him about Caro. She considered deleting it and claiming never to have received it; then thought better of it. She had assured him she would always be his friend. She was under no obligation to reply to him, whatever he said to her.

> *"Dear Ronnie,*
>
> *I thought you should know that Caro has been charged with fraud, both by her company and the Social Services. There was a small paragraph in the paper about her, but no one (so far) has called on me. I feel rather foolish that she also deceived me.*
>
> *I have done some very serious thinking since you told me about her and in retrospect I have to admit that I had my head in the clouds. Why would a girl as attractive and*

personable as Caro (leaving aside her illegal activities) ever find a convenience shop manager interesting?

I decided the time had come to try to move on and better myself. You may think this rather strange, but I have applied to a travel company for a position in their Health and Safety department. I have to admit that I found going on inspections with Caro was fascinating.

If I am accepted I know I would have to undergo training and it is doubtful that I would be sent abroad anywhere for some time, possibly years. I would like to think that I would end up in Crete again one day, but I am equally sure I would find any of the other islands just as beautiful.

Are you planning a visit to England before you return to America for the winter? You know you are always welcome here.

Your friend, Geoff."

Ronnie read the mail through a second time and smiled to herself. At least some good had come out of his affair with Caro; he had at last made an attempt to move away from the convenience store and she hoped his application would be accepted. She replied, telling him that she thoroughly approved of his decision, but that she would not be able to visit England as she had some rather complicated business to sort out with her family. If he wished to visit her in Elounda the following season he should let her know and she could arrange for him to stay at the self catering apartments for a couple of weeks.

Feeling that her immediate duty towards him was done she was now able to turn her attention to the long mail she wanted to write to her mother and uncle, although it as unlikely she would be able to finish it before she joined Nicola and John. She smiled happily; now she was considered as part of the family.

November 2011

Ronnie sat with her great uncle and mother, the old family photographs spread out before them. Ronnie held up the one with her great great grandfather standing beside the donkey, part of the Kastelli house in the back ground.

She shook her head. 'I must have been so stupid not to have recognised the house when you first showed me the photo. It's so obvious.'

'There are probably numerous houses that look like that on Crete. Why should you have immediately recognised it?'

'In the town, but not in the small villages, and Castle – why didn't I associate that name with Kastelli?'

Alexandros shrugged. 'Why should you? Or you could ask why I didn't recognise the village the first time we visited.'

'I'd planned to show you the house, but once Mom hurt her ankle we just concentrated on her. I'm just so delighted that we have found my grandmother. How do you feel, Uncle Alex, now you know she was actually your cousin?'

'It makes no difference to me. Vivi was just Vivi. As a child she could sometimes be a nuisance, tagging along behind me, but as we grew older we became good friends. It would be interesting to know her reaction to her ancestry.'

'I'm rather pleased she doesn't know,' remarked Charlene. 'We're far enough removed to find it fascinating, but I think she could have found the knowledge rather traumatic.'

Ronnie picked up the photograph of the two girls and looked at the faded, almost indecipherable writing on the back. 'Now we know what we are looking at you can just make out their names, Maria and Fotini. I wish they'd put a date on, I'd like to know how old they were at the time. I've asked John if he will look for the man we believe to have been Vivi's father, Aristo Lenandakis. He said he'd try finding him over the winter months, but he doesn't hold out much hope. The lepers had been sent to Spinalonga from all over Greece by then. He could have come from anywhere.'

'How are you planning to spend the winter?' asked Alexandros.

Ronnie shrugged. 'Same as last year. I expect I'll be able to find some temporary office work; then I'll return to Crete at the end of March.'

'You enjoy being over there, don't you?'

Ronnie nodded. 'I feel very much at home; even more now that John and Nicola say I'm included as part of their family due to my Spinalonga association.'

'How do you feel about spending the winter over there?'

'There's not a lot of point in me being there. The visitors who come during the winter are different from the summer tourists. They wouldn't be interested in buying views as souvenirs to take home with them.'

'There could be other work for you to do apart from painting.'

'There's hardly any work for the locals so I'm not likely to find a job.'

Alexandros picked up a folder that had been on the chair beside him. 'You could find you have a good deal of work. After your e-mail to me I contacted Adam Kowalski, the American Embassy man. I relayed all the details to him and his reply was very interesting. He said that provided the house has not been lived in since the death of Sofia Danniakis and as I can prove she was my grandmother the house does belong to me.'

Ronnie gave a nervous giggle. 'In that case you could probably ask the villagers to pay their outstanding rents.'

Alexandros shook his head. 'That may have been my grandfather's way of doing business, but it isn't mine. From all you've told me he cheated them by falsifying their tax figures. No, those houses belong to them and they owe me nothing.'

Ronnie pulled a face. 'I know I wanted to find out about Vivi, but I didn't want him as a relative. Suppose the village priest was right and the sins of the fathers continue to be visited on the children?'

A shadow crossed Alexandros's face. 'I don't think that is very likely.' He had lost his wife when she was in her early fifties, Vivi had been widowed during the Viet Nam war, her daughter's first husband was in prison and her second husband had lost his life in a climbing accident. He hoped that was where the misfortune ended and Ronnie would not suffer.

'So what occupation do you have in mind, Uncle Alex?'

'I told you I would give the house to you and your mother has promised to finance the restoration. You'll need to employ people to carry out the work and you will need to be there to ensure the work is carried out properly. The first job will be to clear out all the old furnishings and you don't want them just dumped. It's possible there could be some more photographs hidden away or something you would want to keep as a souvenir.'

'But I don't speak Greek, Uncle. How am I going to tell workmen what I want them to do?'

'You'll have to employ someone who speaks English.'

'I suppose John might know someone, or maybe Vasi. He has a friend whose father is a builder.'

'There you are then. Find someone reliable and trustworthy and make a start during the winter months whilst the locals have little to occupy them. It will take time for the legal papers to be completed, so I suggest you make plans to return in January.'

'But where will I live? The self catering apartments are closed up in the winter. There's no heating in them and even if Giovanni agreed I could stay there I'd freeze.'

'You must know someone who would rent you a room for a couple of months.'

Ronnie looked doubtful. 'I can e-mail people and ask, I suppose.'

'Failing that there must be proper apartments you could rent for a couple of months. Where do the winter visitors stay?'

'They would be far more expensive than the holiday apartments,' demurred Ronnie.

'It would only be for a couple of months. I think the rent could be added as part of the restoration expenses,' smiled Charlene.

Ronnie left her great uncle in a daze. She had expected to spend three months working at a mundane job in an office, now she had only three weeks to arrange her return to Crete and there was something very important that she felt she needed to do before then.

Hurriedly she composed an e-mail to Giovanni asking if he knew of any apartments she could rent until the self catering unit opened for the season. She sent another mail to Saffron, explaining briefly that she was returning earlier than expected to Elounda and asking if Vasi knew of a builder who spoke English. John and Nicola received a much longer mail, telling them the house in Kastelli now belonged to her and she wanted to restore it to its former glory.

John looked at it and showed it to Nicola. 'Suddenly Ron has become a woman of property.'

'Do you think she really will restore it or just clear it out and patch it up?'

'It probably depends upon the condition of the structure. Remember how Vasi was caught by the Imperia Hotel. Before she does anything she'd be wise to have a structural engineer have a look and take his advice.'

'She must be terribly excited.'

'Thank goodness she only appears to be thinking of the house. She hasn't asked me how I'm getting on with my search for Vivi's father – and I haven't even started.'

Ronnie made copious lists of jobs that she considered would be necessary before she could actually employ a builder to start work. The first item was to purchase a small car to go from Elounda to Kastelli and she hoped she would have enough in her savings account. She certainly did not want to ask her mother for any more money.

She planned to visit the house on her own and examine the cupboards and drawers for anything she considered could be of value to her family. Once she had done that she would arrange for all the old furniture to be removed and employ a structural engineer to give it a comprehensive survey. If he said it was totally unsafe and needed to be raised to the ground she would have to think again about her grand restoration plan.

There she stopped and chewed the end of her pen. Maybe she should ask the structural engineer to inspect the property before she started turning out. She did not want to be inside if the roof was about to collapse. She hoped Vasi might know of someone who could advise her. He had knowledge of property. She smiled to herself. If the house did have to be pulled down she would take photographs of it from all angles so that it could be rebuilt to look exactly as it had when the tax collector and his family had lived there.

Thinking of him made her think about Fotini again and she began to search on her computer for someone locally who gave Greek lessons. There was no way she would be able to learn the language in a few weeks, but she could ask them to make a translation for her and check the pronunciation of the difficult words. She felt too self conscious about her plan to confide in John and ask for his assistance.

January 2012

Ronnie sat in the spare bedroom at Saffron and Vasi's house. They had offered her the use of the room until the self catering apartments reopened at the end of March and she had accepted gratefully. Vasi had been so helpful to her, first by arranging to visit Kastelli with her along with Mr Palamakis, his builder and then negotiating the purchase price of a small car and helping her to complete the necessary forms.

Mr Palamakis had studied the exterior of the house before entering and walking slowly through the ground floor rooms. Ronnie had waited in an agony of impatience until he returned.

'The ground floors are safe enough except for one place where the ceiling is collapsing,' he reported. 'I'm not sure about the stairs or the upper floors. I don't want either of you to come inside until I've checked them out.'

Whilst Ronnie watched him anxiously from the doorway the builder tested each stair before placing his weight on it and he finally disappeared from their sight. When he returned he smiled at Vasi.

'It seems safe enough except for one corner. There's a hole in the roof and the rain has rotted the floorboards. That's where the ceiling below is coming down. I suggest some tape is put round both areas to remind people not to tread there. The roof can be repaired and the rest checked over at the same time. Once the furniture has been removed the floorboards can be replaced.

It's possible a new joist will be needed. After that it will be a question of removing the old plaster from the walls and pulling down the ceilings.'

Vasi nodded and relayed the information to Ronnie.

'Can Mr Palamakis do the work?' she asked and Vasi shook his head.

'Two of his sons would be responsible for the manual labour. He would supervise them, but he's not prepared to climb ladders or shovel up rubble at his age.'

'So I can go in and start sorting out all the old furniture and rubbish now?'

'Why don't you ask Mr Palamakis to clear it all out for you?'

Ronnie shook her head. 'It's just possible there are some old photos or keepsakes. I promised Uncle Alex that I would go through everything. Once I've done that I'll be only too glad if they'll clear everything out for me. I'll come up tomorrow and make a start.'

Ronnie looked around the room, wondering where it would be practical to begin. The house was far larger than she had realised when looking at it from outside. She climbed the stairs gingerly and looked into the upper rooms. One was completely empty. Ronnie felt a pang of sadness. Had this been Fotini's room that had been cleared and all her possessions thrown away when she was taken to Spinalonga?

In the other room there were rag rugs on the floor and on two walls hung large decorative panels of weaving, no doubt for warmth during the winter. Between the windows, their decorative metalwork rusted almost through, hung various religious pictures, the nails knocked carelessly into the walls. Two large chests stood beneath the windows, a small table with two chairs pushed beneath it. Ronnie opened the first chest eagerly. To her disappointment it held only blankets, towels and an old skirt.

She closed the lid and opened the second chest. This was far more interesting. She lifted up the edges of the carefully folded items inside; there were crocheted table mats, embroidered sheets, nightgowns, blouses, skirts and boleros. Despite their age, and a rather musty smell, they did not appear to have been attacked by moths or suffered from damp. She would have to go through them properly and see if they were worth keeping.

She returned to the lower floor and looked around the spacious living room. There was a wide open fireplace and beside it were some smoke blackened pots and pans. In the corner nearest the fire was a large, high, double bed with two wooden steps at the side that would have been used to climb up onto the mattress.

Next to it, taking up most of the remaining space on the wall was the dresser that they had been able to see through the window. In the other corner was a cupboard that stretched from floor to ceiling, two sets of doors dividing it into upper and lower levels and Ronnie had to resist opening it to examine the contents.

Between the windows on the front wall was an old fashioned wash stand, the top tiled and a mirror attached to the back. Ronnie decided this was probably where her great great grandfather has sat to shave each day. She could imagine him sitting there, the mirror propped up against the wall and a bowl of water in front of him. An old brush, still with grey hair caught in the bristles sat there along with a comb that had two teeth missing. They would definitely go into the rubbish Ronnie decided.

On the other side of the window next to the front door was a table with a drawer beneath it and this her Uncle Alex had claimed was his grandfather's desk. Her fingers itched to open the drawer and see if there were papers inside that related to his tax collecting days.

On the back wall there were three woven panels and in front of them was a table, and six chairs, one with a broken leg. The table, although covered in dust, looked sturdy and it would be convenient to place the items she discovered in the cupboard, dresser and desk on it, rather than having to dump them on the floor.

An archway on the far wall led through to a small room that would have been described as a scullery. Wooden shelves, some leaning at precarious angles, held a miscellaneous collection of cooking pots and a box beneath contained cutlery that had obviously been used for the preparation of food. A large sink stood in the corner with a bucket beneath the open waste pipe to catch the water as it was discharged, but there was no tap. Presumably the water had to be collected either from a well or the water cistern in the village, using the large buckets that sat beside it.

The small table bore evidence of cut marks, no doubt where butchery had taken place, and also scorch marks. Beneath the table sat a collection of heavy irons that would have needed to be heated on the fire before they could be used. Hanging on the wall was an old galvanized bath tub, but there was no other sign of either washing or toilet facilities.

Ronnie struggled with the bolt on the back door and finally managed to withdraw it far enough to enable her to open it wide enough to squeeze out of the narrow opening she had created. The door was warped and wedged itself firmly on the stone flagged floor and she hoped she would be able to close it when she left.

Outside the area was surrounded by a high wall inset with a wooden gate. The panels were askew due to rotting over the years and it was only held upright by the chain than ran across it and was fixed into the stone walls at each side. She would need to have that replaced as a priority.

Part of the area beside the far wall was completely covered with weeds and they had begun to spread across the paving stones. There were two outhouses, one larger than the other and as she pulled open the door of the smaller of the two it came away in her hand, the hinges completely rusted through. She struggled to take the weight and then let it drop to the ground. There was nothing inside except a hole in the ground, some stones strategically placed both inside and beside it with some rotting wood on the top. Ronnie stared at it curiously and then the truth dawned on her. This was the toilet. It was the same as the ones that John had shown her on Spinalonga.

Ronnie moved to the other outhouse, opening the door warily, expecting it to fall on her. It stayed upright, despite leaning at an angle where a hinge was broken. As her eyes became accustomed to the interior darkness she could make out the shape of a cart. Other items appeared to have been thrown in at random and Ronnie was loath to investigate further without a torch. There could be rats or even a snake living in there and she did not wish to encounter either. She dragged the door closed as best she could and returned to the primitive kitchen.

She lifted down the bath tub from the wall and as she did so the nail it was hanging on came away bringing a shower of plaster down onto her. She coughed and waved her hand in front of her face. Thank goodness she had thought to cover her hair. The bath would be ideal for placing old cutlery and cooking pots into. She would ask Mr Palamakis to send one of his sons to fit a sturdy gate at the entrance to the back area. At the same time she could ask him to remove the sink and clear the first of the rubbish.

She took the discoloured and rusty cooking pots from the sagging shelves, filling them with bent forks and blunt knives, along with various other implements that were either broken or misshapen with use and in many cases had mould growing on them. She placed each cooking pot into the galvanized bath and there was still some space for more rubbish. Gingerly she collected up the rag rugs from the upper floor, coming across nothing worse than a spider and added them to the accumulation. Those from the living room joined them.

Ronnie looked at the large bed in the corner of the front room. She certainly couldn't face tackling that today. She was tired and was now just wasting her time. It would be sensible to drive down into Elounda and see if there was anywhere open in the village where she could purchase some strong rubbish sacks and a stiff broom. The bedding she could place in a sack and if she removed some of the dust out of the room before she started it should stop it rising in clouds and making her cough.

Ronnie parked easily and walked past the parade of closed shops. She knew up the side road there was a store that sold basic decorating and garden materials. She should be able to purchase both the broom and the sacks from there if it was open.

'Miss Ronnie. What are you doing here?'

Ronnie turned and saw Kyriakos standing before her.

'Hello, Kyriakos. It's a long story and you'll have to forgive my filthy appearance.'

'What have you been doing? You look tired. Have you been digging a garden?'

Ronnie shook her head. 'I think that might be easier and more pleasant than turning out old and mouldy belongings.'

'We will go for a drink and you will tell me.'

'I am in no fit state to go anywhere amongst respectable people,' she protested.

'Come. I know somewhere that will not mind if you are not clean and tidy. You can wash your hands and face and then you will feel respectable.'

'My clothes are dirty.'

'That is no matter.' Kyriakos placed his hand under her elbow and began to lead the way through the back streets of Elounda, finally pushing open the door of a small house.

'Mamma,' he called. 'We have a visitor. Come and meet Miss Ronnie.'

A diminutive woman entered and looked at Ronnie's dishevelled appearance in surprise.

Kyriakos smiled. 'Miss Ronnie is the artist. The lady who painted my sign. She does not usually look like this. She would like to wash and then we will have coffee and she will explain to me why she is tired and dirty.'

Kyriakos's mother smiled and dutifully shook Ronnie's dirty

hand. She beckoned to her to follow her through and indicated the bathroom. From a cupboard she handed Ronnie a clean towel and pointed to the basin. Ronnie looked at the bathroom in surprise. She had not expected to see such modern appliances in an old village house. She managed to say thank you in Greek and Kyriakos's mother closed the door, leaving her to wash her face and hands and comb her hair.

'Thank you, Kyriakos, and please thank your mother. I do feel better now I've had a wash.'

'Then we will drink some coffee and you will tell me what you have been doing.'

Ronnie debated whether to tell Kyriakos the whole story of finding her great grandmother and decided it would be far too long and complicated. He would no doubt tell his mother and the knowledge of her ancestry would be common knowledge throughout Elounda.

'I've been up at the big house in Kastelli, clearing out the old kitchen.'

Kyriakos raised his eyebrows. 'We had heard that an American had claimed the old house but I did not know that was you, Miss Ronnie.'

Ronnie hesitated; then shook her head. 'The house belongs to my great uncle. I am just doing the necessary work as he feels he is too old to deal with it.'

'What are you going to do with it?'

'Clear out the rubbish for a start.'

'You are doing that alone? It is not good for you to be up there alone. If the roof should fall or the floor give way ...' Kyriakos spread his hands.

'Mr Palamakis says the house is safe.'

Kyriakos shook his head. 'No. You are going up again tomorrow?'

Ronnie nodded.

'Then I will come with you. I can help you to move anything that is heavy.'

Ronnie was about to refuse when she realised how hurt Kyriakos would be if she rejected his offer. It would also be reassuring to have Kyriakos there with her. She had seen the suspicious and unwelcoming glances she had received from the villagers and there was no way she would be able to move the mattresses and chests down the stairs unaided.

'I need to go through everything. I'm hoping to find some old photos.'

Kyriakos held up his hands. 'I will touch nothing without your permission.'

'When I have finished clearing it out Mr Palamakis's sons will come and do the repairs.'

'And then your uncle will sell it?'

'Whatever he decides to do with it is up to him,' replied Ronnie evasively.

Kyriakos wanted to start clearing the upper levels of the house, but Ronnie insisted the ground floor was tackled first.

'If we start to move furniture down from upstairs there will be no room to work down here. We can stack the old things to one side as we go. I'll make a start on that cupboard and anything I pass to you can be placed in a rubbish bag. If I think I want to keep anything I'll tell you and it can go on the table for me to look at properly later.'

The cupboard held a miscellaneous collection of glasses and china, mostly cracked or chipped and Kyriakos placed the items dutifully in to the rubbish. Two dishes that looked like silver beneath their tarnish Ronnie placed on the table. A cut throat razor, the leather strop, a chipped basin with a shaving brush and fly blown mirror sat at one side. There were glass chimneys for oil lamps, carefully wrapped in newspaper along with a wooden box containing lace, embroidery silks, buttons, cotton, and needles.

She allowed Kyriakos to stand on a chair and reach down the items that were on the top shelf. The bases to the oil lamps were stored there and again Ronnie placed them on the table as he handed them to her, along with oblongs of embroidered cloth. She was loath to discard them. They had to be the work of either Sofia or her daughters. He handed her two metal boxes, firmly locked and despite him standing on his toes and groping around in the recesses of the cupboard there was no sign of their keys.

Ronnie resisted the urge to ask Kyriakos to force them open. They keys could be in the desk that stood in the corner. She would curb her impatience until there was no other way of inspecting their contents.

She wondered how Kyriakos would feel about her throwing away the faded and damp marked religious pictures that adorned the wall and decided she had to be ruthless.

'I'll obviously save that icon, but those others are rubbish,' she said firmly.

Kyriakos did not argue. 'Shall I remove all of them from the walls?'

'Yes, but can you take them out of the frames? It's possible I could use the frames for some of my paintings.'

Whilst Kyriakos worked away at the nails holding the backing and pictures in place Ronnie turned her attention to the bed. She hoped she would not find that it had been badly soiled and was pleased she had thought to bring some rubber gloves with her.

Cautiously she folded back the moth eaten and mouldy coverlet and placed it on the floor beside her. Beneath it there were blankets, worn thin in places and stained. She folded each one and made a pile of the bedding. The sheets surprised her, they had once been good quality linen and the top hem of each one had been embroidered with flowers. She wondered if they could be cleaned or if they would disintegrate in the process and placed them to one side.

She called a halt to their work. There was still the dresser and the desk to be tackled, but it was too late to make a start on those that day. 'I'll bring a couple of boxes up with me tomorrow and the items on the table can be boxed up until I have the time to examine them properly. No doubt they'll all end up in the rubbish.'

Carefully Ronnie locked the warped back door and locked and padlocked the massive front door. She stood back and looked at the house, envisaging how it would look when she had finally restored it to its former opulence.

'We come again tomorrow?' asked Kyriakos.

'Would you be willing to turn out the outhouse whilst I decide if I want to keep anything we've found so far? I know the cart is in there, but everything else I could see looked like rubbish. If so it can all be placed in a heap outside for Mr Palamakis to take away. There's no point in bringing more rubbish inside.'

'You will be careful, Miss Ronnie.'

'I promise.' Ronnie was amused by his concern for her well being. 'I will only finish stripping the bed when I have boxed up anything I want to keep.'

Ronnie removed the under blanket and exposed the mattress. She would not attempt to move that. The old bedding could be placed on top along with the rubbish sacks. Tentatively she placed her hand on the mattress. It felt hard and unyielding; she would not have wanted to sleep on anything so uncomfortable. What was it stuffed with? At some time it had split in various places along the seam and been haphazardly repaired. Curiosity overcame her and she pulled at the old stitching, the material coming away in her hand. A sheet of newspaper became visible and she smiled. No wonder the mattress felt so hard if it was stuffed with newspaper. She lifted the edge gingerly and gave a gasp. Spread evenly beneath the newspaper were old Greek drachma notes, of various denominations.

Ronnie stood back. Should she remove them or leave them there? Were they of any value? She knew all the old drachmas had been recalled by the banks when the country became part of the European Union and the currency was changed to Euros.

She heard Kyriakos entering the kitchen and hastily threw the blanket back over the mattress. She would keep the discovery to herself for the time being.

'Did you find anything interesting?' she asked.

Kyriakos shook his head. 'I don't think so. There are two old wooden saddles for donkeys in the cart, along with some bits of leather straps hanging on nails. There are old tins and bottles along with some rusty tools and a roll of mouldy carpet. Nothing worth keeping.'

'I'll keep the saddles. I've seen those in the folk museum at Lassithi. Another museum might like to have them.'

'Shall I bring them in?'

'No, they'll not come to any harm by being out there for a few more days. I think we've done enough for today.'

Kyriakos looked at her in surprise. 'It is only mid-day.'

'I have some other jobs I need to do in town when I have cleaned myself up.' She made the excuse quickly. She did not want Kyriakos to know she had found some money hidden in the mattress and tell his mother.

Saffron showered and put on some clean old clothes before entering the lounge where Saffron sat looking at catalogues that offered tourist souvenirs.

'Saffie, would you be able to do me a big favour?'

Saffron looked up with a smile. 'What's that, Ronnie?'

'Would you be willing to come up to the Kastelli house with me?'

'I thought Kyriakos was up there helping you.'

'This is something I don't really want him to know about, but I'd like someone to be there with me.'

'If the villagers worry you I suggest you wait until Vasi comes home. I don't speak enough Greek to explain to them that you are legally entitled to be in there turning out.'

'Kyriakos spoke to them. They still seem very wary of me, but I don't feel threatened by them in any way. When I was stripping off the bed this morning I found a collection of old drachma notes in the mattress. They had to have been hidden deliberately and the mattress sewn up again afterwards. If you would come up with me we could take a knife or scissors and cut the mattress open. I have no idea how much money there is in there.'

'Why do you want me with you?'

'I trust you not to tell everyone in the village and I'd also like some moral support,' admitted Ronnie.

'You've certainly made me very curious. Is it very dirty and dusty up there?'

Ronnie nodded. 'And pretty chilly. Put on some old clothes and bring something to put over your hair.'

'I'll bring some rubber gloves as well.'

Ronnie pulled off the blanket she had thrown over the mattress and lifted the edge where she had pulled away the ticking and exposed the newspaper. 'See.'

Saffron looked into the small space. 'Well, there's certainly some money in there, but it may be valueless. I don't know if the bank is still willing to exchange old drachmas.'

Ronnie slit the side seam and pulled back the cover. Along the length of the mattress were sheets of newspaper and when Ronnie lifted the paper she exposed small piles of drachma notes.

'How long do you think they have been hidden here?'

'Goodness knows. There may be a date on the newspaper.'

'I'm going to open the other seams.' Swiftly Ronnie ran the knife down the mattress seams at the head and foot. She pulled the cover back and spread across the whole of the mattress was the newspaper with drachma notes beneath it.

Saffron gasped in surprise. 'There's an awful lot there. Have you something we can put them into? If we take them back with us Vasi should be able to tell us more about the face value.'

'We'll use a rubbish sack. No one will think twice if they see us putting sacks into the car.'

Saffron donned her rubber gloves and Ronnie placed the notes onto a piece of newspaper, making a rough parcel, before handing it to Saffron to put in the sack. By the time the sack was half full Saffron could only just lift it.

'How much more is there?' she asked.

'Not a lot. We'll start another sack and we can always even out the weight afterwards.'

'Do you think we should turn it over and have a look at the other side?' asked Ronnie.

'I don't think we'd be able to manage it. Mattresses are terribly heavy, even without additional stuffing. Put the blanket back over it for now. You could put the old bedding on top and maybe a chair. That would make it look as if you had no interest in it and were putting things there to be thrown away.'

'Maybe between us we could pull it down so one side is standing on the floor? I'd be able to open up some more of the seams then.'

Together they struggled with the unwieldy mattress until it was propped on its side against the wooden bed base. Whilst Saffron steadied it Ronnie slit the seams and turned back the ticking. There was nothing hidden inside.

Ronnie shrugged. 'Oh, well, it was just a chance. Can we push it back up? When the first load of rubbish has been removed I'll ask Kyriakos to dismantle the base. Why on earth did they make them so high?'

'I expect you'll find their winter or summer clothes and shoes stored underneath, along with spare bedding.'

'Why didn't they use a wardrobe?'

'Where would you put it? Some people had a wooden trunk which they used for storage.'

'There are a couple of trunks upstairs. One is empty and the other has some beautiful embroidered and crocheted items inside.'

'They're probably part of a dowry that one of the girls had started making. The girls usually started preparing their dowry as soon as they could sew decently.'

Ronnie pointed to the sheets she had found with the top hems embroidered. 'Those were on the bed. Would they have been part of a dowry?'

'Possibly, or they may have just passed the evenings sewing and decided to embellish their sheets.'

'I think I could have found a more exciting way to pass my time.'

'Not in those days,' smiled Saffron. 'Do you want to look at anything else whilst we're here?'

'There's still the desk and the dresser I need to turn out, but I can start that job tomorrow.'

'I don't expect you'll find anything like this in either of them.'

'Nor do I,' smiled Ronnie. 'I'm still hoping to find some old photographs, but I'm glad I was curious about the mattress.' She picked up a sack containing the money. 'I shall feel like a bank robber carrying this to the car,' she giggled.

Vasi looked at the neatly sorted notes that Ronnie displayed before him. 'What a shame drachmas are no longer legal currency. You would have a small fortune here, although they are only small denomination notes.'

'Will the bank accept them and change them into Euros?'

'I have no idea. I suggest we make a record of the total amount and I take a note into the bank and ask them. If you are still able to exchange them you might have to fill in a declaration form for each one to say where you found it.'

'What!' Ronnie looked at him in horror. 'That would take me months.'

'It could be financially worth your while. Leave it with me. For the time being I'll put it all into my safe and when I've spoken to the bank I'll tell you their answer.'

Ronnie turned her attention to the dresser, handing Kyriakos the dishes, plates, cups and saucers carefully. 'Most of these are in good condition. I've found one cup without a handle and a cracked plate. My uncle said this was where his grandmother kept the best crockery. Some of it does look very old and he might like to keep it.' Ronnie did not disclose that she was thinking of mounting some of the plates on the walls as decoration eventually.

Just as she thought she had finally emptied the dresser Ronnie felt something at the side. She tried to lift it, but it was a snug fit against the shelf above. She tried to pull it, but her fingers could not get a grip. Sighing in exasperation she wriggled it from side to side until it moved towards the centre of the shelf and she was able to get her fingers behind it. Tied tightly together were a bundle of exercise books. Longing to open them, Ronnie knew she would have no idea of the information they contained.

'I'll take those back with me,' she decided. 'They could well be my great great grandfathers account books and it would be interesting to see how much rent he was charging the villagers.'

Kyriakos's face took on a pained look. 'Your uncle will ask them to pay rent to him again?'

Ronnie shook her head. 'He has no intention of asking them for anything. He says his grandfather cheated them out of their property and he has no right to it.'

A broad smile spread across Kyriakos's face. 'That is true, Miss Ronnie? He will not change his mind?'

'No, definitely not. He would have to go through the lawyers again to prove the houses belonged to him and when it was disclosed that his grandfather had obtained them dishonestly he could well be asked to pay compensation to the villagers. Better to leave things as they are.'

'I can tell the villagers?'

Ronnie looked at him, realisation dawning on her. 'Is that why they've been so unfriendly? They thought they would have to start to pay rent again?'

Kyriakos nodded. 'They thought he would ask for rent that was owed since the old lady died. They do not have that kind of money. If they could not pay what would happen to them? They would have no home and where would they go?'

'Oh, Kyriakos, I had no idea they were worried. Please, tell them, my uncle will not be asking for any rent. The houses belong to them. Can you go and do so now whilst I turn out the desk?'

The desk, as Ronnie called the piece of furniture, was just a table with a drawer underneath. She eased open the drawer and saw it was crammed with pieces of paper, each covered with figures. Ronnie began to examine them, but they gave her no clue to their purpose. There was no date and nothing else written on the scraps, just figures. She smoothed them out as best she could and placed them on the table alongside the exercise books. She would take them back with her and see if Vasi had any idea of their purpose.

Ronnie brushed off the dust and cut the string that had been holding the exercise books together. She opened the first one and saw Greek letters on the page, many of them repeated time and again. This must have been an exercise book used by one of the girls. She opened the next and saw there were Greek words, not just letters written there. In the third the writing had improved and often covered half a page before a line had been drawn beneath it and a new paragraph begun.

Totally fascinated she opened each book in turn, finding all but the first two had pages covered in small Greek writing. These were not her great great grandfather's accounts. It was probable that the books contained passages the girls had been told to copy out by the priest to improve their writing and were of no interest at all, but she would take them to John and ask him if he was able to decipher the cramped hand.

Ronnie decided the time had come to investigate the contents that could be in the cupboard beneath the large wooden bed base. She struggled to open the door on one side of the wooden steps that had been used to climb up onto the mattress.

'I can help, Miss Ronnie?' Kyriakos stood there with a hammer in his hand.

'I don't really want to smash my way in unless it's necessary. There could be something in there that I damage.'

Kyriakos looked at her sceptically. 'I do not think so.' He bent down and examined the door, then straightened up. 'The wood is warped and there is too much weight on the bed. If we remove the mattress and sacks you have put up there we may be able to open it.'

Ronnie sighed in exasperation. 'I thought it was a good idea to put as much as possible on the bed out of the way.' She looked around. 'Suppose we move them in front of the dresser? I think I ought to ask Mr Palamakis to come and collect a load. If we want to start upstairs next week we'll need the space down here.'

Kyriakos nodded. He did not understand why Ronnie was examining everything so diligently. It was all rubbish to be thrown away and Mr Palamakis's sons could have cleared the whole house within a day.

He pointed to the split mattress in disgust. 'Look what they did!'

Ronnie blushed guiltily.

'The Germans always slit open the mattresses. They searched throughout every house for anything of value.'

'Oh! Do you think they would have found anything here?'

'Who knows? They could have taken the old lady's jewellery.'

Ronnie remembered the photograph where her great great grandmother had been wearing a multitude of necklaces and wondered what had become of it. Wherever she had hidden it doubtless the Germans had found it.

The effort of moving everything from the bed and forcing open the doors to the cupboard space beneath had been unrewarding. As Saffron had surmised, there was spare bedding and towels. Next to them, neatly folded, were blouses, skirts, aprons and some old wooden clogs. Behind, pushed towards the back were a collection of shirts, trousers and jackets, along with some old boots. It appeared that Sofia had kept her dead husband's clothes. Despite feeling in all the pockets and tipping out the boots Ronnie found nothing and passed every item to Kyriakos to place in a rubbish sack.

Finally she straightened up. 'I'm sure there's nothing left underneath. If we bring the mattresses down from upstairs we can place them on top along with any other bags of rubbish and I'll ask Mr Palamakis when he can come up to collect them.'

Kyriakos tested the weight of the mattress and shook his head. 'To carry it down the stairs it will need to be folded in half. It is a man's job, Miss Ronnie. Your hands would not be strong enough.'

Ronnie shrugged. 'We could at least take down the wall hangings and the pictures. Again I'll keep the frames if they're any good. Put them on the mattress whilst I roll up these rugs.'

The pictures removed from the walls and the rugs rolled and placed in a rubbish sack Ronnie looked at the wall hangings. 'If I held the weight do you think you could take them off the wall? Provided they're not rotten I'd quite like to keep them.'

Kyriakos shrugged. Miss Ronnie had some strange ideas. It would be better to throw everything away and buy some modern pictures to adorn the walls. He tried to unhook the cumbersome weaving and shook his head.

'I need to be higher. If I pull at them they will tear.'

'Could you reach if we pulled the chest over?' asked Ronnie.

'I will try.'

They moved the empty chest easily and Kyriakos stood on it gingerly, expecting to fall through the lid any minute. 'Are you ready?' he asked. 'Once I take the rod off the hook you will have most of the weight.'

Ronnie bunched the weaving up into her arms. 'I'll stand back a bit and you can just let the rod drop.'

Ronnie bent her head so that any dust or plaster that came down with the rod did not go into her eyes. She heard the rod hit

317

the floor and looked up. On the hook two keys, held together by a piece of wire, dangled tantalizingly.

'Can you reach those keys, Kyriakos?'

He stretched up and handed them down to her. 'Why would you keep your keys up there where it is so difficult to reach them?'

'Maybe no one was supposed to know where they were. I wonder,' Ronnie weighted the keys in her hand. 'These could be the keys to those two old boxes.'

'Shall I bring them up for you to open?' asked Kyriakos and Ronnie shook her head. 'It would be more sensible to take down the other wall hanging and fold them both before we go down. We can put them inside the empty trunk for the time being. If I find something interesting in the boxes I won't want to come back up here again.'

Kyriakos grinned. What did she expect to find? A fortune in gold and jewels?

Ronnie inserted the key into the lock, but it would only turn part of the way before jamming. Ronnie sighed in exasperation. 'I need some oil. Is there any amongst the rubbish from the outhouse?'

'I will find,' Kyriakos assured her and went out of the back door. He had no intention of searching through the rubbish sacks for cans of old oil. He hurried along the road to where the men were gathered beneath the tree as usual and asked if one could provide him with a small can of oil. He promised to return it, once a lock had been oiled and the key made to work.

Ronnie struggled with both locks whilst Kyriakos was away. She was convinced there was something important in the boxes. Why would anybody bother to lock them otherwise? One was heavier than the other and when she shook the lighter of the two or turned it upside down she could hear something moving inside.

To her consternation when Kyriakos returned he had one of the village men accompanying him bearing an oilcan with a long, narrow spout. He waved it at Ronnie and removed the key from the lock. He inserted the nozzle into the keyhole and turned the can upside down, allowing a little oil to dribble in. He scrutinized the key and took a metal file from his back pocket. Carefully he scraped away a thin layer of rust and then placed the key in the lock.

He stood back and looked around the room whilst Ronnie turned the key gently, allowing her to lift the lid and she let out a gasp of delight.

'Photos. I've found some photographs. That's what I've been searching for,' she declared triumphantly and turned to Kyriakos with a delighted smile on her face.

Kyriakos smiled back politely. She had been diligently searching through everything just for a few old photographs! He and the villager exchanged glances and shrugged their shoulders.

'Thank you,' said Ronnie. 'Please thank the gentleman for his trouble.'

'Don't you want him to open the other box?' asked Kyriakos.

'Oh, yes, of course.'

Again the oil was produced and the key touched lightly in places to remove any rust. Both men watched as she opened the second box, expecting to see that it contained more photographs. Inside were envelopes bearing American stamps, some of them were unopened. Ronnie felt tears coming into her eyes.

'These must have been written by my great grandmother to her mother after they arrived in America. How wonderful that they should have survived all this time.'

The man with the oil can shrugged again and touched his head indicating that he thought Ronnie was crazy. Kyriakos smiled. He was tempted to agree with him.

Ronnie could hardly wait to return to Saffron and Vasi and be able to sit and examine the photographs at her leisure. A few appeared identical to the ones that her great uncle had shown her, but there were some that were entirely new to her. She sorted them carefully; looking on the reverse to see if there was a name or date that would give her any further information. Only those taken of her great uncle and grandmother whilst they were children had any details. She could make out their names and the date, but the other wording she could not decipher. She would have to speak to John.

'I've found some old letters from America. Could you translate those for me? I'm sure they're from Maria to her parents telling them what their life was like over there. It must have seemed very alien after the life they were used to here.'

'How many are there?'

'About twenty five.'

'Bring them over and I'll see what I can do.'

'There's also some photographs that have details on the back. I'd like to know what they say, but I feel the letters could be important to me.'

February 2012

John handed Ronnie a ring binder. 'Here are the photos. They were very quick and easy to do. They mostly say things like "Alexandros with his new bike," or "Vivi with her dolls' pram." I don't know that you'll find them very interesting.'

'Thank you, John. I want to show them to Uncle Alex and my mother and they're bound to ask what it says.'

'I've also finished translating the letters. Nick has typed them out and they're in date order with the original letter in a polythene protector behind my translation. There's mention of your Uncle Alex and your grandmother.'

'Really?' Ronnie's eyes lit up. 'I'll start reading them tonight.'

Ronnie read the letters with interest. Maria had described their long sea voyage and subsequent arrival in America. They had been met by Greek speaking officials who had helped them through the formalities and showed them how to fill in their papers giving them permission to live and work in the States.

"I had been frightened that we would not understand what we had to do and they would put us on a boat and send us back to Piraeus. I would not want to spend so long at sea again. I was so thankful it was not rough. I was very scared that the children would fall overboard and would not let them out of our small cabin (that's what they call your bedroom on a ship) if I could help it. They were both rather fretful, but

*now we are on dry land they seem happier. Vivi has stopped
asking for her Mamma and does not cry each night before she
goes to sleep. We are staying in a room in a big house that
they call a hotel whilst Yiorgo looks for work and somewhere
for us to live permanently. Everyone seems very friendly and
helpful, but I do not understand what they are saying to me. I
will write to you again when we have an address."*

The letters continued in the same vein, saying that Yiorgo
had found work in a factory where he would be packing flooring
materials. There were other Greek men working there and they
were helping him to understand the strange language. Alexandros
had started to go to school and at first had cried and stamped his
feet each day and clung to her. Now, three months later he had
accepted, with bad grace, that he had to attend each day. He was
being given special lessons so he could learn the language and
was beginning to be able to make himself understood to the other
children. She and Yiorgo were helping him by asking him to teach
them when he came home each day.

Ronnie was pleased to see that in the third letter she thanked
her father for writing to her and was glad he and her mother were
keeping well. Obviously she had sent them her address and they
were able to communicate regularly.

Mostly the letters described how the children were growing up
and in one she said she had enclosed some photos. Ronnie guessed
they were amongst those she had found in the box. Maria said
that Yiorgo was no longer working in the packing department,
but had been moved so that he now checked that the orders had
been completed correctly.

Ronnie smiled. It must have been hard for him to accept working
as a floor hand after being a clerk in a busy shipping office.

Later Maria described how the people were discussing the war
that was taking place in Europe and how thankful she was that
neither Greece or America were involved. Sadly Maria's relief

was short lived as in her next letter she said she had heard that there was fighting in mainland Greece and was worried that the offensive could spread to Crete. She begged her father to write back to her quickly to reassure her that all was well with them.

It was then that Ronnie reached the letters that appeared never to have been opened by Sofia. She had asked John to do so and she read the contents that he had translated curiously.

"I was told at the post office that I could not send letters to Crete which is why I have not written to you for so long. I am very thankful that the war is over and I do hope that you have not suffered. Being so far away we did not have any fighting over here, but many of the younger men decided they would go to Europe to fight. They seemed to think it would be exciting. It was very sad when we heard that so many did not return. Alexandros is growing fast and now speaks the American language very well. I try to encourage him to speak it to me at home so I can improve. Vivi has no problem at all as we made sure that when she was old enough to start school she had some knowledge of the language. I think she understands more than Yiorgo or I and it is useful when we go shopping. Please write back to me very soon to tell me all is well with you."

Ronnie looked at the date that John had place at the top of the typewritten sheet. Maria's father had been shot by then, but why hadn't her mother written to tell her the news?

The next two letters were far briefer, asking her father to write back and reassure her that all was well with him and her mother. The third brought a tear to Ronnie's eye.

"My dearest Mamma and Pappa
You have not answered my letters to say you are both safe and well. I have heard that Crete suffered badly during

the war and I can only conclude that you both met your deaths at the hands of the wicked invaders. I do hope you did not suffer. I will not write to you again, but remember you each night in my prayers.

   Your loving daughter, Maria."

Ronnie clenched her fists in frustration. Why hadn't Sofia replied to her daughter to say that she was still alive?

'Thank you both so much. I really appreciated the time you took to translate and type out the letters for me. Why, of why, didn't Sofia write back to her daughter? She didn't even open those last letters. What must she have thought when Maria didn't write any more?'

John smiled at her. 'It's quite likely that Sofia was unable to read or write, that was why Maria asked her father to write to her.'

Ronnie looked at him in both horror and amazement. 'Oh, no! Why didn't she ask someone to help her? Surely the village priest would have read them to her and written back on her behalf?'

'She was probably too proud. Her husband had been the tax collector; her son in law had worked as a clerk and both her daughters could read and write. How could she admit that she was the only one in the family who was truly illiterate?'

'But the rents; she continued to collect those after her husband was shot.'

John shook his head. 'Ron, just occasionally even now you will find an old villager who is illiterate. Old Kassie could be and I'm pretty sure her mother was. But,' he wagged his finger at her, 'They can always count money. I expect Sofia asked the villagers for "the same as last time" and they would hand over the same amount to her as they had to her husband.'

'Do you think that was where the money in the mattress came from?'

'Very likely. She would certainly not have trusted a bank with her savings.'

'Poor old lady. I do hope Kassie was kind to her when she looked after her.'

'She probably had an ulterior motive, hoping the old lady would tell her where she had hidden the rent money.'

'She would have stolen it?' Ronnie's eyes opened wide in disbelief.

'That would depend upon her basic honesty. She would probably have given it to the priest and asked him to distribute it amongst the villagers who had paid rent for years. In retrospect it would have been more practical if she had stolen it, rather than it staying hidden in the mattress until it was worthless. A shame your uncle didn't stake his claim to the house before the Euros became the official currency. Apparently it was amazing what poor, penniless people suddenly found they had hidden away. The tax man had a field day!'

'Back to the wicked tax man again.'

John winked at Ronnie. 'Why do you think we do all we can to avoid paying him?'

'So that could be why we didn't find any other money around. I would have expected to have found a small amount in the dresser or desk. Surely she paid Kassie for whatever food she brought in for her.'

'Kassie would not have charged her as such. She would just have cooked a little more than was necessary and taken the surplus over to Sofia. No doubt Kassie helped herself to whatever small amount of money she found lying around feeling she was honestly entitled to it.'

Ronnie hesitated. 'Would you do something else for me, John? Would you take me over to Spinalonga early one morning?'

John raised his eyebrows. Ronnie had shown no inclination to go over there early since her visit with Geoff.

'Painting?' he asked.

Ronnie shook he head. 'No. Just something I feel I have to do. You could say it was laying a ghost.'

Ronnie stood alone in the deserted square. She held a piece of paper in front of her, having read the words until she knew them off by heart. She hoped her poor Greek was understandable.

'Fotini Danniakis, Aristo Lenandakis,' she called softly. 'Are you there? I want to tell you that your daughter, Paraskevi had a happy life with Maria and Yiorgio. They went to America. She married over there and had a daughter. I am your great granddaughter.'

Ronnie stood and listened. There was not a breath of wind, no birdsong, not even the rustle of a beetle in the grass.

She raised her voice. 'Fotini Danniakis, please, if you are there listen to me. I want to tell you that your daughter, Paraskevi had a happy life with Maria and Yiorgio. They went to America. She married over there and had a daughter. I am your great granddaughter.'

From behind her there seemed to come a deep contented sigh and Ronnie whirled round. She was convinced she caught a glimpse of a black skirt and the flash of a white blouse in the doorway across the road and ran across and peered in. There was no one.

She was imagining things again. Slowly she walked back down the path to the old port where John was waiting for her. At the gate way she stopped and looked behind her. She had a distinct feeling that someone was standing a short distance away and watching her.

'Thank you.'

She heard the Geek word spoken quite clearly. She placed her hand on the wall and her face drained of colour.

'You are here. You really are here, Fotini.' Tears dribbled down her face and she brushed them away impatiently as John walked towards her, a concerned look on his face.

'What's wrong? Have you had one of your strange experiences again?'

Ronnie gave him a watery smile. 'I think my great grandmother will be at peace now.' John gave her a puzzled look and she continued. 'When you found out that she had been sent here and my grandmother was born here I realised why I had heard deep sighs and sobbing. It was Fotini crying for her lost daughter. I told her that Vivi had a happy life and that I'm her granddaughter.'

John raised his eyebrows.

'She said thank you to me.' With that Ronnie burst into tears and John placed his arms around her until she quietened. He wished he had accompanied her up to the square and might have been able to experience the ghost of Fotini for himself.

Ronnie looked around the large house in Kastelli. It was far bigger than she had realised. What was she going to do with it? It was far too large for one person. She had considered making one of the upper rooms into a studio, but that would mean either having a window in the roof or enlarging the existing windows. She was loath to make any modern improvements to the exterior.

The upper floors were now completely devoid of furniture and Mr Palamakis's sons were repairing the roof. Once that had been completed Dimitris had agreed to come and start the basic wiring for an electricity supply to be connected. She would have to decide soon where she wanted additional sockets and lights. Should she make the old scullery into a bathroom? That would be practical if she was going to make her home on the ground floor, but if she was going to convert the upper story to a one bedroom apartment for herself it would make more sense to have a modern bathroom installed up there.

She had still not investigated thoroughly the contents of the chests, but along with the antique dresser, wash stand and the original bed the ground floor could become a small museum. There were the old wooden saddles, the silver and china that could be displayed, along with some of the old photographs that she was sure John would be able to enlarge for her. Was that practical? If the house was a museum she would have to spend every day up there or employ someone, hoping enough visitors would come to make it viable.

Ronnie sighed. She had not imagined that restoration of the old house would become so difficult. Originally she had thought she would be moving in by the end of March, but she now realised that would be impossible. She would have to speak to Giovanni and ask if she could continue to rent the self catering apartment for a few more months. When she visited she could ask John if he would be willing to have a look at the old exercise books. Having found the photographs and letters she had pushed the books to one side, considering they were of little importance.

John flicked over the pages quickly. 'Ron, do you realise what this is?'

Ronnie shook her head.

'It's a diary or journal, kept by Maria Roussakis when she was a child.'

'What does it say?'

'Well, it starts when she had just learnt to read and write by the looks of it. It may be of no interest at all; just childhood recollections.'

'John ....'

'I know.' John held up his hands. 'Will I translate it?'

Ronnie smiled hopefully

'I'll give it a go. Nick can help me, but I can't promise that it will be very interesting.'

John turned to Nicola with a grin. 'I'm glad Ronnie didn't unearth the Dead Sea Scrolls. She'd expect me to translate those for her as well.'

'If you type it up on the computer Nick as I read it out to you it will be quicker. She may have been able to read and write, according to the priest, but her spelling is awful and her grammar equally as bad. Listen.

"Pappa C sez I writ wel now but must do mor at home. Terday I stat a dary."

'I'll have to translate it into decent English or it will hardly make sense.'

'Sounds like riveting reading.'

'This is only the start. Who knows what revelations she will make later on?' John picked up a book at random and turned towards the end. 'At least her spelling and grammar had improved when she wrote to her mother from America.'

'Did she make an entry every day?'

'I wouldn't think so, just when she had something to record that she considered important.' John picked up another book and opened it half way through. 'Aha, she mentions Yiorgo on this page. Oh, the naughty girl!'

'What?' asked Nicola eagerly

'She says he touched her breast and she liked it.'

Nicola giggled. 'Of course she did! Do you think she records more about their courtship?

John turned another couple of pages. 'There was obviously something going on between Yiorgo and Maria. She threatens to cut off Fotini's hair if she tells their mother.' John closed the book. 'I mustn't be tempted to start in the middle. We could miss something relevant if we think the first books are just childish scribble. '

If you have enjoyed reading Ronnie, you will be pleased to know that the next book – Maria – is planned for publication in December 2014.

Read on for a 'taster' of what is to come.

MARIA

*"Pappa C sez I writ wel now but must do mor at home.
Terday I stat a dary."*

Maria licked the end of her pencil. What was she going to write
in a diary? Each day was the same.

She would hear her father pulling open the door to the yard
and hurrying across to the tiny outhouse that was their toilet. Her
mother would follow, carrying the slop pail with her. If Fotini had
not been awakened by their movement she would shake her by
the shoulder and both girls would dress hurriedly. It was her job,
being the elder, to carry their slop bucket downstairs and take it
to the outhouse to empty. She was careful to pour the contents
between the stones, wrinkling her nose at the smell as she did so.
They were fortunate not to have to use a corner of the yard in all
weathers, relying on the chickens to peck the area clean.

She and Fotini would wash their hands and face in a bowl of
cold water. The only time that warm water touched their bodies
was on a Saturday night when water would be heated to fill the
tin bath and the family would take turns at immersing themselves
in the water and soaping their bodies. Her father was always first,
whilst the water was at its hottest.

Each morning her father would sit at the washstand and lather
his chin; he would use his cut-throat razor to remove the overnight
stubble, being careful to avoid his moustache. Whilst he did so
she would place four rusks and a few olives into a clean cloth

331

and place them on the table beside his shoulder bag. Once his ritual of shaving was completed he would indicate that she could remove the bowl whilst he used both hands to twist the hairs of his moustache together until the ends were sharp points.

Finally, his toilet complete, Alesandros would place the rusks into his shoulder bag, check he had the money and necessary paper work to hand in to the tax office, collect the donkey's saddle from the outhouse and walk up to the field. She and Fotini would stand outside when they heard the donkey's hoofs on the cobbles and wave to him as he rounded the corner of the village street. Both girls would then return inside to be allocated household chores. Fotini would be sent upstairs to straighten their bedding and sweep the floors, whilst Maria was sent into the village on errands.

Her first task was always to collect water from the village well and carry it back to the house. Some days she had to make four separate journeys as she did not have the strength to carry two full buckets at a time. She was then expected to call at the butcher for whatever meat her mother had requested and then continue to the greengrocer for salad vegetables and fruit. Sofia would indicate to her daughter how many tomatoes or apples she wanted by holding up her fingers. She could not count and nor could most of the villagers so the system worked well. Maria never had any money with her and she had no idea that her father visited the local suppliers at the end of each week and settled the bills.

Once she arrived home with her loaded shopping bag her mother would inspect her purchases. If Sofia was not satisfied Maria would be sent back with the offending item and a replacement requested. She and Fotini could then spend some time together either playing out in the yard or beside the fire during the winter, until their mother called to say Despina had delivered the milk.

Both girls would hurry to the scullery to be given a cup of fresh goat's milk and they would sit and soften some bread left from the previous day in the creamy liquid before drinking the remainder. Whilst they ate and drank their mother would finish kneading the bread dough and shaping it into loaves. Wrapped in a clean cloth, and with Sofia's mark on the side, Maria and Fotini would walk up to the baker and ask him to place it in his oven.

On two afternoons each week, after a lunch of bread and olives, sometimes accompanied by a piece of cheese and a tomato, Maria would walk to the church where Pappa Constantinus would begin teaching a dozen children from the village how to form their letters and numbers. Once he was satisfied they knew their numbers up to ten, the alphabet and the sounds the letters made, he started to teach them to read the Bible. Maria enjoyed the lessons, but wished she was as quick as Yiorgo and Costas. Pappa Constantinus was always telling them they were clever boys.

Two hours later Maria would walk home and help her mother to prepare the vegetables they would have with their evening meal when her father returned. When she was older her mother would teach her how to make the filo pastry she used for cheese pies or how much seasoning she must add to stuffed tomatoes or dolmades; when to add more salt or sugar and which foods had sufficient natural flavouring and needed no addition.

Her father would return the donkey to the field whilst the water was heated on the fire for him to wash his hands and face. Once their meal was over she and Fotini would remove the dishes to the scullery where she used the tepid water left from her father's ablutions to wash out the pots whilst fresh water was heated to wash the plates and give the pots a final rinse. The water would run from the large china sink into a bucket beneath the waste hole and she would take this out to their toilet and tip it between the stones whilst Fotini replaced the plates and dishes on the shelves.

When Maria returned to the living room her father would be sitting at his desk, money spread out before him. As he counted it he would make numbers on a sheet of paper, before finally wrapping the paper around a small bundle of notes which he would place in his bag ready for the next day. The remainder he placed into the drawer beneath the table.

During the evening her mother would sit and either mend their clothes or continue stitching at a blouse or shirt she was making. She and Fotini would play outside with the other village children until the light failed and they would be called and told to go to bed. After bidding their parents a dutiful goodnight, and reminded to say their prayers, Maria would collect the slop bucket they used if necessary during the night, and they would climb the stairs to their bedroom where they shared a mattress. There they would lay side by side, talking quietly and giggling together until one would fall asleep and the other quickly followed suit.

On a Saturday Alesandros did not harness the donkey and ride away from the village. He would walk around the houses collecting the rents that were owed to him, deducting the amounts that were owed to Despina for the goats' milk, for the fruit and vegetables Panayiotis had supplied and the meat from Yiannis. Upon his return he would sit at his desk and enter the amounts into a book and add the figures.

The only day Maria's monotonous routine varied was on a Sunday. She and Fotini would be told to make sure their hands and face were clean, dress in their best skirt and blouse, tie their hair up neatly under their kerchiefs and reminded not to talk or giggle when they were in the Church. They must listen to all that Pappa Constantinus said, even if they did not always understand his sermon.

Maria listened attentively, but one week she had drawn her mother aside afterwards and asked for an explanation.

'Pappas Constantinus says the sins of the father will be visited on the children. Does that mean if Pappa does something wrong I will be punished?' she asked anxiously.

Sofia shook her head. 'Your Pappa would not do anything wrong. You do not need to worry.'

Comforted, but not sure she really understood, Maria

accepted the regular admonishment from the priest with the same equanimity as she did his blessing.

After the church service they would walk slowly home down the village street. Her father would raise his hand to other villagers and they would grudgingly return the greeting although she often heard them hiss at his back after they had passed by. If he heard them he made no acknowledgement of their lack of respect.

Maria licked the lead of her pencil again. She would only write in her diary if something important or exciting happened.

To be continued .....

For up-to-date information about the titles in this continuing saga of a Cretan family, see the website: